Critical Survey of Poetry
Gay and Lesbian Themes

Editor

Rosemary M. Canfield Reisman
Charleston Southern University

Salem Press
A Division of EBSCO Publishing, Ipswich, Massachusetts

Cover photo:
Oscar Wilde (© Corbis)

Copyright © 2012, by Salem Press, A Division of EBSCO Publishing, Inc.
All rights in this book are reserved. No part of this work may be used or reproduced in any manner whatsoever or transmitted in any form or by any means, electronic or mechanical, including photocopy, recording, or any information storage and retrieval system, without written permission from the copyright owner except in the case of brief quotations embodied in critical articles and reviews or in the copying of images deemed to be freely licensed or in the public domain. For information address the publisher, Salem Press, at csr@salempress.com.

ISBN: 978-1-42983-650-0

CONTENTS

Contributors iv

Queer Theory 1

Paula Gunn Allen 9
John Ashbery 15
Elizabeth Bishop. 30
Hart Crane 41
Countée Cullen 54
Allen Ginsberg 64
Thom Gunn 81
A. E. Housman 94
Charlotte Mew 107
Frank O'Hara 112
Adrienne Rich 121
Arthur Rimbaud 135
Sappho 147
Siegfried Sassoon 159
James Schuyler 170
Gertrude Stein 180
Paul Verlaine 193
Alice Walker 203
Walt Whitman 212
Oscar Wilde 228

Checklist for Explicating a Poem 239
Bibliography 242
Guide to Online Resources 245
Geographical Index 249
Category Index 250
Subject Index 253

CONTRIBUTORS

Karley K. Adney
University of Wisconsin, Marathon County

L. Michelle Baker
The Catholic University of America

James John Baran
Louisiana State University-Shreveport

Kate Begnal
Utah State University

Robert G. Blake
Elon University

Peter Carravetta
Queens College, City University of New York

Richard Collins
Xavier University of Louisiana

Frank Day
Clemson University

Desiree Dreeuws
Sunland, California

Jack Ewing
Boise, Idaho

Howard Faulkner
Washburn University

Sarah Fedirka
Arizona State University

Lydia E. Ferguson
Clemson University

Scott Giantvalley
California State University, Dominguez Hills

Dennis Goldsberry
College of Charleston

Daniel L. Guillory
Millikin University

Sarah Hilbert
Pasadena, California

Philip K. Jason
United States Naval Academy

Rebecca Kuzins
Pasadena, California

Leon Lewis
Appalachian State University

Perry D. Luckett
United States Air Force Academy

Evelyn S. Newlyn
Virginia Polytechnic Institute and State University

Allene Phy-Olsen
Austin Peay State University

Jay Ruud
Northern State University

Paul J. Schwartz
Grand Forks, North Dakota

John C. Shields
Illinois State University

Karen F. Stein
University of Rhode Island

QUEER THEORY

The mode of literary and cultural analysis known as queer theory was established in the early 1990's as an outgrowth of numerous theoretical developments from the twentieth century covered by the broad umbrella of poststructuralism. Queer theory began as a reaction to a series of binary distinctions it has questioned, challenged, or outright denied, including male versus female, sex versus gender, nature versus nurture, and heterosexual versus homosexual. The term "queer," as a word of indeterminate meaning and with negative connotations, reinforces the challenges it brings to the texts under investigation. In practice, queer theory demands repeated, nearly infinite, reevaluation of the standard that is established or assumed by texts both literary and cultural. Queer theory is complex, playful, and elusive, making it difficult both to comprehend and to apply, causing some concern about its viability. Because forcing confrontation to expose power relationships is part of its mission, and because it proceeds by testing arguments rather than positing them, queer theory has proven largely indifferent to such accusations.

SEX AND GENDER AND THE BEGINNINGS OF QUEER THEORY

Contributing to queer theory's emergence is the differentiation between sex and gender made by feminist thinkers, including Simone de Beauvoir and Luce Irigaray. Complications to those precepts have been raised by feminist literary and cultural critics such as Eve Kosofsky Sedgwick and Judith Butler. Their arguments are predicated upon premises generally current among postmodernists and specifically articulated by French psychoanalysts Jacques Lacan and Michel Foucault. The fact that queer theory appeared at a historical point in response to specific philosophers suggests to some that it may be culturally bound and might become irrelevant, but its immediate, broad application to a variety of disciplines argues for its continuation as a viable and relevant method of textual analysis.

Beauvoir's claim that "one is not born, but rather becomes, a woman" summarizes for many early feminists the distinction between the biological factors commonly used to identify a person's sex and the social pressures that form a person's gender. While biological sex was then commonly held to be easily categorized and understood, an assumption that would soon be challenged, social constructions were immediately recognized as shifting, variable, and indeterminate. Feminists have since engaged in systematic explorations of the social pressures to which women are subjected, perhaps in complicity with the patriarchy, and which men and women alike, either consciously or otherwise, perpetuate. Lesbian and gay theorists adopt similar models to explore tendencies and behaviors sometimes rooted in biological distinction, other times being culturally conditioned. The distinction has likewise been fostered by those who would like to reduce behaviors and identities to the influence of either nature or nurture so they can "normalize" sexual identities and orientations.

While recent work suggests a more complex model of interaction, early feminist, lesbian, gay, bisexual, and transgender activists tended to hold either a constructionist view, arguing that a person's sexual and gender identities can be formed by his or her environment, or an essentialist view, which claims that sexuality and gender are genetically encoded or biologically self-evident. Both approaches have also been found useful by those who define gender roles in ways they term "traditional" and who advocate male-female, monogamous relationships as the only viable mode of sexual identity or orientation, who consider a genitalia-focused sexual act as the only possible expression of desire, and who treat any person without a clear, binary gender role or sexual orientation as a victim or as willfully disobedient.

At various times, both the constructionist view and the essentialist view have been supported implicitly by the scientific community. Psychoanalysts, psychiatrists, and psychologists embracing the constructionist view engage in inquiries to determine the causes of sexual identification and behavior. In the past, constructionists labeled androgynes, hermaphrodites, and homosexuals as mentally ill; but still today, some clinicians regularly prescribe treatments ranging from counseling to drug therapy aimed at "curing the disease" or "normalizing the subject." Other medical practitioners faced with a wide range of possible combinations among external genitalia, internal sexual organs, and XY chromosomal patterns through which to determine a person's gender prefer to conduct surgery to assign the patient a clear gender, even if doing so means long-term hormone therapy or infertility, coupled with confusion and even anxiety about a gender chosen sometimes by the patient, sometimes by the parents, and sometimes by the surgeon alone. Scientists embracing essentialism continue their search for a master gene that determines sexual identity as well as for a so-called gay gene that determines sexual orientation.

Pushing the Boundaries of Normal versus Queer

Queer theory has generally refused both the constructivist and the essentialist approach as well as the binary logic that governs sexual identification and orientation, preferring to expose the internal logic of each system by locating—often by pushing against it—a boundary between the normal and the deviant, exploring the nature and consequence of deviance and the ways the normal uses the deviant to reinforce its own normality. In these arguments, queer theorists follow poststructuralists, who reject the basis and terms of the Western systems of logic and rational argumentation institutionalized by the dialectic discourses of Plato, who inscribed the Socratic dialogues.

At its foundation, this challenge is brought to language itself, most radically by linguist Ferdinand de Saussure and philosopher Jacques Derrida. Saussure argues that there is no natural connection between a word, which he calls a signifier, and its definition, which he calls the signified. Derrida notes that because the relationship between a word and its definition can only be arbitrary, that relationship is not fixed or stable but subject to what he terms slippage, the process of defining a word by using other words, which in turn have to be defined. So the meaning of an idea is never fixed; it is always in a state of flux that depends on the chain of terms used to elaborate it. Queer theorists apply similar logic to sexual identity, gender roles, and desire, arguing that each depends on a network of relationships established along a specific historical trajectory and resisting fixed definitions that are at the very least arbitrary, are potentially meaningless, and serve an imbalanced and repressive power structure aimed at regulating desire, sex, and thus identity. The term "queer," adopted by analysts working in this mode, is the cause of much debate.

Historically, the term "queer" has been both ambiguous and derogatory. In the field of queer studies, the term "queer" is generally embraced precisely because of its ambiguity and derogatoriness; the term unsettles the audience, provokes argument, and challenges definitions of what is normal. In practice, queer theory seeks to define, first and foremost, itself. The questions it addresses include what is the meaning of the term "queer"; how does the term intersect with and deviate from similar concepts such as gay, lesbian, and transgender; and what is the potential impact of "queer" upon "normal" (for example, of "queering" something). While such definitional strategies generally characterize a burgeoning field of study, queer theory demands that these strategies remain central foci of its analyses so that the mode of inquiry can remain at the margins of disciplinary discourse, constantly questioning what constitutes the standard.

Normalizing Queer Theory

Ironically, queer theory's basis has been threatened by its very popularity. Within a few years of its emergence on the critical field, it has entered the annals of academia as a regular mode of investigation, spawning conferences, books, journals, and courses of study across many disciplines. This proliferation has led some to wonder how such a "trendy" theoretical approach, so readily institutionalized by a historically understood center of power, can continue to define itself as marginal.

This question is further complicated by the potential application of queer theory to any number of intellectual disciplines. For example—greatly simplifying arguments that have taken shape throughout the twentieth century—the Austrian psychoanalyst Sigmund Freud argued that sexuality and desire are key to identity. A student of his school, Lacan, later argued that desire is encoded in language. In turn, Lacan's ideas were modified by French literary theorist Roland Barthes and cultural philosophers Felix Guattari and Gilles Deleuze. Finally, Foucault argued how language functions as the instrument of power. When these arguments are combined, as they are in queer discourse, any linguistic act becomes an instance of power that establishes identity and is subject to a queer analysis. Such a broad application threatens the unity and basis of queer theory by separating it from its original discourses of sex, gender, and desire. Queer theoreticians have recently found themselves in the position of establishing what queer theory is not, trying to prevent a total dissolution of the method that operates by unraveling possible identifications and power relationships.

Still, it remains within queer theory's "nature" to be always teetering on the precipice of oblivion. From the biblical narrative of Sodom and Gomorrah, completely destroyed because of an unidentified history of sexual perversion, to the twentieth century rhetoric surrounding HIV-AIDS, queer discourse has ever hovered at the edges of annihilation. Some argue that obliteration and obsolescence are part of its nature too because homosexual acts are not procreative, thereby separating desire from creation and continuity. While critics charge that the queer model of intellectual inquiry or artistic endeavor is therefore consumptive or even self-destructive, queer theory freely and playfully explores the pleasures found, for example, in both the making and the enjoying of an art object even when devoid of practical application.

The creation of the theory itself is predicated upon two works published in 1990: Sedgwick's *Epistemology of the Closet* and Butler's *Gender Trouble: Feminism and the Subversion of Identity*. Sedgwick's analysis challenges the methodology that separates homosexuality from heterosexuality as the exclusive basis for sexual orientation, locating in the origin of each term an epistemological shift that affects every domain of Western thought. While Sedgwick warns that by historicizing sexuality one runs the risk of eradicating alternate forms of reality, she explores the implications of the ability to precisely date the first use of the term "homosexual" and the fact that its opposite, "heterosexual," while supposedly the normal tendency, was coined many years after and in opposition to the earlier, "deviant" word. Sedgwick argues that by distilling sexual identification to one element of the pleasure paradigm, and that by establishing an oppositional scheme by which to label it, the Western world has reinforced the power structure based squarely upon patriarchy and its ability to control reproduction. This power remains, even though its tenuous hold on society is continually exposed through discourses ranging from the faulty logic governing the U.S. Supreme Court decision to allow states the authority to define and outlaw sexual acts between consenting adults (*Bowers vs. Hardwick*, 1986) to the prejudices feminists routinely discover in the literary canon.

Like Sedgwick, Butler began her career as a feminist theorist and believes that her explorations of sexual orientation and gender identity are warranted both because feminists have historically examined the ways language itself constructs and maintains sexual difference and male power and because feminists must identify the category of person they wish to represent before they can be reasonably expected to achieve their political goals. She speculates on the possibility that by arguing that women are subjected to male power, even by claiming to represent women at all, feminists are actually upholding the very binary logic that divides human beings into two sexual categories—

one dominant, one subservient—thereby perpetrating the patriarchal power they seek to eradicate.

Butler acknowledges the extent to which her arguments depend upon observations made by French theoretician Foucault, who first identified the logic by which binary oppositions operate and subjugate. In *Histoire de la sexualité* (1976-1984; 3 vols.; *The History of Sexuality*, 1978-1987, 3 vols.) Foucault denies the readily accepted explanation for the prevalence of sexual discourse in modern society, that sexuality has been repressed and therefore strives to make itself known. Instead, he argues that even those with the power to repress sexuality generate discourse about it to silence it, not by denying its existence but by enfolding it within its own linguistic structures of confession and inquiry. In his later work *L'Archéologie du savoir* (1969; *The Archaeology of Knowledge*, 1972), Foucault argues that power structures interface with one another and uphold themselves by generating language surrounding the definition of "the normal" but focusing on the abnormal, the disruptive, or the liminal (that which exists at the margins). Foucault notes that these terms are defined only in opposition to a supposed standard, and that they thereby encompass within themselves the norms they supposedly defy. He thus introduces areas of discourse in which the oppositions tend to break down and in which the standards can be exposed and challenged without being simply reversed.

Butler raises several questions about the social construction of gender, but rather than counter these questions with biological arguments, she asserts that social constructions are radically uncertain, almost to the point of unintelligibility. Butler in particular criticizes the distinctions between the mind, the body, and the world; the first two established by Plato, the last added by French philosopher René Descartes, author of the infamous formulation *Cogito, ergo sum*, or "I think, therefore I am." Butler claims that modern discoveries about the roles played by language and perspective in determining truth prove that there can be no distinction between the mental activity, its material substance, and the culture in which it lives, and that, therefore, any notion of sexual identity, whether derived from bodily characteristics or social indoctrination, is necessarily fabricated. Butler speculates that if sex and gender can be distinguished from one another, as they were by earlier feminists, then gender certainly has no causal relationship to sex and may not have any connection to it whatsoever. She opens the possibility that sex itself is not a natural, biological distinction but may be the product of discourse about sex and therefore may be constructed by and for the service of the power that holds some sexes in thrall.

Butler further argues that both sex and gender are subject to the demands and strictures of what she calls performance. Performance is not simply a matter of deciding which sex or gender role one wants to adopt, nor is it the enacting of specific behaviors along a scale of femininity or masculinity. Instead, performance is the product of a complicated interaction between an individual and his or her environment. It is always changing and never definitive, but it is still necessary to the production of identity and the development of relationships. Still, Butler recognizes that people need an identity on which to base their sense of self and to interact with the world in which they live. Therefore, she argues, people construct a gender identity for themselves by performing it. That construction is not stable because people change their performance in response to internal and external pressures. Others interpret the performance and convey their interpretations to the performer, in turn affecting the performance. Butler's argument thus displaces the agent of sexual identification, so that neither the individual nor his or her society is wholly responsible for the construction of sexual identity. Rather, both the person and society work together or in conflict along a scale of gendered possibilities.

Butler's insights dovetail with arguments made by speech-act and reader-reception theorists, who claim that texts perform their meaning in concert with their readers, thus laying the foundation for a broad application of queer theory. By parsing the moves made by a text to constitute the reader's interpretation of sex, gender, and desire, queer theoreticians expose and thereby challenge the power structures that establish and maintain sexual difference. So a "queer reading" might explore the implications of poet and playwright William Shakespeare's sonnets in praise of a young man's physical beauty, in light of the fact that Shakespeare was married and his wife had given birth to three children. A queer analysis, too, could explore the social pressure that keeps pseudonymous female author George Eliot's character Dorothea Brooke (*Middlemarch*, 1872) obligated to her dead husband's scholarship, considering that Eliot was ostracized from learned society for living with a married man. Finally, queer theoreticians may take up seemingly abstract topics such as race, democracy, or the aesthetic and explore how the experiences or perspectives of gays, lesbians, bisexuals, or transgendered persons alter the conceptions of spurious or tacit definitions and standards.

Queer theory's detractors and critics

The methodology of queer theory questions what people believe they know about sex, identity, and desire to expose and challenge unspoken assumptions. Because queer theory refuses the standards adopted by the text and then posits alternatives, often only to undermine them, it has been accused of being petty and querulous, and even illogical. Queer theory both ignores and embraces these accusations in its quest to escape the rules governing philosophical inquiry in the West. Likewise, queer theory has been criticized for its focus on the freakish, abnormal, and fetishist, and for proceeding in a tone alternatively described as campy, hysterical, or "screaming." When they choose to respond, queer theoreticians argue that only by exploring life at the margins can they hope to define the boundaries that uphold power, and that by calling attention to the performative features of argument, they hope to undermine the perhaps more subtle but no more legitimate rhetorical strategies employed by those who claim to be reasonable, rational, and objective.

Finally, in response to charges that queer theory coins terms illogically or unnecessarily, or that it employs complex or even faulty grammatical structures, queer theorists argue that nouns or adjectives used to specify genders or sexual orientations cannot be defined because they refer to such a complex network of objects and experiences. Even the very syntax of language upholds the binary logic of power structures that govern gender and desire, and thus must be defied by those not privileged to speak within or against the system.

Despite the many criticisms that queer theory employs an unnecessary and even exclusionary elitism predicated upon its erudite treatment of texts, that it is overly playful in its handling of serious arguments, and that its intentionally loose treatment of grammar make it unreadable, inapplicable, or irrelevant, queer theory remains a vibrant and productive area of interdisciplinary inquiry. It remains possible that scientific discoveries about sexuality and gender may alter understandings of identity so that its logic becomes utterly nonsensical. Likewise, historical developments may shift the mechanisms of power away from sex and gender. It seems more likely though that the kinds of radical uncertainty, relentless questioning, and rejection of standards performed by queer theory will become the only conceivable model of intellectual inquiry, normalizing queer theory to the point that it too will have to be challenged from an entirely new model.

BIBLIOGRAPHY

Berlant, Lauren, and Michael Warner. "What Does Queer Theory Teach Us About X?" *PMLA* 110, no. 3 (May, 1995): 343-349. An attempt to define queer theory by establishing what it does not do, including the ways it is not useful or practical, while defending that inutility as key to its function.

Butler, Judith. *Gender Trouble: Feminism and the Subversion of Identity*. 1990. Reprint. New York: Routledge, 2008. A foundational text in queer theory that challenges the definitions of "sexuality," "sex," and "gender," locating all three concepts in what Butler describes as performance.

Differences: A Journal of Feminist Cultural Studies 3, no. 2 (Summer, 1991). Special issue on queer theory edited by Teresa de Lauretis. A collection of essays that explores the basis of queer theory and demonstrates its applicability across academic disciplines.

Edelman, Lee. *No Future: Queer Theory and the Death Drive*. Durham, N.C.: Duke University Press, 2004. Edelman questions the viability of a theory—namely queer theory—that opposes convention simply for the sake of opposing convention, exploring the nihilistic impulse and the anti-energy that govern the discipline.

Fuss, Diana, ed. *Inside / Out: Lesbian Theories, Gay Theories*. New York: Routledge, 1991. A collection of essays examining queer identity formation, performance, and interpretation.

Hall, Donald E. *Queer Theories*. New York: Palgrave Macmillan, 2003. A thorough, readable summary of the origins, applications, and range of queer theory.

Halperin, David M. *One Hundred Years of Homosexuality, and Other Essays on Greek Love*. New York: Routledge, 1989. Halperin questions the utility of a historicized perspective for queer theoreticians, particularly the extent to which homosexual identities are culturally constructed and therefore limited and limiting.

Huffer, Lynne. *Mad for Foucault: Rethinking the Foundations of Queer Theory*. New York: Columbia University Press, 2009. Huffer reevaluates Michel Foucault's *Folie et déraison* (1961; *Madness and Civilization*, 1965; fully translated as *History of Madness*, 2006) to argue that it was this early work that should be considered a foundational text in queer theory.

Jagose, Annamarie. *Queer Theory: An Introduction*. 1996. Reprint. New York: New York University Press, 2007. A clear, concise overview of the historical and factual circumstances surrounding the intellectual model.

O'Rourke, Michael. *Derrida and Queer Theory*. New York: Palgrave Macmillan 2010. The first book-length study of critic Jacques Derrida in relation to queer theory. Examines queer theory's "debts to Derrida" and seeks "queer moments" in Derrida's writings.

Rubin, Gayle S. "Thinking Sex." In *The Lesbian and Gay Studies Reader*, edited by Henry Abelove, Michèle Aina Barale, and David M. Halperin. New York: Routledge, 1993. Gayle S. Rubin, in this classic essay, explores whether sex/gender and politics are perhaps the same, and she examines the ways sexual identities are used to enforce power.

L. Michelle Baker

PAULA GUNN ALLEN

Born: Cubero, New Mexico; October 24, 1939
Died: Ft. Bragg, California; May 29, 2008

PRINCIPAL POETRY
The Blind Lion, 1974
Coyote's Daylight Trip, 1978
A Cannon Between My Knees, 1981
Star Child, 1981
Shadow Country, 1982
Wyrds, 1987
Skins and Bones: Poems, 1979-1987, 1988
Life Is a Fatal Disease: Collected Poems, 1962-1995, 1997

OTHER LITERARY FORMS

Paula Gunn Allen's writing helped establish the literature of her American Indian cultural heritage as a legitimate and recognized genre. In addition to her extensive and innovative catalog of poetry, Allen published fiction, nonfiction, biographies, collections of myth and oral tradition, critical essays, pedagogical articles concerning the education of native peoples, and gender and sexuality studies. Allen collected, wrote, and edited personal histories as well as myths and legends of various tribes in her books *The Sacred Hoop: Recovering the Feminine in American Indian Traditions* (1986), *Spider Woman's Granddaughters: Traditional Tales and Contemporary Writing by Native American Women* (1989), and *Grandmothers of the Light: A Medicine Woman's Sourcebook* (1991). Allen's motivation to raise awareness concerning American Indian literature, combined with her innovative academic endeavors, earned her acclaim from critics and readers alike, placing the author at the forefront of the American Indian, feminist, and gay and lesbian literary scenes.

ACHIEVEMENTS

Paula Gunn Allen's literary achievements began in 1978, when the National Endowment for the Arts awarded her a distinguished writing fellowship. She received two postdoctoral fellowships, the first from the University of California in 1981 and the second from the Ford Foundation-National Research Council in 1984. Allen received two awards for her groundbreaking work in 1990: the American Book Award from the Before Columbus Foundation for *Spider Woman's Granddaughters* and the Native American Prize for Literature.

Accolades for Allen's work increased throughout her career, in which she amassed honors such as the Susan Koppelman Award from the Popular Cultural Association and American Culture Association (1991), the Vesta Award for Essay Writing (1991), the Southern California Women for Understanding Award for Literature (1991), an honorary doctorate in humanities from Mills College (1995), the Hubbell Prize for Lifetime Achievement in American Literary Studies (1999), and the Lifetime Achievement Award from the Native Writers' Circle of the Americas (2001). In 2004, Allen's *Pocahontas: Medicine Woman, Spy, Entrepreneur, Diplomat* (2003) was nominated for a Pulitzer Prize, and in 2007, she received the Lannan Literary Fellowship, designed to honor writers whose impact on English-language literature promotes increased interest and readership in both prose and poetry.

Biography

Paula Gunn Allen was born Paula Marie Francis in 1939 in Cubero, New Mexico, and was raised by her mother and grandmother on the Cubero Land Grant, situated between the Laguna and Acoma Pueblo Reservations. The daughter of a Laguna-Sioux-Scottish mother and a Lebanese American father, Allen cultivated her love and appreciation of the myths and lore of her American Indian ancestors and would perpetuate her desire to be a lifelong student of native culture.

Allen began her higher education at Colorado Women's College, where the work of poet Robert Creeley would have a profound influence on her. She took time off from school to marry and have two children, but the marriage ended in divorce a few years later. She transferred to the University of Oregon, earning a B.A. in English in 1966 and an M.F.A. in creative writing in 1968. At the University of New Mexico, Allen wanted to pursue a doctorate in Native American literature, but the dean informed her that this was not possible as Native American literature was not a canonical genre. Instead, in 1975, Allen received a doctorate in American studies with a concentration on Native American literature.

Following the completion of her doctorate, two divorces, and the birth of three children, Allen began writing from a twentieth century lesbian-feminist perspective. She quickly established herself as a prolific writer and has since been acknowledged as the founder of American Indian literary studies. Seeking to rectify the canonical discrepancies regarding ethnic literature, Allen (after publishing five collections of poetry) turned her focus to the retelling of native myths and to lesbian-feminist literary criticism. In subsequent years, Allen kept working, writing many texts that would become staples in the classroom—providing future generations of students with the types of sources that were unavailable to her during her own education.

Analysis

Paula Gunn Allen's first book of poetry, *The Blind Lion*, contains some of the author's most personal work. The poems in its three sections—"The Blind Lion," "The

Amorclast," and "The Separation"—chronicle the dissolution of romantic love, while only subtly referencing her cultural background. The first section records a metamorphosis from the warm comfort of familiarity in "Definition" to colliding and opposing elements in "The Orange on Your Head Is on Fire," in which the man is the "fire/ bird" and the woman is the "cold wind." The lion of the title poem, an animal normally associated with dominance, pride, and courage, is made impotent by its blindness and is transformed into a weeping and pitiable creature. The lion thus becomes a metaphor for the relationship now reduced and defined by isolation. "Cool Life" further elucidates the couple's relationship complications, of which the narrator states: "between us/ we are ice . . ." and "outside of us/ dandelions bloom."

The second section of *The Blind Lion* denotes the irreparable breakage of traditional love and the institution of marriage. The language of the poems becomes increasingly dark and volatile, as the narrator in "The Amorclast" describes, "your fist expresses the rain-/ drops flying around us," culminating with the stark language and imagery of the lover "twisting the handle/ revealing the bone/ of your contempt." Other poems within this section similarly portray the escalating turbulence within the relationship—often represented by aspects of nature such as fog, frost, wind, and shadows. Here, Allen experiments with and reinvents the poetic form in order to fully portray the sporadic and often irrational ways in which people cope with failed relationships.

The third section, "The Separation," portrays the narrator's reclaiming and reinvention of herself, reflected in the increasingly prevalent spiritual and feminist tones of the poems. In "Shadows," the narrator struggles with her sense of identity as "The room comes to me a stranger,/ its familiar things turned/ unfamiliar, as though/ I, a visitor, had just walked in. . . ." Her former life having been forever altered, the narrator cannot recognize where she belongs in her newly realized solitude. "Liebestraume" (German for "dreams of love") is perhaps the darkest piece in the collection, wherein "pestilence," "plague," and "rotting velvet" lie under the covers that "half-hid the empty revolver you cocked and used/ to blow open the bone at the back of my skull. . . ." The romantic title belies the poet's emotions as her dreams of love are displaced by dreams of death. However, the narrator ends the poem expressing expectations of hope and rebirth, from which she will arise transformed.

A CANNON BETWEEN MY KNEES

A Cannon Between My Knees, Allen's third collection, builds on the feelings left unresolved at the end of *The Blind Lion*. The fourteen new poems are more noticeably concerned with spirituality, myth, creation, and the roles of women therein. Allen does include two poems dedicated to her father, "Durango Suite" and "Lament of My Father, Lakota," while further exploring the persistence of memory along with the harsh reality of reservation life in "Wool Season: 1973."

Allen's poetry shows a new maturity in this collection. Her feminist voice becomes increasingly impressive, as in "The Beautiful Woman Who Sings," which depicts a hardworking woman of nature who embodies true beauty. In "Poem for Pat," one of Allen's first pieces representing homosexual love and desire, the narrator reminisces, "we found each other again, she said,/ and we were shivering at what we contemplated/ locked together on the sandstone mesas. . . ." In "Suicid/ing(ed) Indian Woman," the poet retells four stories of jilted, misunderstood, and misused women from various native tribes. From their sadness, she creates strength, and as the collection progresses, so too do the references to woman as creator, mother, grandmother, provider, and nurturer.

Accompanying these representations of female empowerment are references to male weaknesses such as addictions to alcohol and gambling, brought on by the emasculation of native men, just two of the results of white colonization of native lands. These references make the phrase "a cannon between my knees" in the final poem of the collection, "Thusness Before the War," especially poignant, as the symbol of military domination and destruction becomes a phallic symbol of feminine virility and authority.

SHADOW COUNTRY

The meaning behind the title of Allen's fifth poetry collection, *Shadow Country*, welcomes reader interpretation, as its pages contain a world that is somehow universal, yet uniquely hers. Neither dark nor light, the title could represent Allen's feelings about her mixed heritage; it could imply the marginalization of native populations or the diminishing of the country's glory; or it could even signify, as in "Que Cante Quetzal," that the country is engulfed in shadow due to its ongoing participation in brutal military conquests worldwide. Allen does not limit herself by any boundaries in her poetic endeavors, as she explores the themes of creation, consumerism, revolution, apocalypse, resurrection, and celebration.

"Los Angeles, 1980" indicts American vanity and the consumerism that results from people's attempts to achieve the public "ideal." This "death culture" dominates the natural world and pollutes the air, then seeks to use the landscape's true beauty to create organic beauty products, natural-fiber clothes, and herbal nutritional supplements. Despite these urges to improve "naturally," signs reading "Weight and Smoking Control Center" and other such consumer fodder litter the sidewalks. A passerby notices her "average" reflection in the Center's smoky glass, and notes, ". . . death comes in pretty packages too,/ and all around me/ the dying air agreed."

The poems within *Shadow Country*, although certainly concerned with native spirituality, explore the issues of traditional and modern cultures, which are then juxtaposed with political issues. These comparative critiques produce powerful commentary in regard to the conflicting values of white and native societies. Relics and ruins of native cultures, military conquests, and forced removals are present in several poignant poems such as "Another Long Walk," "The Warrior," "Riding the Thunder," and "Off Reservation Blues," in which the dreaming narrator grieves over her imprisonment, which symbolizes the ongoing claustrophobia that resulted from the forced removal of native peoples to reservations, but which gives her poetry meaning: "Open words, openly said/ are not heard."

OTHER MAJOR WORKS

LONG FICTION: *The Woman Who Owned the Shadows*, 1983.

NONFICTION: *Studies in American Indian Literature: Critical Essays and Course Designs*, 1983; *The Sacred Hoop: Recovering the Feminine in American Indian Traditions*, 1986; *Grandmothers of the Light: A Medicine Woman's Sourcebook*, 1991; *As Long as the Rivers Flow: The Stories of Nine Native Americans*, 1996 (with Clark Smith); *Off the Reservation: Reflections on Boundary-Busting, Border-Crossing Loose Canons*, 1998; *Pocahontas: Medicine Woman, Spy, Entrepreneur, Diplomat*, 2003.

EDITED TEXTS: *From the Center—A Folio: Native American Art and Poetry*, 1981; *Spider Woman's Granddaughters: Traditional Tales and Contemporary Writing by Native American Women*, 1989; *Voice of the Turtle: American Indian Literature, 1900-1970*, 1994; *Song of the Turtle: American Indian Literature, 1974-1994*, 1996; *Hozho: Walking in Beauty*, 2001 (with Carolyn Dunn Anderson); *Outfoxing Coyote*, 2002 (with Anderson).

MISCELLANEOUS: *Columbus and Beyond: Views from Native Americans*, 1992 (with others); *Gossips, Gorgons, and Crones: The Fates of the Earth*, 1993 (foreword by Allen; text by Jane Caputi).

BIBLIOGRAPHY

Allen, Paula Gunn. "A Funny Thing Happened on My Way to Press." *Frontiers: A Journal of Women Studies* 23 (2002): 3-6. This short, autobiographical account of Allen's reactions to the stereotypes of American Indians is a quick yet insightful glimpse into the author's personality, both as an American Indian woman and as a poet.

Forbes, Jack. "Colonialism and Native American Literature: Analysis." *Wicazo Sa Review* 3 (1987): 17-23. Forbes's primary objective in this article is to address questions relating to the term "Native American literature." He examines what constitutes native or ethnic literature, who is "allowed" to write it, and what the literature infers or implies within the social construct of a colonial interpretation.

Jahner, Elaine A. "The Style of the Times in Paula Gunn Allen's Poetry." In *Speak to Me Words: Essays on Contemporary American Indian Poetry*, edited by Dean Rader and Janice Gould. Tucson: University of Arizona Press, 2003. In this article, Jahner writes on Allen's use of formal structures in her poems.

Koehler, Lyle. "Native Women of the Americas: A Bibliography." *Frontiers: A Journal of Women Studies* 6 (1981): 73-101. A comprehensive bibliography of authors and works related to various themes in Native American literature and an invaluable go-to guide for those interested in the genre. The author provides subsections on specific topics such as religion, sexuality, and craftswomen.

Rowley, Kelley E. "Re-inscribing Mythopoetic Vision in Native American Studies." *American Indian Quarterly* 26 (2002): 491-500. Mythopoetic vision refers to the process of making myths and how audiences come to perceive them. Rowley uses Allen's four characteristics of a sacred visionary narrative, "the supernatural characters, the nonordinary events, the transcendent powers, and the pour quoi elements," to further expound on the mythopoetics of Native American texts.

Ruppert, Jim. "Paula Gunn Allen and Joy Harjo: Closing the Distance Between Personal and Mythic Space." *American Indian Quarterly* 7, no. 1 (1983): 27-40. Ruppert discusses the poetry of Allen and Joy Harjo and the ways in which their works address the fusion of mundane and mystic/personal and universal spaces, in order to create harmony between earth, mind, and spirit.

Lydia E. Ferguson

JOHN ASHBERY

Born: Rochester, New York; July 28, 1927

PRINCIPAL POETRY
Turandot, and Other Poems, 1953
Some Trees, 1956
The Tennis Court Oath, 1962
Rivers and Mountains, 1966
Selected Poems, 1967
The Double Dream of Spring, 1970
Three Poems, 1972
Self-Portrait in a Convex Mirror, 1975
Houseboat Days, 1977
As We Know, 1979
Shadow Train, 1981
A Wave, 1984
Selected Poems, 1985
April Galleons, 1987
Flow Chart, 1991
Hotel Lautrémont, 1992
Three Books: Poems, 1993
And the Stars Were Shining, 1994
Can You Hear, Bird: Poems, 1995
The Mooring of Starting Out: The First Five Books of Poetry, 1997
Wakefulness: Poems, 1998
Girls on the Run: A Poem, 1999
Your Name Here, 2000
As Umbrellas Follow Rain, 2002
Chinese Whispers, 2002
Where Shall I Wander, 2005
A Worldly Country: New Poems, 2007
Notes from the Air: Selected Later Poems, 2007
Collected Poems, 1956-1987, 2008
Planisphere: New Poems, 2009

OTHER LITERARY FORMS

Although known mainly as a poet, John Ashbery has produced a number of works in various genres. *A Nest of Ninnies* (1969) is a humorous novel about middle-class American life written by Ashbery in collaboration with James Schuyler. His plays include *The Compromise: Or, Queen of the Carabou* (pr. 1956) and *Three Plays* (1978). He also produced a volume of art criticism, *Reported Sightings: Art Chronicles, 1957-1987* (1989). His Charles Eliot Norton Lectures (given at Harvard University) were collected as *Other Traditions* (2000), an engaging volume of literary criticism about six eccentric poets.

Achievements

John Ashbery won three major literary awards for *Self-Portrait in a Convex Mirror:* the National Book Award in Poetry, the Pulitzer Prize, and the National Book Critics Circle Award. Ashbery is a member of the Academy of Arts and Sciences and the American Academy of Arts and Letters (since 1980) and served as chancellor for the Academy of American Poets (1988-1999). He has been honored with two Guggenheim Fellowships, two Fulbright Fellowships, and two National Endowment for the Arts grants. He won the Yale Series of Younger Poets award (1955) for *Some Trees*, Union League Civic and Arts Poetry Prize (1966), an Award in Literature from the American Academy of Arts and Letters (1969), the Shelley Memorial Award (1973), the Levinson Prize (1977), the Jersome J. Shestack Poetry Award (1983), and the Bollingen Prize from Yale University (1985). In 1982, Ashbery was awarded the Fellowship of the Academy of American Poets. In 1985, he was named a winner of both a MacArthur Prize Fellowship and a Lenore Marshall Poetry Prize. He received the Commonwealth Award in Literature (1986), the Ruth Lilly Poetry Prize (1992), the Frost Medal from the Poetry Society of America (1995), the Gold Medal for Poetry from the American Academy of Arts and Letters (1997), the prestigious Antonio Feltrinelli Prize from the Accademia Nazionale dei Lincei in Rome (1992), the Bingham Poetry Prize (1998), theWallace Stevens Award (2001), and the Griffin Poetry Prize (2008). In 2002, he was made an officer of the French Legion of Honor by presidential decree.

Biography

Born in Rochester, New York, in 1927, John Lawrence Ashbery grew up in rural Sodus, New York. He attended Deerfield Academy and Harvard University, where he became friends with poet Kenneth Koch. Ashbery received his B.A. from Harvard in 1949 and his M.A. from Columbia University in 1951. After leaving university life, Ashbery worked for various publishers in New York City until he moved to Paris in 1955. He remained in Paris until 1965, writing for the *New York Herald Tribune*, *Art International*, and *Art News*. From 1965 until 1972, Ashbery worked as executive editor for *Art News* in New York, before becoming a distinguished professor of writing at the Brooklyn College campus of the City University of New York. He has also taught at Harvard University. Ashbery became the Charles P. Stevenson, Jr., Professor of Languages and Literature at Bard College in 1990.

ANALYSIS

As a brief review of his biography would suggest, John Ashbery has had a considerable amount of exposure to the world of art and to the language of art criticism. Ashbery spent a full decade of his life in Paris, the art capital of Europe, where he read deeply in French poetry and immersed himself in the day-to-day life of French culture. Readers of Ashbery's poetry, then, should not be surprised to encounter references to art and occasional snatches of the French language as part of the poetic texts. For example, one of his poems is entitled "Le Livre est sur la table." There are other titles in German, Latin, and Russian, and the poetry as a whole bristles with references from every department of highbrow, middlebrow, and lowbrow culture, including cartoons ("Daffy Duck in Hollywood"), silent movies ("The Lonedale Operator"), literature ("Sonnet," "A Long Novel," and "Thirty-seven Haiku"), history ("The Tennis Court Oath"), and linguistics ("The Plural of 'Jack-in-the-Box'").

Because of its unpredictable style and subject matter, Ashbery's poetry has managed to infuriate, befuddle, amuse, delight, and instruct its readers. His work remains some of the most difficult verse produced, for he refuses to provide the reader with a poetic "reality" that is any less complex than the "reality" of the world outside poetry. Ashbery cannot be simplified or paraphrased because his work has no "content" in the ordinary sense. His poetry is "about" the act of knowing, the process of imagining, the curious associational leaps made by the human mind as it experiences any given moment in time. To read Ashbery is to be teased into a whole range of possible meanings without finally settling on a single one. Although this openness might confuse the reader at the outset, the process of reading Ashbery becomes more pleasurable on each encounter. New meanings appear, and Ashbery's voice comes to seem strangely present, as if he were intoning directly into the reader's ear. These poems are filled with little verbal cues and signals aimed directly at the reader; many of the poems depend on a complicated dialogue or interplay between the author and the reader (a technique he exploits masterfully in *Three Poems*). Thus his work is a kind of half-poetry, always requiring an active reader to make it whole. Ashbery achieves his trademark effect of apparent intimacy while simulating the very process of thought itself.

How Ashbery came to create this new kind of poetry is actually a subchapter in the general history of art and culture in the twentieth century. Certainly he benefited mightily from his study of other artists and thinkers. During his formative years in Paris, he absorbed the French language and the famous paintings of the Louvre while immersing himself in all kinds of printed matter: cheap pamphlets and paperback novels bought from the bookstalls, as well as journalistic prose (in French and English) and the rarefied language of art criticism (which he himself was producing).

In addition, it is clear that a strong line of influence connects Ashbery with writers such as Gertrude Stein, who used disjointed syntax and unorthodox grammar as part of her Surrealistic poetry. He owes a clear debt also to Wallace Stevens, who taught him how to philosophize in poetry and also how to approach subjects obliquely. Stevens, also, was a great lover of French Impressionist painting and Symbolist poetry. From W. H. Auden, who chose Ashbery's *Some Trees* for the Yale Series of Younger Poets, Ashbery learned a conversational naturalness and a lyrical or musical way of phrasing. It might be argued that Ashbery, as a literate artist, was influenced by all the great thinkers of the century, but these poetic debts seem particularly obvious, especially in the early books. He probably learned something from Ludwig Wittgenstein's idea of language as a game, just as he must have responded to Jackson Pollock's expressionist paintings, which use paint in much the same way that Ashbery uses words. Something of the sheer shock value and unpredictability of musicians such as Igor Stravinsky, John Cage, and Anton Webern must have touched him also, since Ashbery is clearly fond of similar effects in his own poems.

These debts to the artistic pioneers of the twentieth century are most obvious in Ashbery's earlier books—that is, those preceding the publication of *Three Poems: Some Trees, The Tennis Court Oath*, and *Rivers and Mountains*. All these books are relatively short and compact, typically containing one long or major poem, often positioned near the end of the volume.

Ashbery's characteristic wonder and inventiveness has proven a hallmark of the several volumes published since 1990. During that period, Ashbery wrote and published more and wrote more of the highest quality than at any other time in his career. With Ashbery, there is no limit to the possibilities inherent in human life and to the sheer fun of the mind's response to them. Regular readers of Ashbery will begin to inhabit a world that is larger, more unpredictable, and infinitely more interesting than anything they have known before.

SOME TREES

Typical of Ashbery's early poems are "The Instruction Manual" from *Some Trees* and the title poem from *Rivers and Mountains*, each of which forces the reader to perform another kind of imaginative leaping, one that is different from the mere shock of the surreal. In "The Instruction Manual," the speaker is bored with his job of writing an instruction manual on the uses of a new metal and, instead, falls into a prolonged aesthetic daydream on the city of Guadalajara, Mexico, which he has never visited. He invents this city in magical detail for the rest of the poem. In like manner, the places described on a map and the map itself become utterly indistinguishable in "Rivers and Mountains," as if Ashbery were suggesting that one's most vivid moments are those that have been rescued or resurrected by the fertile powers of the poetic imagination. Ashbery always emphasizes the primacy of the imagination. In his view, the most vivid reality occurs in the poem itself, because that is the precise point where the inner and outer (spiritual and sensory) experiences of life actually intersect.

Two more early poems bear analysis here, because they also illustrate the poetic techniques favored in many of Ashbery's later poems. "Le Livre est sur la table" and "The Picture of Little J. A. in a Prospect of Flowers" (both from *Some Trees*) are magnificent feats of imaginative power, and each operates on the same principle of aesthetic meditation. In each poem, the poet looks at reality through a work of art, or as if it were a work of art (in "The Picture of Little J. A. in a Prospect of Flowers" a photograph is the medium). The effect is largely the same, because the world is always transformed and made into a work of art by the conclusion of the poem. Stevens is probably the model for this kind of poem, exemplified by his "Thirteen Ways of Looking at a Blackbird" and "A Study of Two Pears." Other poets, particularly William Carlos Williams, Marianne Moore, and Elizabeth Bishop, were to involve themselves passionately in the writing of aesthetically oriented poems, and one can look to some of their pioneering work to explain the sureness and control of Ashbery's similar efforts.

In "Le Livre est sur la table," Ashbery offers the reader a number of aesthetic propositions to contemplate, the most important of which is the notion that beauty results from a certain emptiness or from the placement of an object in an unusual or unaccustomed position. In both instances, the viewer is forced to see the object in a new way. Ashbery again underlines the power of the imagination, giving the example of an imaginary woman who comes alive in her stride, her hair, and her breasts as she is imagined. Most important of all is the artist who creates small artistic catalysts, new and strange relationships that haunt the perceiver with their beauty. Neither the sea nor a simple birdhouse can make for innovative art but placing them together in a fundamental relationship changes them forever:

> The young man places a bird-house
> Against the blue sea. He walks away
> And it remains. Now other
> Men appear, but they live in boxes.

The men in the boxes are the nonartists, who do not realize that the newly created sea is a highlighted thing. All along, the sea has been "writing" a message (with its waves and lines), but only the "young man" (the artist) can read it.

The other "young man," or artist figure, in *Some Trees* is Ashbery himself, described in the snapshot that serves as the aesthetic focal point for the autobiographical poem "The Picture of Little J. A. in a Prospect of Flowers." This little fellow has a head like a mushroom and stands comically before a bed of phlox, but he has the makings of a poet precisely because he appreciates the value of words—especially lost words, those tip-of-the-tongue utterances and slips of the tongue, in which the speaker strains to specify clear meaning. "The Picture of Little J. A. in a Prospect of Flowers" is a typical Ashbery performance, not merely because of its high aesthetic theme but also because of its inclusion of low comedy, irony, and parody. The epigraph—taken from Boris Pasternak's autobiography *Okhrannaya gramota* (1931; *Safe Conduct*, 1945 in *The Collected Prose*

Works)—seemingly contradicts the rest of the poem in what is the first of many jokes (Dick and Jane of childhood books become Dick and Genevieve, conversing in complicated Elizabethan sentences). Childhood is full of jokes and embarrassments, like standing in front of the clicking shutter of a camera, but childhood can also be the beginning of the artist's journey: The poem ends by praising the imagination and its ability to rescue this early phase of life through the power of words. "The Picture of Little J. A. in a Prospect of Flowers" is a bittersweet portrait of a self-conscious and precocious young man who was destined to become a great artist.

THE TENNIS COURT OATH

In *The Tennis Court Oath*, the reader encounters the long quasi-epical poem entitled "Europe," a work related in overall form to T. S. Eliot's *The Waste Land* (1922) and to similar efforts by Ezra Pound, Hart Crane, and Williams. In the most general terms, "Europe" here means the accumulated cultural wealth of European history and its ability—or inability—to help the creative artist in the twentieth century. The decay, or "wasteland," of Europe is juxtaposed to or "intercut" (in film terms) with a trivial story of two travelers, Pryor and Collins, whose unheroic status stands in sharp contrast to the old order. As the poem begins, the poet registers all these complex feelings, while focusing on the shocking blueness of the morning sky, here presented surrealistically:

> To employ her
> construction ball
> Morning fed on the
> light blue wood
> of the mouth

The wrecking ball of construction crews is one of the most visible symbols of the typical cityscape, suggesting simultaneously the twin processes of destruction and re-creation. The sudden, destructive impact of the steel ball approximates the elemental power of the morning light as it, too, rearranges and alters the city and all of its facets. The bystander is left openmouthed and speechless, like the sky itself. This analysis does not fully explicate Ashbery's lines, because, like all dream imagery, they resist final explication. One can describe their suggestiveness and allusiveness, but the dream itself remains a mystery, as does this purely perceived moment of an ordinary morning in the city.

THREE POEMS

Some of the poet's greatness is evident on nearly every page of *Three Poems*, the book that many critics cite as Ashbery's masterpiece. The long, meditative work consists of three interlocking prose poems, "The New Spirit," "The System," and "The Recital," and totals 118 densely packed pages of text. Most of that text is written in prose, a highly interactive prose that constantly urges the reader forward, raises questions, voices doubts and suspicions, and generally plunges the reader headlong into a highly meditative process of thinking and reflecting. *Three Poems* is Ashbery at his most difficult and most satisfying, even though there is virtually no story or tidy paraphrase that can be made of the reading experience itself. Nevertheless, a few elusive details do emerge, and one dimly begins to realize that *Three Poems* is an oblique narrative that in general terms charts a deep relationship between two lovers, one that somehow founders, so that the narrator grows more and more self-possessed. The narrator becomes less and less likely to address the familiar "you" who is called upon again and again in the opening pages of the book. By the end, the "you" has virtually disappeared, as if the loss of love might be charted by the absence of the "you" from pages where only the "I" can finally dominate.

The form of *Three Poems* deserves some attention, because the poems are cast in the form of prose, though their imagery, tonal shifts, and complicated rhythms all suggest poetic (not prosaic) form. To complicate matters even further, Ashbery originally published the second section of the work, "The System," in the *Paris Review* in 1971, the year before the whole work appeared in the form of a book. Ashbery specifically allowed "The System" to be published as a prose work, so by titling the whole three-part composition *Three Poems*, he seems to be teasing the reader again on the simplest level and at the same time calling attention to the arbitrariness of literary labels and taxonomy. As if all those complications were not enough, Ashbery carries the joke further by inserting several poems (or at least texts that look like poems) into the longer work. What counts in the end is the sustained act of mediation and empathy with the narrator that these manipulations of typeface and marginal format will induce in the reader.

The reader, facing *Three Poems*, has a Herculean task to perform: absorbing a long, oblique narrative that requires constant reflection, analysis, and thoughtful mediation. The difficulty is an intentional by-product of Ashbery's stated goal on the first page of the book: to leave out as much as possible in order to create a newer and truer form of communication. Any love story the reader could have encountered would have finally become banal; what Ashbery gives, however, cannot grow stale. To read *Three Poems* is to invent on every page the pain and exaltation that make up the essence of a love story. In that way, the "private" person of the book remains mysterious, as all lovers essentially must remain. Thus, one cannot summarize Ashbery's love story, but one can experience it vicariously.

In "The System," the second and most difficult part of the poem, the narrator becomes utterly preoccupied with himself. In "The New Spirit," even small details of urban life were associated with something the beloved had said or done; here, however, the details and the lover have disappeared. Instead, the narrator is trapped in a kind of mental labyrinth, or "system." In one memorable passage, he imagines the members of the human race boarding a train, which is, of course, their whole life. No one has any idea where the train is going or how fast it is moving. The passengers are ignorant of their journey and—the narrator insists—ignorant of their fundamental situation. The very core of their being is ignorance, yet they fail to recognize this crucial fact. Hence, the narrator views them with contempt.

Three Poems concludes on a lighter note, literally on notes of music, which offer a kind of deliverance for the narrator, who has been trapped in the labyrinth of his doleful thoughts. "The Recital" is important because Ashbery often sees music as an analogue to poetry. Indeed, at one point, he had planned to become a musician, and music has remained a rich source of inspiration throughout his career. The power of music and its essential abstractness make a powerful appeal to the narrator, who at this juncture is exhausted by his Hamlet-like speculations. The poem ends, and with it the whole book, with a description of the power of music (and of art)—the power to inspire new beginnings and new possibilities. In a final jest, Ashbery offers the reader an ending that is actually a beginning: "There were new people watching and waiting, conjugating in this way the distance and emptiness, transforming the scarcely noticeable bleakness into something both intimate and noble." With this brilliant virtuoso effect, Ashbery concludes a poem that is at once a continuance of the great Western tradition of meditative writing (one that includes Saint John of the Cross and Sir Thomas Browne)—and a dramatically arresting rendition of how it feels to be alive in the last decades of the twentieth century. The old and the new come together in a synthesis that is as disturbing, fascinating, and elusive as the century that produced it.

Having reached a kind of artistic plateau with *Three Poems*, Ashbery's career took a new direction. In many ways, *Three Poems* occupies the kind of position in his life that *The Waste Land* did for Eliot. Both works explore psychological traumas and deeply sustained anguish; both plumb the depths of despair until a kind of spiritual nadir is reached. After Eliot completed *The Waste Land*, his work took on a new, spiritual dimension, culminating in the complex Christian poem he called *Four Quartets* (1943). Ashbery's work also changed after the publication of *Three Poems*, but he has not embraced Christian or even theistic belief; he has always insisted on a kind of agnostic or even atheistic vision of life, in which art supplants all conventional notions of divinity. Nevertheless, like Eliot, he has passed through the proverbial dark night of the soul, and his work after *Three Poems* is somehow more confident, less self-consciously experimental, and less opaque. The newer poetry is still impossible to paraphrase, but it is much more accessible and more readable (at least on first sight) than the most extravagant of the early poems, and its subject matter generally seems more central to human experience.

SELF-PORTRAIT IN A CONVEX MIRROR

All these tendencies culminate in a book that won the National Book Award, the Pulitzer Prize, and the National Book Critics Circle Award: *Self-Portrait in a Convex Mirror*. Those prizes and the book itself helped put Ashbery on the literary map, so that he could no longer be summarily dismissed as an eccentric aesthete turning out brilliant but inaccessible work. Readers began to look more closely at what Ashbery was saying and to embrace his message (however complex) as never before.

"Self-Portrait in a Convex Mirror," the title poem, is a brilliant piece of autobiographical writing that does not reveal gritty details of Ashbery's personal life so much as his opinions about art and its power to transform the artist. Self-portraits are as old as art itself, but Ashbery as an art critic and former expatriate had encountered some especially powerful examples of the genre. He must have encountered the great self-portraits of Rembrandt van Rijn and Vincent van Gogh, but the particular work that inspired this poem is a famous masterpiece of the High Renaissance, *Self-Portrait in a Convex Mirror* (1524) by Parmigianino (Girolamo Francesco Maria Mazzola), which hangs in the Kunsthistorisches Museum in Vienna. Ashbery tells the reader that he encountered Parmigianino's famous painting in the summer of 1959, during a visit to Vienna. Parmigianino's self-portrait is uniquely circular in overall form and, as the title suggests, resulted from the artist's close inspection of his visage in a convex mirror, an optical device that creates interesting distortions of scale and distance. Parmigianino's hand, for example, is grossly exaggerated and dominates the foreground of the painting, while his head seems undersized and nearly childlike. It is possible that the Italian artist's childlike appearance appealed to Ashbery because it reminded him of the snapshot of little John Ashbery that had inspired his earlier, much shorter autobiographical lyric, "The Picture of Little J. A. in a Prospect of Flowers."

It is in the nature of self-portraits, then, to conceal and reveal simultaneously—hence the appropriateness of the convex mirror, whose powers of transformation and distortion apply equally to Parmigianino and Ashbery. The poet begins the poem by quoting and paying homage to Giorgio Vasari, the first great art critic. (Ashbery too had been an art critic at the time he saw the painting in Venice.) Vasari explains the complicated arrangements that preceded Parmigianino's actual painting: the use of a barber's convex mirror and the necessity of having a carpenter prepare the circular wooden substratum of the painting. These operations are mere preliminaries, however, to the much more important work of the eyes themselves once the painting has been set up. The eyes cannot penetrate the artificial depth created by this strange mirroring device; therefore, everything that results is a kind of speculation—a word that derives from the Latin word for mirror, *speculum*, as Ashbery points out. Thus in the self-portrait one kind of "mirroring" leads to another; what one sees is not precisely what is there. To hold the paradox in the mind is to enter the world of the artist.

The argument that Ashbery then goes on to develop may perhaps be summarized by the adagelike statement that stability (or order) can be maintained in the presence of instability (or chaos). The movements of time, weather, table tennis balls, and tree branches are all potential elements for the synthesizing and harmonizing power of art, no matter if it distorts something in the process. Perhaps the greatest distortion is that of stability; the stable simply cannot be found in nature, as Isaac Newton showed through his laws of thermodynamics. It is only in the mirror of art (a symbol also favored by William Shakespeare) that stability, order, and form may thrive. Since all art is by definition artificial, then, stability also is an artifice.

Nevertheless, artistic stability is all the artist and the race of human beings can rely on to reveal meaning in an otherwise meaningless space. So Parmigianino's Renaissance painting, like all art, is applicable to all future generations, and Ashbery borrows Parmigianino's technique of mirroring until the world seems to spin around him in a merry-go-round of papers, books, windows, trees, photographs, and desks, and "real life" itself becomes a kind of trick painting. Addressing the Italian master, Ashbery admits that the "uniform substance" or order in his life derives from the Italian genius: "My guide in these matters is your self."

He goes on to quote a contemporary art critic, Sydney Freedberg, who finds the idealized beauty and formal feeling of Parmigianino's self-portrait to depend on the very chaos Ashbery had earlier described. For Freedberg this instability is a collection of bizarre, unsettling aspects of reality that somehow the painting enfolds and harmonizes.

Readers might at this point recall similar discussions—though in radically different language—by John Keats, especially in his great meditation on art, "Ode on a Grecian Urn," which asks the reader to accept art precisely because it transforms the chaos and changeability of human life. Ultimately, this process results in a complete fusion of truth (or reality) and beauty (or art), in Keats's formulation. Ashbery is not Keats, but one has to note the similar posture of the two poets, both contemplating the power of art, both commencing with an art object (the Grecian urn and the Italian self-portrait) and concluding on a note of affirmation. For Ashbery, the power of art is not only magnificent but terrifying, like a pistol primed for Russian roulette with only one bullet in the chamber. Art has the potential to "kill" our old perceptions. Some people might consider this power to be only a dream, but for Ashbery the power remains, and art becomes a kind of "waking dream" in the same unhappy world of human beings that Keats evokes in "Ode on a Grecian Urn." Even in the city, which Ashbery imagines as an insect with multifaceted eyes, art somehow survives. He envisions each person as a potential artist holding a symbolic piece of chalk, ready to begin a new self-portrait.

HOUSEBOAT DAYS

Ashbery continues with this more accessible (and essentially more affirmative) kind of poetry in *Houseboat Days*, the title poem of which likens the mind and its vast storehouse of memory to a boardinghouse that is open to everyone, taking in boarders of every possible type and description. This metaphorical way of describing the sensory, intellectual, and imaginative powers of human beings is a valuable clue for understanding another poem in the volume, one of Ashbery's wittiest and most polished performances, "Daffy Duck in Hollywood," a poem that manages to be tender, lyrical, comic, outrageous, and serious without losing its sense of direction.

An obscure opera serves as a kind of grid or structural framework for this rather freewheeling poem. The poem begins with a stupefyingly absurd collection of mental odds and ends, the flotsam and jetsam of a highly cultured and sophisticated mind that also appreciates the artifacts of popular culture: an Italian opera, Rumford's Baking Powder, Speedy Gonzales, Daffy Duck, Elmer Fudd, the Gadsden Purchase, Anaheim(California), pornographic photographs, and the comic-strip character Skeezix. All these apparent irrelevancies are entirely relevant, because they illustrate the random nature of the mind, its identity as a stream of consciousness. However, these items are also a kind of dodge or subterfuge to block out images of a significant other, possibly a lover. Because of the odd way the mind works through the principle of association, however, these same cartoonlike images also remind the narrator of that other person.

As in so many of his other poems, Ashbery is again insisting that the only reality is the one human beings make, and he concludes by wisely noting that no one knows all the dimensions of this mental life or where the parts fit in. The goal, in Ashbery's opinion, is to keep "ambling" on; thus, each person might remain "intrigued" and open to all the extravagant invitations of life. The mind, with its interminable image making, is strangely cut off from life, but when used properly (that is, aesthetically) it can lay hold of the abundant and unanticipated gifts that always surround and endow impoverished human beings.

A WAVE

This optimistic vein is apparent in most of *A Wave* but especially in the title poem, which seems to contrast crests of positive feelings with troughs of despair. The poem is a long discursive work in which Ashbery creates variations on one essential theme: that a fundamental feeling of security (not to be confused with superficial happiness), a deep and abiding sense of the goodness of life, can, in fact, sustain the person through the pain that life inevitably brings. In this poem, human beings do have final control of their destiny because they are supported by something powerfully akin to older notions of grace or faith. Having this power or "balm," as Ashbery terms it, no one is ever really stripped of autonomy: "we cannot be really naked/ Having this explanation."

APRIL GALLEONS

This mood of sustained hope continues in the exquisitely lyrical *April Galleons*, a book that, like *Houseboat Days*, relies on the metaphor of a boat as a vehicle for psychological as well as physical travel. Included is "Ice Storm," a poem that is highly original yet somehow manages to echo Robert Frost (especially "Birches" and "Design"). As Frost did in "Birches," Ashbery describes winter ice in glittering detail. As Frost did in "Design," Ashbery questions the fate of small things that are out of their accustomed places, such as the rose he stumbles on, growing beside a path entirely out of season.

However, none of these matters disturbs him fundamentally, because he is beginning to get his "bearings in this gloom and see how [he] could improve on the distraught situation all around me, in the darkness and tarnished earth."

AND THE STARS WERE SHINING

Ashbery's wit and virtuosity are often noted by critics, yet his humanity and intelligence are equally important facets of his work. In *And the Stars Were Shining*, this fact becomes readily apparent when in many of the poems his wisdom of age is blended with a great and tender sadness and bursts of wit and vitality. The title poem harks back to the long poems of another age—Roman numerals mark its sections and its cadences recall a past era—but its direct and relaxed language brings it firmly into the late twentieth century. There are fifty-seven more poems in the volume, displaying Ashbery's characteristic wryness and filled with tragicomic snapshots of our time. The works are also philosophical, as he endeavors to find amusement as well as pain in his autumnal themed poems, including the title poem and "Token Resistance."

YOUR NAME HERE

The title of *Your Name Here* aptly hints at the volume's rambunctious, arbitrary themes and pell-mell performances: Poems include "Frogs and Gospels," "Full Tilt," "Here We Go Looby," "Amnesia Goes to the Ball," and "A Star Belched." While his poetic themes are capricious and whimsical, Ashbery's language is intricate, tightly constructed, rhythmic, and sinuous, with a serious undercurrent of memory, time, loss, angst, and desire. Thus, his tone is at once melancholic and comedic, best demonstrated in "What Is Written."

WHERE SHALL I WANDER

Ashbery is reported to have once said that his ambition was "to produce a poem that the critic cannot even talk about." Most of Ashbery's readers would probably agree that he has satisfied this ambition, although some of the poems in *Where Shall I Wander* are more accessible. For example, "Interesting People of Newfoundland" is quite easy to talk about, with its roll call of characters like Larry, who performed foolishly on street corners, and the Russian who said he was a grand duke—and may have been. Doc Hanks was a good "sawbones" when he was not completely drunk; even half drunk he could perform "decent cranial surgery." Walsh's department store had teas and little cakes and rare sherries from all over. The population was small: "But for all that/ we loved each other and had interesting times." Altogether different in conception, "Novelty Love Trot" is hardly transparent, but it musters some explicable philosophical commentary. The poet's taste in books runs to biographies and cultural studies; in music, he likes Liszt's Consolations, "though I've never been consoled/ by them." In the poet's view, for most people, religion is about going to Hell: "I'm probably the only American/

/ who thinks he's going to heaven," but first there is "the steep decline/ into a declivity."

The title of the prose piece "From China to Peru" comes from the first two lines of Samuel Johnson's *The Vanity of Human Wishes* (1749), an imitation of Juvenal's tenth satire: "Let observation with extensive view,/ Survey Mankind, from China to Peru." The vanity of the title stands out clearly in Ashbery's version as the speaker finds himself "taunted" for his dark woolen suit when he arrives at some trivial social occasion where the men appear dressed "to go off on a safari." His only recourse is to the bar, where the "unnerving" events around him make him eager for the cocktail hour. The coherence of this satire then dissolves into a typical Ashbery riff on Japan declaring war on Austro-Hungary and his failure to track down a weather report. "The Red Easel" has a rhymed counterpart in "The Bled Weasel," a *jeu d'esprit* that exemplifies the kind of opaque collection of apparently random lines that frustrates so many readers. No weasel appears in the poem but a caterpillar shows up, "Erect on its parasol," while "Glowworms circulated/ under the trees, confirmed [whatever 'confirmed' means] by whimpering Dobermans." This frivolity collapses, appropriately, in a "crazy quilt of expired pageantry."

A WORLDLY COUNTRY

The title poem of *A Worldly Country*, written in long lines worked into couplets, tells of a city that is riotous by day, with "insane clocks" and "the scent of manure in the municipal parterre." Chickens and geese enjoy the leftover bonbons, but even though "all hell broke loose" in the day, all was calm again by evening. The poet's musings lead him to a moral: "And just as waves are anchored to the bottom of the sea/ we must reach the shallows before God cuts us free." In "Autumn Tea Leaves," it is a partial eclipse that violates the normal day, but the poet cannot discern "what is special about this helix." These phenomena raise questions: What blanket will be sufficient for a freezing night? The dancers who celebrated the celestial occasion revealed "faces/ and senses of humor." However, when it all ended, who knows how many cakes were served, "or leaves collected/ in the hollow of a stump"?

In the fifteen four-line stanzas of "Phantoum," the second line of each stanza is repeated as the first line of the next, with other patterns sneaked in as the stanzas proceed. For example, in stanza 5, the second line, "The auks were squawking, the emus shrieking," becomes line 1 of stanza 6. Little Orphan Annie's adoptive father, Daddy Warbucks, makes a guest appearance in stanza 9 ("Daddy Warbucks was sad, but kept his reasons to himself") with no appreciable gain to the plotless but amiable verses.

A line from Auden's poem "At Last the Secret Is Out" provides the title "The Handshake, the Cough, the Kiss," and it is tempting to interpret the secret as Auden's homosexuality. Even though nothing in the poem speaks directly to a sexual theme, stanza 3 encourages speculation: "We risked it anyway,/ out on the ice where it darkens/ and seems to whisper/ from down below. Watch out, it's the Snow Queen...." The poem then evolves into the poet's reminiscences of childhood in the unnamed "port city of his birth," where he was something of a boy wonder, "the local amateur historian." Rambling thoughts about childhood and the city lead to an apparent climax to the poet's relationship with a coworker in the television industry, a man identified only as "him": "look,/ if that's all you can bring to the table, why are we here?" The speaker concludes his critique by lamenting "an academy/ where losers file past, and the present is unredeemed,/ and all fruits are in season." The poems in this volume show no fading of the wit and bright phrasing of the works first published nearly half a century earlier.

OTHER MAJOR WORKS

LONG FICTION: *A Nest of Ninnies*, 1969 (with James Schuyler).

PLAYS: *Everyman*, pr. 1951; *The Heroes*, pr. 1952; *The Compromise: Or, Queen of the Carabou*, pr. 1956; *The Philosopher*, pb. 1964; *Three Plays*, 1978.

NONFICTION: *The Poetic Medium of W. H. Auden*, 1949 (senior thesis); *Reported Sightings: Art Chronicles, 1957-1987*, 1989; *Other Traditions*, 2000; *John Ashbery in Conversation with Mark Ford*, 2003; *Selected Prose*, 2004.

TRANSLATIONS: *Melville*, 1960 (of Jean-Jacques Mayoux); *Murder in Montarte*, 1960 (of Noel Vixon); *The Deadlier Sex*, 1961 (of Genevieve Manceron); *Alberto Giacometti*, 1962 (of Jacques Dupin); *The Landscape Is Behind the Door*, 1994 (of Pierre Martory); *Giacometti: Three Essays*, 2002 (of Dupin); *The Recitation of Forgetting*, 2003 (of Franck André Jamme).

EDITED TEXT: *Best American Poetry, 1988*, 1988.

BIBLIOGRAPHY

Ashbery, John. "John Ashbery in Conversation with Mark Ford." Interview by Mark Ford. In *Seven American Poets in Conversation: John Ashbery, Donald Hall, Anthony Hecht, Donald Justice, Charles Simic, W. D. Snodgrass, Richard Wilbur*, edited by Peter Dale, Philip Hoy, and J. D. McClatchy. London: Between the Lines, 2008. Ashbery talks about his life and works, including his influences.

_____. "A Kind of Musical Spa." Interview by Craig Burnett. *Frieze* 85 (September, 2004). Ashbery identifies and discusses some of his favorite writers—Ronald Firbank, André Breton, and Frank O'Hara. He praises Guy Maddin's films and says he hated writing art criticism.

Bloom, Harold, ed. *John Ashbery: Comprehensive Research and Study Guide*. Philadelphia: Chelsea House, 2004. Overview of Ashbery's published work, discussing his form, complex linguistics, and vision.

Herd, David. *John Ashbery and American Poetry*. New York: Palgrave, 2000. Herd chronicles Ashbery's poetic career, analyzing his continuities, differences, and improvements over time.

Lehman, David. *The Last Avant-Garde: The Making of the New York School of Poets*.

New York: Doubleday, 1998. Chronicle of New York School of poets, closely tracing Ashbery's life and analyzing elements contributing to the backdrop of his poetry.

MacArthur, Marit J. *The American Landscape in the Poetry of Frost, Bishop, and Ashbery: The House Abandoned*. New York: Palgrave Macmillan, 2008. Examines the poetry of Ashbery, Robert Frost, and Elizabeth Bishop, noting that all three had the subject of the abandoned house.

Malinowska, Barbara. *Dynamics of Being, Space, and Time in the Poetry of Czesław Miłosz and John Ashbery*. New York: Peter Lang, 2000. Malinowska provides a challenging discussion of poetic visions of reality in the works of Miłosz and Ashbery. She works with Martin Heidegger's philosophy of phenomenology and applies key Heideggerian terms—Dasein, space, time, and culture—to explore the reality created by or alluded to in their writings. Jargon heavy but useful.

Milne, Ira Mark, ed. *Poetry for Students*. Vol. 28. Detroit: Thomson/Gale Group, 2008. Contains an analysis of Ashbery's "Self-Portrait in a Convex Mirror."

Shoptaw, John. *On the Outside Looking Out: John Ashbery's Poetry*. Cambridge, Mass.: Harvard University Press, 1994. Abundant and detailed information about Ashbery's life, publication history, and manuscripts make the book valuable. It offers an intriguing but perhaps overworked and insufficiently proven argument that Ashbery's elusiveness derives from his homosexuality.

Vendler, Helen. "Toying with Words." Review of *Plainsphere*. *The New York Times Book Review*, December 13, 2009, p. 14. Vendler reviews the collection dedicated to Ashbery's partner, David Kermani. She notes his wordplay and praises his lyric poems.

Vincent, John Emil. *John Ashbery and You: His Later Books*. Athens: University of Georgia Press, 2007. Examines *And the Stars Were Shining*, *Your Name Here*, and other later works by Ashbery.

Daniel L. Guillory; Philip K. Jason; Sarah Hilbert
Updated by Frank Day

ELIZABETH BISHOP

Born: Worcester, Massachusetts; February 8, 1911
Died: Boston, Massachusetts; October 6, 1979

PRINCIPAL POETRY
North and South, 1946
Poems: North and South—A Cold Spring, 1955
Questions of Travel, 1965
Selected Poems, 1967
The Ballad of the Burglar of Babylon, 1968
The Complete Poems, 1969
Geography III, 1976
The Complete Poems, 1927-1979, 1983

OTHER LITERARY FORMS

In addition to her poetry, Elizabeth Bishop wrote short stories and other prose pieces. She is also known for her translations of Portuguese and Latin American writers. *The Collected Prose*, edited and introduced by Robert Giroux, was published in 1984. It includes "In the Village," an autobiographical revelation of Bishop's youthful vision of, and later adult perspective on, her mother's brief return home from a mental hospital. Like her poetry, Bishop's prose is marked by precise observation and a somewhat withdrawn narrator, although the prose works reveal much more about Bishop's life than the poetry does. Editor Giroux has suggested that this was one reason many of the pieces were unpublished during her lifetime. *The Collected Prose* also includes Bishop's observations of other cultures and provides clues as to why she chose to live in Brazil for so many years.

ACHIEVEMENTS

Elizabeth Bishop was often honored for her poetry. She served as consultant in poetry (poet laureate) to the Library of Congress in 1949-1950. Among many awards and prizes, she received an Award in Literature from the American Academy of Arts and Letters (1951), the Shelley Memorial Award (1953), the Pulitzer Prize in poetry (1956), the Academy of American Poets Fellowship (1969), the National Book Award in Poetry (1970), and the National Book Critics Circle Award in poetry (1976) for *Geography III*. She became a member of the American Academy of Arts and Letters in 1954 and served as chancellor for the Academy of American Poets from 1966 to 1979. However, as John Ashbery said, in seconding her presentation as the winner of the *Books Abroad/ Neustadt International Prize for Literature* in 1976, she is a "writer's writer." Despite her continuing presence for more than thirty years as a major American poet, Bishop never achieved great popular success. Perhaps the delicacy of much of her writing, her restrained style, and her ambiguous questioning and testing of experience made her more difficult and less approachable than poets with showier technique or more explicit philosophies.

Bishop's place in American poetry, in the company of such poets as Marianne Moore, Wallace Stevens, and Richard Wilbur, is among the celebrators and commemorators of the things of this world, in her steady conviction that by bringing the light of poetic intelligence, the mind's eye, on those things, she would enrich her readers' understanding of them and of themselves.

BIOGRAPHY

Elizabeth Bishop is a poet of geography, as the titles of her books testify, and her life itself was mapped out by travels and visits as surely as is her poetry. Eight months after Bishop's birth in Massachusetts, her father died. Four years later, her mother suffered a nervous breakdown and was hospitalized, first outside Boston, and later in her native Canada.

Elizabeth was taken to Nova Scotia, where she spent much of her youth with her grandmother; later, she lived for a time with an aunt in Massachusetts. Although her mother did not die until 1934, Bishop did not see her again after a brief visit home from the hospital in 1916—the subject of "In the Village."

For the rest of her life, Bishop traveled: in Canada, in Europe, and in North and South America. She formed friendships with many writers: Robert Lowell, Octavio Paz, and especially Marianne Moore, who read drafts of many of her poems and offered suggestions. In 1951, Bishop began a trip around South America, but during a stop in Brazil she suffered an allergic reaction to some food she had eaten and became ill. She remained in Brazil for almost twenty years. During the last decade of her life, she continued to travel and to spend time in Latin America, but she settled in the United States, teaching frequently at Harvard, until her death in 1979.

ANALYSIS

In her early poem "The Map," Elizabeth Bishop writes that "More delicate than the historians' are the map-makers' colors." Her best poetry, although only indirectly autobiographical, is built from those mapmakers' colors. Nova Scotian and New England seascapes and Brazilian and Parisian landscapes become the geography of her poetry. At the same time, her own lack of permanent roots and her sense of herself as an observer suggest the lack of social relationships one feels in Bishop's poetry, for it is a poetry of observation, not of interaction, of people as outcasts, exiles, and onlookers, not as social beings. The relationships that count are with the land and sea, with primal elements, with the geography of Bishop's world.

For critics, and certainly for other poets—those as different as Moore and Lowell, or

Randall Jarrell and John Ashbery—Elizabeth Bishop is a voice of influence and authority. Writing with great assurance and sophistication from the beginning of her career, she achieved in her earliest poetry a quiet, though often playful, tone, a probing examination of reality, an exactness of language, and a lucidity of vision that mark all her best poetry. Her later poetry is slightly more relaxed than her earlier, the formal patterns often less rigorous; but her concern and her careful eye never waver. Because of the severity of her self-criticism, her collected poems, although relatively few in number, are of a remarkably even quality.

History, writes Bishop in "Objects and Apparitions," is the opposite of art, for history creates ruins, while the artist, out of ruins, out of "minimal, incoherent fragments," simply creates. Bishop's poetry is a collection of objects and apparitions, of scenes viewed and imagined, made for the moment into a coherent whole. The imaginary iceberg in the poem of that name is a part of a scene "a sailor'd give his eyes for," and Bishop asks that surrender of her readers. Her poetry, like the iceberg, behooves the soul to see. Inner and outer realities are in her poetry made visible, made one.

"Sandpiper"

In Bishop's poem "Sandpiper," the bird of the title runs along the shore, ignoring the sea that roars on his left and the beach that "hisses" on his right, disregarding the interrupting sheets of water that wash across his toes, sucking the sand back to sea. His attention is focused. He is watching the sand between his toes; "a student of [William] Blake," he attempts to see the world in each of those grains. The poet is ironic about the bird's obsessions: He is "finical"; in looking at these details he ignores the great sweeps of sea and land on either side of him. For every point in time when the world is clear, there is another when it is a mist. The poet seems to chide the bird in his darting search for "something, something, something," but then in the last two lines of the poem the irony subsides; as Bishop carefully enumerates the varied and beautiful colors of the grains of sand, she joins the bird in his attentiveness. The reward, the something one can hope to find, lies simply in the rich and multivalent beauty of what one sees. It is not the reward of certainty or conviction, but of discovery that comes through focused attention.

The irony in the poem is self-mocking, for the bird is a metaphor for Bishop, its vision like her own, its situation that of many of her poetic personas. "Sandpiper" may call to mind such Robert Frost poems as "Neither out Far nor in Deep" or "For Once, Then, Something," with their perplexity about inward and outward vision and people's attempt to fix their sight on something, to create surety out of their surroundings. It may also suggest such other Bishop poems as "Cape Breton," where the birds turn their backs to the mainland, sometimes falling off the cliffs onto rocks below. Bishop does share with Frost his absorption by nature and its ambiguities, the ironic tone, and the tight poetic form that masks the "controlled panic" that the sandpiper-poet feels. Frost, however, is in a darker line of American writers: His emphasis is on the transitoriness of the vision, the shallowness of the sea into which one gazes, the ease with which even the most fleeting vision is erased. For Frost's poet-bird, "The Oven Bird," the nature he observes in midsummer is already 90 percent diminished. Bishop, rather, prefers the triumph of one's seeing at all. In her well-known poem "The Fish," when the persona finally looks into the eyes of the fish she has caught—eyes, the poet notes, larger but "shallower" than her own—the fish's eyes return the stare. The persona, herself now caught, rapt, stares and stares until "victory fill[s] up" the boat, and all the world becomes "rainbow, rainbow, rainbow." Like the rainbow of colors that the sandpiper discovers, the poet here discovers beauty; the victory is the triumph of vision.

Like the sandpiper, then, Bishop is an obsessive observer. As a poet, her greatest strength is her pictorial accuracy. Whether her subject is as familiar as a fish, a rooster, or a filling station, or as strange as a Brazilian interior or a moose in the headlights of a bus, she enables the reader to see. The world for the sandpiper is sometimes "minute and vast and clear," and because Bishop observes the details so lucidly, her vision becomes truly vast. She is, like Frost, a lover of synecdoche; for her, the particulars entail the whole. Nature is the matter of Bishop's art; to make her readers see, to enable them to read the world around them, is her purpose. In "Seascape," what the poet finds in nature, its potential richness, is already like "a cartoon by Raphael for a tapestry for a Pope." All that Bishop must accomplish, then, as she writes in "The Fish," is simply "the tipping/ of an object toward the light."

"Objects and Apparitions"

Although the world for the sandpiper is sometimes clear, it is also sometimes a mist, and Bishop describes a more clouded vision as well. She translated a poem by Paz, "Objects and Apparitions," that might indicate the fuller matter of her own work; the objects are those details, the grains of sand that reveal the world once they are tipped toward the light. The apparitions occur when one sees the world through the mist and when one turns vision inward, as in the world of dreams. Here, too, the goal is bringing clarity to the vision—and the vision to clarity. As Bishop writes in "The Weed," about drops of dew that fall from a weed onto a dreamer's face, "each drop contained a light,/ a small, illuminated scene."

Objects and apparitions, mist and vision, land and sea, history and geography, travel and home, ascent and fall, dawn and night—these oppositions supply the tension in Bishop's poetry. The tensions are never resolved by giving way; in Bishop's world, one is a reflection of the other, and "reflection" becomes a frequent pun: that of a mirror and that of thought. Similarly, inspection, introspection, and insight suggest her doubled vision. In "Paris, 7 A.M.," looking down into the courtyard of a Paris house, the poet writes, "It is like introspection/ to stare inside," and there is again the double meaning of looking inside the court and inside oneself.

"The Man-Moth"

No verbs are more prevalent or important in Bishop's poetry than those of sight: Look, watch, see, stare, she admonishes the reader. From "The Imaginary Iceberg," near the beginning of her first book, which compares an iceberg to the soul, both "self-made from elements least visible," and which insists that icebergs "behoove" the soul "to see them so," to "Objects and Apparitions" near the end of her last book, in which the poet suggests that in Joseph Cornell's art "my words became visible," one must first of all see; and the end of all art, plastic and verbal, is to make that which is invisible—too familiar to be noticed, too small to be important, too strange to be comprehended—visible.

In "The Man-Moth," the normal human being of the first stanza cannot even see the moon, but after the man-moth comes above ground and climbs a skyscraper, trying to climb out through the moon, which he thinks is a hole in the sky, he falls back and returns to life belowground, riding the subway backward through his memories and dreams. The poet addresses the readers, cautioning them to examine the man-moth's eye, from which a tear falls. If the "you" is not paying attention, the man-moth will swallow his tear and his most valuable possession will be lost, but "if you watch," he will give it up, cool and pure, and the fruit of his vision will be shared.

Questions of Travel

To see the world afresh, even as briefly as does the man-moth, to gain that bitter tear of knowledge, one must, according to Bishop, change perspectives. In *Questions of Travel*, people hurry to the Southern Hemisphere "to see the sun the other way around." In "Love Lies Sleeping," the head of one sleeper has fallen over the edge of the bed, so that to his eyes the world is "inverted and distorted." Then the poet reconsiders: "distorted and revealed," for the hope is that now the sleeper sees, although a last line suggests that such sight is no certainty. When one lies down, Bishop writes in "Sleeping Standing Up," the world turns ninety degrees and the new perspective brings "recumbent" thoughts to mind and vision. The equally ambiguous title, however, implies either that thoughts are already available when one is upright or, less positively, that one may remain inattentive while erect.

The world is also inverted in "Insomnia," where the moon stares at itself in a mirror. In Bishop's lovely, playful poem "The Gentleman of Shalott," the title character thinks himself only half, his other symmetrical half a reflection, an imagined mirror down his center. His state is precarious, for if the mirror should slip, the symmetry would be destroyed, and yet he finds the uncertainty "exhilarating" and thrives on the sense of "readjustment."

"Over 2000 Illustrations and a Complete Concordance"

The changing of perspectives that permits sight is the theme of Bishop's "Over 2000 Illustrations and a Complete Concordance." The poet is looking at the illustrations in a gazetteer, comparing the engraved and serious pictures in the book with her remembered travels. In the first section of the poem, the poet lists the illustrations, the familiar, even tired Seven Wonders of the World, moving away from the objects pictured to details of the renderings, until finally the "eye drops" away from the real illustrations, which spread out and dissolve into a series of reflections on past travels. These too begin with the familiar: with Canada and the sound of goats, through Rome, to Mexico, to Marrakech. Then, finally, she goes to a holy grave, which, rather than reassuring the viewer, frightens her, as an amused Arab looks on. Abruptly, the poet is back in the world of books, but this time her vision is on the Bible, where everything is "connected by 'and' and 'and.'" She opens the book, feeling the gilt of the edges flake off on her fingertips, and then asks, "Why couldn't we have seen/ this old Nativity while we were at it?" The colloquial last words comprise a casual pun, implying physical presence or accidental benefit. The next four lines describe the nativity scene, but while the details are familiar enough, Bishop's language defamiliarizes them.

The poet ends with the statement that had she been there she would have "looked and looked our infant sight away"—another pun rich with possibilities. Is it that she would have looked repeatedly, so that the scene would have yielded meaning and she could have left satisfied? Do the lines mean to look away, as if the fire that breaks in the vision is too strong for human sight? The gazetteer into which the poet first looked, that record of human travels, has given way to scripture; physical pictures have given way to reflected visions and reflections, which, like the imaginary iceberg, behoove the soul to see.

"THE RIVERMAN"

Bishop participates in the traditional New England notion that nature is a gazetteer, a geography, a book to be read. In her poem "The Riverman," the speaker gets up in the night—night and dawn, two times of uncertain light, are favorite times in Bishop's poetic world—called by a river spirit, though at first the dolphin-spirit is only "glimpsed." The speaker follows and wades into the river, where a door opens. Smoke rises like mist, and another spirit speaks in a language the narrator does not know but understands "like a dog/ although I can't speak it yet." Every night he goes back to the river, to study its language. He needs a "virgin mirror," a fresh way of seeing, but all he finds are spoiled. "Look," he says significantly, "it stands to reason" that everything one needs can be obtained from the river, which draws from the land "the remedy." The image of rivers and seas drawing, sucking the land persists in Bishop's poetry. The unknown that her poems scrutinize draws the known into it. The river sucks the earth "like a child," and the riverman, like the poet, must study the earth and the river to read them and find the remedy of sight.

PICTORIAL POETRY

Not only do the spirits of nature speak, but so too for Bishop does art itself. Her poetry is pictorial not only in the sense of giving vivid descriptions of natural phenomena but also in its use of artificial objects to reflect on the self-referential aspect of art. Nature is like art, the seascape a "cartoon," but the arts are like one another as well. Bishop is firmly in the *ut pictura poesis* tradition—as is a painting, so a poem—and in the narrower tradition of ekphrasis: Art, like nature, speaks.

In "Large Bad Picture," the picture is an uncle's painting, and after five stanzas describing the artist's attempt to be important by drawing everything oversized—miles of cliffs hundreds of feet high, hundreds of birds—the painting, at least in the narrator's mind, becomes audible, and she can hear the birds crying.

In the much later "Poem," Bishop looks at another but much smaller painting by the same uncle (a sketch for a larger one? she asks), and this time the painting speaks to her memory. Examining the brushstrokes in a detached and slightly contemptuous manner, she suddenly exclaims, "Heavens, I recognize the place, I know it!" The voice of her mother enters, and then she concludes, "Our visions coincided"; life and memory have merged in this painting as in this poem: "how touching in detail/ —the little that we get for free."

"The Monument"

Most explicitly in "The Monument," Bishop addresses someone, asking her auditor to "see the monument." The listener is confused: the assemblage of boxes, turned catty-corner one on the other, the thin poles hanging out at the top, the wooden background of sea made from board and sky made from other boards: "Why do they make no sound?... What is that?" The narrator responds with "It is the monument," but the other is not convinced that it is truly art. The voice of the poet again answers, insisting that the monument be seen as "artifact of wood" which "holds together better than sea or cloud or sand could." Acknowledging the limitations, the crudeness of it, the questions it cannot answer, she continues that it shelters "what is within"—presenting the familiar ambiguity: within the monument or within the viewer? Sculpture or poem, monument or painting, says the poet, all are of wood; that is, all are artifacts made from nature, artifacts that hold together. She concludes, "Watch it closely."

Thus, for Bishop, shifting perspectives to watch the natural landscape (what she quotes Sir Kenneth Clark as calling "tapestried landscape") and the internal landscape of dream and recollection are both the matter and the manner of art, of all arts, which hold the world together while one's attention is focused. The struggle is to see; the victory is in so seeing.

Poems of questioning

Bishop's poetry is not unequivocally optimistic or affirmative, however. There are finally more ambiguities than certainties, and—like her double-edged puns—questions, rhetorical and conversational, are at the heart of these poems. Bishop's ambiguity is not that of unresolved layers of meaning in the poetry, but in the unresolvable nature of the world she tests. "Which is which?" she asks about memory and life in "Poem." "What has he done?" the poet asks of a chastised dog in the last poem of *Geography III.* "Can countries pick their colors?" she asks in "The Map." *Questions of Travel* begins with a poem questioning whether this new country, Brazil, will yield "complete comprehension"; it is followed by another poem that asks whether the poet should not have stayed at home: "Must we dream our dreams/ and have them, too?" Bishop poses more questions than she answers. Indeed, at the end of "Faustina," Faustina is poised above the dying woman she has cared for, facing the final questions of the meaning that death gives to life: Freedom or nightmare?, it begins, but the question becomes "proliferative," and the poet says that"There is no way of telling./ The eyes say only either."

Knowledge, like the sea, like tears, is salty and bitter, and even answering the questions, achieving a measure of knowledge, is no guarantee of permanence. Language, like music, drifts out of hearing. In "View of the Capitol from the Library of Congress," even the music of a brass band "doesn't quite come through." The morning breaks in "Anaphora" with so much music that it seems meant for an "ineffable creature." When he appears, however, he is merely human, a tired victim of his humanity, even at dawn. However, even though knowledge for Bishop is bitter, is fleeting, though the world is often inscrutable or inexplicable, hers is finally a poetry of hope. Even "Anaphora" moves from morning to night, though from fatigue to a punning "endless assent."

POETIC FORM

Bishop's poetry is often controlled by elaborate formal patterns of sight and sound. She makes masterful use of such forms as the sestina and villanelle, avoiding the appearance of mere exercise by the naturalness and wit of the repetitions and the depth of the scene. In "The Burglar of Babylon," she adopts the ballad form to tell the story of a victim of poverty who is destroyed by his society and of those "observers" who watch through binoculars without ever seeing the drama that is unfolding. Her favorite sound devices are alliteration and consonance. In "The Map," for example, the first four lines include "shadowed," "shadows," "shallows," "showing"; "edges" rhymes with "ledges," "water" alliterates with "weeds." The repetition of sounds suggests the patterning that the poet finds in the map, and the slipperiness of sounds in "shadows"/"shallows" indicates the ease with which one vision of reality gives place to another. The fifth line begins with another question: "Does the land lean down to lift the sea?," the repeated sound changing to a glide. "Along the fine tan sandy shelf/ is the land tugging at the sea from under?" repeats the patterning of questions and the *sh* and *l* alliteration, but the internal rhyme of "tan" and "sandy," so close that it momentarily disrupts the rhythm and the plosive alliteration of "tan" and "tugging," implies more strain.

Being at the same time a pictorialist, Bishop depends heavily on images. Again in "The Map," Norway is a hare that "runs south in agitation." The peninsulas "take the water between thumb and finger/ like women feeling for the smoothness of yard-goods." The reader is brought up short by the aptness of these images, the familiar invigorated. On the map, Labrador is yellow, "where the moony Eskimo/ has oiled it." In the late poem "In the Waiting Room," a young Elizabeth sits in a dentist's waiting room, reading through a *National Geographic*, looking at pictures of the scenes from around the world. The experience causes the young girl to ask who she is, what is her identity and her similarity, not only with those strange people in the magazine but also with the strangers there in the room with her, and with her Aunt Consuela, whose scream she hears from the inner room. Bishop's poetry is like the pictures in that magazine; its images offer another geography, so that readers question again their own identity.

Use of conceit

This sense of seeing oneself in others, of doubled vision and reflected identities, leads to another of Bishop's favorite devices, the conceit. In "Wading at Wellfleet," the waves of the sea, glittering and knifelike, are like the wheels of Assyrian chariots with their sharp knives affixed, attacking warriors and waders alike. In "The Imaginary Iceberg," the iceberg is first an actor, then a jewel, and finally the soul, the shifting of elaborated conceits duplicating the ambiguous nature of the iceberg. The roads that lead to the city in "From the Country to the City" are stripes on a harlequin's tights, and the poem a conceit with the city the clown's head and heart, its neon lights beckoning the traveler. Dreams are armored tanks in "Sleeping Standing Up," letting one do "many a dangerous thing," protected. In the late prose piece "12 O'Clock News," each item on a desk becomes something else: the gooseneck lamp, a moon; the typewriter eraser, a unicyclist with bristly hair; the ashtray, a graveyard full of twisted bodies of soldiers.

Formal control, a gently ironic but appreciative tone, a keen eye—these are hallmarks of Bishop's poetry. They reveal as well her limitation as a poet: a deficiency of passion. The poetry is so carefully controlled, the patterns so tight, the reality tested so shifting, and the testing so detached, that intensity of feeling is minimized. Bishop, in "Objects and Apparitions," quotes the painter Edgar Degas: "'One has to commit a painting . . . the way one commits a crime.'" As Richard Wilbur, the writer whom she most resembles in her work, has pointed out, Degas loved grace and energy, strain coupled with beauty. Strain is absent in Bishop's work.

Character sketches

Although there are wonderful character sketches among her poems, the poetry seems curiously underpopulated. "Manuelzinho" is a beautiful portrait of a character whose account books have turned to dream books, an infuriating sort whose numbers, the decimals omitted, run slantwise across the page. "Crusoe in England" describes a man suddenly removed from the place that made him reexamine his existence. These are people, but observers and outsiders, themselves observed. The Unbeliever sleeps alone at the top of a mast, his only companions a cloud and a gull. The Burglar of Babylon flees a society that kills him. Cootchie is dead, as is Arthur in "First Death in Nova Scotia," and Faustina tends the dying. Crusoe is without his Friday, and in "Sestina," although a grandmother jokes with a child, it is silence that one hears, absence that is present. There is little love in Bishop's poetry. It is true that at the end of "Manuelzinho," the narrator confesses that she loves her maddening tenant "all I can,/ I think. Or do I?" It is true that at the end of "Filling Station," the grubby, but "comfy" design of the family-owned station suggests that "Somebody loves us all," but this love is detached and observed, not felt. Even in "Four Poems," the most acutely personal of Bishop's poems and the only ones about romantic love, the subject is lost love, the conversation internal. "Love should be put into action!" screams a hermit at the end of "Chemin de Fer," but his only answer is an echo.

OTHER MAJOR WORKS

SHORT FICTION: "In the Village," in *Questions of Travel*, 1965.

NONFICTION: *The Diary of "Helena Morley,"* 1957 (translation of Alice Brant's *Minha Vida de Menina*); *Brazil*, 1962 (with the editors of *Life*); *One Art: Letters*, 1994; *Words in Air: The Complete Correspondence Between Elizabeth Bishop and Robert Lowell*, 2008 (with Robert Lowell).

EDITED TEXT: *An Anthology of Twentieth Century Brazilian Poetry*, 1972 (with Emanuel Brasil).

MISCELLANEOUS: *The Collected Prose*, 1984 (fiction and nonfiction); *Edgar Allan Poe and the Juke-Box: Uncollected Poems, Drafts, and Fragments*, 2006 (Alice Quinn, editor); *Poems, Prose, and Letters*, 2008.

BIBLIOGRAPHY

Bishop, Elizabeth. Interviews. *Conversations with Elizabeth Bishop*. Edited by George Monteiro. Jackson: University Press of Mississippi, 1996. These interviews with Bishop reveal the unusual artistic spheres in which she moved. Monteiro's lucid introduction respects the complexities of both Bishop and her repressive historical moment.

Bloom, Harold. *Elizabeth Bishop: Modern Critical Views*. New York: Chelsea House, 1985. Bloom has gathered fifteen previously published articles on separate poems and on Bishop's poetry as a whole, as well as a new article, "At Home with Loss" by Joanne Feit Diehl, on Bishop's relationship to the American Transcendentalists. "The Armadillo," "Roosters," and "In the Waiting Room" are some of the poems treated separately. A chronology and a bibliography complete this useful collection of criticism from the 1970's and early 1980's.

Costello, Bonnie. *Elizabeth Bishop: Questions of Mastery*. Cambridge, Mass.: Harvard University Press, 1991. Provides a comprehensive view of Bishop's visual strategies and poetics, grouping poems along thematic lines in each chapter. She examines the poet's relationship to spirituality, memory, and the natural world by exploring her metrical and rhetorical devices.

Goldensohn, Lorrie. *Elizabeth Bishop: The Biography of a Poetry*. New York: Columbia University Press, 1992. Analyzing Bishop's life through the lens of her verse, Goldensohn probes the lesbianism and alcoholism that Bishop wished to conceal in her life and examines the role that Brazil played in shaping Bishop's works.

Harrison, Victoria. *Elizabeth Bishop's Poetics of Intimacy*. New York: Cambridge University Press, 1993. Harrison's application of critical theory to Bishop's work reveals new facets of Bishop's art. She examines Bishop's language, poetics, and prosody via postmodern theory, feminist theory, and cultural anthropology. Takes advantage of the ample manuscript materials available.

Miller, Brett C. *Elizabeth Bishop: Life and the Memory of It*. Berkeley: University of California Press, 1993. The first critical biography of Bishop, this resource combines the subject's life and writings. Numerous notebook entries and letters are uncovered as sources for later poems, and Bishop's alcoholism is discussed.

_____. *Flawed Light: American Women Poets and Alcohol*. Urbana: University of Illinois Press, 2009. Miller studies how drinking and alcoholism affected certain prominent American women poets, and how their struggles were reflected in their poetry.

Parker, Robert Dale. *The Unbeliever: The Poetry of Elizabeth Bishop*. Urbana: University of Illinois Press, 1988. Parker has the advantage of a longer view of Bishop's writings and criticism. His wide grasp of her life and work leads him to shape her development into three stages: poems of wish and expectation, resignation into poems of place, and finally, as is natural with maturity, poems of retrospection. He focuses on the major poems in each area, with a last chapter on the later poems, some of which, such as "The Moose," had been in her mind for twenty years. Includes particularly fine notes and an index.

Schwartz, Lloyd, and Sybil P. Estess. *Elizabeth Bishop and Her Art*. Ann Arbor: University of Michigan Press, 1983. This valuable source gathers critical articles from admirers, as well as interviews, introductions at poetry readings, explications of specific poems, and a bibliography (1933-1981). Some of Bishop's journal passages demonstrate why she is a preeminent American poet—her realism, common sense, lack of self-pity over losses—as James Merrill calls her, "our greatest national treasure."

Travisano, Thomas. *Elizabeth Bishop: Her Artistic Development*. Charlottesville: University Press of Virginia, 1988. This comprehensive study of Bishop's career traces the evolution of her prose and poetry through three phases. The first, "Prison," uses enclosure as its metaphor; the second, "Travel," breaks through into engagement with people and places; and the third, "History," reconciles her life of loss and displacement to a calm, mature mood of courage and humor. Complemented by a chronology, a bibliography, and an index.

Howard Faulkner

HART CRANE

Born: Garrettsville, Ohio; July 21, 1899
Died: Gulf of Mexico; April 27, 1932

PRINCIPAL POETRY
White Buildings, 1926
The Bridge, 1930
The Collected Poems of Hart Crane, 1933 (Waldo Frank, editor)

OTHER LITERARY FORMS

Hart Crane's principal literary production was poetry. Other writings include reviews, several essays on literature, and two essays on poetry: "General Aims and Theories" and "Modern Poetry." His letters have been published, including those between Crane and the critic Yvor Winters and Crane's letters to his family and friends.

ACHIEVEMENTS

Hart Crane is acknowledged to be a fine lyric poet whose language is daring, opulent, and sometimes magnificent. Although complaints about the difficulty and obscurity of his poetry persist, the poems are not pure glittering surface. When Harriet Monroe, editor of *Poetry*, challenged metaphors of his such as the "calyx of death's bounty" in "At Melville's Tomb," Crane demonstrated the sense within the figure. In 1930, Crane received the Levinson Prize from *Poetry* magazine.

Crane is significant, moreover, in being a particularly modern poet. He wrote that poets had to be able to deal with the machine as naturally and casually as earlier poets had treated sheep and trees and cathedrals. His aim was to portray the effects of modern life on people's sensibilities. In his poetry, Crane caught the frenzied rhythms and idioms of the jazz age.

Crane's stature also rests on his having created a sustained long poem, *The Bridge*. Early critics looking for a classical epic deplored the poem's seeming lack of narrative structure. Some critics also objected to Crane's joining the party of Walt Whitman at a time when Whitman and optimism were in disfavor. Later critics, however, have seen *The Bridge* as one of the great poems in modern American literature. They find in it a more Romantic structure, the structure of the poet's consciousness or the structure of human consciousness.

BIOGRAPHY

Hart Crane was born Harold Hart Crane to Grace Hart, a Chicago beauty, and C. A. (Clarence Authur) Crane, a self-made businessman who became a successful candy

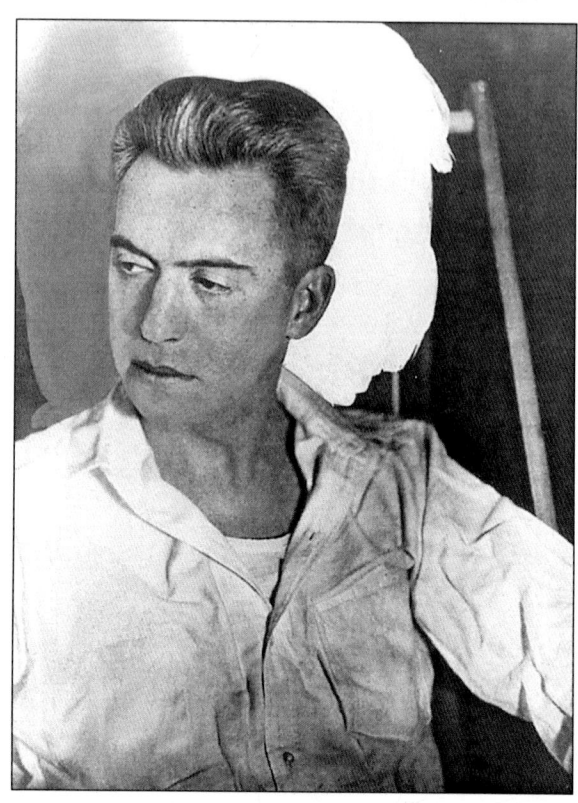

Hart Crane
(Library of Congress)

manufacturer. An only child, Crane felt that he was made the battleground of his parents' conflicts. When Crane was fifteen years old, a family trip to his grandmother's Caribbean plantation, the Isle of Pines, erupted in quarreling. Crane subsequently made two suicide attempts.

When he was seventeen, Crane went to New York to become a poet, not to prepare to enter college as his father thought. In the next several years, Crane alternated between living in Cleveland and New York, working at low-paying jobs, primarily in advertising, jobs that drained his energy for writing poetry. Crane received little financial support from his father, who wanted Crane to commit himself to a business career. In 1917, siding with his mother in a family argument, Harold Crane began using the name Hart Crane.

In this period, Crane's poems were being published in "little" magazines. To stimulate his creativity, Crane often relied on drink and music, a habit that led him to later problems with alcohol. (His poem "The Wine Menagerie" pays tribute to the connection he found between intoxication and poetic vision.) Crane's homosexuality, which involved him in brawls and run-ins with the police, also provided him the experience of love.

"For the Marriage of Faustus and Helen" was published in 1923, a breakthrough for Crane, who previously had written only short lyrics. Poor and often unemployed, he applied in 1925 for a grant from Otto Kahn, a financier and patron of the arts. Crane received money to help support him while he worked on *The Bridge*, a poem that was to be a synthesis of the American identity. The next summer, Crane wrote a major part of his masterwork at his grandmother's plantation on the Isle of Pines, Cuba. In 1926, a collection of his poetry, *White Buildings*, was published.

Crane's stormy family life continued. In 1928, in California, after helping to nurse his sick grandmother, Crane had a final quarrel with his mother, Grace, and they never saw each other again. Shortly thereafter, Crane received a legacy from his grandmother Hart's estate, and he traveled to London and Paris. There he met Harry and Caresse Crosby, who offered to publish *The Bridge* in a special edition. In 1930 in Paris and then in New York, *The Bridge* was published.

That winter, Crane was reconciled with his father. A few months later in 1931, Crane received a fellowship from the Guggenheim Foundation. He spent a year in Mexico preparing to write a poetic drama on the conquest of Mexico. The year was marked by drinking sprees and trouble with the police for brawling and homosexuality. After traveling back briefly to Ohio for his father's funeral, Crane returned to Mexico.

At the end of his stay in Mexico, Crane had a close relationship with Peggy Cowley, who was being divorced from Malcolm Cowley. The two had plans to be married, but Crane had fits of despondency, fears about his difficulty with writing, and anxieties about the quality of his latest poem, "The Broken Tower." After a suicide attempt that Crane feared would attract police attention, he and Peggy Cowley set sail for New York on the *Orizaba*. A stop at Havana during which Crane and Cowley lost track of each other was followed by a night on board ship during which Crane went on a violent drinking spree and was robbed and beaten. The next day at noon, Crane jumped overboard from the deck of the *Orizaba* and was never found.

Analysis

Hart Crane's characteristic mode of poetry is visionary transformation. His language is that of transformation aimed at a reality beyond the surface of consciousness. Crane called the technique that subtly converts one image into another the "logic of metaphor." Like that of the French Symbolist poets—Charles Baudelaire, Arthur Rimbaud, Jules Laforgue, and Paul Verlaine—Crane's language is often vivid and obscure, a "jeweled" style that juxtaposes apparently alien entities. It is a poetry of indirection, not naming but suggesting objects or using them for an evocation of mood, for their magic suggestiveness. Sometimes choosing words for their music or texture, Crane employs the technique of synaesthesia, the correspondence between different sense modalities. Symbolists such as Crane, intuiting a correspondence between the material world and spiritual realities, aim to elicit a response beyond the level of ordinary consciousness.

Influenced by T. S. Eliot (but wanting to counteract the pessimism of the early Eliot), Crane used ironic mythological, religious, and literary echoes interspersed with snatches of banal conversation and lines from popular songs and slang. His method of achieving various perspectives almost simultaneously by the juxtaposition of such unlikely elements has been called cubist. The tension between his cubist and Symbolist methods and his Whitmanian sentiments accounts for the unique quality of Crane's style.

Crane's poetry uses visionary transformations in an attempt to encompass the modern experience. In *The Bridge*, historical figures such as Christopher Columbus, legendary characters such as Rip Van Winkle, and mythic figures such as Maquokeeta (the consort of Pocahontas) are made part of the poet's consciousness, associated with personal memories of his childhood and with scenes of modern urban soullessness. The modern scene is transmuted by the elements, which provide a standard of value and a range of alternatives. In "For the Marriage of Faustus and Helen," the classic figure of Helen of Troy is brought together with the Renaissance figure of Dr. Faustus, and the two figures with their complex contexts bring a new perspective to the streetcar, the nightclub, and the aerial battle they visit in Crane's poem. Crane learned from the Symbolists that an image can become symbolic within a private context, calling up a dense network of meanings, emotions, and associations. Such images, unlike traditional symbols, draw on the cumulative force of the poet's personal associations—his personal "language"—rather than on the common cultural heritage. Crane's poetry fuses such personal symbols with traditional symbols from the sweep of Western culture.

"For the Marriage of Faustus and Helen"

"For the Marriage of Faustus and Helen," a poem of almost 140 lines, is Crane's first long poem. It is a marriage song for Faustus, the poet in search of spiritual fulfillment, and Helen, a figure of ideal beauty. The poem begins, however, in the tawdry modern world with the mind fettered by artificial distinctions and smothered with the trivial: stock quotations, baseball scores, and office memos. "Smutty wings" in the first stanza becomes "sparrow wings" in the second as evening brings freedom from the strictures of the office.

The poet enters his experience by getting lost, forgetting his streetcar fare and forgetting to get a transfer. Between green and pink advertisements, he sees Helen's eyes across the aisle from him, half laughing. The poet wants to touch her hands as a sign of love. Helen offers him words, inspiring his poetry. The poet's promise of love makes Helen ecstatic, and like a Romantic poet, the modern poet dedicates his vision to her praise.

The setting of the next section is a rooftop nightclub with dancers cavorting to jazz played by black musicians. The scene of wild revelry is Dionysian. The abandon of the dancers is contrasted with the passivity of relatives, sitting home in rocking chairs. The poet invites the reader to experience a fortunate fall "downstairs" into sensual abandon. ("National Winter Garden" in *The Bridge* presents a much more somber and sordid version of the Fall.) Here the scene is a fallen world where people titter at death. The flapper who is the incarnation of Helen in the fallen realm should not be frowned on, however; even though it is "guilty song," sensual love, that she inspires, she is young and still retains some of the innocence of the ideal Helen.

The scene changes again in the third section, with the poet addressing a fighter pilot as an emissary of death (a problem that Crane would explore again in *The Bridge*). Crane treats war and the desecration of the heavens as the ultimate problem for the poet who would love the world and see beauty in it. It is not only eternity and abstract beauty that the poet praises but also the years, and beauty in and out of time, to which the bleeding hands of the poet pray. More advanced than business or religion, the imagination of the poet reaches beyond despair.

THE BRIDGE

The Bridge, a poem of more than twelve hundred lines, is Crane's masterwork, comparable to T. S. Eliot's *The Waste Land* (1922) and William Carlos Williams's *Paterson* (1946-1958). Although it is not a classical epic because it is not a narrative, the poem's seriousness and magnitude are reflected in its theme: The poet tries to find in himself and in the United States the possibility of the redemption of love and vision. Crane wanted the poem to be not an expression of narrow nationalism but a synthesis of the spiritual reality of the United States.

The central symbol of the poem is the Brooklyn Bridge, a product of contemporary technology that seemed in its beauty to embody humanity's aspirations for transcendence. In the poem, the bridge is seen as a musical instrument, a harp; as the whitest flower, the anemone; as a ship, a woman, a world. In a letter to Otto Kahn, his patron, Crane said that the bridge symbolizes "consciousness spanning time and space." It is a figure of power in repose, a quality that Crane ascribes in the poem to God. The bridge also symbolizes all that joins and unifies, as the bridge unites the material and the spiritual in its existence.

"TO BROOKLYN BRIDGE"

"To Brooklyn Bridge," the proem, is an invocation to the bridge, in which the central opposition of the poem is sketched out—the life-giving spirituality of the bridge versus the deadening influence of the materialistic, commercial city. The freedom of the soaring seagull in the sky is contrasted with the destructive compulsion of the "bedlamite" who jumps from the bridge, amid the jeering onlookers. The poet asks the bridge to "lend a myth to God," to be the means of belief and transcendence in the city that seems to have no ideals and nothing in which to believe.

"Ave Maria"

In the next section, "Ave Maria," Crane goes back to the beginnings of America and to an age of faith, to Columbus after his discovery. Journeying back to Spain, Columbus meditates that he will tell the queen and her court that he is bringing back "Cathay." He will announce his discovery of a new reality, something that the poet accomplishes in his journey into history and myth. (In this section the sea acts as a bridge between the two continents.) Columbus's dedication has its counterweight, however, in Fernando, Isabella's husband, who anticipates a "delirium of jewels." Even in the discovery of America, the motive for its exploitation was present.

"Powhatan's Daughter"

The next section of the poem, "Powhatan's Daughter," includes five sections. The first part, "The Harbor Dawn," is set in the present, with the sounds of fog horns, trucks passing, and stevedores yelling—back by the Brooklyn Bridge but enshrouded in fog. The blurring of sights and sounds by fog and water is in preparation for a blurring of time and space for a visionary journey with the poet. In the sanctuary of his room by the bridge or in his dream, the poet has an experience of love, in which his beloved is portrayed in mythic terms. Her eyes drink the dawn, and there is a forest in her hair. The mythic past lives in the present or at least in the love of the poet.

"Van Winkle"

The next section, "Van Winkle," shifts abruptly with the mention of macadam roads that leap across the country and seem to take the poet back to his childhood as well as to figures in American history that he learned about in school: Francisco Pizarro, Hernán Cortés, Priscilla Alden, Captain John Smith, and Rip Van Winkle. Van Winkle, who was legendary rather than historical, was a man out of time, displaced, because he refused to grow up. Here Van Winkle forgets the office hours and the pay and so ends up sweeping a tenement. He can get only menial work in a commercial society that demands a dedication to materialistic values. Van Winkle has a different, uncommercial vision. He looks at Broadway and sees a springtime daisy chain. Instead of the lifeless city, he sees a beautiful natural world.

Lines about Van Winkle are interspersed with memories of the poet's own childhood. The memories pick up equivalents for recurring symbols of the poem—the eagle for space and the snake for time. The poet remembers stoning garter snakes that "flashed back" at him. Instead of eagles, his space figures were paper airplanes, launched into the air.

Mythic journeys often involve the search for the father or the mother as a part of the search for identity. Crane introduces a possible need for that search in recounting two memories of disjunction from his parents: a glimpse of his father whipping him with a lilac switch and a more subtle denial by his mother, who once "almost" brought him a smile from church and then withheld it. Together with the smile, the mother seems to be withholding her approval and love. The final image of the section is of Van Winkle, ready for a streetcar ride, warned that it is getting late. It is time for the journey to continue.

"The River"

"The River" begins with a jumble of sounds, fragments of conversations—perhaps on the streetcar—mention of commercial products such as Tintex and Japalac, and slogans from advertising, with fragments slapped against one another, making no sense. A misplaced faith links "SCIENCE—COMMERCE and the HOLY GHOST." Unlike the sermons in stones that William Shakespeare's world could find, the slogans and jingles are meaningless.

From the streetcar, the scene switches to a magnificent train, the Twentieth Century Limited, roaring cross-country. The poem focuses on the hoboes who ride the rails and who, like Van Winkle, refuse to grow up. The men who did grow up, however, killed the last bear in the Dakotas and strung telegraph wires across the mountain streams. Those who want progress and a world of "whistles, wire, and steam" have a different time-sense from that of the wanderers. Although people like the poet's father would call the hoboes useless clods, the wanderers sense some truth and know the body of the land as alive and beautiful. In that knowledge, they are like the poet who knows the land "bare"—intimately—and loves it. The eagle of space and the serpent of time appear, adorning the body of the beloved land, but the old gods need to be propitiated because the iron of modern civilization (and especially of the railroad) has split and broken the land and the mythic faith.

The train seems now to follow the river or to become the river. Everyone becomes part of the river, which is timeless because eternal; lost in the river, each one becomes his father's father. The poet and the poem are not only traveling across the country but are journeying back into time as well. Affirming again the possibility of love, the river whose one will is to flow is united with the gulf in passion.

"The Dance"

In "The Dance," the poet returns to the time of Native American greatness, the time of Pocahontas. The poet imagines himself a Native American, initiated into the worldview of the brave, at home in nature, speeding over streams in his canoe. He salutes Maquokeeta, the medicine man and priest. He commands Maquokeeta to dance humankind back to the tribal morning, to a time of harmony between humankind and nature when he had power even over rainbows, sky bridges. Maquokeeta is named the snake that lives before and beyond, the serpent Time itself. The time that he creates in his dance is the time of mythic wholeness. Pocahontas, the earth, is his eternal bride, and in the dance he possesses her; time and space are made one. The poet has become one with Maquokeeta by calling him up and participating imaginatively in the dance.

"Indiana"

The next section, "Indiana," a transitional one, is a letdown of poetic energy and drama. The verse is more prosaic and the rhymes seem strained. The explicit function of the piece is to have the national spirit passed from the Native American to the white settlers in a continuation of American history. It also chronicles the parting of a mother from a son, who is now to be independent (an important struggle in Crane's own life). The mother's pleas and clinging continue to the end of the section and almost beyond, binding the son by his pledge. Unwilling to let go, she begs for remembrance, naming the young man "stranger," "son," and finally "my friend." The relationship of friend, however, seems more request than fact, and nothing is related from the son's point of view.

"Cutty Sark"

Once the poet has succeeded in getting away, in the "Cutty Sark" section, his verse returns to the energy and style of "The River" and earlier sections. The narrator is again the poet, introducing a tall, eerie sailor he has met in a South Street bar. Like the hoboes and perhaps like the poet, the sailor is an outcast. (In various ways he resembles Herman Melville's Captain Ahab and Samuel Taylor Coleridge's Ancient Mariner.) Like the hoboes in "The River," this sailor has a different sense of time from that of the commercial city. Instead of being tuned to the cycles of nature, the sailor's time-sense has been disturbed by the expanse of Arctic white, eternity itself. The sailor, who says he cannot live on land any more, is almost run down by a truck as he tries to cross the street, a sign of the break between the inarticulate, prophetic sailor and the cynical city.

The poet starts walking across the Brooklyn Bridge to get home, and his thoughts are still filled with memories of the clipper ships, related to the bridge in shape by being called parabolas. Just as Fernando's greed was part of Columbus's discovery of America, part of the motive for the sailing ships was "sweet opium" and the tea the imperial British sought. The poet's experience and the American experience are still a mixture of the ideal and the sordid.

"Cape Hatteras"

"Cape Hatteras" is a substantial section of almost 250 lines. It begins with a primitive setting, with a dinosaur sinking into the ground and coastal mountains rising out of the land. In contrast to the impersonal geological processes, the poet, who has been wandering through time and space, tells the reader that he has returned home to eat an apple and to read Walt Whitman. From Marseille and Bombay, he is going home to the United States, to the body of Pocahontas and the sweetness of the land under the "derricks, chimneys," and "tunnels." He is returning to try to get a perspective on the exotic experiences he has had.

Next, the poet contemplates the infinity of space that is not subjugated by time and the actions of humanity, even though modern humanity can know space by "an engine in a cloud." The poet invokes Whitman and asks if infinity was the same when Whitman walked on the beach in communion with the sea. The poet's answer is that Whitman's vision lives even in the stock-market society of the present and in the free paths into the future. Opposed to Whitman's vision, however, is the fallen world of the machine, a demoniac world of unleashed power. The din and the violence of slapping belts and frogs's eyes that suddenly appear, vulnerable in the midst of such uncontrolled machinery, make the world a nightmare, an apocalyptic vision. The dance of the machines is a devilish parody of the heavenly, creative dance of the poet as the Native American priest, and America as Pocahontas.

The poet presents the scene of Wilbur and Orville Wright at Kitty Hawk with their silver biplane, praising their daring but deploring the use of the invention for war. A demoniac image that is parallel to the later image of the bridge as an anemone is the grenade as a flower with "screaming petals." Such terrible power is rationalized with theories as destructive as hail to the fertile earth. Imaginative vision cannot control the machines that have splintered space, even as the iron railroad split the land. The poet reminds the pilot that at the great speed of the airplane, the pilot has no time to consider what doom he is causing: He is intoxicated with space. The pilot's real mission is to join the edges of infinity, to bring them together in a loving union, to conjugate them. The poet follows his warning with a scene of the fighter pilot's destruction. Hit by a shell, the plane spirals down in a dance of death, and all that bravery becomes "mashed and shapeless debris."

If the fighter pilot represents a false relationship with space and infinity, Whitman is a figure with the right relationship, one whose vision of the earth and its renewal makes possible a new brotherhood. Whitman makes himself a living bridge between the sky and humanity through song. Whitman is also chief mourner of the men lost in wars, from the Civil War to Crane's time.

The next part of "Cape Hatteras" reads like a Romantic poet's declaration of his awakening to the beauty and inspiration of nature in its rhapsodic description of flowers and of heights that the poet has climbed. The declaration is followed by an apostrophe to Whitman as the awakener of the poet. Whitman is named his poetic master, the bread of angels in a eucharistic sense, and the one who began work on the bridge, the myth or imaginative construction that the poet is here creating. In Whitman, the poet seems to have claimed his poetic father: He says that Whitman's vision has passed into his hands.

"THREE SONGS"

In the next section, "Three Songs," the poet tries to work through his relationship with the feminine. In the first song, "Southern Cross," he says that he yearns for a relationship that would be heavenly, ideal, and also real. (He pictures night and the constellation of the Southern Cross.) What he has found, however, is not woman, nameless and ideal, but Eve and Magdalene, fallen women, and a Venus who is subhuman and ape-like. All the women lead to one grave, to death. The poet seems to feel disgust at the physical being of woman. He next pictures woman as a ship. Like the Ancient Mariner in Coleridge's poem, he is revolted by the generative (physical-sexual) nature of the sea. In Crane's poem, however, it is the feminine ship that is pictured as promiscuous, defiled by the masculine sea. The feminine also has qualities of a sea monster that can sting man. The Southern Cross, the poet's idealization of the feminine, drops below the horizon at dawn, and what is left is woman's innumerable spawn, evidence of her indiscriminate sexuality.

The next song, "National Winter Garden," may seem to be a continuation of the poet's disgust with women, but it is different in being given an actual, rather than an archetypal, setting. The scene is a striptease in a burlesque show. The stripper's dance is a vulgar parody of sexuality and another parody of the creative, ecstatic dance of the Indian priest-poet and Pocahontas. The burlesque queen awakens sexual appetite, but she is only pretending to have youth and beauty. Her pearls and snake ring are also fake, and the poet, who is waiting for someone else, runs away from the final "spasm." Here, however, the poet can make a reconciliation with Magdalene, with feminine sexuality, admitting its finality. Both men and women are physical and sexual; their natures are inescapable. If a woman is an agent of death, she is also an agent of birth. If each man dies alone in sexual union with her, he is also somehow born back into life, into his own sexual nature.

A third song for woman is "Virginia." The woman, Mary, is young, childlike, and possibly innocent. The poet seems to be using echoes of a popular song. Mary is working on Saturday at an office tower. She is described in chivalric terms; the poet is serenading her, and she is at least temporarily inaccessible. Flowers are blooming and bells are ringing, even if they are "popcorn bells." Like Rapunzel in the fairy tale, Mary is asked to let down her golden hair. All seems light and graceful (even though in the fairy tale the prince pays for his courtship with Rapunzel with a period of wandering in the forest, blinded). At the end of the song, the poet calls the girl "Cathedral Mary," sanctifying her, perhaps ironically.

"QUAKER HILL"

In "Quaker Hill," the tone changes from the light, playful tone of the previous song. The section begins with a diatribe against weekenders descending on the countryside. Self-absorbed, they are out of tune with nature. They also have a distorted relation with time, being eager to buy as an expensive antique a cheap old deal table whose finish is being eaten by woodlice. The poet says that time will make strange neighbors.

Meditating on time as a destroyer, the poet asks where his kinsmen, his spiritual fathers are. To find his heritage, he has to look past the "scalped Yankees" to the mythic world of the Native Americans and accept his "sundered parentage." The poet says that men must come down from the hawk's viewpoint to that of the worm and take on their tongues not the Eucharist but the dust of mortality.

This humiliation is associated with the artist's abject position in modern society. Emily Dickinson and Isadora Duncan are introduced as examples of artists scorned in their day, and the only consolation the poet offers is that pain teaches patience. He asserts that patience will keep the artist from despair, implying that time will vindicate him. The section closes with a motif that is parallel to the fall of the fighter pilot to shapeless debris. Like the plane spiraling down, a leaf breaks off from a tree and descends in a whirling motion, but the leaf is part of a natural cycle, and the poet has put his faith in time and nature.

"THE TUNNEL"

The scene shifts back to the city in the next section, "The Tunnel." The natural world is left behind, and the poet is in the center of the gawdy theater district. References to hell, death, and "tabloid crime-sheets" make the area a wasteland. The subway, the fastest way home, is a descent into hell. The traveler cannot look himself in the eye without being startled and afraid. The sound of the subway is a monotone, but fragments of conversation are lewdly suggestive. The subway riders are the walking dead, living on like hair and fingernails on a corpse, yet "swinging" goes on persistently "somehow anyhow." The sounds of the subway make a phonograph of hell that plays within the poet's brain. This labyrinth of sound even rewinds itself; from this hell there is no exit. Love is a "burnt match." In "For the Marriage of Faustus and Helen," the flapper, the modern embodiment of beauty, was like a skater in the skies. Here the discarded match is skating in the pool of a urinal.

Suddenly the poet sees a disembodied head swinging from a subway strap. The apparition, figure of the artist scorned and destroyed by his society, is Edgar Allan Poe. Poe's eyes are seen below the dandruff and the toothpaste ads. In this banal setting, death reaches out through Poe to the poet. At this point, the subway comes to a dead stop. A sight of escape is momentary, and then the train descends for the final dive under the river.

As the train lurches forward again, the poet sees a "wop washerwoman." In the midst of the inferno, there is a positive figure of a woman. Although she is not a discoverer like Columbus, her work has dignity: She cleans the city at night. A maternal figure, she brings home to her children her eyes and hands, Crane's symbols of vision and love. A victim like Poe and the poet, the cleaning woman is bandaged. Other birth imagery here is demoniac: A day being born is immediately slaughtered. The poet's greatest agony is that in this nightmare, he failed to preserve a song.

In his great agony, the poet feels the train start to ascend. Both the poet and the train are, like Lazarus, resurrected. They are returning to the natural world above ground. His vocation renewed, the poet can affirm the everlasting word. Once above ground again, the poet is at the river bank, ready to turn to the bridge.

"Atlantis"

With the poet resurrected, "Atlantis"—the final section of the poem—is a song of deliverance. It is an ecstatic paean to the bridge, seen as music, light, love, joy, and inspiration. More dynamic than the music of the spheres, the music of the bridge creates a divinity. It is a myth that kills death: It gives death its utter wound, just by its light, its lack of shadow. By the myth of the bridge, the cities are endowed with ripe fields. They have become natural, organic, and fruitful. The bridge is the city's "glittering pledge" forever. It is the answerer of all questions. In the poet's vision and in the poem, it is unutterably beautiful.

"Atlantis" acts as a synthesis, subsuming earlier motifs such as stars, seagulls, cities, the river, the flower, grass, history and myth, and circles and spirals. The question "Is it Cathay?" links the end of *The Bridge* with Columbus's discovery of America in the beginning, not in a mood of anxiety but in wonder at an America transfigured. The final two lines bring together time and space—the serpent and the eagle— with the music and radiance and energy of the bridge transcendent.

Other major works

NONFICTION: *The Letters of Hart Crane*, 1952 (Brom Weber, editor).

MISCELLANEOUS: *The Complete Poems and Selected Letters and Prose of Hart Crane*, 1966 (Weber, editor); *O My Land, My Friends: The Selected Letters of Hart Crane*, 1997 (Langdon Hammer and Brom Weber, editors); *Complete Poems and Selected Letters*, 2006.

Bibliography

Berthoff, Warner. *Hart Crane: A Re-Introduction.* Minneapolis: University of Minnesota Press, 1989. This is a solid, concise, generally accurate discussion of Crane's life and work that corrects misrepresentations of earlier books.

Bloom, Harold, ed. *Hart Crane: Comprehensive Research and Study Guide.* Philadelphia: Chelsea House, 2003. Contains a biography of Crane and extensive analysis of works including "Voyages," "Repose of Rivers," "To Brooklyn Bridge," "The Tunnel," and "The Broken Tower."

Crane, Hart. *O My Land, My Friends: The Selected Letters of Hart Crane.* Edited by Langdon Hammer and Brom Weber. New York: Four Walls Eight Windows, 1997. This expanded and revised edition *The Letters of Hart Crane* (1952) includes separate introductions to the periods of Crane's life and an analytical index. One-third of the letters are new, and all are uncensored.

Fisher, Clive. *Hart Crane.* New Haven, Conn.: Yale University Press, 2002. A biography of the poet that uses extant documents to exhaustively examine his personal life, including his homosexuality, to link his turbulent existence with his poetic talent. Looks at the suicidal tendencies of the poet's mother and re-creates the scene of his death.

Gabriel, Daniel. *Hart Crane and the Modernist Epic: Canon and Genre Formation in Crane, Pound, Eliot, and Williams.* New York: Palgrave Macmillan, 2007. Examines the importance of Crane in modernism and in creating a new version of the epic.

Hammer, Langdon. *Hart Crane and Allen Tate: Janus-Faced Modernism.* Princeton, N.J.: Princeton University Press, 1993. Called a "brilliant study" by the reviewer for the *Times Literary Supplement*, this book focuses on the friendship between Crane and Tate, analyzing modern American poetry's progress toward professionalism and institutionalization. Includes an index.

Mariani, Paul L. *The Broken Tower: A Life of Hart Crane.* New York: W. W. Norton, 1999. Examines the life of Crane, who held a pivotal role in the development of American literature's avant-garde. Quotations from Crane's letters and poems are included throughout the narrative.

Reed, Brian M. *Hart Crane: After His Lights.* Tuscaloosa: University of Alabama Press, 2006. An examination of the poet that looks at how to interpret his works, as well as the lyric and epic form.

Tapper, Gordon A. *The Machine That Sings: Modernism, Hart Crane, and the Culture of the Body.* New York: Routledge, 2006. An analysis of Crane's work that focuses on his preoccupation with the body. Examines "The Wine Merchant," "Voyages," and "Possessions," as well as three section of *The Bridge*— "National Winter Garden," "The Dance," and "Cape Hatteras."

Kate Begnal

COUNTÉE CULLEN

Born: New York, New York; or Louisville, Kentucky; or Baltimore, Maryland;
  May 30, 1903
Died: New York, New York; January 9, 1946

PRINCIPAL POETRY
Color, 1925
The Ballad of the Brown Girl: An Old Ballad Retold, 1927
Copper Sun, 1927
The Black Christ, and Other Poems, 1929
The Medea, and Some Poems, 1935
On These I Stand: An Anthology of the Best Poems of Countée Cullen, 1947

OTHER LITERARY FORMS

Countée Cullen (KUH-lehn) wrote nearly as much prose as he did poetry. While serving from 1926 through most of 1928 as literary editor of *Opportunity*, a magazine vehicle for the National Urban League, Cullen wrote several articles, including book reviews, and a series of topical essays for a column called "The Dark Tower" about figures and events involved in the Harlem Renaissance. He also wrote many stories for children, most of which are collected in *My Lives and How I Lost Them* (1942), the "autobiography" of Cullen's own pet, Christopher Cat, who had allegedly reached his ninth life. Earlier, in 1932, the poet had tried his hand at a novel, publishing it as *One Way to Heaven* (1932). In addition to articles, reviews, stories, and a novel, the poet translated or collaborated in the writing of four plays, one of them being a musical. In 1935, Cullen translated Euripides' *Medea* for the volume by the same name; in 1942, Virgil Thomson set to music the seven verse choruses from Cullen's translation. With Owen Dodson, Cullen wrote the one-act play *The Third Fourth of July*, which appeared posthumously in 1946. The musical was produced at the Martin Beck Theater on Broadway, where it ran for 113 performances; this production also introduced Pearl Bailey as the character Butterfly.

ACHIEVEMENTS

Countée Cullen's literary accomplishments were many. While he was a student at DeWitt Clinton High School, New York City, he published his first poems and made numerous and regular contributions to the high school literary magazine. From DeWitt, whose other distinguished graduates include Lionel Trilling and James Baldwin, Cullen went to New York University. There he distinguished himself by becoming a member of Phi Beta Kappa and in the same year, 1925, by publishing *Color*, his first collection of

Countée Cullen
(Library of Congress)

poems. In June, 1926, the poet took his second degree, an M.A. in English literature from Harvard University. In December, 1926, *Color* was awarded the first Harmon Gold Award for literature, which carried with it a cash award of five hundred dollars. Just before publication in 1927 of his second book, *Copper Sun*, Cullen received a Guggenheim Fellowship for a year's study and writing in France. While in France, he worked on improving his French conversation by engaging a private tutor and his knowledge of French literature by enrolling in courses at the Sorbonne. Out of this experience came *The Black Christ, and Other Poems*. In 1944, the poet was offered the chair of creative literature at Nashville's Fisk University, but he refused in order to continue his teaching at the Frederick Douglass Junior High in New York City.

BIOGRAPHY

Countée Cullen was born Countée LeRoy Porter, although scholars remain uncertain as to the place of his birth. He was raised by Elizabeth Porter, who is thought to be his grandmother and who brought him to Harlem. When Porter died in 1918, Cullen was adopted by the Reverend and Mrs. Frederick A. Cullen; the Reverend Cullen was minister of the Salem Methodist Episcopal Church of Harlem. The years spent with the Cullens in the Methodist parsonage made a lasting impression on the young poet; although he experienced periods of intense self-questioning, Cullen appears never to have discarded his belief in Christianity.

During his undergraduate years at New York University, the young poet became heavily involved with figures of the Harlem Renaissance; among these Harlem literati were Zora Neale Hurston, Langston Hughes, Carl Van Vechten (a white writer who treated black themes), and Wallace Thurman. After the appearance of *Color* in 1925 and the receipt of his Harvard M.A. in June, 1926, Cullen assumed the position of literary editor of *Opportunity*. At the end of October, 1926, he wrote one of the most important of his "Dark Tower" essays about the appearance of that great treasure of the Harlem Renaissance, the short-lived but first black literary and art quarterly *Fire* (issued only once). He contributed one of his best poems, "From the Dark Tower," to *Fire*. About the solitary issue, Cullen wrote that it held great significance for black American culture, because it represented "a brave and beautiful attempt to meet our need for an all-literary and artistic medium of expression."

On April 10, 1928, Cullen married Nina Yolande Du Bois, daughter of one of the most powerful figures of twentieth century black American culture, W. E. B. Du Bois; the two were married at Salem Methodist Episcopal Church. This union proved to be of short duration, however; while Cullen was in Paris on his Guggenheim Fellowship, his wife was granted a decree of divorce. The marriage had not lasted two years. Much of Cullen's poetry deals with disappointment in love, and one senses that the poet was himself often disappointed in such matters.

In 1940, however, after Cullen had taught for several years at the Frederick Douglass Junior High School of New York, he married a second time; on this occasion he chose Ida Mae Roberson, whom he had known for ten years. Ida Mae represented to the poet the ideal woman; she was intelligent, loyal, and empathetic, if not as beautiful and well-connected as his former wife.

When Cullen died of uremic poisoning on January 9, 1946, only forty-two years old, the New York newspapers devoted several columns to detailing his career and praising him for his distinguished literary accomplishments. However, nearly thirty years after Cullen's death, Houston A. Baker deplored (in *A Many-Colored Coat of Dreams: The Poetry of Countée Cullen*, 1974) the fact that no collection of his poetry had been published since the posthumous *On These I Stand*, nor had any of his previously published volumes been reprinted. Indeed, many volumes of this important Harlem Renaissance poet can be read only in rare-book rooms of university libraries.

Analysis

In his scholarly book of 1937, *Negro Poetry and Drama*, Sterling A. Brown, whose poems and essays continue to exert formidable influence on black American culture, remarked that Countée Cullen's poetry is "the most polished lyricism of modern Negro poetry." About his own poetry and poetry in general, Cullen himself observed, "Good poetry is a lofty thought beautifully expressed. Poetry should not be too intellectual. It should deal more, I think, with the emotions." In this definition of "good poetry," Cullen reflects his declared, constant aspiration to transcend his color and to strike a universal chord. However, the perceptive poet, novelist, essayist and critic James Weldon Johnson asserted that the best of Cullen's poetry "is motivated by race. He is always seeking to free himself and his art from these bonds."

The tension prevalent in Cullen's poems, then, is between the objective of transcendence—to reach the universal, to enter the "mainstream"—and his ineluctable return to the predicament his race faces in a white world. This tension causes him, on one hand, to demonstrate a paramount example of T. S. Eliot's "tradition and the individual talent" and, on the other, to embody the black aesthetic (as articulated during the Harlem Renaissance). In his best poems, he achieves both. Transcending the bonds of race and country, he produces poetry that looks to the literature and ideas of the past while it identifies its creator as an original artist; yet, at the same time, he celebrates his African heritage, dramatizes black heroism, and reveals the reality of being black in a hostile world.

"YET DO I MARVEL"

"Yet Do I Marvel," perhaps Cullen's most famous single poem, displays the poet during one of his most intensely lyrical, personal moments; however, this poem also illustrates his reverence for tradition. The sonnet, essentially Shakespearean in rhyme scheme, is actually Petrarchan in its internal form. The Petrarchan form is even suggested in the rhyme scheme; the first two quatrains rhyme *abab, cdcd* in perfect accord with the Shakespearean scheme. The next six lines, however, break the expected pattern of yet another quatrain in the same scheme; instead of *efef* followed by a couplet *gg*, the poem adopts the scheme *eeffgg*. While retaining the concluding couplet (*gg*), the other two (*eeff*) combine with the final couplet, suggesting the Petrarchan structure of the sestet. The poem is essentially divided, then, into the octave, wherein the problem is stated, and the sestet, in which some sort of resolution is attempted.

Analysis of the poem's content shows that Cullen chose the internal form of the Petrarchan sonnet but retained a measure of the Shakespearean form for dramatic effect. By means of antiphrastic statements or ironic declaratives in the first eight lines of the poem, the poem's speaker expresses doubt about God's goodness and benevolent intent, especially in his creation of certain limited beings. The poem begins with the assertion that "I doubt not God is good, well-meaning, kind" and then proceeds to reveal that the speaker actually believes just the opposite to be true; that is, he actually says, "I do doubt God is good." For God has created the "little buried mole" to continue blind and "flesh that mirrors Him" to "some day die." Then the persona cites two illustrations of cruel, irremediable predicaments from classical mythology, those of Tantalus and Sisyphus. These mythological figures are traditional examples: Tantalus, the man who suffers eternal denial of that which he seeks, and Sisyphus, the man who suffers the eternal drudgery of being forced to toil endlessly again and again only to lose his objective each time he thinks he has won it.

The illustration of the mole and the man who must die rehearses the existential pathos of modern human beings estranged from God and thrust into a hostile universe. What appeared to be naïve affirmations of God's goodness become penetrating questions that reveal Cullen himself in a moment of intense doubt. This attitude of contention with God closely resembles that expressed by Gerard Manley Hopkins in his sonnet "Thou Art Indeed Just, Lord." The probing questions, combined with the apparent resolve to believe, are indeed close; one might suggest that Cullen has adapted Hopkins's struggle for certainty to the black predicament, the real subject of Cullen's poem. The predicaments of Tantalus and Sisyphus (anticipating Albert Camus's later essay) comment on a personal problem, one close to home for Cullen himself. The notion of men struggling eternally toward a goal, thinking they have achieved it but having it torn from them, articulates the plight of black artists in the United States. In keeping with the form of the Petrarchan sonnet, the ninth line constitutes the *volta* or turn toward some sort of resolution. From ironic questioning, the persona moves to direct statement, even to a degree of affirmation. "Inscrutable His ways are," the speaker declares, to a mere human being who is too preoccupied with the vicissitudes of his mundane existence to grasp "What awful brain compels His awful hand," this last line echoing William Blake's "The Tyger." The apparent resolution becomes clouded by the poem's striking final couplet: "Yet do I marvel at this curious thing:/ To make a poet black, and bid him sing!"

The doubt remains; nothing is finally resolved. The plight of the black poet becomes identical with that of Tantalus and Sisyphus. Like these figures from classical mythology, the black poet is, in the contemporary, nonmythological world, forced to struggle endlessly toward a goal he will never, as the poem suggests, be allowed to reach. Cullen has effectively combined the Petrarchan and the Shakespearean sonnet forms; the sestet's first four lines function as an apparent resolution of the problem advanced by the octave. The concluding couplet, however, recalling the Shakespearean device of concentrating the entire poem's comment within the final two lines, restates the problem of the octave by maintaining that, in the case of a black poet, God has created the supreme irony. In "Yet Do I Marvel," Cullen has succeeded in making an intensely personal statement; as Johnson suggested, this poem "is motivated by race." Nevertheless, not only race is at work here. Rather than selecting a more modern form, perhaps free verse, the poet employs the sonnet tradition in a surprising and effective way, and he also shows his regard for tradition by citing mythological figures and by summoning up Blake.

REGARD FOR TRADITION

Cullen displays his regard for tradition in many other poems. "The Medusa," for example, by its very title celebrates once again the classical tradition; in this piece, another sonnet, the poet suggests that the face of a woman who rejected him has the malign power of the Medusa. In an epitaph, a favorite form of Cullen, he celebrates the poetry of John Keats, whose "singing lips that cold death kissed/ Have seared his own with flame." Keats was Cullen's avowed favorite poet, and Cullen celebrates him in yet a second poem, "To John Keats, Poet at Spring Time." As suggested by Cullen's definition of poetry, it was Keats's concern for beauty which attracted him: "in spite of all men say/ Of Beauty, you have felt her most."

"HERITAGE"

Beauty and classical mythology were not the only elements of tradition that Cullen revered. Indeed, he forcefully celebrated his own African heritage, exemplifying the first of the tenets of the black aesthetic. "Heritage" represents his most concentrated effort to reclaim his African roots. This 128-line lyric opens as the persona longs for the song of "wild barbaric birds/ Goading massive jungle herds" from which, through no fault of his own, he has been removed for three centuries. He then articulates Johnson's observation that this poet is ever "seeking to free himself and his art" from the bonds of this heritage. The poem's speaker remarks that, although he crams his thumbs against his ears and keeps them there, "great drums" always throb "through the air." This duplicity of mind and action force upon him a sense of "distress, and joy allied." Despite this distress, he continues to conjure up in his mind's eye "cats/ Crouching in the river reeds," "silver snakes," and "the savage measures of/ Jungle boys and girls in love." The rain has a particularly dramatic effect on him; "While its primal measures drip," a distant, resonant voice beckons him to "'strip!/ Off this new exuberance./ Come and dance the Lover's Dance!'" Out of this experience of recollection and reclaiming his past comes the urge to "fashion dark gods" and, finally, even to dare "to give You [the one God]/ Dark despairing features."

THE BLACK CHRIST

The intense need expressed here, to see God as literally black, predicts the long narrative poem of 1929, *The Black Christ*. This poem, perhaps more than any other of Cullen's poems, represents his attempt to portray black heroism, the second tenet of the black aesthetic. Briefly the poem tells the tale of Jim, a young black man who comes to believe it is inevitable that he will suffer death at the hands of an angry lynch mob. Miraculously, after the inevitable lynching has indeed occurred, the young man appears to his younger brother and mother, much as Jesus of Nazareth, according to the Gospels, appeared before his disciples. Christ has essentially transformed himself into black Jim. Although the poem contains such faults as a main character who speaks in dialect at one point and waxes eloquent at another, and one speech by Jim who, pursued by the mob, speaks so long that he cannot possibly escape (one may argue that he was doomed from the start), it has moments of artistic brilliance.

Jim "was handsome in a way/ Night is after a long, hot day." He could never bend his spirit to the white man's demands: "my blood's too hot to knuckle." Like Richard Wright's Bigger Thomas, Jim was a man of action whose deeds "let loose/ The pent-up torrent of abuse," which clamored in his younger brother "for release." Toward the middle of the poem, Jim's brother, the narrator, describes Jim, after the older brother has become tipsy with drink, as "Spring's gayest cavalier"; this occurs "in the dim/ Half-light" of the evening. At the end, "Spring's gayest cavalier" has become the black Christ, Spring's radiant sacrifice, suggesting that "Half-light" reveals only selective truths, those one may be inclined to believe are true because of one's human limitations, whereas God's total light reveals absolute truth unfettered. Following this suggestion, the image "Spring's gayest cavalier" becomes even more fecund. The word "cavalier" calls up another poem by Hopkins, "The Windhover," which is dedicated to Christ. In this poem, the speaker addresses Christ with the exclamation, "O my chevalier!" Both "cavalier" and "chevalier" have their origins in the same Latin word, *caballarius*. Since Cullen knew both French and Latin and since Hopkins's poems had been published in 1918, it is reasonable to suggest a more than coincidental connection. At any rate, "Spring's gayest cavalier" embodies an example of effective foreshadowing.

Just before the mob seizes Jim, the narrator maintains that "The air about him shaped a crown/ Of light, or so it seemed to me," similar to the nimbus so often appearing in medieval paintings of Christ, the holy family, the disciples, and the saints. The narrator describes the seizure itself in an epic simile of nine lines. When Jim has been lynched, the younger brother exclaims, "My Lycidas was dead. There swung/ In all his glory, lusty, young,/ My Jonathan, my Patrocles." Here Cullen brings together the works of John Milton, the Bible, and Homer into one image that appears to syncretize them all. Clearly, the poet is attempting to construct in Jim a hero of cosmic proportions while at the same time managing to unify, if only for a moment, four grand traditions: the English, the biblical, the classical, and, of course, the African American.

"HARLEM WINE"

While *The Black Christ* dramatizes black heroism, it also suggests what it means to be black in a hostile, white world. Not all the black experience, however, is tainted with such unspeakable horror. In "Harlem Wine," Cullen reveals how blacks overcome their pain and rebellious inclinations through the medium of music. The blues, a totally black cultural phenomenon, "hurtle flesh and bone past fear/ Down alleyways of dreams." Indeed, the wine of Harlem can its "joy compute/ with blithe, ecstatic hips." The ballad stanza of this poem's three quatrains rocks with rhythm, repeating Cullen's immensely successful performance in another long narrative poem, *The Ballad of the Brown Girl*.

"FROM THE DARK TOWER"

Although not as notable a rhythmic performance as "Harlem Wine" or *The Ballad of the Brown Girl*, "From the Dark Tower" is, nevertheless, a remarkable poem. It contains a profound expression of the black experience. Important to a reading of the poem is the fact that the Dark Tower was an actual place located on New York's 136th Street in the heart of Harlem; poets and artists of the Harlem Renaissance often gathered there to discuss their writings and their art. Perhaps this poem grew out of one of those gatherings. The poem is more identifiably a Petrarchan or Italian sonnet than "Yet Do I Marvel"; as prescribed by the form, the octave is arranged into two quatrains, each rhyming *abbaabba*, while the sestet rhymes *ccddee*. The rhyme scheme of the sestet closely resembles that in "Yet Do I Marvel."

The octave of "From the Dark Tower" states the poem's problem in an unconventional, perhaps surprising manner by means of a series of threats. The first threat introduces the conceit of planting, to which the poem returns in its last pair of couplets. The poet begins, "We shall not always plant while others reap/ The golden increment of bursting fruit." The planting conceit suggests almost immediately the image of slaves working the fields of a Southern plantation. Conjuring up this memory of the antebellum South but then asserting by use of the future tense ("We *shall* not") that nothing has changed—that is, that the white world has relegated modern African Americans to their former status as slaves, not even as good as second-class citizens—Cullen strikes a minor chord of deep, poignant bitterness felt by many blacks during his lifetime. However, what these blacks produce with their planting is richly fertile, a "bursting fruit"; the problem is that "others reap" this "golden increment." The poet's threat promises that this tide of gross, unjust rapine will soon turn against its perpetrators.

The next few lines compound this initial threat with others. These same oppressed people will not forever bow "abject and mute" to such treatment by a people who have shown by their oppression that they are the inferiors of their victims. "Not everlastingly" will these victims "beguile" this evil race "with mellow flute"; the reader can readily picture scenes of supposedly contented, dancing "darkies" and ostensibly happy minstrel men. "We were not made eternally to weep" declares the poet in the last line of the octave. This line constitutes the *volta* or turning point in the poem. All the bitterness and resentment implied in the preceding lines is exposed here. An oppressed people simply will not shed tears forever; sorrow and self-pity inevitably turn to anger and rebellion.

The first four lines of the sestet state cases in defense of the octave's propositions that these oppressed people, now identified by the comparisons made in these lines as the black race, are "no less lovely being dark." The poet returns subtly to his planting conceit by citing the case of flowers that "cannot bloom at all/ In light, but crumple, piteous, and fall." From the infinite heavens to finite flowers of Earth Cullen takes his reader, grasping universal and particular significance for his people and thereby restoring and bolstering their pride and sense of worth.

Then follow the piercing, deep-felt last lines: "So, in the dark we hide the heart that bleeds,/ And wait, and tend our agonizing seeds." As with "Yet Do I Marvel," Cullen has effectively combined the structures of the Petrarchan and Shakespearean sonnets by concluding his poem with this trenchant, succinct couplet. The planting conceit, however, has altered dramatically. What has been "golden increment" for white oppressors will yet surely prove the "bursting fruit" of "agonizing seeds." The poem represents, then, a sort of revolutionary predeclaration of independence. This "document" first states the offenses sustained by the downtrodden, next asserts their worth and significance as human beings, and finally argues that the black people will "wait" until an appropriate time to reveal their agony through rebellion. Cullen has here predicted the anger of James Baldwin's *The Fire Next Time* (1963) and the rhetoric of the Black Armageddon, a later literary movement led by such poets as Amiri Baraka, Sonia Sanchez, and Nikki Giovanni.

Whereas these figures of the Black Armageddon movement almost invariably selected unconventional forms in which to express their rebellion, Cullen demonstrated his respect for tradition in voicing his parallel feelings. Although Cullen's work ably displays his knowledge of the traditions of the Western world, from Homer to Keats (and even Edna St. Vincent Millay), it equally enunciates his empathy with black Americans in its celebration of the black aesthetic. At the same time that his poetry incorporates classicism and English Romanticism, it affirms his black heritage and the black American experience.

OTHER MAJOR WORKS

LONG FICTION: *One Way to Heaven*, 1932.

PLAYS: *Medea*, pr., pb. 1935 (translation of Euripides); *One Way to Heaven*, pb. 1936 (adaptation of his novel); *St. Louis Woman*, pr. 1946 (adaptation of Arna Bontemps's novel *God Sends Sunday*); *The Third Fourth of July*, pr., pb. 1946 (one act; with Owen Dodson).

CHILDREN'S LITERATURE: *The Lost Zoo (A Rhyme for the Young, but Not Too Young)*, 1940; *My Lives and How I Lost Them*, 1942.

EDITED TEXT: *Caroling Dusk*, 1927.

MISCELLANEOUS: *My Soul's High Song: The Collected Writings of Countee Cullen, Voice of the Harlem Renaissance*, 1991 (Gerald Early, editor).

BIBLIOGRAPHY

Baker, Houston A., Jr. *A Many-Colored Coat of Dreams: The Poetry of Countée Cullen*. Detroit: Broadside Press, 1974. This brief and somewhat difficult volume examines Cullen's poetry in the context of a black American literature that is published and criticized largely by a white literary establishment. Presents a new view of Cullen's poetry by holding it up to the light of black literary standards.

Ferguson, Blanche E. *Countée Cullen and the Negro Renaissance*. New York: Dodd, Mead, 1966. The only book-length study of Cullen for many years, this volume is a highly fictionalized biography. In a pleasant and simple style, Ferguson walks readers through major events in Cullen's life. Includes eight photographs, a brief bibliography, and an index.

Hutchinson, George, ed. *The Cambridge Companion to the Harlem Renaissance*. New York: Cambridge University Press, 2007. This work on the Harlem Renaissance contains a chapter comparing Cullen and Langston Hughes.

Onyeberechi, Sydney. *Critical Essays: Achebe, Baldwin, Cullen, Ngugi, and Tutuola*. Hyattsville, Md.: Rising Star, 1999. A collection of Onyeberechi's criticism and interpretation of the work of several African American authors. Includes bibliographic references.

Perry, Margaret. *A Bio-Bibliography of Countée Cullen*. Westport, Conn.: Greenwood Press, 1971. After a brief biographical sketch, Perry offers a valuable bibliography of Cullen's works and a sensitive reading of the poetry.

Pettis, Joyce. *African American Poets: Lives, Works, and Sources*. Westport, Conn.: Greenwood Press, 2002. This work on African American poets contains an entry describing the life and works of Cullen.

Schwarz, A. B. Christa. *Gay Voices of the Harlem Renaissance*. Bloomington: Indiana University Press, 2003. Schwarz examines the work of four leading writers from the Harlem Renaissance—Cullen, Langston Hughes, Claude McKay, and Richard Bruce Nugent— and their sexually nonconformist or gay literary voices.

Shucard, Alan R. *Countée Cullen*. Boston: Twayne, 1984. A basic biography detailing the life and works of Cullen.

Tuttleton, James W. "Countée Cullen at 'The Heights.'" In *The Harlem Renaissance: Revaluations*, edited by Amritjit Singh, William S. Shiver, and Stanley Brodwin. New York: Garland, 1989. Examines Cullen's years at New York University and analyzes his senior honors thesis on Edna St. Vincent Millay. Tuttleton argues that this period was very important to Cullen's emergence as a poet.

Washington, Shirley Porter. *Countée Cullen's Secret Revealed by Miracle Book: A Biography of His Childhood in New Orleans*. Bloomington, Ind.: AuthorHouse, 2008. This work by Cullen's niece asserts that Cullen was born James S. Carter, Jr., in New Orleans to James S. Carter, Sr., the first licensed African American dentist in Louisiana, and to Gussie Yeager Carter.

John C. Shields

ALLEN GINSBERG

Born: Newark, New Jersey; June 3, 1926
Died: New York, New York; April 5, 1997

PRINCIPAL POETRY
Howl, and Other Poems, 1956, 1996
Empty Mirror: Early Poems, 1961
Kaddish, and Other Poems, 1958-1960, 1961
The Change, 1963
Reality Sandwiches, 1963
Kral Majales, 1965
Wichita Vortex Sutra, 1966
T.V. Baby Poems, 1967
Airplane Dreams: Compositions from Journals, 1968
Ankor Wat, 1968
Planet News, 1961-1967, 1968
The Moments Return, 1970
Ginsberg's Improvised Poetics, 1971
Bixby Canyon Ocean Path Word Breeze, 1972
The Fall of America: Poems of These States, 1965-1971, 1972
The Gates of Wrath: Rhymed Poems, 1948-1952, 1972
Iron Horse, 1972
Open Head, 1972
First Blues: Rags, Ballads, and Harmonium Songs, 1971-1974, 1975
Sad Dust Glories: Poems During Work Summer in Woods, 1975
Mind Breaths: Poems, 1972-1977, 1977
Mostly Sitting Haiku, 1978
Poems All over the Place: Mostly Seventies, 1978
Plutonian Ode: Poems, 1977-1980, 1982
Collected Poems, 1947-1980, 1984
White Shroud: Poems, 1980-1985, 1986
Hydrogen Jukebox, 1990 (music by Philip Glass)
Collected Poems, 1992
Cosmopolitan Greetings: Poems, 1986-1992, 1994
Making It Up: Poetry Composed at St. Marks Church on May 9, 1979, 1994 (with Kenneth Koch)
Selected Poems, 1947-1995, 1996
Death and Fame: Poems, 1993-1997, 1999
Collected Poems, 1947-1997, 2006

Other Literary Forms

Allen Ginsberg recognized early in his career that he would have to explain his intentions, because most critics and reviewers of the time did not have the interest or experience to understand what he was trying to accomplish. Consequently, he published books that include interviews, lectures, essays, photographs, and letters to friends as means of conveying his theories about composition and poetics.

Achievements

The publication of "Howl" in 1956 drew such enthusiastic comments from Allen Ginsberg's supporters, and such vituperative condemnation from conservative cultural commentators, that a rift of immense proportions developed, which has made a balanced critical assessment very difficult. Nevertheless, partisan response has gradually given way to an acknowledgment by most critics that Ginsberg's work is significant, if not always entirely successful by familiar standards of literary excellence. Such recognition was underscored in 1974, when *The Fall of America* shared the National Book Award in Poetry. Ginsberg was awarded a Los Angeles Times Book Prize (1982) and the Frost Medal by the Poetry Society of America (1986). Included among the many honors he garnered during his lifetime were an Academy Award in Literature from the American Academy of Arts and Letters in 1969, the Woodbury Poetry Prize, Guggenheim fellowships, the National Arts Club Medal of Honor, the Before Columbus Foundation award for lifetime achievement, the University of Chicago's Harriet Monroe Poetry Award, an American Academy of Arts and Sciences fellowship, and the Medal of Chevalier de l'Ordre des Arts et Letters.

The voice Ginsberg employed in "Howl" not only has influenced the style of several generations of poets, but also has combined the rhythms and language of common speech with some of the deepest, most enduring traditions in American literature. In both his life and his work, Ginsberg set an example of moral seriousness, artistic commitment, and humane decency that made him one of the most popular figures in American culture. The best of his visionary and innovative creations earned for him recognition as one of the major figures of the twentieth century.

Biography

Allen Ginsberg was born Irwin Allen Ginsberg, the second son of Naomi Levy Ginsberg, a Russian-born political activist and communist sympathizer, and Louis Ginsberg, a traditional lyric poet and high school English teacher. He attended primary school in the middle-class town of Paterson, New Jersey. He grew up in a conventional and uneventful household, with the exception of his mother's repeated hospitalizations for mental stress. He entered Columbia University in 1943, intending to pursue a career in labor law, but the influence of such well-known literary scholars as Lionel Trilling and Mark Van Doren, combined with the excitement of the Columbia community, which included fellow student Jack Kerouac and such singular people as William Burroughs and Neal Cassady, led him toward literature as a vocation. He was temporarily suspended from Columbia in 1945 and worked as a welder and apprentice seaman before finishing his degree in 1948. Living a "subterranean" life (to use Kerouac's term) that incorporated drug use, a bohemian lifestyle, and occasional antisocial acts of youthful ebullience, Ginsberg was counseled to commit himself for several months to Columbia Presbyterian Psychiatric Institute to avoid criminal charges associated with the possession of stolen goods; there, in 1949, he met Carl W. Solomon, to whom "Howl" is dedicated. During the early 1950's, he began a correspondence with William Carlos Williams, who guided and encouraged his early writing, and Ginsberg traveled in Mexico and Europe.

In 1954, Ginsberg moved to San Francisco to be at the center of the burgeoning Beat movement. He was living there when he wrote "Howl," and he read the poem for the first time at a landmark Six Gallery performance that included Gary Snyder, Philip Whalen, and Michael McClure. His mother died in 1956, the year *Howl, and Other Poems* was published, and he spent the next few years traveling, defending *Howl* against charges of obscenity, working on "Kaddish"—his celebration of his mother's life, based on a Hebrew prayer for the dead—and reading on college campuses and in Beatnik venues on both coasts.

The growing notoriety of the Beat generation drew Ginsberg into the media spotlight in the early 1960's, and he was active in the promotion of work by his friends. He continued to travel extensively, visiting Europe, India, and Japan; he read in bars and coffeehouses, and published widely in many of the prominent literary journals of the counterculture. His involvement with various hallucinatory substances led to the formation of LeMar (Organization to Legalize Marijuana) in 1964 with the poet, songwriter, and publisher Ed Sanders, and his continuing disaffection with governmental policies took him toward active political protest. In 1965, he was invited to Cuba and Czechoslovakia by Communist officials, who mistakenly assumed that his criticism of American society would make him sympathetic to their regimes, but Ginsberg's outspoken criticism of all forms of tyranny and suppression led to his expulsion from both countries.

His political activism—particularly in reaction to the Vietnam War—and close association with the counterculture continued throughout the 1960's and 1970's. During the 1960's, he invented the nonviolent concept of "flower power" in an attempt to neutralize martial aggression. In 1967, he was one of the organizers of the first "Human Be-In." The following year, he was arrested in Chicago at the Democratic National Convention with many other demonstrators, and in 1969, he testified at the Chicago Seven trials; that same year, he was at the center of a semi-serious effort to exorcise the Pentagon. In the early 1970's, he spent some time on a farm in rural New York, formally accepted the teachings of Buddhism from Chögyam Trungpa, who initiated him with the name "Lion of Dharma," and afterward cofounded, with Anne Waldman, a school of literary inquiry, the Jack Kerouac School of Disembodied Poetics at the Naropa Institute in Colorado. He was inducted into the American Institute of Arts and Letters in 1974, an indication of recognition as an artist in the mainstream of American culture, and he further confirmed this status by traveling with Bob Dylan's Rolling Thunder Review as a "poet-percussionist" in 1975. Continuing to combine artistic endeavor with a commitment to social justice, Ginsberg took part—with longtime lover Peter Orlovsky—in protests at the Rocky Flats Nuclear Facility in 1978 and wrote the "Plutonium Ode," which expressed his concern about the destructive forces humans had unleashed.

During the 1980's, Ginsberg continued to travel, teach, write, and perform his work. The publication of his *Collected Poems, 1947-1980* in 1984 was received with wide attention and respect, and he was appointed distinguished professor at Brooklyn College in 1986, the year he published *White Shroud*, which includes an epilogue to "Kaddish" along with other poems from the 1980's. His ability as a teacher was clearly demonstrated in his appearance on the Public Broadcasting Service series *Voices and Visions* in 1987. As the decade drew to a close, he was involved in collaboration with composer Philip Glass on a chamber opera called *Hydrogen Jukebox* (a phrase from "Howl"), which was performed in 1990. Continuing to write with energy while teaching a graduate-level course on the Beats at the City University of New York Graduate Center, Ginsberg described his goals in the 1990's, in a poem called "Personals Ad," as similar to the ones he had always pursued: "help inspire mankind conquer world anger & guilt." It was an appropriate task for a "poet professor in his autumn years." Afflicted with diabetes, hepatitis, and liver cancer, he died at age seventy following a stroke on April 5, 1997, in New York City.

Analysis

"Howl," the poem that carried Allen Ginsberg into public consciousness as a symbol of the avant-garde artist and as the designer of a verse style for a postwar generation seeking its own voice, was initially regarded as primarily a social document. As Ginsberg's notes make clear, however, it was also the latest specimen in a continuing experiment in form and structure. Several factors in Ginsberg's life were particularly important in this breakthrough poem, written as the poet was approaching thirty and still drifting through a series of jobs, countries, and social occasions. Ginsberg's father had exerted more influence than was immediately apparent. Louis Ginsberg's very traditional, metrical verse was of little use to his son, but his father's interest in literary history was part of Ginsberg's solid grounding in prosody. Then, a succession of other mentors—including Williams, whose use of the American vernacular and local material had inspired him, and great scholars such as art historian Meyer Shapiro at Columbia, who had introduced him to the tenets of modernism from an analytic perspective—had enabled the young poet to form a substantial intellectual foundation.

In addition, Ginsberg was dramatically affected by his friendships with Kerouac, Cassady, Burroughs, Herbert Hunke, and other noteworthy denizens of a vibrant underground community of dropouts, revolutionaries, drug addicts, jazz musicians, and serious but unconventional artists of all sorts. Ginsberg felt an immediate kinship with these "angelheaded hipsters," who accepted and celebrated eccentricity and regarded Ginsberg's homosexuality as an attribute, not a blemish. Although Ginsberg enthusiastically entered into the drug culture that was a flourishing part of this community, he was not nearly as routed toward self-destruction as Burroughs or Hunke; he was more interested in the possibilities of visionary experience. His oft-noted "illuminative audition of William Blake's voice simultaneous with Eternity-vision" in 1948 was his first ecstatic experience of transcendence, and he continued to pursue spiritual insight through serious studies of various religions—including Judaism and Buddhism—as well as through chemical experimentation.

His experiments with mind-altering agents (including marijuana, peyote, amphetamines, mescaline, and lysergic acid diethylamide, or LSD) and his casual friendship with some quasi-criminals led to his eight-month stay in a psychiatric institute. He had already experienced an unsettling series of encounters with mental instability in his mother, who had been hospitalized for the first time when he was three. Her struggles with the torments of psychic uncertainty were seriously disruptive events in Ginsberg's otherwise unremarkable boyhood, but Ginsberg felt deep sympathy for his mother's agony and also was touched by her warmth, love, and social conscience. Although not exactly a "red diaper baby," Ginsberg had adopted a radical political conscience early enough to decide to pursue labor law as a college student, and he never wavered from his initial convictions concerning the excesses of capitalism. His passionate call for tolerance and fairness had roots as much in his mother's ideas as in his contacts with the "lamblike youths" who were "slaughtered" by the demon Moloch: his symbol for the greed and materialism of the United States in the 1950's. In conjunction with his displeasure with what he saw as the failure of the government to correct these abuses, he carried an idealized conception of "the lost America of love" based on his readings in nineteenth century American literature, Walt Whitman and Henry David Thoreau in particular, and reinforced by the political and social idealism of contemporaries such as Kerouac, Snyder, and McClure.

Ginsberg brought all these concerns together when he began to compose "Howl." However, while the social and political elements of the poem were immediately apparent, the careful structural arrangements were not. Ginsberg found it necessary to explain his intentions in a series of notes and letters, emphasizing his desire to use Whitman's long line "to *build up* large organic structures" and his realization that he did not have to satisfy anyone's concept of what a poem should be, but could follow his "romantic inspiration" and simply write as he wished, "without fear." Using what he called his "Hebraic-Melvillian bardic breath"—a rhythmic pattern similar to the cadences of the Old Testament as employed by Herman Melville—Ginsberg wrote a three-part prophetic elegy, which he described as a "huge sad comedy of wild phrasing."

"HOWL"

The first part of "Howl" is a long catalog of the activities of the "angelheaded hipsters" who were his contemporaries. Calling the bohemian underground of outcasts, outlaws, rebels, mystics, sexual deviants, junkies, and other misfits "the best minds of my generation"—a judgment that still rankles many social critics—Ginsberg produced image after image of the antics of "remarkable lamblike youths" in pursuit of cosmic enlightenment, "the ancient heavenly connection to the starry dynamo in the machinery of night." Because the larger American society had offered them little support, Ginsberg summarized their efforts by declaring that these people had been "destroyed by madness." The long lines, most beginning with the word "who" (which was used "as a base to keep measure, return to and take off from again"), create a composite portrait that pulses with energy and excitement. Ginsberg is not only lamenting the destruction—or self-destruction—of his friends and acquaintances, but also celebrating their wild flights of imagination, their ecstatic illuminations, and their rapturous adventures. His typical line, or breath unit, communicates the awesome power of the experiences he describes along with their potential for danger. Ginsberg believed that by the end of the first section he had expressed what he believed "true to eternity" and had reconstituted "the data of celestial experience."

Part 2 of the poem "names the monster of mental consciousness that preys" on the people he admires. The fear and tension of the Cold War, stirred by materialistic greed and what Ginsberg later called "lacklove," are symbolized by a demon he calls Moloch, after the Canaanite god that required human sacrifice. With the name Moloch as a kind of "base repetition" and destructive attributes described in a string of lines beginning with "whose," the second part of the poem reaches a kind of crescendo of chaos in which an anarchic vision of frenzy and disruption engulfs the world.

In part 3, "a litany of affirmation," Ginsberg addresses himself to Solomon, a poet he knew from the Psychiatric Institute; he holds up Solomon as a kind of emblem of the victim-heroes he has been describing. The pattern here is based on the statement-counterstatement form of Christopher Smart's *Jubilate Agno* (1939; as *Rejoice in the Lamb*, 1954), and Ginsberg envisioned it as pyramidal, "with a graduated longer response to the fixed base." Affirming his allegiance to Solomon (and everyone like him), Ginsberg begins each breath unit with the phrase "I'm with you in Rockland" followed by "where . . ." and an exposition of strange or unorthodox behavior that has been labeled "madness" but that to the poet is actually a form of creative sanity. The poem concludes with a vision of Ginsberg and Solomon together on a journey to an America that transcends Moloch and madness and offers utopian possibilities of love and "true mental regularity."

During the year that "Howl" was written, Ginsberg wondered whether he might use the same long line in a "short quiet lyrical poem." The result was a poignant tribute to his "old courage teacher," Whitman, which he called "A Supermarket in California," and a meditation on the bounty of nature, "A Strange New Cottage in Berkeley." He continued to work with his long-breath line in larger compositions as well, most notably the poem "America," which has been accurately described by Charles Molesworth as "a gem of polyvocal satire and miscreant complaint." This poem gave Ginsberg the opportunity to exercise his exuberant sense of humor and good-natured view of himself in a mock-ironic address to his country. The claim "It occurs to me that I am America" is meant to be taken as a whimsical wish made in self-deprecating modesty, but Ginsberg's growing popularity through the last decades of the century cast it as prophetic as well.

"Kaddish"

Naomi Ginsberg died in 1956 after several harrowing episodes at home and in mental institutions, and she was not accorded a traditional orthodox funeral because a *minyan* (a complement of ten men to serve as witnesses) could not be found. Ginsberg was troubled by thoughts of his mother's suffering and tormented by uncertainty concerning his own role as sometime caregiver for her. Brooding over his tangled feelings, he spent a night listening to jazz, ingesting marijuana and methamphetamine, and reading passages from an old bar mitzvah book. Then, at dawn, he walked the streets of the lower East Side in Manhattan, where many Jewish immigrant families had settled. A tangle of images and emotions rushed through his mind, organized now by the rhythms of ancient Hebrew prayers and chants. The poem that took shape in his mind was his own version of the Kaddish, the traditional Jewish service for the dead that had been denied to his mother. As it was formed in an initial burst of energy, he saw its goal as a celebration of her memory and a prayer for her soul's serenity, an attempt to confront his own fears about death, and ultimately, an attempt to come to terms with his relationship to his mother.

"Kaddish" begins in an elegiac mood, "Strange now to think of you gone," and proceeds as both an elegy and a kind of dual biography. Details from Ginsberg's childhood begin to take on a sinister aspect when viewed from the perspective of an adult with a tragic sense of existence. The course of his life's journey from early youth and full parental love to the threshold of middle age is paralleled by Naomi's life as it advances from late youth toward a decline into paranoia and madness. Ginsberg recalls his mother "teaching school, laughing with idiots, the backward classes—her Russian speciality," then sees her in agony "one night, sudden attack . . . left retching on the tile floor." The juxtaposition of images ranging over many years reminds him of his own mortality, compelling him to probe his subconscious mind to face some of the fears that he has suppressed about his mother's madness. The first part of the poem concludes as the poet realizes that he will never find any peace until he is able to "cut through—to talk to you—" and finally to write her true history.

The central incident of the second section is a bus trip the twelve-year-old Ginsberg took with his mother to a clinic. The confusion and unpredictability of his mother's behavior forced him to assume an adult's role, for which he was not prepared. For the first time, he realizes that this moment marked the real end of childhood and introduced him to a universe of chaos and absurdity. As the narrative develops, the emergence of a nascent artistic consciousness, poetic perception, and political idealism is presented against a panorama of life in the United States in the late 1930's. Realizing that his growth into the poet who is revealing this psychic history is closely intertwined with his mother's decline, Ginsberg faces his fear that he was drawing his newfound strength from her as she failed. As the section concludes, he squarely confronts his mother's illness, rendering her madness in disjointed scraps of conversation while using blunt physical detail as a means of showing the body's collapse: an effective analogue for her simultaneous mental disorder. There is a daunting authenticity to these details, as Ginsberg speaks with utter candor about the most intimate and unpleasant subjects (a method he also employs in later poems about sexual contacts), confirming his determination to bury nothing in memory.

This frankness fuses Ginsberg's recollections into a mood of great sympathy; he is moved to prayer, asking divine intervention to ease his mother's suffering. Here he introduces the actual Hebrew words of the Kaddish, the formal service that had been denied his mother because of a technicality. The poet's contribution is not only to create an appropriate setting for the ancient ritual but also to offer a testament to his mother's most admirable qualities. As the second section ends, Ginsberg sets the power of poetic language to celebrate beauty against the pain of his mother's last days. Returning to the elegiac mode (after Percy Bysshe Shelley's "Adonais"), Ginsberg has a last vision of his mother days before her final stroke, associated with sunlight and giving her son advice that concludes, "Love,/ your mother," which he acknowledges with his own tribute, "which is Naomi."

The last part of the poem, "Hymmnn," is divided into four sections. The first is a prayer for God's blessing for his mother (and for all people); the second is a recitation of some of the circumstances of her life; the third is a catalog of characteristics that seem surreal and random but coalesce toward the portrait he is producing by composite images; and the last part is "another variation of the litany form," ending the poem in a flow of "pure emotive sound" in which the words "Lord lord lord," as if beseeching, alternate with the words "caw caw caw," as if exclaiming in ecstasy.

By resisting almost all the conventional approaches to the loaded subject of motherhood, Ginsberg has avoided sentimentality and reached a depth of feeling that is overwhelming, even if the reader's experience is nothing like the poet's. The universality of the relationship is established by its particulars, the sublimity of the relationship by the revelation of the poet's enduring love and empathy.

The publication of "Kaddish" ended the initial phase of Ginsberg's writing life. "Howl" is a declaration of poetic intention, while "Kaddish" is a confession of personal necessity. With these two long, powerful works, Ginsberg completed the educational process of his youth and was ready to use his craft as a confident, mature artist. His range in the early 1960's included the hilarious "I Am a Victim of Telephone," which debunked his increasing celebrity, the gleeful jeremiad "Television Was a Baby Crawling Toward That Deathchamber," the generously compassionate "Who Be Kind To," and the effusive lyric "Why Is God Love, Jack?" A tribute to his mentor, "Death News," describes his thoughts on learning of Williams's demise.

"Kral Majales"

In 1965, after he had been invited to Cuba and Czechoslovakia, Ginsberg was expelled from each country for his bold condemnation of each nation's policies. In Prague, he had been selected by students (including young Václav Havel) as Kral Majales (king of May), an ancient European honor that has lasted through centuries of upheaval. In the poem "Kral Majales"—published accompanied by positive and negative silhouettes of the smiling poet, naked except for tennis shoes and sporting three hands bearing finger cymbals, against a phallic symbol—he juxtaposed communist and capitalist societies at their most dreary and destructive to the life-enhancing properties of the symbolic May King: a figure of life, love, art, and enlightenment. The first part of the poem is marked by discouragement, anger, and sorrow mixed with comic resignation to show the dead end reached by governments run by a small clique of rulers. However, the heart of the poem, a list of all the attributes that he brings to the position of Kral Majales, is an exuberant explosion of joy, mirth, and confidence in the rising generation of the mid-1960's. Written before the full weight of the debacle in Vietnam had been felt and before the string of assassinations that rocked the United States took place, Ginsberg reveled in the growth of what he thought was a revolutionary movement toward a utopian society. His chant of praise for the foundations of a counterculture celebrates "the power of sexual youth," productive, fulfilling work ("industry in eloquence"), honest acceptance of the body ("long hair of Adam"), the vitality of art ("old Human poesy"), and the ecumenical spirit of religious pluralism that he incarnates: "I am of Slavic parentage and Buddhist Jew/ who worships the Sacred Heart of Christ the blue body of Krishna the straight back of Ram the beads of Chango." In a demonstration of rhythmic power, the poem builds until it tells of the poet's literal descent to earth from the airplane he took to London after his expulsion. Arriving at "Albion's airfield" with the exultation of creative energy still vibrating through his mind and body, he proudly presents (to the reader or listener) the poem he has just written "on a jet seat in mid Heaven." The immediacy of the ending keeps the occasion fresh in the poet's memory and alive forever in the rhythms and images of his art.

"Witchita Vortex Sutra"

The Prague Spring that was to flourish temporarily in events such as the 1965 May Festival was crushed by Soviet tanks in 1968. By then, the United States had become fully involved in the war in Southeast Asia, and Ginsberg had replaced some of his optimism about change with an anger that recalled the mood of the Moloch section of "Howl." In 1966, he was in Kansas to read poetry, and this trip to the heartland of the United States became the occasion for a poem that is close to an epic of American life as the country was being torn apart. "Witchita Vortex Sutra," one of Ginsberg's longest poems, combines elements of American mythological history, personal psychic exploration, multicultural interaction, and prophetic incantation. The poem is sustained by a twin vision of the United States: the submerged but still vital American spirit that inspired Whitman and the contemporary American realities by which "many another has suffered death and madness/ in the Vortex." A sense of a betrayal informs the narrative, and the poet is involved in a search for the cause and the cure, ultimately (and typically) discovering that only art can rescue the blighted land.

The first part of the poem depicts Kansas as the seat of American innocence, where the spirit of transcendental idealism is still relatively untouched by American actions in Vietnam. Whitman's dream of an open country and worthy citizens seems to remain alive, but events from the outside have begun to reach even this sheltered place. The land of Abraham Lincoln, Vachel Lindsay, William Jennings Bryan, and other American idealists is being ruined by the actions of a rogue "government" out of touch with the spirit of the nation. The poet attempts to understand why this is happening and what consequences it has for him, for any artist. After this entrance into the poem's geopolitical and psychic space, the second part presents, in a collage form akin to Ezra Pound's *Cantos* (1925-1972), figures, numbers, names, and snatches of propaganda about the conflict in Vietnam. Following Pound's proposal that a bad government corrupts a people by its misuse of language, Ginsberg begins an examination of the nature of language itself to try to determine how the lies and deceptions in "black language/ writ by machine" can be overcome by a "lonesome man in Kansas" who is "not afraid" and who can speak "with ecstatic language": that is, the true language of human need, essential human reality. Calling on "all Powers of imagination," Ginsberg acts as an artist in service to moral being, using all the poetic power, or versions of speech, that he has worked to master.

Ginsberg's "ecstatic language" includes, in particular, the lingo of the Far Eastern religions he has learned in his travels. To assist in exorcising the demons of the West, he implores the gods of the East (fitting, since the war is in the East) to merge their forces with those of the new deities of the West, whose incarnation he finds in such American mavericks as the musician Dylan. He summons them as allies against the Puritan death-wish he locates in the fanaticism of unbending, self-righteous zealots such as Kansas's Carrie Nation, whose "angry smashing ax" began "a vortex of hatred" that eventually "defoliated the Mekong Delta." Through the poem, Ginsberg has cast the language artist as the rescuer, the visionary who can restore the heartland to its primal state as a land of promise and justice. In an extraordinary testament to his faith in his craft, Ginsberg declares, "The war is over now"—which, in a poem that examines language in "its deceits, its degeneration" (as Charles Molesworth says), "is especially poignant being only language."

THE FALL OF AMERICA

Other poems, such as "Bayonne Entering NYC," further contributed to the mood of a collection titled *The Fall of America*, but Ginsberg was also turning again toward the personal. In poems such as "Wales Visitation," a nature ode written in the spirit of the English Romantics, and "Bixby Canyon," which is an American West Coast parallel, Ginsberg explores the possibilities of a personal pantheism, attempting to achieve a degree of cosmic transcendence to compensate for the disagreeable situation on earth. His loving remembrance for Beat poet Cassady, "On Neal's Ashes," is another expression of this elegiac inclination, which reaches a culmination in *Mind Breaths*.

MIND BREATHS

"Mind Breaths," the title poem of the collection *Mind Breaths*, is a meditation that gathers the long lines of what Ginsberg has called "a chain of strong-breath'd poems" into a series of modulations on the theme of the poet's breath as an aspect of the wind-spirit of life. As he has often pointed out, Ginsberg believes that one of his most basic principles of organization is his ability to control the rhythms of a long line ("My breath is long"). In "Mind Breaths," he develops the idea that the voice of the poet is a part of the "voice" of the cosmos—a variant on the ancient belief that the gods spoke directly through the poet. Ranging over the entire planet, Ginsberg gradually includes details from many of the world's cultures, uniting nations in motive and design to achieve an encompassing ethos of universality. Beneath the fragmentation and strife of the world's governments, the poet sees "a calm breath, a silent breath, a slow breath," part of the fundamentally human universe that the artist wishes to inhabit.

PLUTONIAN ODE

In the title poem of *Plutonian Ode*, Ginsberg offers another persuasive poetic argument to strengthen the "Mind-guard spirit" against the death wish that leads some to embrace "Radioactive Nemesis." Recalling, once again, "Howl," in which Moloch stands for the death-driven impulses of humankind gone mad with greed, Ginsberg surveys the history of nuclear experimentation. The poem is designed as a guide for "spiritual friends and teachers," and the "mountain of Plutonian" is presented as the dark shadow-image of the life force that has energized the universe since "the beginning." Addressing himself, as well, to the "heavy heavy Element awakened," Ginsberg describes a force of "vaunted Mystery" against which he brings, as always, the "verse prophetic" to "wake space" itself. The poem is written to restore the power of mind (which is founded on spiritual enlightenment) to a civilization addicted to "horrific arm'd, Satanic industries"—an echo of Blake's injunctions at the dawn of an era in which machinery has threatened human well-being.

"Birdbrain"

The tranquility of such reveries in poems such as "Mind Breaths" did not replace Ginsberg's anger at the social system but operated more as a condition of recovery or place of restoration, so that the poet could venture back into the political arena and chant, "Birdbrain is the ultimate product of Capitalism/ Birdbrain chief bureaucrat of Russia." In the poem "Birdbrain," published in *Collected Poems, 1947-1980*, Ginsberg castigates the idiocy of organizations everywhere. His humor balances his anger, but there is an implication that neither humor nor anger will be sufficient against the forces of "Birdbrain [who] is Pope, Premier, President, Commissar, Chairman, Senator!" In spite of his decades of experience as a political activist, Ginsberg never let his discouragement overcome his sense of civic responsibility. The publication of *Collected Poems, 1947-1980* secured Ginsberg's reputation as one of the leading writers of late twentieth century American literature.

White Shroud

The appearance in 1986 of *White Shroud* revived Ginsberg's political orations; in this work, he identifies the demons of contemporary American life as he sees them: "yes I glimpse CIA's spooky dope deal vanity." There is a discernible sense of time's passage in "White Shroud," which is a kind of postscript to "Kaddish." Once again, Ginsberg recollects the pain of his family relationships: His difficulties in dealing with aging, irascible relatives merges with his responsibility to care for those who have loved him, and his feeling for modern America fuse with his memories of the Old Left past of his immigrant family. The poem tells how Ginsberg, in search of an apartment, finds himself in the Bronx neighborhood where his family once lived. There he meets the shade of his mother, still berating him for having abandoned her, but now offering him a home as well. There is a form of comfort for the poet in his dream of returning to an older New York to live with his family, a return to the "lost America," the mythic America that has inspired millions of American dreams.

Cosmopolitan Greetings

Ginsberg in the 1990's expressed his introspective side with lyric sadness in such poems as "Personals Ad" (from *Cosmopolitan Greetings*), in which he communicates his quest for a ". . . companion protector friend/ young lover w/empty compassionate soul" to help him live "in New York alone with the Alone." With the advent of his seventh decade, he might have settled for a kind of comfortable celebrity, offering the substance of his literary and social experiences to students at the Graduate Center of the City University of New York and to countless admirers on reading tours throughout the nation. Instead, he accepted his position as the primary proponent and spokesperson for his fellow artists of the Beat generation, and he continued to write with the invention and vigor that had marked his work from its inception. Acknowledging his perspective as a "poet professor in autumn years" in "Personals Ad," Ginsberg remains highly conscious of ". . . the body/ where I was born" (from "Song," in *Howl, and Other Poems*), but his focus is now on the inescapable consequences of time's passage on that body in poems that register the anxieties of an aging man trying to assess his own role in the cultural and historical patterns of his era.

The exuberance and the antic humor that have always been a feature of Ginsberg's poetry of sexual candor remain, but there is a modulation in tone and mood toward the rueful and contemplative. Similarly, poems presenting strong positions about social and governmental policies often refer to earlier works on related subjects, as if adding links to a chain of historical commentaries. Although few of Ginsberg's poems are as individually distinctive as the "strong-breath'd poems" such as "Howl," "Kaddish," or "Witchita Vortex Sutra," which Ginsberg calls "peaks of inspiration," Ginsberg's utilization of a characteristic powerful rhythmic base figure drives poems such as "Improvisation in Beijing," "On Cremation of Chogyam Trungpa, Vidadhara," "Get It," and "Graphic Winces" offer statements that are reflections of fundamental positions that Ginsberg has been developing throughout his work.

"Improvisation in Beijing," the opening poem, is a poetic credo in the form of an expression of artistic ambition. Using the phrase "I write poetry . . ." to launch each line, Ginsberg juxtaposes ideas, images, data, and assertion in a flux of energetic intent, his life's experiences revealing the desire and urgency of his calling. Ginsberg has gathered his responses to requests for his sources of inspiration: from the explicitly personal "I write poetry to make accurate picture my own mind" to the overtly political ". . . Wild West destroys new grass & erosion creates deserts" to the culturally connected "I write poetry because I listened to black Blues on 1939 radio, Leadbelly and Ma Rainey" to the aesthetically ambitious in the concluding line, "I write poetry because it's the best way to say everything in mind with 6 minutes or a lifetime."

"On Cremation of Chogyam Trungpa, Vidadhara," a tribute to a spiritual guide, reverses the structural thrust of "Improvisation in Beijing" so that the lines beginning "I noticed the . . ." spiral inward toward a composite portrait built by "minute particulars," Ginsberg's term for Williams's injunction "No ideas but in things." Ginsberg concentrates on specifics in tightly wound lines that present observations of an extremely aware, actively thoughtful participant: "I noticed the grass, I noticed the hills, I noticed the highways,/ I noticed the dirt road, I noticed the cars in the parking lot." Eventually, the poet's inclusion of more personal details reveals his deep involvement in the occasion, demonstrating his ability to internalize his guide's teaching. The poem concludes with a summation of the event's impact, a fusion of awe, delight, and wonder joining the mundane with the cosmic. Typically at this time in his life, Ginsberg acts from a classic poetic position, speaking as the recorder who sees, understands, and appreciates the significance of important events and who can find language adequate for their expression.

The collection, like Ginsberg's other major volumes, contains many poems that are not meant to be either especially serious or particularly profound. These works include poems written to a musical notation ("C.I.A. Dope Calypso"), poetic lines cast in speech bubbles in a "Deadline Dragon Comix" strip, three pages of what are called "American Sentences" (which are, in effect, a version of haiku), and a new set of verses to the old political anthem, "The Internationale," in which Ginsberg pays homage to the dreams of a social republic of justice while parodying various manifestations of self-important propagandists and salvationists.

The poems in the volume that show Ginsberg at his most effective, however, occur in two modes. Ever since his tribute to Whitman, "A Supermarket in California," Ginsberg has used the lyric mode as a means of conveying his deeply romantic vision of an idealized existence set in opposition to the social disasters he has resisted. These are poems of appreciation and gratitude, celebrating the things of the world that bring delight. "To Jacob Rabinowitz" is a letter of thanks for a translation of Catullus. "Fun House Antique Store" conveys the poet's astonishment at finding a "country antique store, an/ oldfashioned house" on the road to "see our lawyer in D.C." The lovingly evoked intricate furnishings of the store suggest something human that is absent in "the postmodern Capital." Both of these poems sustain a mood of exultation crucial to a lyric.

The other mode that Ginsberg employs is a familiar one. Even since he described himself as "Rotting Ginsberg" in "Mescaline" (1959), Ginsberg has emphasized physical sensation and the extremes of sensory response as means for understanding artistic consciousness, a mind-body linkage. Some of the most despairing lines Ginsberg has written appear in these poems— understandable considering the poet's ailments, including the first manifestations of liver cancer, which Ginsberg endured for years before his death. Nonetheless, the bright spirit that animates Ginsberg's work throughout is present as a counterthrust.

"In the Benjo," which has been placed at the close of the collection, expresses Ginsberg's appreciation for Snyder's lessons in transcendent wisdom and epitomizes a pattern of affirmation that is present in poems that resist the ravages of physical decline ("Return to Kral Majales"), the loss of friends ("Visiting Father & Friends"), the sorry state of the world ("You Don't Know It"), and the fraudulent nature of so-called leaders ("Elephant in the Meditation Hall"). In these poems, as in many in earlier collections, Ginsberg is conveying the spirit of an artistic age that he helped shape and that his work exemplifies. As Snyder said in tribute, "Allen Ginsberg showed that poetry could speak to our moment, our political concerns, our hopes and fears, and in the grandest style. He broke that open for all of us."

COLLECTED POEMS, 1947-1997

Collected Poems, 1947-1997 is a massive chronological compilation—combining *Collected Poems, 1947-1980, White Shroud, Cosmopolitan Greetings,* and *Death and Fame*—that gathers virtually every poem Ginsberg ever wrote, from his first published effort, "In Society" (1947), to his last written work, "Things I'll Not Do (Nostalgia)," finished just days before he died. The volume incorporates drawings, photographs, sheet music, calligraphy, notes, acknowledgments, introductions, appendixes, and all the other addenda included in the previous publications that collectively reveal Ginsberg's far-reaching interests and his enormous skill. Ginsberg's entire body of work portrays the poet's growth as a craftsperson, a seeker of truth, a spokesperson for his generation, and ultimately as a human being.

Even in his earliest work, "In Society"—which alludes to his homosexuality and includes epithets that polite society would deem vulgar—Ginsberg demonstrated that no subject was unworthy of consideration, no phrase taboo. Though his topics from the beginning were sometimes controversial, the format of his poems was still restrained and formal because he had not yet rejected his father's traditionalist ways. Such poems as "Two Sonnets" (1948), with their conventional fourteen-line structures and rhyme schemes, would not look out of place in collections of William Shakespeare or Edmund Spenser. Indeed, much of Ginsberg's early work (in the first section, "Empty Mirror: Gates of Wrath, 1947-1952") constitutes rhyming verse as the poet experimented with meter, line length, and language in his fledgling efforts to find a unique voice. Subject matter, too, is fairly traditional: love poems, contemplation of nature, and musings on life, death and religion. With few exceptions, the titles of these poems—"A Very Dove," "Vision 1948," "Refrain," "A Western Ballad," "The Shrouded Stranger," "This Is About Death," "Sunset," "Ode to the Setting Sun"— give little indication of Ginsberg's pixie-like humor or his coming break with literary convention.

Part 2 of the collection ("The Green Automobile, 1953-1954") provides the first inkling that Ginsberg was beginning to discover the appropriate form of expression for ideas too large to be otherwise contained. The long poem "Siesta in Xbalba and Return to the States," an impressionistic work based on Ginsberg's travels in Mexico, sets the stage for the angry, dynamic, no-holds-barred compositions that would follow and characterize the bulk of his poetic career. The main part of Ginsberg's career is collected in eleven sections: "Howl, Before and After: San Francisco Bay Area (1955-1956)," "Reality Sandwiches: Europe! Europe!" (1957-1959)," "Kaddish and Related Poems (1959-1960)," "Planet News: To Europe and Asia (1961-1963)," "King of May: America to Europe (1963-1965)," "The Fall of America (1965-1971)," "Mind Breaths All over the Place (1972-1977)," "Plutonian Ode (1977-1980)," "White Shroud: Poems, 1980-1985," "Cosmopolitan Greetings: Poems, 1986-1992," and "Death and Fame: Poems, 1993-1997."

At the very end of his life, as he lay dying, Ginsberg, like someone reviewing the span of his existence in clarifying flashes, seemed to return full circle to where he had begun. Brief bursts of inspiration, such as "American Sentences," are whimsical, epigram-like in nature. Other final thoughts, including "Sky Words," "Scatological Observations," "My Team Is Red Hot," "Starry Rhymes," "Thirty State Bummers," and "Bop

Sh'bam," are almost childlike ditties in conventional verse forms such as rhyming couplets and quatrains.

Collected Poems, 1947-1997 captures the essence of an artist who, like Whitman before him, exploded the notion of what poetry could or should be. Mostly, though, it lays bare the mind and soul of an individual of consummate craft, a person of fierce intelligence and insatiable curiosity, a human blessed with playful wit, undying optimism, all-encompassing compassion and unstinting generosity for other people.

OTHER MAJOR WORKS

NONFICTION: *Indian Journals*, 1963; *The Yage Letters*, 1963 (with William Burroughs); *Indian Journals, March 1962-May 1963: Notebooks, Diary, Blank Pages, Writings*, 1970; *Allen Verbatim: Lectures on Poetry, Politics, Consciousness*, 1974; *Gay Sunshine Interview*, 1974; *Visions of the Great Rememberer*, 1974; *To Eberhart from Ginsberg*, 1976; *As Ever: The Collected Correspondence of Allen Ginsberg and Neal Cassady*, 1977; *Journals: Early Fifties, Early Sixties*, 1977, 1992; *Composed on the Tongue: Literary Conversations, 1967-1977*, 1980; *Allen Ginsberg Photographs*, 1990; *Snapshot Poetics: A Photographic Memoir of the Beat Era*, 1993; *Journals Mid-Fifties, 1954-1958*, 1995; *Deliberate Prose: Selected Essays, 1952-1995*, 2000; *Family Business: Selected Letters Between a Father and Son*, 2001 (with Louis Ginsberg); *Spontaneous Mind: Selected Interviews, 1958-1996*, 2001; *The Letters of Allen Ginsberg*, 2008 (Bill Morgan, editor); *The Selected Letters of Allen Ginsberg and Gary Snyder*, 2009 (Morgan, editor).

EDITED TEXT: *Poems for the Nation: A Collection of Contemporary Political Poems*, 2000.

MISCELLANEOUS: *Beat Legacy, Connections, Influences: Poems and Letters by Allen Ginsberg*, 1994; *The Book of Matyrdom and Artifice: First Journals and Poems, 1937-1952*, 2006.

BIBLIOGRAPHY

Baker, Deborah. *A Blue Hand: The Tragicomic, Mind-Altering Odyssey of Allen Ginsberg, a Holy Fool, a Lost Muse, a Dharma Bum, and His Prickly Bride in India.* New York: Penguin, 2009. A well-researched study of the life-changing travels in India undertaken by Ginsberg and various companions in search of enlightenment, and the aftereffects of the journeys on the poet's work and attitudes.

Edwards, Susan. *The Wild West Wind: Remembering Allen Ginsberg.* Boulder, Colo.: Baksun Books, 2001. A fond and enlightening reminiscence from an author, teacher, artist, and metaphysician who worked for twenty years alongside Ginsberg at Naropa University.

Felver, Christopher, Lawrence Ferlinghetti, and David Shapiro. *The Late Great Allen Ginsberg: A Photo Biography.* New York: Running Press, 2003. A compendium of images and impressions of the poet from all stages of his life, with contributions from many of those who knew him and worked or performed alongside him, including Philip Glass, Ray Manzarek, Ed Sanders, Norman Mailer, Peter Orlovsky, Gary Snyder, Gregory Corso, William Burroughs, and Lawrence Ferlinghetti.

Ginsberg, Allen. *Howl: Original Draft Facsimile, Transcript, and Variant Versions, Fully Annotated by Author, with Contemporaneous Correspondence, Account of First Public Presentation*. New York: Harper Perennial Modern Classics, 2006. An in-depth examination of Ginsberg's first important work, which resulted in charges of obscenity—eventually dismissed—and which made the poet a household name.

Landas, John. *The Bop Apocalypse*. Champaign: University of Illinois Press, 2001. An illuminating account of the religious aspects and elements of the work of Ginsberg, Jack Kerouac, and William Burroughs. Particularly good on the historical dynamics operating in the writers' lives.

Miles, Barry. *The Beat Hotel: Ginsberg, Burroughs, and Corso in Paris, 1958-1963*. New York: Grove Press, 2000. A narrative chronicle of the Beats in Paris from the "Howl" obscenity trial to the invention of the cut-up technique. Based on firsthand accounts from diaries, letters, and many original interviews.

Morgan, Bill. *I Celebrate Myself: The Somewhat Private Life of Allen Ginsberg*. New York: Viking Press, 2006. Morgan drew on unpublished letters and journals to create an extensive, full-length biography, the first to be published after Ginsberg's death. Morgan veers away from lending his own opinion and chronicles rather than interprets Ginsberg's life; however, he manages to highlight the events that inspired Ginsberg to write his unique brand of poetry.

Podhoretz, Norman. *Ex-Friends: Falling Out with Allen Ginsberg, Lionel and Diana Trilling, Lillian Hellman, Hannah Arendt, and Norman Mailer*. New York: Encounter Books, 2000. Podhoretz, the conservative editor of *Commentary*, presents a different and highly entertaining perspective on the infighting that went on among the New York intellectual community of which Ginsberg was a part during the 1950's and 1960's.

Raskin, Jonah. *American Scream: Allen Ginsberg's "Howl" and the Making of the Beat Generation*. Berkeley: University of California Press, 2006. Describes Ginsberg's composition and presentation of his groundbreaking poem against the twin backdrops of the poet's personal life and the era in which it was created.

Trigillo, Tony. *Allen Ginsberg's Buddhist Poetics*. Carbondale: Southern Illinois University Press, 2007. This scholarly study focuses on the poet's adoption of Buddhism and its effect on Ginsberg's work, in terms of form, content, and spirituality.

Leon Lewis
Updated by Jack Ewing

THOM GUNN

Born: Gravesend, Kent, England; August 29, 1929
Died: San Francisco, California; April 25, 2004

PRINCIPAL POETRY
Fighting Terms, 1954, 1962
The Sense of Movement, 1957
My Sad Captains, and Other Poems, 1961
Selected Poems, 1962 (with Ted Hughes)
A Geography, 1966
Positives, 1966 (with photographs by Ander Gunn)
Touch, 1967
The Garden of the Gods, 1968
The Explorers, 1969
The Fair in the Woods, 1969
Poems, 1950-1966: A Selection, 1969
Sunlight, 1969
Last Days at Teddington, 1971
Moly, 1971
Moly and My Sad Captains, 1971
Poems After Chaucer, 1971
Mandrakes, 1973
Songbook, 1973
To the Air, 1974
Jack Straw's Castle, 1975
Jack Straw's Castle, and Other Poems, 1976
The Missed Beat, 1976
Bally Power Play, 1979
Games of Chance, 1979
Selected Poems, 1950-1975, 1979
Talbot Road, 1981
The Menace, 1982
The Passages of Joy, 1982
Undesirables, 1988
The Man with Night Sweats, 1992
Collected Poems, 1993
In the Twilight Slot, 1995
Boss Cupid, 2000
Site Specific: Seventeen "Neighborhood" Poems, 2000

Other literary forms

Thom Gunn was best known for his poetry as well as his essays that present criticism and autobiographical information. *The Occasions of Poetry: Essays in Criticism and Autobiography* (1982) collects Gunn's reviews and essays on poets from Fulke Greville and Ben Jonson to Robert Creeley and Robert Duncan. It also contains four valuable essays on the composition and inspiration of Gunn's own poetry, including the autobiographical sketch "My Life up to Now" (1977).

Achievements

Thom Gunn was richly honored for his work during his lifetime. He won the Levinson Prize in 1955, the Somerset Maugham Award in 1959, the Arts Council of Great Britain Award in 1959, a National Institute of Arts and Letters Award in 1964, and a Rockefeller Foundation award in 1966. He won a Gold Medal in poetry from the Commonwealth Club of California in 1976 for *Jack Straw's Castle*. *The Passages of Joy* earned the W. H. Smith Award (1980), two Northern California Book Awards in poetry (1982, 1992), and the PEN/Los Angeles Prize for poetry (1983). In 1988, he won the Robert Kirsch Award for body of work from the *Los Angeles Times* as well as the Sara Teasdale prize. He was honored with the Shelley Memorial Award of the Poetry Society of America and the Lila Wallace-*Reader's Digest* Writers' Award in 1990. *The Man with Night Sweats* earned him the Lenore Marshall Poetry Prize and the PEN Center USA West Poetry Award, both in 1993. He received a Lambda Literary Award in 1994 and the Award of Merit from the American Academy of Arts and Letters in 1998. He held a Guggenheim Fellowship in 1971 and a MacArthur Fellowship in 1993. In 2001, he received the Thom Gunn Award for Gay Poetry for *Boss Cupid*.

Biography

Born Thomson William Gunn, Thom Gunn grew up in the London suburb of Hampstead Heath, "forever grateful" that he was "raised in no religion at all." During the Blitz, he read John Keats, Alfred, Lord Tennyson, and George Meredith, who have all influenced his verse in various ways. His parents—both journalists, although his mother had stopped working before his birth—were divorced when he was eight or nine. After two years in the British army, Gunn went to Paris to work in the offices of the Metro. He attended Trinity College, University of Cambridge, during the early 1950's; there he attended the lectures of F. R. Leavis and began to write poetry in earnest, publishing his first book, *Fighting Terms*, in 1954, while still an undergraduate. He worked briefly on the magazine *Granta* and, as president of the English Club, met and introduced Angus Wilson, Henry Green, Dylan Thomas, and William Empson, among others. Here he also became a pacifist, flirted with socialism, hitchhiked through France during a summer vacation, and met Mike Kitay, his American companion, who influenced his decision to move to the United States.

After graduation, Gunn spent a brief period in Rome and Paris. At the suggestion of the American poet Donald Hall, Gunn applied for and won a creative writing fellowship to Stanford University, where he studied with the formalist poet and critic Yvor Winters. After a short teaching stint in San Antonio, Texas, where he first rode a motorcycle ("for about a month"), heard Elvis Presley's songs, and saw James Dean's movies, Gunn accepted an offer to teach at the University of California, Berkeley, in 1958.

Gunn returned to London for a year (1964-1965) just as the Beatles burst on the scene. Back in San Francisco, he gave up tenure in 1966, only a year after it was granted, and immersed himself in the psychedelic and sexual revolution of the late 1960's. While teaching at Princeton University in 1970, Gunn lived in Greenwich Village when the first art galleries began to appear in SoHo. He moved to San Francisco and began his tenure at University of California, Berkeley, first as a lecturer and then, beginning in 1973, as an associate professor of English. He continued to teach on a part-time basis to allow him, as he says, to write relatively unfettered by academic demands. Gunn died in San Francisco on April 25, 2004.

Analysis

Thom Gunn first achieved notoriety in England, as part of what was called the Movement, an unofficial tag applied to some poets of the 1950's who were, in Gunn's words, "eschewing Modernism, and turning back, though not very thoroughgoingly, to traditional resources in structure and method." Poets of the Movement included Philip Larkin, Kingsley Amis, and Donald Davie, among others. Gunn continued to achieve critical acclaim by approaching a diverse number of subjects previously excluded from poetry, with a similar regard for structure and meter.

Having moved to the United States in the late 1950's, Gunn is somewhat of an amphibious poet. One might say that while his poetry has its formal roots in the English tradition, his subject matter has been taken largely from his American experience. He is known particularly for his exploration of certain counterculture movements from the 1950's to the 1980's. He is comfortable on the fringes of society, where popular culture thrives; rock music, motorcycle gangs, leather bars, and orgies have been his milieu. He is also considered one of the poets who deal most frankly with gay subject matter and themes. What distinguishes Gunn from other poets working with the same material is that he has refused to abandon structure and meter, preferring to impose form on chaotic subjects. Since the mid-1960's, however, Gunn has been increasingly influenced by American poets, notably William Carlos Williams; he turned first to the flexible meters of syllabic verse and subsequently to free verse, without sacrificing his demanding sense of form.

A poet interested in the possibilities of identity, Gunn is best known for his explorations into the existential hero, who takes many guises in his poetry, including the soldier and the motorcyclist. The greatest influence on his thought in these matters has been the existentialism espoused by Jean-Paul Sartre in his philosophical treatise *L'Être et le néant* (1943; *Being and Nothingness*, 1956). For Sartre, humanity is condemned to freedom to make its own meaning in an absurd universe. For Gunn, poetry has been the vehicle of this creation.

Fighting Terms

Gunn began his poetic career while still at Cambridge, with the publication of *Fighting Terms*. The image of the soldier is first of all, Gunn has written, "myself, the national serviceman, the 'clumsy brute in uniform,' the soldier who never goes to war, whose role has no function, whose battledress is a joke," but it is also the "attractive and repellant" real soldier, who kills but also quests, like Achilles and Odysseus. Above all, the soldier is the poet, "an existential conqueror, excited and aggressive," trying to make sense of his absurd situation.

These poems show Gunn's propensity to try, not always successfully, to make meaning of action in the intervals between action. "The Wound" is a good example. While recuperating, a soldier remembers the engagement of battle. As "the huge wound in my head began to heal," he remembers the Trojan War, but it is unclear whether this was his actual experience or only a hallucination. It could be that he is a contemporary soldier reverting to myth in the damaged and "darkened" valleys of his mind. When he rises to act again, his wound "breaks open wide," and he must again wait for "those storm-lit valleys to heal." His identity is thus never resolved.

Similarly, in "Looking Glass," the narrator is a kind of gardener who observes his life under glass. He compares it to a Garden of Eden in which "a fine callous fickleness" sent him in search of pleasure, "gratification being all." Yet there is no God present in this world to give the world an a priori meaning: "I am the gardener now myself.... I am responsible for order here." In the absence of God, "risks are authorized"—a theme that imbues Gunn's later poems of experience. He is also alienated from society and does not "care if villagers suspect" that his life is going "to seed." He takes a kind of pride in his status as outsider: "How well it goes to seed." The act of observing the wild garden of his life is a pleasure in itself, even though he is an outcast, "damp-booted, unemployed."

In "The Beach Head," the narrator is a would-be conqueror planning a campaign into his own society: "I seek a pathway to the country's heart." Again the alienated outsider ("I, hare-brained stranger") is heard making sense of his life, wondering whether to enter history through a fine gesture, "With little object other than panache/ And showing what great odds may be defied." His alternative to action is to watch and "wait and calculate my chances/ Consolidating this my inch-square base." This conflict is at the heart of Gunn's poetry, early and late: whether to risk the heroic act or succumb to the passivity of contemplation. Yet the latter too has its risk—namely, that his failure to act may cause society's "mild liking to turn to loathing."

The Sense of Movement

The Sense of Movement continues Gunn's exploration of the active versus the contemplative existential hero. Here the pose, poise, or panache of the hero is more important than the goal of the action, the movement constituting its own meaning. The volume introduces Gunn's idealized "American myth of the motorcyclist, then in its infancy, of the wild man part free spirit and part hoodlum"; his motorcyclist series is based on Andrew Marvell's mower poems. Gunn admits that the book is largely derivative ("a second work of apprenticeship"), partaking of Yvor Winters's formalism, William Butler Yeats's theory of the mask, and Jean-Paul Sartre's existentialist philosophy of engaged action.

The opening poem of the volume, "On the Move," explores the conflict between "instinct" and "poise." This is a key dichotomy in Gunn's work. The natural world of instinct is largely unavailable to thinking human beings, who, unlike birds, must create a kind of surrogate impetus for the meaningful movement. The motorcyclists become the focus for this conflict because of their assumed pose of wildness; yet it is a pose, a posture that is only "a part solution, after all," to the problem. Riding "astride the created will," they appear "robust" only because they "strap in doubt... hiding it." The doubt has to do with their destination, as they "dare a future from the taken routes." The absurdity of action (a notion central to existential thought) is emphasized in that the person can appeal neither to natural instinct nor to metaphysics for the meaning he must himself create: "Men manufacture both machine and soul." Unlike "birds and saints," the motorcyclists do not "complete their purposes" by reaching a destination. The movement is its own excuse: "Reaching no absolute, in which to rest,/ One is always nearer by not keeping still."

"In Praise of Cities" affirms the disorderly evolution of human attempts to create meaning in the cityscape, which is personified as a woman, "indifferent to the indifference which conceived her." She withholds and offers herself to the one who wants to discover her secrets. "She wanders lewdly, whispering her given name,/ Charing Cross Road, or Forty-Second Street." Yet the city is really a mirror in which the narrator sees his "own designs, peeling and unachieved" on her walls, for she is, finally, "extreme, material, and the work of man." As in "On the Move," however, the narrator does not so much comprehend as simply embrace the city, with "a passion without understanding." His movement is its own excuse, but the communion with humankind, through his created cityscape, is real.

My Sad Captains, and Other Poems

My Sad Captains, and Other Poems marks a turning point in Gunn's career, a border crossing that is evident in the book's two-part structure. The first half is concerned with the conflict between the "infinite" will and the "confined" execution, and the meter is suitably traditional. The epigraph from William Shakespeare's *Troilus and Cressida* (pr. c. 1601-1602) suggests that while "desire is boundless," "the act is a slave to limit." Limit is represented by the formalist quality of the poems in this first part of the book.

The second half of the book is much less theoretical, more concerned with direct experience, as its epigraph from F. Scott Fitzgerald suggests: "It's startling to you sometimes—just air, unobstructed, uncomplicated air." This thematic quality is reflected in the breathy technique of syllabic verse, in which the line is determined by the number of syllables rather than accents; the rhymes are random or, when regular, slant. The syllabic form is well suited to the direct apprehension of experience in such poems as "Light Among Redwoods," where "we stand/ and stare—mindless, diminished—/ at their rosy immanence."

Thematically, the volume continues to develop Gunn's "existential conqueror" motif in poems such as "The Book of the Dead" and "The Byrnies," while expanding his poetic repertoire to include snails and trucks as well as some more exotic familiars: tattoo parlors in "Blackie, the Electric Rembrandt" and gay and leather bars in "Modes of Pleasure" (two poems, one title) and "Black Jackets."

"A Map of the City" is perhaps even more successful than "In Praise of Cities" in affirming the human chaos of the city by its treatment of the theme within a traditional form. The speaker stands on a hill at night, looking at the "luminous" city like a map below. Like William Blake's "London," Gunn's city is a maze of drunks, transients, and sailors. From this vantage point, he can "watch a malady's advance," while recognizing his "love of chance." He sees the city's concrete boredom and suffering but also its abstract "potential" for both satisfaction and danger. From this perspective, he can, if only for a moment, get his bearings in relation to the city as a whole, as a map, so that when he descends into the maze again, he will be able to navigate his way through its dangers and flaws. He embraces the "crowded, broken, and unfinished" as the natural concomitants to the riches of city life, as he concludes: "I would not have the risk diminished."

The title poem, "My Sad Captains," is a tribute to all those friends who have inspired the poet, "a few with historical/ names." These men who were immersed in experience once seemed to him to have lived only to "renew the wasteful force they/ spent with each hot convulsion"; yet now they exist "apart" from life, "winnowed from failures," and indeed above life, "and turn with disinterested/ hard energy, like the stars."

Though this poem closes the volume, it can be profitably read together with any number of poems from the book, but especially the opening poem, "In Santa Maria del Popolo," which describes a painting of the "one convulsion" of "Saul becoming Paul" by the sixteenth century artist Caravaggio (Michelangelo Merisi). Here Paul becomes "the solitary man," "resisting, while embracing, nothingness." Yet it is to Caravaggio that Gunn looks for this revelation, the artist being one of his "sad captains."

Although Gunn did not do much more with syllabic verse after *My Sad Captains, and Other Poems*, it was, he said, a way of teaching himself about "unpatterned rhythms," or free verse. From this point onward, he worked in both traditional and "open" forms.

POSITIVES

Positives is written entirely in open forms. These poems were written to accompany his brother Ander's photographs of life in London. Poems about other works of art are common, especially in modern poetry. W. H. Auden's "Musée des Beaux Arts" (1939) and John Ashbery's "Portrait in a Convex Mirror" (1964) are examples of poems that interpret paintings from a distant time and place, as is Gunn's own "In Santa Maria del Popolo." In *Positives*, however, the collaboration is very much contemporary. The poems are written with the photographs, which seem to have taught Gunn to pay attention to the details of street life, pubs, construction sites, abandoned houses, and bridges in a way he never had before. As a result, Gunn gives up the symbolism of Yeats for luminous realities: "It is not a symbolic/ bridge but a real bridge;/ nor is the bundle/ a symbol." This quality makes *Positives* the least philosophical of his early works, even though the theme is large: the progress from birth and "doing things for the first time" to old age and "the terror of full repose." Written to face the photographs, the poems are freed of the burden of description, so that they have a transparent quality, a light touch, and, on the whole, a positive tone.

The poems and photographs depict the "memoirs of the body" in the lines of a face or a stance or gesture. In most cases, "an ambiguous story" can be read there: either as "the ability to resist/ annihilation, or as the small/ but constant losses endured/ but between the lines/ life itself!" These moments of activity in the present—human beings absorbed in the space between past and future—are Gunn's subjects: a child bathing, boys waiting to grow up, motorcyclists riding, a bride overwhelmed by the weight of lace, an old woman balancing a bundle on her head. Each has a history and a destiny, but these are components of their present hopes and fears.

TOUCH

Touch similarly reaches out to a real humanity. By making choices one may cut off other possibilities, but one also affirms a commitment to the individual experience. In "Confessions of the Life Artist," the narrator is "buoyant with the sense of choice." Having chosen, one finds that the death of possibilities unchosen only fortifies "one's own identity."

The opening poem addresses the "Goddess" of loneliness—Proserpine, the fruitful goddess confined away from human touch in the underworld. When she arises in a park, one of Gunn's ever-present soldiers is waiting for "a woman, any woman/ her dress tight across her ass/ as bark in moonlight." The final line seems to reject the idea that myth can enrich human lives; rather, it is persons, "vulnerable, quivering," who lend to myth their own "abundance."

The movement explored in previous volumes here becomes not linear motion through time but the spatial, encircling movement of the imagination wedded to emotion. In the "turbulence" of "The Kiss at Bayreuth," there is a paradoxical moment in which two "may then/ be said to both move and be still." The egotism of the "inhuman eye" of contemplation is overcome in the moment that two are able to "not think of themselves."

Similarly, in the title poem, touch is what Gunn's narrators seem to have been gravitating toward all along. As the narrator slips into the familiar space of a shared bed, he discovers an "enclosing cocoon... where we walk with everyone." This personal communion implies a larger community of sleepers who partake in the "continuous creation" of humanity.

There is not room here for a full discussion of the long poem "Misanthropos," but it is in this poem of seventeen sections that the theme of *Touch* is most fully explored. The protagonist is the last man on Earth after a great holocaust, or at least he seems to be. The problem of identity in the absence of others to validate one's existence is explored as the man sheds old values, memories, and emotions as he sheds his former clothes. When he at last loses the distinctions of language, he encounters other survivors, and direct sensation, experienced anew, is shocking.

MOLY

The background informing *Moly* is Gunn's experience with lysergic acid diethylamide (LSD), which, he said, "has been of the utmost importance to me, both as a man and as a poet." Although he recognized the acid trip to be "essentially non-verbal," it was important and "possible to write poetry about any subject that was of importance to you." Unlike other drug-induced poetry, which tends to mimic the diffusion and chaos of the raw experience in free verse, the poems in *Moly* attempt to present "the infinite through the finite, the unstructured through the structured." These poems are highly controlled by structure and meter, while dealing with strange transformations.

The title poem, "Moly," is a dramatic monologue in the voice of one of Odysseus's men who has been turned into a pig by the witch Circe. Its rhymed couplets underscore the dual nature of man, part human and part beast, in search of the essential and magical "root" that will restore his humanity: "From this fat dungeon I could rise to skin/ And human title, putting pig within." The herb he is seeking is moly ("From milk flower to the black forked root"), which rhymes with "holy." The influence of Yeats's "Leda and the Swan" (1924) is evident, yet the swine-man of Gunn's poem is a typically contemporary twist on the mythological theme of the beast-god of Yeats's modernist poem.

Gunn's 1973 essay "Writing a Poem" discusses the conception and composition of "Three," but it is illuminating as a more general discussion of how a poem comes to be. Gunn says that he encountered a naked family on the beach and wanted to preserve them on paper as a kind of "supersnapshot," to find "an embodiment for my haunting cluster of concepts" about them. He calls his desire to preserve this feeling a sense of "decorum"—that is, a description that would be true to his direct experience of them, not the "pat" theme of "innocence and repossession."

Jack Straw's Castle, and Other Poems

This idea of decorum seems to dominate the poems in *Jack Straw's Castle, and Other Poems*. Here there is a kind of easy humor and simplicity of emotion only glimpsed in the earlier poems. In "Autobiography," perhaps influenced by Robert Creeley, the speaker desires (and achieves) "the sniff of the real." "Last Days at Teddington" tells of a return to a house that "smelt of hot dust through the day," and all sensation is clear and complete, like the garden that "fell back on itself."

The title poem, however, is a nightmarish version of a fairy tale, in which Gunn confronts his own worst enemy, himself: "I am the man on the rack/ I am the man who puts the man on the rack/ I am the man who watches the man who puts the man on the rack." Yet by confronting the demons of the imagination in this way, he seems to clear the air for a renewed apprehension of experience, to recognize that the "beauty's in what is, not what may seem." In this way, "Jack's ready for the world."

The Passages of Joy

The Passages of Joy is the world the poet of "Jack Straw's Castle" has readied himself for. In "The Menace," the speaker discovers "the stifling passages" of the mind, where "the opposition lurks" not outside himself, but within: "I am, am I,/ the one-who-wants-to-get-me." The joys seem less simple, more problematic after the decades of easy sex and drugs. This volume, in fact, contains Gunn's frankest expression of gay concerns in the era of acquired immunodeficiency syndrome (AIDS), although its focus shifts away from leather bars and orgies to long-standing relationships of shared domesticity.

The title is taken from Samuel Johnson's *The Vanity of Human Wishes* (1749), a satire on the tragic and comic elements of human hopes and errors. One of the poems ("Transients and Residents") bears an epigraph from Johnson's poem:

> Time hovers o'er, impatient to destroy,
> And shuts up all the Passages of Joy.

The very personal poems of this volume show Gunn, now past fifty, dealing with the effects of age—in a person, in a generation, and perhaps in the race.

The three parts of the book show Gunn in a range of moods, from what might be called the meditative poems of the first and third parts to the hip pop-culture poems of part 2. Part 2 begins with a poem for Robert Mapplethorpe, the controversial photographer of the more dangerous elements of the gay scene. Another poem features a "dead punk lady," the murdered girlfriend of Sid Vicious of Sex Pistols fame.

The poet of "A Map of the City" still "would not have the risk diminished," for in the risks are to be found certain "passages of joy." In addition to the literal underground passages of "Another All Night Party," in which orgies occur, there are also the symbolic rites of passage of "Adultery" and "Talbot Road."

"Talbot Road" is a poetic treatment of Gunn's "year of great happiness" in London during the Beatles era, when, according to his almost-identical prose account in "My Life up to Now" (1977), "barriers seemed to be coming down all over." One of these barriers had to do with Gunn's own sexuality. The centerpiece of the five-part poem is a return to Hampstead Heath, where he meets "my past self" in the form of a nineteen-year-old. "This was the year," he says, "the year of reconciliation," but it is unclear whether he means his own nineteenth year of 1964-1965; the ambiguity is intentional, for he means both. Hampstead Heath had been for him the scene of childish play and vague adolescent longings, where by day he "had played hide and seek/ with neighbor children"; in 1964, however, he could see the dark side that had always been there, since by night the Heath had long been a notorious venue for promiscuous sexual encounters, and there he now "played as an adult/ with troops of men whose rounds intersected/ at the Orgy Tree."

The central poem of the volume, however, is "Transients and Residents," in which these literal and figurative passages give way to the real passage of time. The four poems that make up this sequence stand in their own right as powerful and timely meditations on the passage of joy in the age of AIDS. Subtitled "An Interrupted Sequence," these four portraits of gay men in different roles explore the passing of a time of carefree sexual awakening and put the reader in the midst of sickness and death. The last portrait is of the poet himself at his desk, catching a glimpse of himself writing—which interrupts the sequence. This interruption perhaps provides a clue into the poet's view of the other portraits he has been drawing, for like the drug dealer in "Crystal," "he puts his soul/ Into each role in turn, where he survives/ Till it is incarnation more than role."

On the streets of "Night Taxi," a cabdriver takes his "fares like affairs/ — no, more like tricks to turn:/ quick, lively, ending up/ with a cash payment." As in the earlier motorcycle poems, Gunn remains obsessed with movement. The cabdriver is intent on maneuvering his way gracefully through the maze of the city, one with his machine. There is still a sense of independence, yet there is also a sense of community; the driver's movement depends on others, even is subservient to the wishes of others: "It's all on my terms but/ I let them think it's on theirs." It is an appropriate poem to end this book that focuses mostly on the importance of other people.

UNDESIRABLES

Gunn's later poems, such as those in *Undesirables*, return to the gritty side of city life in the 1980's, observing characters and situations with an edge of black humor, like scenes reflected in a switchblade. He has not given up his preoccupation with Yeats—"Old Meg" is an incarnation of Yeats's Crazy Jane—but all sense of imitation is gone. Gunn has renounced the Yeatsian pronouncement for the rabbit punch and the belly laugh. "Punch Rubicundus," for example, is a ribald poem about an aging gay man, in which the satire is all self-directed. The host, Mr. Punch, enters one of his "vaudeville of the sexual itch" parties, riding on a donkey, and says, "But this *can't* be Byzantium. (Though/ they do say Uncle Willie's ghost got an invite)." The irreverent reference to Yeats's "Sailing to Byzantium" (1927) and "Byzantium" (1932) is clear: Uncle Willie is William Butler Yeats, whose spirits were supposed to ride "astraddle on the dolphin's mire and blood" to "the holy city of Byzantium."

The poetry of Gunn continued to develop as an up-to-the-minute report on the contemporary scene. Yet his roots in the tradition of poetry were deep, and his dialogue with the poets and forms of the past was as much a part of his evolution as a poet as was his keen eye for the realities of his time.

THE MAN WITH NIGHT SWEATS

Gunn received critical acclaim for *The Man with Night Sweats*, recognized for its unsentimental examination of AIDS, death, and neglected members of contemporary American society. He wrote the poems during 1982 to 1988, a period when the AIDS epidemic was devastating the gay community and the global community shared widespread homophobia and concerns over its transmission. Here the topic of AIDS seemed a theme to which Gunn could attach a particular passion and poetic craft, a place to offer heartbreaking poems of young men struggling with a disease that consumes them with fear and its cruelty. The skepticism of his past poetry here gives way to elegy and lament, lyrical meditation, and a form of rage that is finely tooled with his poetic balance.

In this collection, Gunn acts as both a witness to the devastation of AIDS as well as one deeply involved with it. He writes in "The Renaissance," "You came back in a dream./ I'm all right now you said." His witnessing of the suffering also takes on a ferocity, a compulsion to attest to the wreckage of AIDS, almost as a way to provide a kind of defense:

> I shall not soon forget
> . . . .
> The angle of his head,
> Arrested and reared back
> On the crisp field of bed,...

One of the strongest poems of the collection is "Lament," an elegy of more than one hundred lines in which the speaker describes in great detail the slow dying of a close friend in a hospital ward. Rather than elevate the dying friend with praise and abstraction as does traditional elegy, this piece repeats that death is a "difficult enterprise" and chronicles the tedium and pain experienced by his friend—the "clumsy stealth" that has "distanced" him "from the habits of health." "Lament" is a perfect example of Gunn's tightly channeled, yet deeply felt elegies that form this collection.

BOSS CUPID

Boss Cupid echoes the elegiac style of *The Man with Night Sweats*, its three sections examining the loss of friends, lovers, and even, in one case, a lifestyle. Rather than focusing entirely on loss, however, the collection also explores the sexual allure of youth, and renewal and recovery. Frank references to "the sexual New Jerusalem" of Gunn's younger years are here, and in "Saturday Night," he writes a genuinely affecting lament for the sex and drugs scene of the mid-1970's. It moves beyond the endpoints referenced in *The Man with Night Sweats* and his subsequent *Collected Poems* by pushing the boundaries of his poetry to include, in one loose whole, the makings of legend, myth, phantasmagoria, and autobiography. Historic, mythic figures such as Arachne and King David make appearances here, as well as the homeless, college students, and social deviants (as in his five "songs for Jeffrey Dahmer" grouped under the title "Troubadour"). His edgy wit, lyric versatility, and adept caricatures of personas help make this collection a powerful reminder that every life is "dense/ with fine compacted difference."

OTHER MAJOR WORKS

NONFICTION: "My Life up to Now," 1977; *The Occasions of Poetry: Essays in Criticism and Autobiography*, 1982, 1985 (Clive Wilmer, editor); *Shelf Life: Essays, Memoirs, and an Interview*, 1993; *Thom Gunn in Conversation with James Campbell*, 2000.

EDITED TEXTS: *Poetry from Cambridge 1951-52: A Selection of Verse by Members of the University*, 1952; *Five American Poets*, 1963 (with Ted Hughes); *Selected Poems of Fulke Greville*, 1968; *Ben Jonson*, 1974; *Ezra Pound*, 2000; *Selected Poems*, 2003 (by Yvor Winters).

MISCELLANEOUS: *Thom Gunn at Seventy*, 1999.

BIBLIOGRAPHY

Brown, Merle E. *Double Lyric: Divisiveness and Communal Creativity in Recent English Poetry*. New York: Columbia University Press, 1980. Brown argues that poetry is the result of the dialectic between the poet's thinking and speaking selves, the poem being a communal expression of that double consciousness. The theory bears fruit in the two chapters devoted to Gunn's work. The first explores the idea of "inner community" in the long poem "Misanthropos," the second the idea of "authentic duplicity" in Gunn's poetry up to *Jack Straw's Castle, and Other Poems*.

Gunn, Thom. "Thom Gunn." Interview by Christopher Hennessy. In *Outside the Lines: Talking with Contemporary Gay Poets*, edited by Hennessy. Ann Arbor: University of Michigan Press, 2005. Gunn explores his works, technical and emotional development, and the links between his sexuality and verse.

Guthmann, Edward. "A Poet's Life, Part 1: Reserved but Raw, Modest but Gaudy, Thom Gunn Covered an Enormous Amount of Ground in His Exquisite Work and His Raucous Life." *San Francisco Chronicle*, April 25, 2005, p. C1. On the one-year anniversary of Gunn's death, Guthmann wrote a two-part profile of the poet that described his life largely through conversations with friends and colleagues.

_____. "A Poet's Life, Part 2: As Friends Died of AIDS, Thom Gunn Stayed Healthy—Until His Need to Play Hard Finally Killed Him." *San Francisco Chronicle* April 26, 2005, p. E1. The second installment in a profile of the deceased Gunn reveals much about his life in San Francisco with partner Mike Kitay.

King, P. R. *Nine Contemporary Poets: A Critical Introduction.* London: Methuen, 1979. The chapter devoted to Gunn, "A Courier After Identity," discusses five distinct personas in Gunn's poetic development: the "embattled" stance of *Fighting Terms*, "a life of action and of pose" in *The Sense of Movement*, the "divided self" of *My Sad Captains, and Other Poems*, the striving for "contact" with humankind and nature in *Touch*, and the "widening sympathies" of *Moly* and *Jack Straw's Castle, and Other Poems*. An excellent overview.

Leader, Zachary, ed. *The Movement Reconsidered: Essays on Larkin, Amis, Gunn, Davie, and Their Contemporaries.* New York: Oxford University Press, 2009. A collection of essays on the Movement poets, including one on Gunn and one discussing Gunn and Donald Davie.

Michelucci, Stefania. *The Poetry of Thom Gunn: A Critical Study.* Jefferson, N.C.: McFarland, 2009. Michelucci finds a desire for freedom in Gunn's early poetry that leads to his vindication of his closeted sexuality.

Weiner, Joshua, ed. *At the Barriers: On the Poetry of Thom Gunn.* Chicago: University of Chicago Press, 2009. A collection of critical essays examine Gunn's poetry, including "Meat," "Considering the Snail," and "Duncan."

Richard Collins
Updated by Sarah Hilbert

A. E. HOUSMAN

Born: Fockbury, Worcestershire, England; March 26, 1859
Died: Cambridge, England; April 30, 1936

PRINCIPAL POETRY
A Shropshire Lad, 1896
Last Poems, 1922
More Poems, 1936
Collected Poems, 1939

OTHER LITERARY FORMS

A. E. Housman (HOWS-muhn) created a single work of prose fiction, *A Morning with the Royal Family*, a youthful fantasy printed without his permission in 1882 in the *Bromsgrovian* and unpublished elsewhere. His translations total 102 lines from Aeschylus's *Hepta epi Thēbas* (467 B.C.E.; *Seven Against Thebes*), Sophocles' *Oidipous epi Kolōnōi* (401 B.C.E.; *Oedipus at Colonus*), and Euripides' *Alkēstis* (438 B.C.E.; *Alcestis*) and first appeared in A. W. Pollard's *Odes from the Greek Dramatists* in 1890. They have since been included in the *Collected Poems*. Henry Maas has collected more than eight hundred of Housman's letters, which, though not in the great tradition of English letter-writing, shed considerable light on the poet's enigmatic personality.

ACHIEVEMENTS

Although A. E. Housman's fame today rests on a handful of poems, it was to classical scholarship that he devoted most of his life. For nearly fifty years, he was a professor of Latin, first at University College, London, and later at Cambridge University. A profound and prolific scholar fluent in five languages, he published in that time approximately two hundred critical papers and reviews spanning the entire spectrum of classical literature from Aeschylus to Vergil. This work consists mainly of textual emendations of corrupt manuscripts and is highly technical, providing a stark contrast to the lucid simplicity of his poetry. Titles such as "Emendationes Propertianae," "The Codex Lipsiensis of Manilius," and "Adversaria Orthographica" abound in *The Classical Papers of A. E. Housman* (1972), collected and edited by J. Diggle and F. R. D. Goodyear in three volumes. In addition, Housman has left behind editions of Ovid, Juvenal, Lucan, and Marcus Manilius and several major lectures, including *The Confines of Criticism* (1969) and *The Name and Nature of Poetry* (1933).

Housman held no illusions either about the power of classical knowledge to influence human character or the extent of its appeal, but he nevertheless placed the highest premium on learning for its own sake and was a relentless seeker after truth using the method of textual criticism, which he defined in *The Application of Thought to Textual Criticism* (1922) as "the science of discovering error in texts and the art of removing it." This was for him "an aristocratic affair, not communicable to all men, nor to most men." The one thing most necessary to be a textual critic "is to have a head, not a pumpkin, on your shoulders, and brains, not pudding, in your head." He applied to others the same rigorous standards of scholarship that he set for himself, and he had no sympathy for incompetence in any form. He was particularly annoyed by the practice of modern criticism of following one manuscript whenever possible instead of weighing the relative merits of alternative manuscripts, a practice, he writes in his preface to Juvenal (1905), designed "to rescue incompetent editors alike from the toil of editing and from the shame of acknowledging that they cannot edit." His harshest words are reserved for self-complacent and insolent individuals masquerading as sane critics. His vituperative attacks on Elias Stoeber and Friedrick Jacob in his 1903 preface to Manilius may be taken as typical: "Stoeber's mind, though that is no name to call it by, was one that turned as unswervingly to the false, the meaningless, the unmetrical, and the ungrammatical, as the needle to the pole," and "Not only had Jacob no sense for grammar, no sense for coherency, no sense for sense, but being himself possessed by a passion for the clumsy and the hispid he imputed this disgusting taste to all the authors whom he edited." The extent of Housman's learning and the unbridled candor of his judgments made him a respected and feared polemicist and perhaps the most formidable classicist of his age. W. H. Auden called him "The Latin Scholar of his generation."

Throughout his career Housman repeatedly denied having any talent for literary criticism, and he turned down the Clark Lectureship in English Literature at Trinity College, Cambridge, on the ground that he did not qualify as a literary critic, who, he wrote in *The Confines of Criticism*, is rarer than "the appearance of Halley's comet." When he was at University College, London, he delivered papers on various English poets including Matthew Arnold, Algernon Charles Swinburne, and Alfred, Lord Tennyson, but he refused to allow them to be published and apparently resented the demands the Literary Society made on him, writing in his preface to Arthur Platt's *Nine Essays* (1927) that "Studious men who might be settling *Hoti*'s business and properly basing *Oun* are expected to provide amusing discourses on subjects of which they have no official knowledge and upon which they may not be titled even to open their mouths." Nevertheless, Housman's several excursions into literary criticism reflect a great sensitivity to such central concerns as the integrity of literary texts and the debasement of language. In its emphasis on the numinous intractability of great poetry, *The Name and Nature of Poetry* is an oblique repudiation of the intellectualism of T. S. Eliot and I. A. Richards. Housman's criticism shows the influence of Matthew Arnold, but the importance he attached to the undergirding of impressionistic judgments with sound scholarship goes beyond that Victorian sage.

As a poet, Housman was successful to the point of celebrity. *A Shropshire Lad* was initially slow to catch on with the reading public, but after Grant Richards took over as Housman's publisher, it became a great success on both sides of the Atlantic. Its moody *Weltschmerz* caught the fin de siècle state of mind, just as *Last Poems* captured the ennui of a war-weary generation. Today the inevitable reaction has set in, and Housman's poetry is not as highly regarded as it once was. The melancholy of his poems too often seems uninformed by spiritual struggle, but the plaintive lyricism of his best work has a universal and enduring appeal.

Biography

Alfred Edward Housman was born on March 26, 1859, in Fockbury, Worcestershire, into an ancient family of preachers and farmers whose English roots extended back to the fourteenth century. His great-grandfather on his father's side, an evangelical preacher who lived out his life with a wife and eight children in genteel poverty, was shy and unassertive in manner but inwardly tough, capable of bearing up under the hardships of life with manly fortitude. Housman was able to observe at first hand that stoicism, which informs so much of his mature poetry, in his own mother, Sarah, whose prolonged suffering and death after bearing seven children was a model of quiet courage. In the words of George L. Watson, "With his grimly stoical demeanor, Housman often recalled some ancestral farmer, glowering at the inclement weather" (*A. E. Housman: A Divided Life*, 1957). No such family precedent exists for Housman's career as a scholar unless it be a distant cousin on his father's side who was a lecturer in Greek and Divinity at Chichester College, and still less exists for the poet's rejection of the Church within a year of his mother's death.

The death of Housman's mother on his twelfth birthday brought a traumatic end to his childhood and left him with a profound sense of loss from which he never fully recovered. He had adored the witty, intelligent woman who took pride in her descent from Sir Francis Drake, and her death created a vacuum that could not be filled by his father, Edward, a lackluster solicitor who took increasingly to drink during Sarah's illness and who, two years after her death, married his cousin Lucy and began a long slide into poverty, dying after many years of broken health in 1894. Alfred was never close to his father. He regarded his drunkenness and general improvidence as intolerable weaknesses and held him in barely concealed contempt. He was, however, close to his six brothers and sisters during his early life and, as the oldest, conducted literary parlor games for them, taking the lead in writing nonsense verse, a practice that continued during summer vacations through his college years.

Sarah's death was not permitted to interrupt for long Housman's studies at nearby Bromsgrove School, where he had enrolled on a scholarship in the fall of 1870. Bromsgrove was an old and reputable public school and provided an excellent foundation in the classics, English, and French. As a student, Housman was introspective and shy and was known as Mouse by his classmates. Throughout his childhood, he was afflicted with a nervous disorder, and while a student at Bromsgrove, he had violent seizures that the headmaster attributed to Saint Vitus's dance (chorea). Later in life this nervous condition took the form of occasional facial contortions that might "incongruously reappear in the course of the most impersonal lectures, as he read aloud one of the odes of Horace, leaving his astonished students 'afraid the old fellow was going to cry,'" in the words of George L. Watson. His nervous affliction notwithstanding, Housman seemed to thrive on the rigorous eleven-hour-a-day regimen at Bromsgrove School. In 1874, he appeared for the first time in print with a poem in rhymed couplets about the death of Socrates for which he won the prize for composition in English verse and which he delivered on Commencement Speech Day. It was published in the *Bromsgrove Messenger* on August 8, 1874, much to his later chagrin. In adult life, Housman was always jealous of his reputation and forbade the publication of his juvenilia and occasional addresses, which he felt did not meet the high standards he set for himself.

Housman's career at Bromsgrove School ended in triumph as he won the Lord Lyttelton prize for Latin verse, the honorarium for Greek verse, and the Senior Wattell prize, along with a generous scholarship to St. John's College, Oxford. At least some of Housman's success at this time can be attributed to Herbert Millington, who became headmaster at Bromsgrove School in 1873. A man of keen intellect, Millington presented a formidable figure to the students, and Housman felt some hero-worship for him, referring to him much later as a good teacher for a clever boy. Millington was the most important role model of Housman's youth.

In the fall of 1877, Housman entered Oxford and, within a few days, was writing irreverently to his stepmother about the solemn Latin ceremony of matriculation. He joined the Oxford Union, and although he was inactive, he was "an avowed member and staunch champion of the Conservative faction" (Watson). Generally, however, Housman remained uninvolved in the life of the university. He was unimpressed by its professors and attended only one lecture by the illustrious Benjamin Jowett. Housman came away disgusted by Jowett's disregard for the "niceties" of scholarship. A lecture by John Ruskin also left Housman unimpressed. Housman later wrote that "Oxford had not much effect on me." This was not entirely the case, for it was at Oxford that he began to develop in earnest his capacity for classical scholarship. Passively resisting the conventional curriculum, Housman early in his Oxford career decided to devote his energies to the text of the Latin poet Sextus Propertius, whose garbled works required extensive editorial attention. He continued to work on Propertius for the remainder of his time at Oxford. Watson writes that Housman was already "embarking on those problems of conjectural emendation which are the acme of classical learning." It was also at this time that Housman began keeping a commonplace book of his favorite quotations, which tended toward the sepulchral, as one might expect of a young man whose only adornments for his college rooms were Albrecht Dürer's "Melancholia" and "The Knight,

Death and the Devil." Housman's favorite poem during his early Oxford years was Arnold's "Empedocles on Etna" (1852), which he said contained "all the law and the prophets." He was attracted to Thomas Hardy's early novels for their gloomy stoicism. For a time, Housman flirted with the poetry of Swinburne and wrote an antiecclesiastical poem, "New-Year's Eve," modeled on Swinburne's style.

Clearly the most important thing that happened to Housman during these years was his friendship with Moses Jackson, which had a deep and lasting effect on him. Among the first people he met at Oxford were A. W. Pollard and Jackson. He liked them both, but he was especially attracted to the latter. Jackson was everything that Housman was not: sociable, handsome, athletic, and charismatic. A brilliant student of engineering, he excelled with ease at everything he did. The three became fast friends, and in 1879, Housman won a first class in Moderations but his failure to win either the Hertford Classical Scholarship or the Newdigate Prize for English verse was an omen of worse to come. In his last year at Oxford, Housman shared rooms with Pollard and Jackson, and according to Watson, this "was to be the most perturbed and momentous period of his life." There is convincing evidence that at this time Housman developed a passionate attachment for Jackson, which he kept hidden from everyone at great psychic cost to himself. He became irritable and moody, but his friends apparently suspected nothing. He failed his examination in Greats, and in the summer of 1881, he returned to his family in disgrace. Andrew S. Gow in his *A. E. Housman: A Sketch* (1936) attributes Housman's failure to the nature of the curriculum, which emphasized history and philosophy at the expense of literature, but the weight of later opinion places the blame on Housman's changed feelings for Jackson.

Housman returned to Oxford in the fall of 1881 to qualify for the lowly pass degree. He worked occasionally as a tutor in Greek and Latin at his old school and studied intensively for the Civil Service Examination. In December, 1882, he moved to London to share lodgings with Jackson and Jackson's younger brother, Adalbert, and went to work in the Patent Office, where he spent the next ten years registering trademarks. From this point until 1885, not one letter emerged from Housman, and not even a brother and sister could gain access to him when they came to live in London. In 1886, Housman, seeking the peace of solitude, took private rooms in Highgate, and from this time on, his "invariable mode of life," according to Watson, would be "monastic seclusion." Only the Jackson brothers were encouraged to intrude on his privacy.

In 1888, Housman broke on the scholarly world with an avalanche of brilliant critical articles that won for him an international reputation (and would secure for him the chair in Latin at University College, London, in 1892). Given that these early scholarly publications were researched in the evenings at the British Museum after a full day at the Patent Office, his accomplishment must be seen as nothing short of heroic. His *Introductory Lecture* (1937) was given on October 3, 1892, at University College and earned for him the lasting respect of his colleagues. Housman's scholarly writing continued unabated during his years there. He continued to work on the manuscripts of Propertius, edited works by Ovid and Juvenal, and in 1897 came out with a brilliant series of papers on the *Heroides*. In the meantime, Moses Jackson had gone to live in India and Adalbert had died, plunging Housman into near suicidal gloom that was to persist at intervals for the rest of his life and that could be relieved only by creative activity. In 1896, *A Shropshire Lad* appeared, published at his own expense, and 1899 saw the first paper on Manilius, the poet who was to become the object of Housman's most important work of scholarship. His edition of Manilius appeared in five books over a twenty-seven-year period, "a monument of incomparable skill and thankless labour."

The eventual success of *A Shropshire Lad* and Hous man's recognized position as a scholar of the first rank made him something of a celebrity, and during his last ten years at University College, he would dine at the Café Royal with a select circle of friends that included his brother Laurence, his publisher Grant Richards, his faculty colleague Arthur Platt, and a few others. By now Housman was a connoisseur of fine food and wine and an accomplished dinner conversationalist. He remained aloof from the London literary scene, however, and had little appreciation for the serious writers of his day, including the poet William Butler Yeats. On a lesser level, he intensely disliked the novels of John Galsworthy, and when James Joyce's *Ulysses* (1922) was published, Housman sniffed, "I have scrambled and waded through and found one or two half-pages amusing." Nor did he display any interest in music or painting. About such composers as Ralph Vaughan Williams and Charles Butterworth, who set some of his poems to music, Housman remarked, "I never hear the music, so I do not suffer."

In October, 1911, Housman was elected Kennedy Professor of Latin at Cambridge University and a fellow of Trinity College. His brilliant inaugural lecture on *The Confines of Criticism* remained unpublished during his lifetime because he was unable to verify a reference in it to Percy Bysshe Shelley. At the university, Housman became a member of a select group of the faculty known as The Family, which met twice a month for dinner. At these ritual banquets, Housman proved a good raconteur and was a well-accepted member of the group, but he held himself back from intimate friendships with his colleagues for fear of rejection or disappointment. He was equally distant toward his students; and his lectures, which he gave twice weekly in all three academic terms, were sparsely attended both because of the highly technical nature of his subject matter and the coldness of his demeanor on the platform. Throughout his twenty-five years at Cambridge, Housman continued to publish widely, directing his major efforts to the edition of Manilius. He was both respected as a great scholar and feared as a devastating polemicist. *Last Poems*, which appeared in 1922, was a great success. In the spring of 1933, Housman was prevailed on to give the Leslie Stephen Lecture. He delivered *The Name and Nature of Poetry* on the twenty-second anniversary of his inaugural lecture as Kennedy Professor of Latin. In the summer of 1935, an ill Housman rallied enough strength for one last trip to France, where he had vacationed regularly since 1897.

Weakened by heart disease, he died in Cambridge on April 30, 1936. In the words of Watson, he "wore in absolute repose a look of 'proud challenge.'"

Analysis

A. E. Housman once remarked, with that scathing condescension of which he was a master, that Swinburne "has now said not only all he has to say about everything, but all he has to say about nothing." Actually, when Housman was at Oxford he fell under Swinburne's powerful spell. His "New Year's Eve" (*Additional Poems*, 21), written about 1879, celebrates the death of the gods in a labored imitation of the "Hymn to Proserpine": "Divinities disanointed/ And kings whose kingdom is done." The poem is interesting but uninspired, and it is good that Housman early rejected Swinburne as a model. Still, one wishes that Housman had possessed more of the older poet's exuberance of imagination and richness of rhetoric, for it is in these qualities that his poetry is most deficient.

Practically all his poems are variations on the related themes of mortality and the miseries of the human condition; while a close reading reveals considerably more variety than at first appears, it is nevertheless true that the body of Housman's poetry is slighter than that of any other English poet of comparable reputation. The authorized canon consists of only three small volumes, which were published separately: *A Shropshire Lad*, *Last Poems*, and the posthumous *More Poems*. The twenty-three *Additional Poems* and three verse translations have been added to the *Collected Poems* for a total of 175 original poems. All are short, some no more than a stanza in length. The predominant form is the lyric. The tone is characteristically mournful and the mood elegiac. It is useless to look for any kind of development, either of substance or technique, in these poems, for most of them were written in the 1890's when Housman was under great psychological stress. They are intensely autobiographical inasmuch as they spring from the deep well of Housman's psyche, but few refer to specific events in his life. Housman's passion for privacy was as great as Robert Browning's, and he was attracted to the lyric as a verse form largely because of its essential impersonality. The emotion of his poems is usually general, an undifferentiated *Weltschmerz*, and such dramatic elements as may occur as persona and setting are characteristically undefined. The extremely personal and revealing "The world goes none the lamer" (*More Poems*, 21) and "Because I liked you better" (*More Poems*, 31) are exceptional.

Doomed love

In the world of Housman's poetry, which is more obviously consistent than that of more complex poets, youth fades into dust, lovers are unfaithful, nature is lovely but indifferent, and death is the serene end of everything. These great archetypal themes have given rise to some of the world's finest poetry, from Sir Walter Ralegh's "The Nymph's Reply to the Shepherd" to William Butler Yeats's "Sailing to Byzantium." What makes them interesting in Housman's poetry are the particular forms in which they are cast. "With rue my heart is laden" (*A Shropshire Lad*, 54), a poem sometimes set to music, may be taken as exemplary of his lyricism:

> With rue my heart is laden
> For golden friends I had,
> For many a rose-lipt maiden
> And many a lightfoot lad.
> By brooks too broad for leaping
> The lightfoot boys are laid;
> The rose-lipt girls are sleeping
> In fields where roses fade.

In this lyric of studied simplicity there is a classical blending of form and substance. The simple and inventive diction; the Latinate syntax, parallelism, and balance; the alternating seven- and six-syllable lines restrain still further the already generalized emotion; and while the poem is cold and artificial, it has a kind of classical grace. A comparison with William Wordsworth's "A Slumber Did My Spirit Seal" will reveal the power of a great sensibility working through the constraints of classical form to convey a sense of profound personal feeling.

In too many of Housman's lyrical poems, including the well-known "When I was one-and-twenty" (*A Shropshire Lad*, 13) and "When first my way to fair I took" (*Last Poems*, 35), the feeling is severely attenuated by a mannered flatness, and the passion that the poet undoubtedly experienced is swallowed up by the generalization of the emotion. At worst, the feeling degenerates into the bathos of "Could man be drunk for ever" (*Last Poems*, 10) or the histrionic posturing of "Twice a week the winter thorough" (*A Shropshire Lad*, 17), but at their best there is a genuine communication of feeling, as in "Yonder see the morning blink" (*Last Poems*, 11) and "From far, from eve and morning" (*A Shropshire Lad*, 32). There is a thin line between the expression of the poignancy of existence and sentimentality, and it is a tribute to Housman's tact that he so seldom crosses it.

Housman's poems work best when the emotion is crystallized by a dramatic context, as in some of the love pieces and the poems about soldiers in which the oracular pronouncements about the miseries of living that so easily lapse into an unacceptable didacticism are subordinated to more concrete situations. "Oh see how thick the goldcup flowers" (*A Shropshire Lad*, 5) is a clever and humorous dialogue between a young blade and a girl who spurns his advances, but beneath the surface gaiety there is the slightest suggestion of the mortality and faithlessness of lovers. In "Delight it is" (*More Poems*, 18) the youthful speaker addresses the maiden in words of reckless honesty—"Oh maiden, let your distaff be/ And pace the flowery meads with me/ And I will tell you lies"—and one is to assume that he is a prototype of all young lovers.

In "Spring Morning" (*Last Poems*, 16), the idyllic beauty of an April morning and the universal renewal of life in the spring place in ironic relief the "scorned unlucky lad" who "Mans his heart and deep and glad/ Drinks the valiant air of dawn" even though "the girl he loves the best/ Rouses from another's side." The speaker of "This time of year" (*A Shropshire Lad*, 25) is more fortunate, but only because the former lover of his sweetheart has died. "Is my team ploughing" (*A Shropshire Lad*, 27) dramatizes a similar situation in which the surviving youth has taken his dead friend's girl. In a dialogue that extends beyond the grave, the living lover tells his dead friend: "I cheer a dead man's sweetheart/ Never ask me whose." One of the most effective of Housman's love poems is "Bredon Hill" (*A Shropshire Lad*, 21), in which the sound of the church bells reminds the speaker of the untimely death of his sweetheart. The poem ends ambiguously with the distraught lover saying to the humming steeples: "Oh, noisy bells, be dumb/ I hear you, I will come." Also with death in mind is the speaker of "Along the field" (*A Shropshire Lad*, 26), who a year before had heard the aspen predict the death of his sweetheart. The prediction fulfilled, he now walks beside another girl, and under the aspen leaves he wonders if they "talk about a time at hand/ When I shall sleep with clover clad/ And she beside another lad."

In all these poems love is doomed to transience by infidelity or death. This, they say, is the human condition. In virtually all of them, death has supplanted sex as the major ingredient, making them unique in English love poetry.

DEATH

Death is also, less surprisingly, the main element in most of Housman's military poems. The poems about soldiers, with the exception of the frequently anthologized "Epitaph on an Army of Mercenaries" (*Last Poems*, 37), are not as well known as some of Housman's other poetry. At first sight they may seem somewhat out of place, but it is not surprising that an introverted classical scholar of conservative convictions should glamorize the guardians of the empire. The attitude toward the soldier is consistently one of compassion and respect and the poems convey a depth of sincerity not always felt elsewhere. The prospect of young men going to die in foreign lands in the service of the queen takes on an added poignancy from the death of Housman's younger brother, Herbert, who was killed in the Boer War. On another level, a soldier's death is an honorable form of suicide and a way to attain lasting fame. "The Deserter" (*Last Poems*, 13) and "The Recruit" (*A Shropshire Lad*, 3) may be taken as typical. In the first, the lass, rejected by her lover so that he may rejoin his comrades, upbraids him and others like him for scouring "about the world a-wooing/ The bullet to their breast"; in the second, the lad is promised eternal fame either as a returning hero or as a slain comrade. In "Lancer" (*Last Poems*, 6), the speaker affirms his coming death with the ringing refrain of "*Oh who would not sleep with the brave?*" In these poems Housman succeeds in investing Thanatos, characteristically an enervated and sterile attitude, with a singular vitality.

The placid stoicism of the soldiers makes these ultimately the least melancholy of all of Housman's poems.

The melancholy that permeates virtually every line of Housman's poetry is a matter of temperament more than of a well-wrought metaphysics. He affirms the existence of the soul in such poems as "The Immortal Part" (*A Shropshire Lad*, 43) and "Be still, my soul" (*A Shropshire Lad*, 48) even as he denies its immortality, the agnostic "Easter Hymn" (*More Poems*, 1) notwithstanding. Such monologues to the dead as "To an Athlete Dying Young" (*A Shropshire Lad*, 19) and "Shot? so quick, so clean an ending?" (*A Shropshire Lad*, 44) are intended as no more than poetic license. Death is seen as the final, desirable release from the Sisyphean exhaustion of living. Thanatos ultimately leads to suicide, which in several of the poems is prescribed as the best antidote for the illness of life. Other strategies for coping with the suffocating consciousness of "our long fool's-errand to the grave" are hedonism and, more logically, stoicism.

HEDONISM AND STOICISM

In Housman's hedonistic poems, the traditional sexuality of the carpe diem theme has been eliminated. In his most rousing invitation to pleasure, "Think no more lad" (*A Shropshire Lad*, 49), the lad is told to "be jolly/ Why should men make haste to die?" Such pleasures as "jesting, dancing, drinking" stave off the darkness, since "'tis only thinking/ Lays lads underground." The other exercises in hedonism are more subdued. The speaker of "Loveliest of trees" (*A Shropshire Lad*, 2), aware of his limited time, will go about the woodlands "To see the cherry hung with snow," and "The Lent Lily" (*A Shropshire Lad*, 79) invites anyone who will listen to enjoy the spring and gather all the flowers that die on Easter Day. In "Reveille" (*A Shropshire Lad*, 4), the lad is enjoined to rise and enjoy the morning, for "Breath's a ware that will not keep/ Up, lad: when the journey's over/ There'll be time enough to sleep." "Ho, everyone that thirsteth" (*More Poems*, 22) makes an effective use of the living waters of Scripture as a metaphor of fulfillment. The poem concludes that "he that drinks in season/ Shall live before he dies," but the "lad that hopes for heaven/ Shall fill his mouth with mold."

Stoicism is a more satisfying way of coming to grips with the human condition, and it provides the basis for several of Housman's most rewarding poems, including "The Oracles" (*Last Poems*, 25), "The Sage to the Young Man" (*More Poems*, 4), and "The chestnut casts his flambeaux" (*Last Poems*, 9). In this last poem, an embittered young man drinking in a tavern deplores the passing of another spring and curses "Whatever brute and blackguard made the world" for cheating his "sentenced" soul of all that it has ever craved. Then with dramatic suddenness, he sees that "the troubles of our proud and angry dust/ Are from eternity," and this leads to his stoic affirmation that "Bear them we can, and if we can we must." The idea here that human misery is both certain and universal is the central focus of such powerful poems as "The First of May" (*Last Poems*, 34), "Westward on the high-hilled plains" (*A Shropshire Lad*, 55), and "Young is the blood"

(*More Poems*, 34). In "Young is the blood," the speaker identifies his own pain in a youth he espies whistling along the hillside highway and proclaims in the succession of the generations "that the sons of Adam/ Are not so evil-starred/ As they are hard." This is the heart of Housman's stoicism, and this is one of his more honest and successful poems.

In a number of Housman's poems, the universalization of the existential predicament embodies a vision of the remote past that suggests the ultimate insignificance of everything. The speaker of "When I watch the living meet" (*A Shropshire Lad*, 12) is reminded by the moving pageant filing through the street of the dead nations of the past where "revenges are forgot/ And the hater hates no more," just as the speaker of "On Wenlock Edge" (*A Shropshire Lad*, 31) is put in mind by a storm of "the old wind in the old anger" threshing the ancient Roman city of Uricon. He knows the storm will pass even as "the Roman and his trouble," both now "ashes under Uricon." The perspective shifts to the future in "I wake from dreams" (*More Poems*, 43) and "Smooth between sea and land" (*More Poems*, 45), which present visions of apocalyptic dissolution.

The poetry of Housman is the poetry of negation. Most of it is shot through with a nameless melancholy and much of it is pessimistic. His lyrics invite comparison with Hardy's, with which they are often included in anthologies, but they reflect none of Hardy's moral depth. They are closer in spirit to those of Heinrich Heine, whom Housman mentioned as one of the three major influences on his work, along with the English ballads and the songs of William Shakespeare. Housman's *Weltschmerz* struck a deep chord in two generations of English readers, making *A Shropshire Lad* and *Last Poems* two of the most popular volumes of poetry of their period. Today, Housman's reputation is tempered by the knowledge that his poetry, though capable of creating haunting moods, neither expands nor deepens one's self-awareness nor one's awareness of life, despite his claim in "Terence, this is stupid stuff" (*A Shropshire Lad*, 62) that it prepares one for life's rigors. For this reason, Housman must be considered a minor poet.

OTHER MAJOR WORKS

LONG FICTION: *A Morning with the Royal Family*, 1882.

NONFICTION: *The Application of Thought to Textual Criticism*, 1922; *The Name and Nature of Poetry*, 1933; *Introductory Lecture*, 1937; *Selected Prose*, 1961 (John Carter, editor); *The Confines of Criticism*, 1969; *The Letters of A. E. Housman*, 1971 (Henry Maas, editor); *The Classical Papers of A. E. Housman*, 1972 (J. Diggle and F. R. D. Goodyear, editors).

EDITED TEXTS: *M. Manilii Astronomicon Liber Primus*, 1903; *Ivnii Ivvenalis Satvrae*, 1905; *M. Manilii Astronomicon Liber Secundus*, 1912; *M. Manilii Astronomicon Liber Tertius*, 1916; *M. Manilii Astronomicon Liber Quartus*, 1920; *M. Annaei Lvcani Belli Civilis Libri Decem*, 1926; *M. Manilii Astronomicon Liber Quintus*, 1930.

BIBLIOGRAPHY

Bayley, John. *Housman's Poems.* New York: Oxford University Press, 1992. An analysis of the poetic works of Housman.

Bloom, Harold, ed. *A. E. Housman.* Philadelphia: Chelsea House, 2003. Collection of essays on Hous man that covers topics such as masculine relationships and the gay subtext and Housman's divided persona. Contains considerable analysis of *A Shropshire Lad.*

Corcoran, Neil, ed. *The Cambridge Companion to Twentieth-Century English Poetry.* New York: Cambridge University Press, 2007. Contains a chapter discussing Housman's poetry and comparing it with that of Hardy, Charlotte Mew, and Edward Thomas Peter Howarth.

Efrati, Carol. *The Road of Danger, Guilt, and Shame: The Lonely Way of A. E. Housman.* Madison, N.J.: Fairleigh Dickinson University Press, 2002. This examination of Housman's life and works focuses on the effect of his presumed homosexuality on his poetry and lifestyle.

Graves, Richard Perceval. *A. E. Housman: The Scholar- Poet.* London: Routledge & Kegan Paul, 1979. A fine, balanced biography, drawing on material previously unpublished from public and private sources. Especially significant is Graves's reconciliation of Housman's romantic poetry and classical scholarship. Extensive notes and a bibliographical essay make this volume an especially useful study.

Holden, Alan W., and J. Roy Birch. *A. E. Housman: A Reassessment.* New York: St. Martin's Press, 2000. A collection of both biographical and critical essays that uncover the deceptive simplicity of Housman's poetry and life. Includes bibliographical references and index.

Leggett, B. J. *Housman's Land of Lost Content: A Critical Study of "A Shropshire Lad."* Knoxville: University of Tennessee Press, 1970. Contending that *A Shropshire Lad* contains most of Housman's enduring poems, Leggett provides a painstaking analysis of its structure and its theme ("the problem of change"). Leggett aims to shift discussion away from Housman's personality.

———. *The Poetic Art of A. E. Housman.* Lincoln: University of Nebraska Press, 1978. A useful study divided by topics: the use of metaphor, nature poetry, structural patterns, Housman, T. S. Eliot, and "critical fashion in the thirties." Leggett devotes two chapters to Housman's theory and practice of poetry because this has been a contested point in literary criticism. Supplemented by extensive notes but no bibliography.

Naiditch, P. G. *Problems in the Life and Writings of A. E. Housman.* Beverly Hills, Calif.: Krown & Spellmam, 1995. A lucid and readable biographical account with lasting contributions to knowledge of a great and controversial scholar. Includes a bibliography and index.

Page, Norman. *A. E. Housman: A Critical Biography.* New York: Schocken Books,

1983. A succinct account drawing on published and unpublished sources, with separate chapters on Housman's classical scholarship and the development of his poetry. The introduction is especially helpful on the biographer's method, on his evaluation of previous biographies, and on his decision to separate discussions of the life and the work.

Robert G. Blake

CHARLOTTE MEW

Born: London, England; November 15, 1869
Died: London, England; March 24, 1928

PRINCIPAL POETRY
The Farmer's Bride, 1916, 1921 (also known as *Saturday Market*, 1921)
The Rambling Sailor, 1929
Collected Poems of Charlotte Mew, 1953
Collected Poems and Prose, 1981
Selected Poems, 2008

OTHER LITERARY FORMS

Though primarily known for her poetry, Charlotte Mew (myew) also wrote short stories and essays. Her first story to appear in print was "Passed" (1894), published in John Lane and Elkin Mathews's *The Yellow Book*, which also published works by Henry James and Max Beerbohm and the drawings of Aubrey Beardsley. From 1899 to 1905, Mew was a regular contributor to *Temple Bar*, a magazine for middle-class Victorians, which published the stories "The China Bowl" (1899), "An Open Door" (1903), "A White Night" (1903), and "Mark Stafford's Wife" (1905), as well as the essays "Notes in a Brittany Convent" (1901) and "The Poems of Emily Brontë" (1904). "An Old Servant" (1913), Mew's tribute to her childhood nurse, Elizabeth Goodman, appeared in *The New Statesmen*. Mew rewrote "The China Bowl" as a one-act play, which was broadcast by the British Broadcasting Corporation posthumously in 1953. That same year, *Cornhill Magazine* published her story "A Fatal Fidelity."

ACHIEVEMENTS

Although Charlotte Mew's work never won any awards, her poetry did win accolades from major literary figures, including Virginia Woolf, Thomas Hardy, Siegfried Sassoon, Rebecca West, H. D., and novelist May Sinclair. In 1923, Hardy, John Masefield, and Walter de la Mare secured for her a Civil List pension of seventy-five pounds per year.

BIOGRAPHY

Charlotte Mew was born in 1869 in the Bloomsbury section of London, where she would live her whole life, much of it at 9 Gordon Street. She was the first girl born to Frederick Mew and Anna Maria Kendall. Originally from the Isle of Wight, Frederick Mew had been sent to London by his father to train as an architect. He became an assistant to architect H. E. Kendall, Jr. In 1863, he married Kendall's daughter, Anna Maria.

Anna Maria, an invalid much of her life, saw her marriage as beneath her. Frederick's death in 1898 put the family into financial crisis. Of the seven Mew children, only Charlotte, her older brother, Henry, and two younger siblings, Anne and Freda, survived to adulthood. Henry and Freda were both institutionalized for mental illness, a situation that strained the family's limited resources and haunted Mew's poetry.

Following her father's death, Mew lived with her sister Anne and her mother at Gordon Street. Eventually they lived in the basement, having rented out the upper rooms for additional income. Mew was particularly devoted to Anne, a painter who attended the Royal Female School of Art and later rented a studio, 6 Hogarth Studios. In 1909, the year Mew published "Requiescat," her sister Anne had a painting accepted by the Royal Academy. As girls, they attended the Gower Street School and later lectures at University College, London.

At Gower Street, Mew developed a crush on Miss Lucy Harrison, the school's headmistress. Mew's unrequited love for Harrison anticipates her most important adult female relationships. Of particular importance were her relationships with Ella D'Arcy, assistant literary editor of *The Yellow Book*, whom she met in 1894, a year before composing "The China Bowl," and novelist and suffragette May Sinclair, whom she met in 1913 through Mrs. Dawson "Sappho" Scott, an arts patron and founder of International PEN. Sinclair brought Mew's work to the attention of Ezra Pound, who published "The Fête" in *The Egoist*. Mew wrote "Madeleine in Church," which many consider her best poem, during the years of her friendship with Sinclair. While in love with both D'Arcy and Sinclair, Mew repressed her desire because of a strict sense of sexual propriety. Perhaps for the same reason and out of fear that any offspring would suffer mental illness, Mew and her sister Anne decided to never marry.

In 1915, Mew met Alida Monro (née Klemantaski), whose husband, Harold, owned the Poetry Bookshop (Bloomsbury), where Mew read her work. After reading Mew's poem "The Farmer's Bride" in *The Nation* (1912), Monro convinced her husband to publish a collection of Mew's poetry. In 1916, the Poetry Bookshop printed five hundred copies of *The Farmer's Bride*. Five years later, it brought out a revised edition with eleven additional poems. Despite unflagging support from the Monros and positive reviews from H. D. and West, the book did not sell well. In 1929, the Poetry Bookshop posthumously published Mew's poetry collection, *The Rambling Sailor*.

In 1923, the same year Mew was awarded the Civil List pension, her mother died of bronchial pneumonia. Unable to continue paying rent on their house, now in Delancey Street, Mew and her sister Anne lived temporarily at Anne's studio. Anne's health was seriously declining, and in June, 1927, she died of cancer. On February 15, 1928, devastated by the loss of her sister and perhaps fearing for her own mental health (she had become obsessed with germs and the possibility that her sister had been buried alive), Mew agreed to enter a nursing home near the Baker Street Station. Less than one month later, on March 24, 1928, she committed suicide by drinking half a bottle of Lysol.

ANALYSIS

At times autobiographical, Charlotte Mew's poetry frequently takes the themes of longing, death, insanity, and loneliness. It often addresses passion, religious and sexual, as well as sin and the distance between a heavenly God and individual human suffering on Earth. Her work frequently contains tensions created through binaries of inside/outside, freedom/confinement, nature/society. Her deeply emotional verse contains jarring juxtapositions of images and is marked by irregular rhyme and meter. Writing in the last decade of the nineteenth century and the first decades of the twentieth, Mew's poetry straddles the fin de siècle and early modernist periods.

THE FARMER'S BRIDE

The poems in *The Farmer's Bride* reflect Mew's dominant themes. "Ken" and "On the Asylum Road" provide moving depictions of madness and the isolation that results from mental illness. "Ken" closes with the lines, "... when they took/ Ken to that place, I did not look./ After he called and turned on me/ His eyes. These I shall see—" The final dash suggests that the speaker remains haunted by Ken's gaze. In "The Narrow Door," death disrupts a game of "shop" as a coffin is carried out through the narrow door before which the "café children" play. Images of death appear in the partially autobiographical "The Changeling," in which "the little pale brother" has been "called away," and "The Quiet House," which opens with "the old Nurse" and concludes with the speaker's revision of the famous line from René Descartes, "some day I *shall* not think; I shall not *be*!" In "Fame," Mew's speaker mediates on whether she could renounce her fame, represented by "the over-heated house," "Where no one fits the singer to his song,/ Or sifts the unpainted from the painted faces," and return to her previous life, symbolized in "The folded glory of the gorse, the sweet-briar air." Choosing Fame, the speaker fantasizes taking her "To our tossed bed." A still birth, "A frail, dead, new-born lamb," "The moon's dropped child," results from their union, a consequence of ambition and sexual passion.

The title poem, "The Farmer's Bride," tells of a young bride, who, having developed a fear of men, runs away. Chased after and returned by the villagers, she is locked away where she "does the work about the house" "like a mouse." The bride's imprisonment, symbolic of women's confinement in marriage, is contrasted against her natural self, which the narrator associates with "wild violets" and the "beasts in stall." In the lines "Sweet as the first wild violets, she,/ To her wild self. But what to me?," the break between "self" and "me," illustrates this broken and unconsummated union. The farmer laments that there are no children: "What's Christmas-time without there be/ Some other in the house than we!" The poem ends with the farmer overcome by his grief and sexual desire: "Oh! my God! the down,/ The soft young down of her, the brown,/ The brown of her—her eyes, her hair, her hair!"

The Farmer's Bride also contains the two-hundred-line free-verse poem, "Madeleine in Church," a dramatic monologue spoken by a woman who prefers to kneel not before Jesus, but rather a "plaster saint" "... more like [her] own clay,/ Not too divine." Too high on the cross, Jesus appears distant from the realities of her life, her marriage and divorce, the death of her child, her fading youth. She challenges him, "What can You know, what can You really see/ Of this dark ditch, the soul of me!" Unlike the traditional "fallen woman," Mew's Madeleine is unrepentant, insisting twice, "We are what we are" and that she will not be among the "broken things" held in God's "everlasting wings." The poem offers two versions of love through which Mew repeats the human/divine binary represented by the saint and Jesus. Mew invites readers to compare the perfect yet unattainable passion of Mary Magdalene for Jesus, "a passion" "so far from earthly cares and earthly fears" that one can only look "at it through tears," to the marriage of the speaker's mother, who was "yoked to the man that Father was." Looking to bridge this chasm between the heavenly and the earthly, the speaker longs for a human Jesus, who would notice or even speak to her: "If He had ever seemed to notice me/ Or, if, for once, He would only speak."

THE RAMBLING SAILOR

This posthumous collection of thirty-two poems was edited by Alida Monro and contains six of Mew's "Early Poems," including "Requiescat." While the collection continues themes of loss, loneliness, and death, particularly the death of children, these poems express resignation and a fragile hope. They are poems of remembrance, of things, places, and people lost. The speaker in "The Trees Are Down" observes the cutting down of "the great plane-trees at the end of the gardens," and in "Fin de Fête," the speaker recalls how she and an anonymous "you" "should have slept" together like children in a fairy tale, but now there is only the speaker's "lonely head."

Stylistically these poems are more restrained; there are more sonnets, and fewer free-verse lines overspill the page. In a mirroring of form and content, the sexual and religious passion, the grief and despair is also contained, though tentatively. The speakers in these poems appear less consumed with earthly desires, meditating instead on the afterlife. The speaker in "In the Fields," reflecting the "lovely things which pass," asks, "Can I believe there is a heavenlier world than this?," and "Not for That City" claims, "We strain our eyes beyond this dusk to see/ What, from the threshold of eternity/ We shall step into...." Facing their own death or the death of someone they love, the speakers in these poems look to nature, particularly spring, for solace. Having previously "... liked Spring last year/ Because you were here," the speaker of "I So Liked Spring," decides, "I'll like Spring because it is simply Spring/ As the thrushes do," and the war poem, "May, 1915," assures its readers, "Let us remember Spring will come again."

BIBLIOGRAPHY

Dowson, Jane, and Alice Entwistle. "'I Will Put Myself, and Everything I See, upon the Page': Charlotte Mew, Sylvia Townsend Warner, Anna Wickham and the Dramatic

Monologue." In *A History of Twentieth-Century British Women's Poetry*. New York: Cambridge University Press, 2005. Contains considerable analysis of Mew's poetry, finding the poet's hallmark to be an ability to summon "felt absence."

Fitzgerald, Penelope. *Charlotte Mew and Her Friends*. 1992. Reprint. London: Flamingo, 2002. In this book-length biography, Fitzgerald examines Mew's life in the context of her friendships with Ella D'Arcy, Mrs. Dawson Scott, and May Sinclair. Contains selected poems and bibliography.

Goss, Theodora, ed. *Voices from Fairyland: The Fantastical Poems of Mary Coleridge, Charlotte Mew, and Sylvia Townsend Warner*. Seattle: Aqueduct Press, 2008. Presents the poetry of Mew, Coleridge, and Warner, with some critical analysis.

Hamilton, Ian. *Against Oblivion: Some Lives of the Twentieth-Century Poets*. New York: Viking, 2002. Contains a biography essay on Mew that looks at her poetry. Hamilton edited a selection of Mew's poetry.

Katz, Jon, and Kevin Prufer, eds. *Dark Horses: Poets on Overlooked Poems—An Anthology*. Urbana: University of Illinois Press, 2007. Contains Mew's poem "The Trees Are Down," with a commentary by Molly Peacock.

Kendall, Tim. *Modern English War Poetry*. Oxford: Oxford University Press, 2006. The chapter on Mew compares her war poetry to that of Edward Thomas, analyzing the trope of spring in each.

Leighton, Angela. *Victorian Women Poets: Writing Against the Heart*. New York: Harvester Wheatsheaf, 1992. The chapter on Mew in this introduction to eight nineteenth century women poets provides a biography and analysis of her work, identifying her as a Victorian and drawing comparisons to writer and artist Christina Rossetti.

Rice, Nelljean McConeghey. *A New Matrix for Modernism: A Study of the Lives and Poetry of Charlotte Mew and Anna Wickham*. New York: Routledge, 2003. Rice views both Mew and Wickham, who both published through the Poetry Bookshop, to be modern poets.

Sarah Fedirka

FRANK O'HARA

Born: Baltimore, Maryland; June 27, 1926
Died: Mastic Beach, New York; July 25, 1966

PRINCIPAL POETRY
A City Winter, and Other Poems, 1952
Oranges, 1953
Meditations in an Emergency, 1957
Odes, 1960
Lunch Poems, 1964
Love Poems (Tentative Title), 1965
In Memory of My Feelings: A Selection of Poems, 1967 (Bill Berkson, editor)
The Collected Poems of Frank O'Hara, 1971, 1995 (Donald Allen, editor)
Selected Poems, 1974 (Allen, editor)
Early Poems, 1946-1951, 1976
Poems Retrieved, 1951-1966, 1977, 1996
Selected Poems, 2008 (Mark Ford, editor)

OTHER LITERARY FORMS

Frank O'Hara was always a poet, no matter what he wrote. His plays (published in *Selected Plays*, 1978), only a few of which are actually capable of being produced with any degree of dramatic effectiveness, are more often plays with words and visual effects than exploration of character or idea through dramatic conflict. Some juxtapose a vast variety of characters (from O'Hara's own friends to Benjamin Franklin, Marlene Dietrich, William Blake, and Generalissimo Franco), most with only a single short speech, with connections nonexistent outside O'Hara's fertile imagination. Others of these short plays offer sustained characters speaking in non sequiturs or in monologues unheard by other characters. In one play, *Try! Try!* (pr., pb. 1951), the monologues work in an interesting way, since there is a plot with a recognizable triangle of characters and actual dialogue, besides some poetic and psychologically suggestive monologues. Another produced play, *The General Returns from One Place to Another* (pr. 1964), uses verbal, visual, and dramatic means to satirize the American military abroad, particularly in the person of Douglas MacArthur.

O'Hara's prose has been collected in *Standing Still and Walking in New York* (1975, Donald Allen, editor). The volume consists chiefly of miscellaneous pieces on modern art and contains a small quantity of literary criticism as well.

Besides writing for *Art News*, O'Hara worked on the catalogs for various exhibits at the Museum of Modern Art, including those on contemporary American painters Jack-

Frank O'Hara

son Pollock and Robert Motherwell. His art criticism tends to be impressionistic rather than technical, but it effectively conveys the essence of contemporary painting.

Achievements

Other than the advent of the Beat movement, probably the most exciting thing to happen to American poetry in the mid-twentieth century is the ascendance of vital and natural voices, with all the immediacy of actual human talk, through the work of the New York School of poets. Heading them were Frank O'Hara, John Ashbery, and Kenneth Koch, with O'Hara's voice being the dominant one. Drawing elements from Walt Whitman, William Carlos Williams, Gertrude Stein, French Surrealists such as Guillaume Apollinaire and Pierre Reverdy, and the Russian poets Vladimir Mayakovsky and Boris Pasternak, O'Hara shattered the prevailing poetic standards regarding language, form, and content and forged his own verse with tremendous vigor and fire. He did not want to produce the sort of pristine, shapely work that could be found in scores of other volumes, admired by the literary establishment of New Critics for their traditional forms, metaphoric complexities, and mythic overtones. O'Hara rejected all these familiar ingredients, writing in unfettered free verse, shifting images and metaphors wildly throughout a poem, and dealing with earthy subject matter or very personal experiences without any effort to make them seem universally significant. He received the Avery Hopwood Major Award in Poetry in 1951 and the National Book Award in Poetry in 1972 for *The Collected Poems of Frank O'Hara*.

Most of O'Hara's poems flow, without any attempt to structure them formally, through the free association of his surrealistic poems, where one image or word leads to another, however logically unrelated, or through the simple recording of his actual activities, thoughts, and feelings on special occasion (or not-so-special ones). Because he was so keenly in tune with his feelings, such poems work splendidly in conveying the moods that generated them, especially through the marvelously vivid vocabulary that dances across his pages.

Not least among his achievements is his lively sense of humor, sometimes just a light tone that flavors much of his work as he playfully recounts his activities or observations, sometimes satiric views of various cultural and political icons (including the movies), sometimes raucous comedy full of delightful surprises, such as the sun appearing to chat with the poet abed or a vision of bugs walking through the apartment "carrying a little banner/ which says 'in search of lanolin.'" Delight in words and experience, surprise at the variety of existence: These are the keynotes of O'Hara's poetry, which retains its freshness and appeal far beyond the attempts of so many others to imitate it.

Biography

Although born in Baltimore and reared in rural Massachusetts, Francis Russell O'Hara discovered a more appropriate milieu first among fellow poets and aficionados of the other arts at Harvard (where he received his B.A. degree in English literature in 1950) and subsequently in New York City. In the meantime, he had spent two years in the U.S. Navy in the South Pacific and a year at the University of Michigan, where he received his M.A. in 1951 and the Avery Hopwood Major Award in Poetry for a manuscript collection of poetry (his master's thesis). Once in New York, he rejoined fellow Harvard graduates Ashbery and Koch and involved himself in various arts in assorted capacities, while remaining, with the others, quite apart from the literary establishment of the day. He worked for the Museum of Modern Art, advancing from a staff position working on circulating exhibitions to an associate curatorship, selecting numerous exhibitions of contemporary American and Spanish artists and being responsible for the catalogs published in conjunction with the exhibits. He also wrote occasional articles and reviews for *Art News* and had several plays performed. He adopted a very casual attitude toward his poetry, sending poems off to friends without keeping a copy, stuffing them in drawers, gathering material only under pressure from eager editors such as John Bernard Myers. He was intensely involved (whether as friend or lover) with many different and interesting women and men throughout these New York years until his death after a freak accident on Fire Island.

Analysis

To enter the world of Frank O'Hara is to abandon familiar road maps, to give up hope for a straight and clear way through, for easily recognizable landmarks that indicate where one is going, where one has been. With "no revolver pointing the roadmarks," the reader is free to travel without preconceptions and without insistent points made by the poet. O'Hara's world is closer to Lewis Carroll's than to Robert Frost's, being constantly full of surprises, byways, sharp turns, cul-de-sacs, a grotesquerie of roadside attractions, and few places to stop or rest, so that one ends up nowhere near one's anticipated goal, perhaps not even at an ending at all but simply at a halt, like running out of gas. For that is how many O'Hara poems conclude—with neither a bang nor a whimper, but only a sudden cessation of the impetuous, rapid drive of words and images and feelings that has made up the poem. His poetry is exciting, startling, dizzying, frightening, overwhelming, demanding, involving, crude, elaborate, stark, disorderly, sexy, and sometimes very funny. As a poet crafting his art, O'Hara had as much gleeful fun—even when dealing with feelings considerably less than euphoric—as the liveliest child or the most daredevil racer.

O'Hara was the epitome of the New York poet: fast, frenzied, jazzy, upbeat, smart-aleck, shrewd, unzipped, down-to-earth, open, and full of action. Like his fellow New York poets (friends, some contemporaries, some followers or students from a workshop he offered), he thrived on the bustle of the city and participated in its multitude of activities. Far from being a poetic hermit in an ivory tower, he actively involved himself with people and with the other arts—notably with painters, but also with dancers and musicians. The kind of painting he favored was action painting, a style indigenous to New York and led by Jackson Pollock. Its random quality, abstractness, and emphasis on the process of painting rather than the static permanence demonstrated in a still life or a portrait all have their correspondences in O'Hara's poetry.

This poetry pulses with action of all sorts—sexual, mental, emotional, physical, natural, industrial, transportational—all the types of action, in fact, that make up the United States. Action itself is the subject of some of his poems, such as his self-styled "I do this I do that" poems. The action of the poem may be expressed in vocabulary (colorful concrete nouns and vivid active verbs expressing dynamic movement); in syntax (whether conventional—using such devices as piled-up participial phrases, short sentences, and parataxis, though quite grammatically—or unconventional—omitting parts of a sentence or letting a single word or phrase serve two different but simultaneous functions in two adjacent syntactical units); in interjections ("Hey!," "Yeah!"); or in rapid shifts of subject, place, or time—from stanza to stanza, sentence to sentence, line to line, and even from one word or phrase to the next.

"My Heat"

"My Heat" provides evidence of all these. The opening stanza is filled with verbs denoting vigorous action: four finite verbs ("committed," "fell off the balcony," "I'd force the port!/ Violate the piers"), one infinitive ("to refountain myself"), and two present participles ("jetting," "turning in air"). Unconventional syntax and punctuation give a sensation of dizziness fitting this turning and falling: The "if" clause seems to have two main verbs unseparated by a conjunction or comma, both with "I" as subject; then O'Hara does not set off what is presumably his main clause by a comma after the subordinate clause, so that the infinitive could be regarded as part of either the subordinate or the main clause. The verb's unfamiliarity ("refountain") also sharpens the reader's attention, as does the unclearness of its connection with the rest of the sentence. This main clause seems to end with the exclamation point after "port," yet the next word is another verb, presumably another main verb for the subject "I"—unless it is an imperative for the two vocatives ending the stanza ("you bores! you asses!"). Keeping readers alert, the very next word, "geology," at the beginning of the next stanza, not only has nothing to do with "the balcony," "the port," or "the piers," but also is punctuated by a question mark.

The punctuation is certainly not completely unorthodox, though it is surprising. What would give the traditional poetry reader more trouble are the rapid shifts in imagery, but this is part of O'Hara's point: the pleasure he takes in "jetting" from one image to whatever it suggests, the pleasure he takes in "jetting" such words and phrases from his typewriter—all as opposed to the "you" in this poem, who always seems a few steps behind poet "Frank," who proclaims, with another surprising but apt and active verb choice, "I've kayoed your popular cant/ I'd rather jet!"

A New Critic such as John Crowe Ransom would probably throw up his hands at the untidiness of O'Hara's metaphorical maneuverings. There is no clear one-to-one correspondence between tenors and vehicles here; there is certainly no single picture provided out of which the meaning derives, no identifiable incident that gives rise to the poetic expression. The meaning, rather, resides in the exuberant movement of the poem and its words, images that—in themselves and in their transformations throughout the poem—suggest the force of creativity as well as that of sexuality.

This poem is, in fact, only one of the most compressed treatments of sexuality among O'Hara's work, from the ejaculatory "jetting" of its opening line on to the final line: "'That's no furnace, that's my heart!'" The heat of passion is inflated to the power of a furnace. The diffuse jetting rampant throughout the poem amply reflects the exuberant sexuality—not a sexual desire directed at a single person and thus capable of being satisfied, but rather directed at no one in particular, an all-pervasive urge, reveling in the fact of sexuality and the pleasure of the sexual feeling itself. O'Hara's images are used not as specific metaphors—he mixes them too outrageously for that—but rather as evocations of the many flavors and feelings of sexuality (or, in other poems, whatever has motivated that poetic outburst): its sweetness and beauty in roses, its violence (in violating the piers), its power (as a volcano "to melt everyone into syrup"), its self-containment, its richness, even its humor ("laughing like an old bedspring," a simile that makes a believable aural comparison as well as fitting the sexual subject matter).

JOYFUL SEXUALITY, IMAGISTIC FERTILITY

O'Hara's eroticism is far from fin de siècle decadence, which hints at more than it tells; nor does it explicitly depict sexual acts, as in pornography. Rather, it revels in a joyous sexuality that fellow gay poet Whitman would certainly recognize and appreciate. Only rarely does O'Hara depict an actual sexual act, as in "Twin spheres full of fur and noise/ rolling softly up my belly" for an act of fellatio. A lively choice of images ("my mouth is full of suns") and abstractions ("that softness seems so anterior to that hardness"), with a climactic hint of Apollo's chariot of the sun, raises the experience to a mythic level, but not for long. O'Hara's poetry must constantly move, never rest, and of course the moment of sexual ecstasy dissolves, even as it is achieved: "It must be discovered soon and disappear."

Sex is not, however much it may appear so from these examples, O'Hara's only concern; like Whitman, he felt intense pleasure simply in living, and since sex represents the most intense form of physical pleasure, he naturally perceived a sexual quality in his relationship with living—in all its aspects—and hence with the rest of the world. He could penetrate the world—make an impact on it, enter its multifarious experiences—just as he could penetrate a lover; he could also be penetrated by experience, by the myriad sensory impressions all around him—just as a lover might penetrate him. This openness to both roles parallels his sexual orientation; his homosexuality, indicating openness to nonstandard sexual practices, may have a share in O'Hara's imagistic fertility, as he presents (in "Easter," for example) nonhuman and inanimate nature surging with sexuality ("it's the night like a love it all cruisy and nelly"). Such images, which cannot be deciphered into metaphorical correspondences of tenor and vehicle with an "underlying" subject behind the metaphorical development, serve to suggest sexuality in O'Hara's more public poems (as contrasted with private poems such as "Twin Spheres," written for his lover Vincent Warren) without having to be gender-specific.

In most of his poems, the images shift constantly; the reader is meant to flow with the stream of O'Hara's free associations, which is often remarkably easy to do because of his vivid and emotionally evocative choice of nouns, verbs, and adjectives, even when the precise meaning of a passage remains indecipherable. "Savoy" shifts ground even more rapidly than "My Heat," yet it conveys a rich sequence of moods.

"SAVOY"

"Savoy" opens with a feeling of terror, although its cause is unclear. Like other O'Hara poems, it begins with an image that he proceeds to join to a simile—a logical enough poetic device—but the simile proceeds to take over as the poem's main concern. However, O'Hara writes elsewhere, "How I hate subject matter!," and the reader realizes that actually neither simile nor its tenor is the subject of the poem. Looking at the extended so-called simile ("like a bespectacled carapaceous witch doctor of Rimini/ beautifying an adolescent tubbed in entrails of blue cement . . .") reveals that it is hardly to be apprehended in the manner of a metaphysical conceit. What is a witch doctor doing in Rimini, on the Italian seacoast? How can anyone be beautified in a bath of "blue cement"? A few lines down, who is the "you" suddenly addressed? The rapid changes mirror those of a dream or nightmare, in which identities shift inexplicably. This is the method of Surrealist poetry, which O'Hara brought into American poetry with a new force after it had flourished in Europe several decades earlier. O'Hara clearly indicates a romance with the word and whatever lively images it evokes rather than with its specific literal denotation. Even in describing terrors and dangers in "Savoy," O'Hara is having fun; the pleasure is in the movement of the poem, not in discerning its "meaning."

"I DO THIS I DO THAT" POEMS

O'Hara's less surrealistic poems, however, which record his actions, are not hard to understand at all. Simple in form and structure, the "I do this I do that" poems, as he calls them in "Getting Up Ahead of Someone (Sun)," are, at their best, more than a mere transcription of the day's activities; they convey the quality of the poet's conscious mind and the shifting moods stirred by his activities. The most famous—and most moving—example of this sort of poem is "The Day Lady Died," which pays tribute to singer Billie Holiday upon her death but is hardly a standard elegy with explicit presentation of grief and concentration on praise for the deceased. Instead, O'Hara begins the poem—and carries on for the bulk of it—with an account of his movements, fairly random, around New York on a Friday afternoon. Suddenly he is caught short by "a NEW YORK POST with her face on it," and he is reminded of hearing Holiday ("Lady Day") sing "in the 5 SPOT," when "everyone and I stopped breathing." This last action (or rather lack of it) stunningly conveys the whole impact not only of Holiday's art but also of her death and is especially effective in stopping movement and thought after such a bustling buildup. The rest of the poem does not prepare the reader for such a conclusion at all.

Most of his "I do this I do that" poems are much less serious, and often poke fun at himself or take a delightfully lighthearted approach to the addressee, a friend or a lover, and the particular relationship they share. In fact, O'Hara's humor is one of his most characteristic traits; however, his work is quite different from light verse because it rarely satirizes and certainly does not use rhyme and rhythm. Rather, it is based on surprise, giving his readers the unexpected, as his Surrealist pieces do. Those, however, are rarely comic because they so constantly shift ground that the reader has no solid base to stand on, a necessity if comic surprise is to hit with true effectiveness.

"POEM (LANA TURNER HAS COLLAPSED!)"

A true comic gem is "Poem (Lana Turner has collapsed!)," a delightful little poem that O'Hara wrote on the spur of the moment on a ferryboat to a poetry reading. Written in the conversational tone at which he was so adept, it enters the world of comedy with the very first line, with its hysterical exclamation point like a sensationalistic headline (as the poem later reveals it in fact to be). The reader knows not to take this as seriously as Lady Day's death, first because of the exclamation point, then because this announcement appears at the beginning of the poem rather than at its climax.

The second line continues the humorous tone with O'Hara's verb choice—"I was trotting along." The speaker is obviously not a horse, nor does this verb have the intensity of suggestion of those in "My Heat"; it merely gives the reader a funny sense of the light, frolicsome quality of the poet's movements. The humor continues—and builds—stylistically with the paratactic structure of short clauses joined by coordinating conjunctions, then in content with the poet's slight disagreement with his friend about the weather (whether it was raining and snowing or hailing), and further, with the surprising apparent shift in position of the "you," who at first appears to be with the speaker and then is seen as the goal he is walking toward. The poet notes the traffic "acting exactly like the sky," using the humorous idiom of very mild outrage ("isn't that exactly like so-and-so?"). Then comes the appearance of the headline—to complete what now appears to be a flashback after the poem's opening line. The poet proceeds to assure the motion-picture star that she has no reason to collapse, there being no snow or rain in Hollywood; moreover, he refers to his own behavior at parties, where he himself has never collapsed. He concludes with an actual address to the actress—comically unpunctuated, although it encompasses an interjection, a vocative, and two short clauses not joined by conjunctions: "oh Lana Turner we love you get up." This last line suggests that all the motion-picture star needs here is reassurance of her fans' love and an affectionately authoritative encouragement. O'Hara is implying that he cannot take this inflated problem seriously, nor should anyone else; he is gently mocking the superhuman status accorded celebrities. Of course this is a poem simply to be enjoyed, hardly to be pondered seriously. Although O'Hara certainly took poetry seriously, he also believed in enjoying it, as he did life.

Living in a throbbing city, he had countless experiences to enjoy, from attending films and ballet to walking the streets (as in the poems just discussed) to meeting with a wide range of acquaintances, for a Coke, a trip to a museum, a party, or even sex. All these experiences are celebrated in his vital poetry, through which he has vividly conveyed not only a sense of the excitement of life but also a rich sense of himself as a living person: As with Whitman, it is not a mere book one encounters when reading O'Hara: "Who touches this touches a man."

OTHER MAJOR WORKS

PLAYS: *Try! Try!*, pr., pb. 1951; *The General Returns from One Place to Another*, pr. 1964; *Selected Plays*, 1978.

NONFICTION: *Jackson Pollock*, 1959; *New Spanish Painting and Sculpture*, 1960; *Robert Motherwell, with Selections from the Artist's Writings*, 1965; *Standing Still and Walking in New York*, 1975 (Donald Allen, editor).

MISCELLANEOUS: *Early Writing*, 1977.

BIBLIOGRAPHY

Cappucci, Paul R. *William Carlos Williams, Frank O'Hara, and the New York Art Scene*. Madison, N.J.: Fairleigh Dickinson University Press, 2010. Examines the New York School of poets and O'Hara, as well as Williams and his influence on the poet.

Feldman, Alan. *Frank O'Hara*. Boston: Twayne, 1979. This book introduces O'Hara as a New York poet. His language, style, and degrees of coherence are analyzed. Themes of "the self," varieties of feelings, and humor are examined in succeeding chapters. Includes chronology, select bibliography, and index.

Gooch, Brad. *City Poet: The Life and Times of Frank O'Hara*. New York: Harper-Perennial, 1994. This biography of O'Hara details his life from his Massachusetts Catholic boyhood to Harvard University and to New York, where his art criticism became seminal to the abstract expressionist painters and sculptors.

Perloff, Marjorie. *Frank O'Hara: Poet Among Painters*. Rev. ed. Chicago: University of Chicago Press, 1998. This revised edition of a 1977 work adds a new introduction. Perloff analyzes O'Hara's "aesthetic of attention" and surveys the early poems. Her central chapter looks at his "poem-paintings," and then his "great period" is presented. Includes illustrations, notes, a bibliographical note, and an index.

Shaw, Lytle. *Frank O'Hara: The Poetics of Coterie*. Iowa City: University of Iowa Press, 2003. Argues that O'Hara is a coterie poet in that he valued relationships and linkages between people, including the mock family that consisted of his friends, and that being a coterie poet is not a negative thing in the case of O'Hara.

Ward, Geoff. *Statutes of Liberty: The New York School of Poets*. New York: Palgrave, 2001. An acclaimed account of the New York School and its key figures, John Ashbery, O'Hara, and James Schuyler, and their growing influence on postmodern poetics.

Scott Giantvalley

ADRIENNE RICH

Born: Baltimore, Maryland; May 16, 1929

PRINCIPAL POETRY
A Change of World, 1951
The Diamond Cutters, and Other Poems, 1955
Snapshots of a Daughter-in-Law, 1963
Necessities of Life, 1966
Selected Poems, 1967
Leaflets, 1969
The Will to Change, 1971
Diving into the Wreck, 1973
Poems: Selected and New, 1950-1974, 1975
Twenty-one Love Poems, 1976
The Dream of a Common Language, 1978
A Wild Patience Has Taken Me This Far: Poems 1978-1981, 1981
Sources, 1983
The Fact of a Doorframe: Poems Selected and New, 1950-1984, 1984
Your Native Land, Your Life, 1986
Time's Power: Poems, 1985-1988, 1989
An Atlas of the Difficult World: Poems, 1988-1991, 1991
Collected Early Poems, 1950-1970, 1993
Dark Fields of the Republic: Poems, 1991-1995, 1995
Selected Poems, 1950-1995, 1996
Midnight Salvage: Poems, 1995-1998, 1999
Fox: Poems, 1998-2000, 2001
The School Among the Ruins: Poems, 2000-2004, 2004
Telephone Ringing in the Labyrinth: Poems, 2004-2006, 2007

OTHER LITERARY FORMS

Adrienne Rich is known primarily for her poetry, but she has produced essays on writing and politics as well: *Of Woman Born: Motherhood as Experience and Institution* (1976) is an analysis of the changing meanings of childbirth and motherhood in Anglo-American culture, in which Rich draws on personal experience as well as sources in mythology, sociology, economics, the history of medicine, and literature to develop her analysis. *On Lies, Secrets, and Silence: Selected Prose, 1966-1978* (1979) is a collection of essays on women writers (including Anne Bradstreet, Anne Sexton, Charlotte Brontë, and Emily Dickinson) and feminism. *Blood, Bread, and Poetry: Selected*

Prose, 1979-1985 (1986) followed with further essays on women writers and feminist criticism. *What Is Found There: Notebooks on Poetry and Politics* (1993) delivers just what the title promises. For several years Rich also coedited, with Michelle Cliff, the lesbian feminist journal *Sinister Wisdom*.

Achievements

Adrienne Rich's work has been at the vanguard of the women's movement in the United States. Her poems and essays explore her own experience and seek to develop a "common language" for women to communicate their values and perceptions. She has received numerous awards, including two Guggenheim Fellowships, the National Institute of Arts and Letters Award for Poetry (1960), the Shelley Memorial Award of the Poetry Society of America (1971), and the National Book Award (1974) for *Diving into the Wreck*. Other recognitions include the Ruth Lilly Poetry Prize (1986), the Northern California Book Award in poetry (1989), the Bill Whitehead Award (1990), Lambda Literary Awards (1991, 1995, 2001), the Lenore Marshall Poetry Prize (1992), the Academy of American Poets Fellowship (1992), the *Los Angeles Times* Book Prize (1992), the Frost Medal (1992), a MacArthur Fellowship, the Poets' Prize (1993), the Fred Cody Award for lifetime achievement (1994), the Wallace Stevens Award (1996), the Lifetime Achievement Award from the Lannan Foundation (1999), the Bollingen Prize (2003), and the Medal for Distinguished Contribution to American Letters from the National Book Foundation (2006). In 2004, *The School Among the Ruins* earned Rich the National Book Critics Circle Award, the Gold Medal from the Commonwealth Club of California, and the Poetry Center Book Award. She served as chancellor for the Academy of American Poets from 1999 to 2001.

Biography

Adrienne Cecile Rich was born in 1929, into a white, middle-class southern family. Her Jewish father, Arnold Rice Rich, taught medicine at The Johns Hopkins University. Her southern Protestant mother, Helen Jones Rich, was trained as a composer and concert pianist but gave up her career to devote herself to her husband and two daughters. She carried out their early education at home, until the girls began to attend school in fourth grade. Her father encouraged his daughter to read and to write poetry. In his library, she found the work of such writers as Matthew Arnold, William Blake, Thomas Carlyle, John Keats, Dante Gabriel Rossetti, and Alfred, Lord Tennyson. Rich graduated from Radcliffe College in 1951, the year her first volume of poetry was published. She traveled in Europe and England on a Guggenheim Fellowship in 1952-1953.

Rich married Alfred H. Conrad in 1953 and in the next few years gave birth to three sons, David (1955), Paul (1957), and Jacob (1959). She lived with her family in Cambridge, Massachusetts, from 1953 to 1966, but spent 1961-1962 in the Netherlands on

Adrienne Rich
(Library of Congress)

another Guggenheim Fellowship. In 1964, Rich began her involvement in the New Left, initiating a period of personal and political growth and crisis. In 1966, the family moved to New York, where Conrad taught at City College of New York. Rich also began to teach at City College, where she worked for the first time with disadvantaged students. In 1970, Rich ended her marriage, and later the same year, Conrad ended his life. Rich continued teaching at City College and then Rutgers University until 1979, when she moved to western Massachusetts. Poems of these years explore her lesbian relationships.

Rich eventually moved to northern California to continue her active career as poet, essayist, and sought-after speaker. Rich spent time in the 1980's and early 1990's at numerous California colleges and universities, acting as visiting professor and lecturer. Her stops included Scripps College, San Jose State University, and Stanford University. In 1992, she accepted the National Director of the National Writer's Voice Project. In the 1990's, she joined several advisory boards, including the Boston Woman's Fund, National Writers Union, Sisterhood in Support of Sisters in South Africa, and New Jewish Agenda.

Analysis

Adrienne Rich's successive volumes of poetry chronicle a contemporary female artist's odyssey. Her earliest work is a notable contribution to modern poetry. Her later work has broken new ground as she redefines and reimagines women's lives to create a female myth of self-discovery. In her life and work, she has been struggling to break out of patriarchal social and literary conventions, to redefine herself and to create new traditions. W. H. Auden praised her first volume for its stylistic control, its skillful use of traditional themes such as isolation, and its assimilation of influences such as the work of Robert Frost and William Butler Yeats. He wrote: "The poems . . . in this book are neatly and modestly dressed, speak quietly but do not mumble, respect their elders but are not cowed by them, and do not tell fibs."

Since then, however, Rich has been reshaping poetic conventions to develop her own themes and to create her own voice, often a radical (and sometimes a jarring) one. Reviewer Helen Vendler termed *Diving into the Wreck* "dispatches from the battlefield." Central concerns of Rich's poetry include the uses of history and language, the relationship of the individual to society, and the individual's quest for identity and meaning. The home is often a site for the working out of these themes.

A Change of World

Auden chose Rich's first volume of poetry, *A Change of World*, for the Yale Younger Poets Award. Despite the title, the poems have to do with resisting change. Rich's early training at her father's hands reinforced her allegiance to a literary tradition of meticulous craft, of "beauty" and "perfection." Accordingly, these poems are objective, carefully crafted, and rhymed, with echoes of W. H. Auden, T. S. Eliot, and Robert Frost. A recurring image is that of the home as a refuge that is threatened by social instability ("The Uncle Speaks in the Drawing Room") or natural forces ("Storm Warnings"). The women in these poems remain at home, occupied with women's tasks such as embroidering ("Aunt Jennifer's Tigers"), weaving ("Mathilde in Normandy"), and caring for their families ("Eastport to Block Island"). A central theme of these poems is the use of art as a technique for ordering experience ("Aunt Jennifer's Tigers" and "At a Bach Concert"). "At a Bach Concert" is written in a musically complex form, a variant of the intricate terza rima stanza used by Dante. Rich's poem weaves together many strands of poetic technique (assonance, consonance, internal rhyme, off-rhyme, alliteration) and rhetorical devices (oxymoron and parallelism) into a rich textural harmony to develop the theme that formal structure is the poet's gift of love: "Form is the ultimate gift that love can offer—/ The vital union of necessity/ With all that we desire, all that we suffer."

The Diamond Cutters

The theme of artistic control and craft is repeated in Rich's second book, *The Diamond Cutters*. Written when Rich was traveling in Europe as the recipient of a

Guggenheim Traveling Fellowship, this volume is a tourist's poetic diary. Landscape and scenery are prominent. The book blends two moods, nostalgia for a more beautiful past and ironic disillusionment with a present that falls short of perfection (as in "The Ideal Landscape," "Lucifer in the Train," or "The Strayed Village." In a profound way, all the characters in this book are exiles, aliens, uneasy in the places they inhabit. The heroines of poems such as "Autumn Equinox," "The Prospect," and "The Perennial Answer" are dissatisfied with their lives but unable to change. They hold on to history and to the social structures it has produced, refusing to question present conditions. Suppressed anger and unacknowledged tensions lie just beneath the surface of all the poems; the book's tone is passive, flat. Eight years passed before Rich's next book appeared. Its stylistic and thematic changes reflect changes in her outlook.

SNAPSHOTS OF A DAUGHTER-IN-LAW

In her next two books, *Snapshots of a Daughter-in-Law* and *Necessities of Life*, Rich begins to move from conventional poetic forms, to develop her own style, and to deal more directly with personal experience. Her attitudes toward literary tradition, history, and the home have changed markedly. She questions traditional attitudes toward home and family. As she found the patriarchal definitions of human relationships inadequate, her work became more personal and more urgent.

Snapshots of a Daughter-in-Law is written in a looser form than Rich's previous work. Language is simpler, texture less dense. The title poem is a series of vignettes of women's experiences. It fairly bristles with quotations drawn from Rich's wide-ranging reading. According to the poem, male authorities have always defined women in myths and literature. Thus, women lacked a literature of their own in which to define themselves. Rich wrote that she composed the poem "in fragments during children's naps, brief hours in a library, or at 3 A.M. after rising with a wakeful child." Because of these interruptions, she wrote the poem over a two-year period. In this poem, she wrote, "for the first time, directly about experiencing myself as a woman" rather than striving to be "universal." As the title indicates, these are static, fixed vignettes: The women are trapped, denied scope for action and choice.

Another poem in this volume, "The Roofwalker," speaks again of entrapment. The poem's speaker is a builder or architect who is no longer satisfied with the enclosure he has built. The role of the artist is here redefined. Whereas "At a Bach Concert" celebrated the need for objectivity, distance, and form, the speaker of "The Roofwalker" feels constrained by forms: "Was it worth while to lay—/ with infinite exertion—/ a roof I can't live under?" The poet begins to wonder whether her tools—rhyme, alliteration, meter, poetic conventions—are stifling her imagination.

The well-planned house that Rich rejects in "The Roofwalker" is the house of formalist poetry as well. She finds the measured stanzas, rhymed couplets, and blank verse rhythms of her earlier books too rigid for her present purposes. Writing a poem no longer means finding a form for a preconceived idea. Instead, each experience informs its own expression; the poem is not product, but process. The poet, like "The Roofwalker," must break out of the stultifying traditional structure. Like most of her contemporaries, she has come to write in freer forms. Yet Rich never abandons rational structure or rootedness in social context as do some experimental writers.

NECESSITIES OF LIFE

Rich's next book, *Necessities of Life*, continues her movement toward a freer poetic line and toward subjectivity. Where she formerly spoke of history in terms of objects and products of tradition, she now identifies with historical persons (Antinous, Emily Dickinson, and others). A struggle between death and life, between winter and spring, is in process. Indoor-outdoor imagery carries the weight of these tensions. Poems of death and disappearance take place indoors; the expansive, life-enhancing experiences occur outdoors.

These poems are a retreat from the angry stance of "Snapshots of a Daughter-in-Law" and the daring escape of "The Roofwalker." In *Necessities of Life*, Rich feels oppressed by the human world, so she turns to nature for sustenance. *Necessities of Life* establishes a deep relationship with the world of nature; it is one of the "bare essentials" that preserve the heroine in her difficulties. Through a bond with the vegetable and animal world, the world of warmth and light, the book is able to bring life to bear against death and darkness. Nature's cyclical pattern provides clues for survival. Plants move from winter's icy grip into spring's renewal by learning to exist on little. To achieve similar rebirth, humans must consciously will change and force themselves into action. This is the pattern of death and rebirth that structures the book.

LEAFLETS

Rich's first four books are built on linear oppositions. Balanced groups of stanzas articulate dichotomies between art and emotion, control and chaos, passivity and action, indoors and outdoors. Often characters must choose between alternatives. Tension between polarities becomes a controlling force, focusing the poems' energies. In her next books of poetry, Rich would modify the dualistic structure of the earlier books. At the end of *Leaflets*, she introduces the *ghazal*, a series of two-line units that conflate many ideas. These poems are collagelike, offering multiple perspectives.

Prompted by her increasing social concern and the leftist political critique evolving in the middle and later 1960's, Rich turned from personal malaise to political struggle, from private meditation to public discourse. Her jarring tone reflects her anger and impatience with language. Rhythms are broken, speech is fragmented. The poems suggest hurried diary entries. Images of violence, guerrilla warfare, and global human suffering suggest an embattled society. Yet anger is close kin to hope: It asserts the wish to effect change. Therefore, alongside the destruction, symbols of fertility and rebirth appear.

Rich writes of an old tradition dying and a new one struggling to be born. Fear of change dominated her earlier books, but the "will to change" is paramount here. The poems of this period describe Rich's heroines casting off traditional roles and preparing for journeys. The titles of the next three books represent steps in this process. *Leaflets* is a manifesto for public involvement, *The Will to Change* is the determination to move forward, and *Diving into the Wreck*, the first title to contain a verb, is the act itself.

The evolution of *Leaflets* epitomizes Rich's movement from the personal to the political. The first poem, "Orion," is written in regular six-line stanzas and built on a typical pattern of balanced contrast. Indoors and outdoors, feminine and masculine, stagnation and adventure are the poles. The poem is a monologue in which the speaker blames herself for her failures as a woman. In contrast, the last poem in the book, "Ghazals," is a series of unrhymed couplets arranged in a seemingly random conflation of ideas and images. "Ghazals" is a multivoiced political critique of contemporary America. The heroes and heroines of the book are revolutionaries, protesters, and challengers of an old order: Frantz Fanon, Walt Whitman, Galileo, LeRoi Jones (Amiri Baraka), Eldridge Cleaver, and Dian Fossey. Turning her back on a political tradition that she now equates with death and destruction, Rich is saddened and estranged. However, she not only wants to last until the new tradition begins but also will attempt to create that new tradition. To do so, she must substitute new ideas and modes of expression for the old, wishing "to choose words that even you/ would have to be changed by" ("Implosions"). Because the values and attitudes she wants to modify are so deeply entrenched in people's most fundamental assumptions, language itself must be reshaped to provide a vocabulary equal to her task of reconstruction. Consequently, language becomes a crucial issue.

Rich believes that "only where there is language is there world" ("The Demon Lover"). She fears, however, that the English language is "spoiled." If the poet is using the "oppressor's language," how may her words avoid contamination?

THE WILL TO CHANGE

Rich's powerful meditation on language and power "The Burning of Paper Instead of Children" (in *The Will to Change*) draws on her classroom experience with disadvantaged students. Unlike the poet, whose privileged childhood opened the possibilities of language to her, the children of the ghetto find the worlds of literacy and power closed to them. Rich quotes a student whose grammatical awkwardness lends his description of poverty a pointed eloquence: "a child steal because he did not have money to buy it: to hear a mother say she do not have money to buy food for her children . . . it will make tears in your eyes." Because she mistrusts rhetoric, the poet closes her meditation with a prose passage of bald statement.

> I am in danger. You are in danger. The burning of a book arouses no sensation in me. I know it hurts to burn. There are flames of napalm in Catonsville, Maryland. I know it hurts to burn.

The typewriter is overheated, my mouth is burning, I cannot touch you and this is the oppressor's language.

Her simple syntax affirms her identification with the disadvantaged student, the oppressed. In her refusal to use complex diction or traditional metrics she argues by implication for a rhetoric of honesty and simplicity.

DIVING INTO THE WRECK

Rich's poetry revises the heroic myth to reflect women's experiences. *Diving into the Wreck* presents questing female heroes for the first time in her work. On their quests, they reconnect with lost parts of themselves, discover their own power, and build commonality with other women. Women's lives are the central focus as Rich's project becomes that of giving voice to women's experience, developing a "common language" that will bring the "dark country" of women's lives into the common light of day. Yet Rich also claims another task for women: They must struggle to redeem an endangered society. She argues that patriarchy's exaggerated aggressiveness, competition, and repression of feeling have led Western civilization to the brink of extinction. The task of reconstruction must be taken up by women. Working for change, the women in this book seek to turn civilization from its destructive paths by persuasion, creation of new myths, or redirection of anger.

To understand and overcome patriarchy's suicidal impulses, Rich attempts to open a dialogue. Almost all the poems in *Diving into the Wreck* are cast as dialogue. Conversation is the book's central metaphor for poetry. The book begins with "Trying to Talk with a Man," a poem that deals with the dangers of an accelerating arms race but also has a deeper subject: the creation of a dialogue between men and women. Considering gender a political issue, Rich calls on men to join her in rethinking gender questions.

The book, however, comes to question the possibility of real communication. "Translations" examines the gulf between the languages spoken by women and men. In "Meditations for a Savage Child," the concluding poem, scientists cannot teach the child to speak.

POEMS: SELECTED AND NEW, 1950-1974

Poems: Selected and New, 1950-1974 includes early unpublished poems and several new ones. In the final poem of this book, "From an Old House in America," Rich uses the home image as a starting point for a reconsideration of American history from a woman's point of view. She reimagines the lives of women, from immigrants to pioneers to the new generation of feminist activists. All are journeying. Simple and direct in language, written in stanzas of open couplets, the poem is a stream-of-consciousness meditation that builds in force as it imagines the unwritten history of North American women and reaches a profound celebration of sisterhood.

Thus, by the end of the book, the woman at home is transformed from the cautious door-closer of "Storm Warnings" (*A Change of World*) into the active participant in history and the questing adventurer eager to define herself by exploration and new experience.

THE DREAM OF A COMMON LANGUAGE

Transformation is the cornerstone of *The Dream of a Common Language* and *A Wild Patience Has Taken Me This Far*. The poet wishes to effect fundamental changes in social arrangements, in concepts of selfhood, in governmental politics, in the meanings of sexuality, and in language. To that end, transformation supplants her earlier idea of revolution.

The title *The Dream of a Common Language* suggests vision, community, and above all a language in which visions and shared experience may be conceived and expressed. Dream is the voice of the nocturnal, unconscious self breaking into daytime existence. The terrain Rich explores here is the unknown country of the self, discovered in dream, myth, vision, and ritual. Like dreams, the poems telescope time and space to make new connections among past, present, and future, between home and world. "Common" signifies that which is communal, habitual, shared, widely used, and ordinary. Rich sets great value on the common, choosing it over the extraordinary.

In *The Dream of a Common Language*, the poet affirms that poetry stems from "the drive/ to connect. The dream of a common language." The book's central section, "Twenty-One Love Poems," orchestrates the controlling themes of women's love, power, language, world. Images of light and dark, dream and reality, speech and silence, home and wanderer structure the sequence. There are in fact twenty-two poems, for Rich has included an unnumbered "Floating Poem." Drawing from the sonnet tradition, Rich breaks formal conventions by varying the poems' lengths and departing from strict rhyme and meter. The sequence records a particular lesbian relationship, its joyous beginnings, the difficulties encountered, and the termination of the relationship. The poems ask questions about the meanings of self, language, and love between women, and about the possibilities of sustaining love in a hostile world. Rich insists on grounding her explorations in the quotidian as well as the oneiric world. To be "at home" in the world requires coming to terms with the ugliness and brutality of the city, the pain and wounds, as well as the beauty of love and poetry. Deliberately, Rich situates the first sonnet of her sequence "in this city," with its "rainsoaked garbage."

Because she wishes to escape false romanticism, Rich seeks to connect the poems firmly to the world of daily life, to avoid sentimentality, and to speak honestly of her feelings. Because she wishes to transform the self-effacing behavior that has typically characterized women in love, she stresses self-awareness and deliberate choice. Caves and circles—images of roundness, completeness, and wholeness—are dominant. Like the homes of Rich's earlier work, they are enclosures; however, the meaning of encirclement has been transformed, for in her new vision, the poet no longer escapes from the world in her narrow room but reaches out to include the world, to bring it within her protected circle.

Poem 21, the final poem of the sequence, is a complex network of dreamlike associations, of ritual and archetypal memory. In the sonnet, Rich moves from dark into light, from the prehistoric into the present, from inanimate nature ("the color of stone") into purposeful consciousness ("more than stone"). She becomes by choice "a figure in the light." The clarity of intelligence—"a cleft of light"—shapes her purpose. In drawing the circle, she deliberately chooses her place.

Particularly in the last three poems of the book, there is a sacramental quality, as Rich affirms her fusion with a world of women working together throughout time. Weaving, cooking, and caring for children, they are crafting beautiful and utilitarian objects such as ceramic vessels, quilts, and clothing. Through these tasks, they create mementos of their lives and carry out the work of making a world.

"Transcendental Etude" is a long meditative poem of great richness and power. It traces the course of birth, death, and rebirth through a creativity that heals splits in the natural world and within the self. The poem begins in the pastoral imagery of an August evening and ranges over the realms of nature and of human life. Rich's vision here transforms the poet's craft. As a poet, she need not be, as she had once feared, an egocentric artist seeking undying fame at the expense of those she loves. Instead, through participation in the life of the physical universe, she articulates the patterns of her own being, of life itself. Thus, Rich's new metaphor of the poet is at once the most daring and the most simple: The poet is a common woman.

Achieving a selfhood that encompasses both creative work and human relationships, egotism and altruism, Rich and her women heal their psychic split in the symbolic return to home, to the full self represented by the circle. The voyage into history, the unconsciousness, the mind is completed in the return.

EXPLORING WOMEN'S SHARED PASTS

The next group of books—*A Wild Patience Has Taken Me This Far*, *Sources*, *The Fact of a Doorframe*, *Your Native Land, Your Life*, and *Time's Power*—continue to develop the themes broached in *The Dream of a Common Language*: exploration of women's shared past, the struggle to be "at home" in a strife-torn world, the vision of transforming the self and the world. Here again the imagery is that of simple, ordinary objects important to women's lives: books, kettles, and beets. Yet these books speak in a more muted voice, the voice of resolution, acceptance, accomplishment, with less anger.

A Wild Patience Has Taken Me This Far is to a large extent a dialogue with nineteenth century women writers and thinkers: the Brontës, Susan B. Anthony, Elizabeth Barrett Browning. "Culture and Anarchy" takes its title from Matthew Arnold's essay on nineteenth century culture. Arnold longed for a literate, elite, verbal culture; Rich, on the other hand, celebrates a world of women's work, both verbal and nonverbal. Here, growing and cooking vegetables, responding to nature's seasonal rhythms, the simple tasks of women's lives, form a valuable cultural matrix out of which arise the heroic actions of individual women.

Rich's poem is a quilting together of the words of historical women (derived from the diaries and letters of Emily Dickinson, Susan B. Anthony, Elizabeth Barrett Browning, and Jane Addams) and meditation on her own life and work. The women's voices here replace the quotations of male words in "Snapshots of a Daughter-in-Law." Again, Rich telescopes time, bringing the earlier women into the circle of her life, joining them in their acts and visions.

In *Sources*, Rich returns to her past and engages in a dialogue with her dead father and husband. She is trying to come to terms with her own life and to put the lives of the others into perspective. *Your Native Land, Your Life* and *Time's Power* continue to develop the persona of the poet as representative woman facing the issues of her country and time. Language and poetry and their relation to history remain foci of concern: in "North American Time" she writes

> Poetry never stood a chance
> of standing outside history.
> . . . .
> We move   but our words stand
> become responsible
> for more than we intended

In the ruefully ironic "Blue Rock" she writes

> Once when I wrote poems they did not change
> left overnight on the page
> . . . .
> But now I know what happens while I sleep
> and when I wake the poem has changed:
> the facts have dilated it, or cancelled it.

Time's Power is a book of dialogue, with the poet's mother, her lover, and a cast of historical figures. "Letters in the Family" is a series of imagined letters written by fictionalized historical persons, such as a friend of the Hungarian partisan Chana Senesh or a South African mother writing to her child. The book ends with "Turning," a poem of quest for knowledge. It articulates a question the poet-speaker asks as she tries to understand her ongoing quest: "So why am I out here, trying/ to read your name in the illegible air?"

Midnight Salvage

Rich subtly moves toward a quieter wisdom in *Midnight Salvage*, passing the torch and trying to impart to future readers and writers what she has learned and how she learned it. In doing so, she reminisces of her girlhood and her past selves' varied goals and causes, perhaps best captured in the title poem, an ambitious, eight-section piece that sorts through her history. Her experience with aging and illness brings forth the subject matter of physical torture. "Shattered Head" ranges from one body's devastation ("a life hauls itself uphill") to the betrayal of the many, and by the end of the poem, to the victims of torture or warfare ("who did this to us?"). Her work continues to be combative, yet in this volume, it is in a quiet, more indirect way.

Fox

Fox continues to meld Rich's art with conviction, her familiar attentions to social injustice and intense personal introspection still present. She praises, commemorates, and questions friends and public figures, while also probing what political action means. Her usual strident tone makes a small retreat here, however, and her voice is less edgy, a little more malleable, than in previous collections. As she declares in "Regardless," a poem about loving a man, "we'd love/ regardless of manifestoes I wrote or signed." Yet familiar themes are present, whether she is writing about war in the long, provocative poem "Veterans Day," female identity in the searing title poem, or the violence witnessed by a woman in "Second Sight," and Rich continues to give voice to the most fundamental of feelings.

Poetic evolution

Rich's successive volumes of poetry reveal her development as poet and as woman. As she breaks out from restrictive traditions, her voice is achieving power and authenticity. From a poet of isolation and withdrawal, of constraint and despair, she has become a seer of wide-ranging communal sympathy and great imaginative possibility. She is redefining in her life and poetry the meanings of language, poetry, love, power, and home. In her earlier life and work, she accepted patriarchal definitions. Consequently, she felt trapped in personal and poetic conventions: a marriage that curbed her creativity, an aesthetic that split form and feeling, a language that ignored her experience, a position of powerlessness.

At first, she spoke in a derivative voice, the language of the "universal." Reluctant to speak as a woman, she echoed the tone of her male poetic ancestors. Because she hesitated to voice her own experience, her early poems are highly polished but avoid emotional depth. She grew to mistrust a language that seemed alien. The fragmented, provisional, stark poems of *Leaflets*, *The Will to Change*, and *Diving into the Wreck* record her groping toward a new language in which to voice her deepest concerns. In subsequent books, she wrote in a freer form, viewing poems as "speaking to their moment."

This stance is particularly noticeable in such works of the 1990's as *An Atlas of the Difficult World*, with its powerhouse title poem, *Dark Fields of the Republic*, and *Midnight Salvage*. These volumes, produced almost on schedule every three or four years, also suggest less urgency and a more relaxed authority as a voice at once personal and representative. In *Fox*, there seems to be a gradual falling off of intensity, a quieter wisdom, as Rich moves into her seventies.

Through the major phases of her career, the transformations of Rich's home imagery parallel her growth of poetic force and political awareness. In early poems, the home was entrapping, because patriarchal voices defined women's roles. As Rich's women became more self-defining, the old relationships were abandoned or modified to fit the real needs of the persons involved. Achieving selfhood, Rich's female heroes came to seize control of their homes, their lives. Through metaphorical journeys exploring the world, women's history, and their own psychic heights and depths, they struggle for knowledge and self-mastery. Healing their tormenting self-division, they grow more "at home" in the world. They recognize and cherish their links to a women's tradition of great power and beauty and to the natural world. In this process, the idea of home has acquired new significance: from frail shelter or painful trap it has grown to a gateway, the starting point for journeys of self-exploration, and the magic circle to which women return so that they may participate in the work of "making and remaking" the world.

OTHER MAJOR WORKS

NONFICTION: *Of Woman Born: Motherhood as Experience and Institution*, 1976; *On Lies, Secrets, and Silence: Selected Prose, 1966-1978*, 1979; *Blood, Bread, and Poetry: Selected Prose, 1979-1985*, 1986; *What Is Found There: Notebooks on Poetry and Politics*, 1993, 2003; *Arts of the Possible: Essays and Conversations*, 2001; *Poetry and Commitment: An Essay*, 2007; *A Human Eye: Essays on Art in Society, 1997-2008*, 2009.

EDITED TEXTS: *The Best American Poetry, 1996*, 1996; *Selected Poems / Muriel Rukeyser*, 2004.

MISCELLANEOUS: *Adrienne Rich's Poetry and Prose: Poems, Prose, Reviews, and Criticism*, 1993 (Barbara Chartesworth Gelpi and Albert Gelpi, editors).

BIBLIOGRAPHY

Cooper, Jane Roberta, ed. *Reading Adrienne Rich: Review and Re-visions, 1951-1981*. Ann Arbor: University of Michigan Press, 1984. A useful collection of reviews and critical studies of Rich's poetry and prose. It includes Auden's foreword to *A Change of World* and other significant essays. The aim is for breadth and balance.

Dickie, Margaret. *Stein, Bishop, and Rich: Lyrics of Love, War, and Place*. Chapel Hill: University of North Carolina Press, 1997. Examination of the poets Rich, Gertrude Stein, and Elizabeth Bishop. Three of the book's nine chapters are devoted to Rich. Bibliography, index.

Estrin, Barbara L. *The American Love Lyric After Auschwitz and Hiroshima.* New York: Palgrave, 2001. Estrin finds a connection between the language of the love lyric and hate speech. Using the specific examples of Rich, Wallace Stevens, and Robert Lowell, she expresses a revisionist critique of twentieth American poetry, supporting the theory that the love lyric is political.

Gelpi, Barbara Charlesworth, and Albert Gelpi, eds. *Adrienne Rich's Poetry and Prose.* New York: W. W. Norton, 1993. This volume in the Norton Critical Edition series presents a significant sampling of Rich's work, biographical materials, and a carefully representative selection of essays (sometimes excerpted) and reviews. It provides a chronology and a list of selected criticism for further study.

Keyes, Claire. *The Aesthetics of Power: The Poetry of Adrienne Rich.* Athens: University of Georgia Press, 1986. Keyes discusses Rich as a feminist poet. Introduction provides a biographical and historical overview. Each of the ten chapters discusses one of Rich's books, from *A Change of World* through *A Wild Patience Has Taken Me This Far.*

Langdell, Cheryl Colby. *Adrienne Rich: The Moment of Change.* Westport, Conn.: Praeger, 2004. This biography of Rich traces her several transformations through analyses of her poems.

Ratcliffe, Krista. *Anglo-American Feminist Challenges to the Rhetorical Traditions: Virginia Woolf, Mary Daly, Adrienne Rich.* Carbondale: Southern Illinois University Press, 1996. A feminist perspective on the rhetoric and literary devices of writers-critics Rich, Virginia Woolf, and Mary Daly. Bibliography, index.

Templeton, Alice. *The Dream and the Dialogue: Adrienne Rich's Feminist Poetics.* Knoxville: University of Tennessee Press, 1994. Templeton finds each of Rich's volumes both responsive to and party to the dominant critical issues at the time of publication. Templeton's exploration of Rich's "feminist poetics" posits feminism as a way of reading literature, so that reading in itself becomes a political act.

Waddell, William S., ed. *"Catch If You Can Your Country's Moment": Recovery and Regeneration in the Poetry of Adrienne Rich.* Newcastle, England: Cambridge Scholars, 2007. A collection of eight essays on Rich's poetry that focuses on the themes of recovery and regeneration. Looks at her development from a poet dealing with feminist personal topics to one dealing with public, political issues.

Yorke, Liz. *Adrienne Rich: Passion, Politics, and the Body.* Newbury Park, Calif.: Sage, 1998. This accessible introduction to Rich's work reviews the process and development of her ideas, tracing her place in the major debates within second-wave feminism. Yorke assesses Rich's contribution to feminism and outlines her ideas on motherhood, heterosexuality, lesbian identity, Jewish identity, and issues of racial and sexual otherness.

Karen F. Stein; Philip K. Jason
Updated by Sarah Hilbert

ARTHUR RIMBAUD

Born: Charleville, France; October 20, 1854
Died: Marseilles, France; November 10, 1891

PRINCIPAL POETRY
Une Saison en enfer, 1873 (*A Season in Hell*, 1932)
Les Illuminations, 1886 (*Illuminations*, 1932)

OTHER LITERARY FORMS
The impact of Arthur Rimbaud (ram-BOH) on the literary world stems entirely from his poetry.

ACHIEVEMENTS
Arthur Rimbaud's meteoric career has forever earned for him a place as the brilliant *enfant terrible* of French verse. Since his death, he has attracted more critical attention than any French poet save Stéphane Mallarmé. A revolutionary both in his life and in his art, Rimbaud exerted a radical influence on the scope and direction of French poetry. He has been credited with introducing *vers libre* (free verse), which would come to dominate modern poetry, and his systematic cultivation of dreams, hallucinations, and madness anticipated modern interest in the irrational side of the human mind. He became, for a time, the patron saint of André Breton and the Surrealists. Rimbaud's conception of the poetical "I" as "other" ("Je est un autre") has been acclaimed as an intuitive perception of the unconscious that predated its mapping bySigmund Freud. Finally, Rimbaud was the first French literary figure to sound a distinctly feminist note in his writings, condemning the cultural repression of women and looking forward to a future day of liberation when they would assume their rightful place in society and art. Faithful to his own precept, "Il faut être absolument moderne" ("We must be absolutely modern"), he prefigured key trends in modern art and thought.

BIOGRAPHY
Jean-Nicolas-Arthur Rimbaud was born in the provincial town of Charleville on the Franco-Prussian border. His mother, Vitalie Cuif, was of peasant stock and a devout Jansenist; his father, Captain Frédéric Rimbaud, was an itinerant army officer who abandoned the family when Rimbaud was only six years old. A brilliant student, Rimbaud completed nine years of schooling in eight, earning numerous literary prizes in the course of his studies. His earliest attempts at verse were in Latin, followed by his first poem in French, "Les Étrennes des orphelins" ("The Orphans' New Year's Day Gifts"), published in January, 1870. Encouraged by his teacher, Georges Izambard,

Arthur Rimbaud
(Library of Congress)

Rimbaud sent off three poems to the Parnassian poet Théodore de Banville, who, however, failed to express any interest.

The outbreak of the Franco-Prussian War in July, 1870, put an end to Rimbaud's formal schooling. Alienated by the hypocrisy of provincial society, which he satirized in various poems composed in the early months of 1870, he ran away from home three times: first to Paris, then to Belgium, and again to Paris. He was back in Charleville when the Paris Commune was declared on March 18, 1871. Although much critical attention has been devoted to Rimbaud's possible ties with the Commune, there is no clear evidence that he ever left Charleville during the crucial period of the Paris uprising. On May 15, Rimbaud composed his celebrated "Lettre du voyant" ("Seer Letter"), addressed to a friend, Paul Demeny. Rimbaud's break with traditional poetry was by this time already complete, and on August 15, he again wrote to Banville, enclosing a new poem, "Ce qu'on dit au poète à propos de fleurs" ("What One Says to the Poet in Regard to Flowers"), a vitriolic attack on Parnassian poetics. Shortly thereafter, Rimbaud also sent off eight new poems, in two installments, to Paul Verlaine, who responded with the famous phrase "Venez, chère grande âme, on vous appelle, on vous attend" ("Come, dear great soul, we call to you, we await you").

Rimbaud arrived in the capital with a copy of his newly composed poem, "Le Bateau ivre" ("The Drunken Boat"), which brought him some notoriety among the Parisian literary crowd. The young poet's obnoxious behavior soon alienated him, however, both from Verlaine's family and his fellow artists, and March , 1872, found him back in Charleville. Rimbaud returned to Paris in May and there began a series of escapades with Verlaine that some have characterized as simply youthful exuberance and others as an unhappy love affair. The pair fled first to Brussels, then to London, where a quarrel erupted. Verlaine returned to Brussels, where he was soon followed by Rimbaud.

In Brussels, events soon took a tragic turn. In a moment of drunken rage, Verlaine fired on Rimbaud, wounding him slightly in the hand. The incident might have ended there, but Verlaine later accosted Rimbaud in the street, and the frightened youth sought help from a passing police officer. The authorities intervened, and Verlaine was sentenced to two years in prison. Rimbaud returned to his mother's family farm at Roche, where he completed *A Season in Hell*, begun in April. In late 1873, Rimbaud again visited Paris, where he made the acquaintance of the young poet Germain Nouveau, with whom he traveled to London in the early months of 1874. Almost nothing is known of this second friendship beyond the fact that it ended with Nouveau's abrupt return to Paris in June of that year.

In 1875, Rimbaud embarked on a new series of travels that led him to Stuttgart, across the Swiss Alps on foot into Italy, and back to Charleville via Paris. After visiting Vienna in April, 1876, he enlisted in the Dutch colonial army on May 19 and set sail for Java. He deserted ship in Batavia (modern Djakarta) and returned to Charleville. In May, 1877, Rimbaud was in Bremen, where he attempted (in vain) to enlist in the American Marines. Subsequent travels the same year took him to Stockholm, Copenhagen, Marseilles, Rome, and back to Charleville. In early 1878, he visited Hamburg, returning during the summer to work on the family farm at Roche. In October, he again traversed Switzerland on foot, crossing the Alps into Italy. There he took the train to Genoa and embarked for Alexandria, later departing for Cyprus, where he worked as a foreman in a marble quarry. Stricken with typhoid, he returned to Charleville in May, 1879 , once again spending the summer at Roche. In March, 1880, he was back in Cyprus, where he found work as a construction foreman. An intemperate climate and a salary dispute soon forced him to resign his position and to seek employment elsewhere.

Rimbaud spent the remaining eleven years of his life as the business agent of a French colonial trading company in the remote wilds of Abyssinia (modern-day Ethiopia) and Aden. At the end of this time, he had amassed, through agonizing labor and in the face of constant adversity, the modest sum of 150,000 francs (approximately 30,000 dollars). In February, 1891, intense pain in his right knee forced him to return to France for medical treatment. Doctors in Marseilles diagnosed his illness as cancer and ordered the immediate amputation of the infected right leg. The cancer proved too widespread to check, however, and Rimbaud died in a state of delirium on November 10, 1891. According to a tradition spawned by his devout sister, Isabelle, who was with the poet in his final moments, Rimbaud returned to Catholicism on his deathbed. Since Isabelle is, however, known to have tampered with her brother's personal letters, critics have given little credence to her testimony.

Analysis

Arthur Rimbaud's early verse (of which he published only three short pieces in various academic bulletins) falls into two general categories. First, there is his satiric verse, exemplified by such poems as "Les Premières Communions" ("First Communions") and "Les Assis" ("The Seated Ones"), which attacks religious hypocrisy and the sterility of bourgeois society. Second, there is his erotic verse, typified by such poems as "Vénus anadyomène" ("Venus Emerging from the Waves") and "Le Coeur volé" ("The Stolen Heart"), which speaks of the trauma of sexual coming-of-age. A pastiche of traditional styles and forms, these initial works nevertheless evidence a brilliant gift for verbal expression and announce the theme of revolt which informs all Rimbaud's writings.

"Seer Letter"

On May 15, 1871, Rimbaud declared his emancipation from traditional poetics in his celebrated "Seer Letter," addressed to his friend Paul Demeny. This letter, Rimbaud's *ars poetica*, begins with a contemptuous denunciation of all previous poetry as nothing more than rhymed prose. Only Charles Baudelaire, "un vrai dieu" ("a true god"), is spared and, even then, only partially—he frequented a self-consciously artistic milieu, and he failed to find new forms of expression. Rimbaud then calls for a radically new conception of the poet's mission: "Car je est un autre" ("For I is an other"). It is the essential task of the poet to give voice to the repressed, unconscious "other" that lies concealed behind the mask of the rational, Cartesian "I"—the "other" that societal restrictions have condemned to silence. This can be accomplished only by "un long, immense et raisonné dérèglement de tous les sens" ("a long, immense and reasoned derangement of all the senses"). Unlike his Romantic predecessors and such Symbolist contemporaries as Mallarmé, who passively awaited the return of the muse, Rimbaud insists on the active role the poet must take: "Le Poète se fait voyant" ("The poet makes himself a seer"). The poet must actively cultivate dreams, hallucinations, and madness. In so doing, he becomes the great liberator of humanity, a Prometheus who steals fire from the gods, the spokesperson for all those whom society has ostracized: "Il devient entre tous le grand malade, le grand criminel, le grand maudit—et le grand Savant!" ("He becomes, more than anyone, the great sick one, the great criminal, the great accursed one—and the great Learned One!"). Such a poet will be "un multiplicateur de progrès" whose genius, unrestrained by societal taboos and the limitations of rational thought, will lead humankind into a new golden age.

Throughout the remaining months of 1871 and the following year, Rimbaud endeavored to give form to this poetic vision in a new series of songs and verse that are best exemplified by two poems that critics have universally acclaimed as masterpieces: "Le Bateau ivre" ("The Drunken Boat") and "Voyelles" ("Vowels").

"The Drunken Boat"

Perhaps the best known of Rimbaud's works, "The Drunken Boat" was composed during the summer of 1871 and presented to Verlaine in September of that same year. Although the work borrows from a wide variety of sources (Victor Hugo, Baudelaire, Jules Verne, and Vicomte Chateaubriand, to name but a few), it remains a stunning and original tour de force—particularly for a young poet of sixteen. The poem, composed of twenty-five quatrains in classical Alexandrines and narrated in the first person, is a symbolic drama in three acts. In the first act (quatrains 1 through 4), set on a vast river in the New World, the boat recounts its escape from its haulers, who are massacred by screaming natives, and its subsequent descent toward the sea. There follows a brief, transitional interlude (quatrain 5) in which the boat passes through a ritual purification: Its wooden shell is permeated by the seawater that cleanses it of wine stains and vomit and bears off the boat's rudder and anchor.

The second and central act (quatrains 6 through 22) tells of the boat's intoxicating maritime adventures and its fantastic, hallucinatory vision of a transcendental reality that ordinary mortals have only glimpsed in passing. Yet, the boat's long and frenetic voyage of discovery ultimately begins to turn sour. After braving whirlpools, hurricanes, raging seas, and Leviathans from the deep, the boat unexpectedly declares its nostalgia for the ancient parapets of Europe.

In the third and final act (quatrains 23 through 25), the boat's delirious optimism turns to anguished despair. Its quest for the absolute has at length proved futile, and the boat now seeks dissolution in death. If it desires a return to European waters, it is to the cold, black puddle into which a sad, impoverished child releases a boat as frail as a May butterfly. At the same time, the boat realizes the impossibility of any turning back to its previous mode of existence. It can no longer follow in the wake of the merchant ships, nor bear the haughty pride of the military gunboats, nor swim beneath the horrible eyes of the prison ships that lie at anchor in the harbor.

"The Drunken Boat" reflects both Rimbaud's new conception of the poet as "seer" and the influence of the French Symbolists, such as Verlaine and Baudelaire, who sought to replace the effusive, personalized verse of the Romantics with a symbolic, impersonal mode of expression. Critics have generally equated the work's "protagonist," the boat, with the poet himself, reading the poem as a symbolic account of Rimbaud's own efforts to transcend reality through language. Most critics are also agreed that the poem's final two stanzas, while they suggest the advent of a new self-awareness, evince a disillusionment with the "seer" experiment and prefigure Rimbaud's later renunciation of poetry.

"Vowels"

Rimbaud's celebrated sonnet "Vowels," written in decasyllabic verse, dates from the same period as "The Drunken Boat" and was similarly presented to Verlaine in September, 1871. Another of Rimbaud's "seer" poems, the work postulates a mystic correspondence between vowels and colors: "A noir, E blanc, I rouge, U vert, O bleu" ("A black, E white, I red, U green, O blue"). The poem has its literary source in Baudelaire's famous sonnet "Correspondences," which had asserted an underlying connection between sounds, perfumes, and colors and had popularized the concept of synesthesia. Another probable source for the work has been found in an illustrated alphabet primer that Rimbaud may have read as a child and that has served to elucidate some of the sonnet's enigmatic imagery.

Perhaps the most ingenious interpretation of the poem is that of the critic Lucien Sausy, who argued that the work exploits correspondences not between sound and color (there are, in fact, few traces of such matching within the phonetic content of the poem) but rather between the visual form of the vowels themselves and the images to which the latter are linked: *A*, if inverted, thus suggests the delta-shaped body of a fly; *E* (written as a Greek epsilon in the manuscript), if turned on its side, suggests vapors, tents, and glaciers; and so on. (Sausy's interpretation, first advanced in *Les Nouvelles Littéraires*, September 2, 1933, is available in the notes to the Pléiade edition of Rimbaud's works.) As a counterbalance, however, one might mention Verlaine's explanation of the sonnet: "Rimbaud saw things that way and that's all there is to it."

A Season in Hell

By his own account, Rimbaud composed *A Season in Hell* during the period from April to August of 1873. Rimbaud supervised the book's publication, and it was printed in Brussels in the fall of 1873 in an edition of five hundred copies. Rimbaud was unable, however, to pay the printing costs, and this first edition, save for six author's copies that circulated among his friends, remained in the attic of a Brussels publishing house until discovered in 1901 by a Belgian bibliophile, who did not make his discovery public until 1914.

The text, which Rimbaud had originally intended to entitle "Livre païen" (pagan book) or "Livre nègre" (Negro book—the French adjective is pejorative), consists of nine prose poems and seven poems in verse, the latter all contained within the section "Délires II" ("Deliria II"). The work has been variously acclaimed by critics for its original and stunning verbal display, its fantastic, visionary imagery, and its prophetic pronouncements concerning Rimbaud's own future. As the title indicates, *A Season in Hell* is Rimbaud's poetic attempt to come to grips with his recent "dark night of the soul"—his unhappy adventure with Verlaine and his anguished experience as "seer." Viewed from the perspective of Rimbaud's own metaphysical dictum—"I is an other"—the work, narrated in the first person, recounts a confrontation between the rational, conscious "I" and the irrational, unconscious "other" which the poet had systematically worked to cultivate.

The text opens with a brief introductory section (untitled) in which the poet evokes with longing his lost state of childhood innocence. He recalls his frenzied flight from reason, his revolt against traditional concepts of beauty and morality, his pursuit of crime, and his cultivation of madness. He momentarily dreams of regaining his former state of innocence through a return to Christian charity but immediately rejects the latter as an empty illusion. Inescapably condemned to death and damnation, he dedicates his opus not to the traditional poetic Muse but rather to Satan. This introductory segment serves to announce the key themes that the body of the work will subsequently develop: the abandonment of the "seer" experiment, the nostalgia for the comfort afforded by traditional Christian values, and the attainment of a new self-awareness that, however, prevents any naïve return to the past.

"BAD BLOOD"

In the following prose poem, "Mauvais Sang" ("Bad Blood"), the poet attributes his failure to transcend the vulgar world or reality to some inherited defect that now condemns him to a life of manual toil. Nor does he envision any hope in the progress promised by Cartesian rationalism and the advent of science. The world may yet be headed toward total destruction. Disillusioned with Western civilization, he seeks imaginative shelter in what he perceives as the savage freedom of black African society. His amoral utopia is, however, destroyed by the arrival of the white colonialists, who impose their debilitating Christian ethics by force of arms. Momentarily seduced by Christianity, the poet ultimately rejects it as an infringement on human freedom and refuses to embark on a honeymoon with Jesus Christ as father-in-law. Rather than remain enslaved, he hurls himself to his death beneath the horses of the conquering Europeans.

"NIGHT IN HELL"

The conflict between Christianity and paganism is further developed in "Nuit de l'enfer" ("Night in Hell "). Here, the poet is engulfed in the fires of Hell, to which his parents have condemned him through baptism and catechism lessons. His suffering derives from his inability to choose between the absolute but terrible freedom offered by Satan and the serene but limited freedom promised by the Christian God. Hell, in short, is a state of eternal and lucid alienation.

"Deliria I"

"Délires I" ("Deliria I") introduces a "Viérge folle" ("Foolish Virgin") who recounts her difficult life with "l'Époux infernal" ("The Infernal Spouse") who seduced her with the false promise of an amoral and transcendent Paradise. Numerous critics have found in this passage a mythic retelling of Verlaine's intellectual and erotic seduction by Rimbaud; other critics have preferred to read the passage as emblematic of the seduction of the poet's rational and moral self by his own irrational and amoral unconscious. In either case, the poem is a bitter indictment of Rimbaud's failed efforts to transform reality.

"Deliria II"

In "Délires II" ("Deliria II"), subtitled "L'Alchimie du verbe" ("Verbal Alchemy"), the poet looks back on what he now views as an act of folly: his attempt to transcend reality through the systematic cultivation of the irrational and the invention of a new language that would draw in all the human senses and give voice to everything in humans that had previously been barred from expression. He gives as tangible examples of this enterprise six verse poems, the visionary imagery of which speaks symbolically of his hunger and thirst for the absolute, his frustration with past theology and future technology, and his fervent conviction that he has indeed found the mystic line of juncture between sea and sky, body and soul, the known and unknown. This metaphysical quest has ultimately failed, the poet says, for he has been damned by the rainbow—an ironic allusion to the rainbow sent by God to Noah as a sign of future redemption. As his dream-filled night draws to a close, and morning approaches, the poet awakes to hear the strains of the hymn "Christus venit" (Christ has come) resounding through the somber cities of the world. His career as "seer" has ended with the bleak dawn of reality.

"The Impossible," "Lightning," "Morning," and "Farewell"

The four remaining prose poems, all of them brief, further expand on major themes in the work. In "L'Impossible" ("The Impossible"), the poet tells of his futile efforts to reconcile Christianity and Eastern mysticism and his ultimate rejection of both. In "Éclair" ("Lightning"), the poet finds momentary comfort in the dignity of work but cannot avoid perceiving the vanity of all human efforts in the face of death and dissolution. "Matin" ("Morning") announces the end of the poet's night in Hell. In spite of the limitations imposed by the human condition, he chooses life over death. Although all men are slaves, they should not curse life. In the final passage, "Adieu" ("Farewell"), the poet renounces his unsuccessful career as "seer" in favor of a newfound divine clarity, the anguished self-knowledge that his experience has brought him. There will be no turning back to the past for solace, nor any attempt to seek oblivion in the love of a woman. Humans must be absolutely modern, the poet declares; for himself, he is content to possess the truth that humans are both body and soul.

ILLUMINATIONS

Illuminations was published in 1886, without Rimbaud's knowledge. Some years earlier, he had left a manuscript of the work with Verlaine, whence it passed through several hands before it was published in the Symbolist periodical *La Vogue*, appearing in book form (edited and with a preface by Verlaine) later in the same year.

Although a century has passed since the first appearance of *Illuminations*, a number of fundamental questions concerning the collection remain to be resolved and perhaps will never be definitely resolved. First there is the matter of the title. The manuscript itself is untitled, and the only evidence for the title by which the collection is known is the statement of Paul Verlaine, a notoriously unreliable witness. In a letter written in 1878 to his brother-in-law, Charles de Sivry, Verlaine says: "Have re-read *Illuminations* (painted plates)...." Later, in the preface to the first edition of *Illuminations*, he adds that "the word [that is, "illuminations"] is English and means *gravures coloriées*, colored plates," claiming that this was the subtitle that Rimbaud had chosen for the work.

The question of the title and subtitle may seem a mere scholarly quibble, but it is more than that, for at issue is the significance that Rimbaud himself attached to the title and, by extension, the spirit in which he intended the work to be read. Some critics, accepting Verlaine's testimony without qualification, suggest that by "painted plates" or "colored plates," Rimbaud meant the cheap colored prints that had recently become widely available. The tone of the title, then, would be highly ironic. Other critics suggest that Verlaine garbled Rimbaud's meaning—that Rimbaud had in mind the illuminated manuscripts of the Middle Ages. Still others reject Verlaine's testimony on this matter as another of his fabrications, arguing that by "illuminations" Rimbaud meant moments of spiritual insight; some readers have seen in the title a reference to the occult doctrines of Illuminism.

Another important debate concerns the date of composition. It was long believed that *Illuminations* preceded *A Season in Hell*, but later this assumption was seriously challenged. Again, the question of dating may appear to be of interest only to specialists, but such is not the case. The conclusion to *A Season in Hell* has been widely regarded as Rimbaud's farewell to poetry. If, in fact, he wrote *Illuminations* after *A Season in Hell*, many existing critical interpretations are invalid or in need of substantial revision.

This argument for dating *Illuminations* after *A Season in Hell* is primarily based on the pioneering research of Henri de Bouillane de Lacoste. Bouillane de Lacoste's graphological analysis of the manuscript, in conjunction with other, more subjective, arguments, has persuaded many scholars to accept Verlaine's once-rejected assertion that the work was written during the period from 1873 to 1875 in the course of Rimbaud's European travels. On the other hand, there are a number of reputable Rimbaud scholars who find Bouillane de Lacoste's analysis inconclusive at best and who thus retain the old chronology. In any case, one cannot know with certainty the date of composition of the individual poems themselves, nor is there any clear indication of the final order in which Rimbaud intended them to appear. The reason for Rimbaud's prolongation of his poetic career beyond his abdication from poetry in *A Season in Hell* seems destined to remain a mystery.

Illuminations is regarded by many critics as Rimbaud's most original work and his consummate contribution to French poetry. Although it represents a continuation of the "seer" experiment conducted in his earlier verse, it also marks a radical departure from the narrative, anecdotal, and descriptive modes of expression to be found in his previous poetry and in that of his contemporaries. The poems in *Illuminations* are strikingly modern in that each forms a self-contained, self-referential unit that stands independent of the collection as a whole and remains detached from any clear point of reference in the world of reality. They do not purport to convey any didactic, moral, or philosophical message to the reader. Ephemeral and dreamlike, each emerges from the void as a spontaneous flow of images generated by free association. They are works in which the rational "I" allows the unconscious "other" to speak. As manifestations of the unconscious, they reveal an almost infinitely rich condensation of meaning that defies any linear attempts at interpretation. They thus elucidate Rimbaud's earlier remark in *A Season in Hell* that he "reserved all translation rights." They are, again in the poet's own words, "accessible to all meanings." If they are coherent, it is in the way dreams are coherent, and like dreams, they speak from the hidden recesses of the mind. Hermetic in form, they lead down a different path from that charted by the Symbolist verse of Rimbaud's contemporary, Mallarmé: They reflect not an aesthetic obsession with the problematics of language but a perpetual striving to give voice to all that reason and social mores have condemned to silence.

Although *Illuminations* consists of a discontinuous series of pieces devoid of any central narrative plot, critics have drawn attention to a number of major recurring themes to be found within the text. Given the work's dreamlike qualities and its close affinity with the unconscious, it is not surprising that the theme most often cited by critics is that of childhood. Numerous passages in the work evoke the blissful innocence of childhood, Rimbaud's "paradise lost," irrevocably destroyed by the advent of civilization and Christianity. The theme is developed at particular length in the two prose poems "Enfance" ("Childhood") and "Après le déluge" ("After the Deluge"). In the first, the child-poet tells of his Satanic fall from a state of divine omniscience and absolute freedom into a subterranean prison, where he is condemned to silence. In the second, which ironically alludes to the biblical story of the Flood and the promise of divine redemption, the poet sees the natural innocence of childhood as being progressively corrupted by the rise of civilization, and he ends by conjuring up new floods that will sweep away the repressive work of society.

A second and related major theme, exemplified by such prose poems as "Villes I" ("Cities I"), "Villes II" ("Cities II"), and "Métropolitain" ("Metropolitan"), is that of the city. Although modeled in part on the Paris and London of Rimbaud's own time, the cities in *Illuminations* are phantasmagoric, shimmering cities of the future that present a vision of technological wonder and bleak sterility. Promised utopias, they repeatedly and rapidly degenerate into vast urban wastelands that devour their pitiful human prey. In the end, they are bitterly renounced by their creator and verbally banished back to the void from which they emerged.

A third major theme is that of metamorphosis—a theme that is a logical outgrowth of Rimbaud's own assertion that "I is an other." For Rimbaud, as his "Seer Letter" makes clear, the seemingly stable Cartesian I is merely an illusion that masks the presence of a multiplicity of repressed others. Humans have no central, defining essence. In *Illuminations*, the poet thus undergoes a continual series of metamorphoses. In "Parade," he appears as a procession of itinerant comedians; in "Antique," as the son of the pagan god Pan, at once animal, man, and woman; in "Bottom," as the character in William Shakespeare's *A Midsummer Night's Dream* (pr. c. 1595-1596) who seeks to appropriate all the other characters' roles; and finally, in "Being Beauteous," as the incarnation of beauty itself. There are no limits to humanity's being, Rimbaud suggests, if people will only realize the vast potential within them.

OTHER MAJOR WORKS
MISCELLANEOUS: *Œuvres complètes*, 1948 (*Complete Works, Selected Letters*, 1966); *Rimbaud Complete*, 2002-2003 (2 volumes; Wyatt Mason, editor).

BIBLIOGRAPHY
Ahearn, Edward J. *Rimbaud: Visions and Habitations*. Berkeley: University of California Press, 1983. Discusses the influence of Rimbaud's early life and surroundings on his brief poetic career, including the anticlerical and anticonventional guidance he received during his teen years, when he began writing poetry. Points out links between Rimbaud's poetic images and his actual physical environment.

Cohn, Robert Greer. *The Poetry of Rimbaud*. 1973. Reprint. Columbia: University of South Carolina Press, 1999. A critical analysis of the poetry that Rimbaud wrote during his short life.

Hackett, Cecil Arthur. *Rimbaud: A Critical Introduction*. New York: Cambridge University Press, 1981. A good introduction for those beginning to explore Rimbaud's poetry. Contains much poem-by-poem explication, as well as analyses of Rimbaud's overall poetic achievement and cultural influence.

Lawler, James R. *Rimbaud's Theatre of the Self*. Cambridge, Mass.: Harvard University Press, 1992. A unique book that translates Rimbaud's work into a theatrical progression, explaining why the poet stopped writing to explore the dark side of his personality.

Oxenhandler, Neal. *Rimbaud: The Cost of Genius*. Columbus: Ohio State University Press, 2009. An examination of the life of Rimbaud that argues that his talent had a destructive side to it.

Perloff, Marjorie. *The Poetics of Indeterminacy: Rimbaud to Cage.* Evanston, Ill.: Northwestern University Press, 2000. This work contains only one chapter on Rimbaud but is highly useful in placing him within his historical context. Discusses his influence on modernist poets such as Gertrude Stein, Ezra Pound, and William Carlos Williams, as a transitional force between Symbolism and modernism.

Robb, Graham. *Rimbaud: A Biography.* New York: W. W. Norton, 2000. Presents a "reconstruction of Rimbaud's life"; discusses the revolutionary impact his poetry had on twentieth century writers and artists, especially since Rimbaud's admirers primarily arose after his early death. Examines the influence of Rimbaud's early family life, in particular his stormy relationship with his mother, and presents thoroughly his checkered career after his abandonment of poetry at the age of twenty-one.

Steinmetz, Jean-Luc. *Arthur Rimbaud: Presence of an Enigma.* Translated by Jon Graham. New York: Welcome Rain, 2001. A comprehensive biography, this work focuses on Rimbaud's numerous self-contradictions and extremes of behavior, particularly in his stormy relationship with the older poet Paul Verlaine. The author analyzes Rimbaud's poetry primarily in its relation to the poet's life.

James John Baran

SAPPHO

Born: Eresus, Lesbos, Asia Minor (now in Greece); c. 630 B.C.E.
Died: Mytilene, Lesbos, Asia Minor (now in Greece); c. 580 B.C.E.
Also known as: Psappho

PRINCIPAL POETRY
Poetarum Lesbiorum Fragmenta, 1955
Lyra Graeca, 1958 (volume 1)
Sappho: A New Translation, 1958
Sappho: Poems and Fragments, 1965
The Poems of Sappho, 1966
The Sappho Companion, 2000 (Margaret Reynolds, editor)
If Not, Winter: Fragments of Sappho, 2002 (Anne Carson, editor)

OTHER LITERARY FORMS
Sappho (SAF-oh) is known only for her poetry.

ACHIEVEMENTS
One of the most admired poets of the ancient world, Sappho was widely popular not only during her lifetime but also for centuries after. Although she wrote nine books of poetry, very little of the corpus remains. Except for a very few phrases on vase paintings or papyri, Sappho's poetry has been preserved primarily in small bits that happened to be quoted by other writers. Some 170 of these fragments are extant, and although there may be among them one or two complete poems, most of the fragments consist of only a few lines or a few words. For Sappho's poem fragments, the numerical system of Edgar Lobel and Denys Page, *Poetarum Lesbiorum Fragmenta*, is used.

These fragments indicate that Sappho's poems were largely lyrical, intended to be sung and accompanied by music and perhaps dance. Although her poetry was thus traditional in form, it differed significantly in content from the larger body of Greek verse, which was written primarily by men. Whereas other Greek poets were mainly concerned with larger and more public issues and with such traditional masculine concerns as war and heroism, Sappho's poems are personal, concerned with the emotions and individual experiences of herself and her friends. In exploring and describing the world of passion, in particular, Sappho departed from conventional poetic themes. Perhaps that is one of the reasons that her poetry was so popular in the ancient world.

Sappho's work has continued to be popular, however, not only because of the timelessness of her subject matter but also because of the exactness of her imagery and the intensity of her expression. Although her style is simple, direct, and conversational, her poems are powerful in creating an impression or evoking an emotion. Her world is therefore not the larger world of politics or warfare, but the smaller world of personal feeling; nevertheless, in depicting the outer limits of that world—the extremes of jealousy as well as tenderness, the depths of sorrow as well as the heights of ecstasy—Sappho's poetry sets a standard to which all later writers of lyrics must aspire.

In addition to being well known for her subject matter, Sappho has come to be associated with a particular metrical form. Although she was probably not the inventor of Sapphic meter, it has been so named because of her frequent use of it. In Sapphic meter, the stanza consists of three lines, each of which contains five feet—two trochees, a dactyl, and two more trochees—with a concluding fourth line of one dactyl and one trochee. The first line of the "Ode to Aphrodite" in the original Greek illustrates this meter. This ode is thought to have been accompanied by music written in the Mixolydian mode, a musical mode with which Sappho is also associated. Plutarch, in fact, claims that this mode, which is said to arouse the passions more than any other, was invented by Sappho.

Sappho's enduring reputation is based, however, on the fragments of her poetry that remain. Although those fragments themselves indicate her poetry's worth, ther e is in addition the testimony of other writers regarding the greatness of her accomplishment. She was praised and revered by a long line of ancients, including Solon, Plato, Aristotle, Horace, Catullus, Ovid, and Plutarch. Proving that imitation is the highest form of praise, some later poets actually incorporated her verse into their own compositions; Catullus's Poem 51, for example, is a slight reworking of a poem by Sappho. Plutarch, who, like Catullus, admired this particular ode, described it as being "mixed with fire," a metaphor that could accurately be applied to the entire body of Sappho's remaining poetry.

Biography

There are few details about Sappho's life that can be stated with certainty; the only evidence is what other writers said about her, and there is no way of knowing whether what they said is true. She is thought to have been of an aristocratic family of the island of Lesbos and to have had three brothers and a daughter named Cleis; dates of her birth and death, however, are not known. Athenaeus, writing around 200 c.e., claimed that Sappho was a contemporary of Alyattes, who reigned in Lydia from 610 to 560 b.c.e.; Eusebius of Caesarea, who was writing in the late third and early fourth centuries c.e., refers to Sappho (also known as Psappho) in his chronicle for the year 604 b.c.e. Other writers indicate that Sappho lived at the time of another poet, Alcaeus of Lesbos, who seems to have been born around 620 b.c.e. It seems safe, therefore, to conclude that Sappho was born sometime during the last quarter of the seventh century and lived into the first half of the sixth century b.c.e.

Sometime between 604 and 592 b.c.e., Sappho seems to have been sent into exile in

Sappho

Sicily by Pittacus, who was then a democratic ruler of Mytilene on Lesbos ; an inscription on the Parian marbles of the third century B.C.E. provides confirmation. Although it seems likely that such an exile would have been for political reasons, there are no clear references in any of the fragments of Sappho's poems to indicate that she was specifically concerned with political matters; in fact, based on those fragments, her poetry appears to have been very much apolitical.

Whether Sappho was married is also uncertain; some say that she had a husband named Cercylas, but others believe this report to be a creation of the Greek comic poets. More suspect is the story that Sappho committed suicide by leaping from the Leucadian Cliff when rejected by a sailor named Phaon. To begin with, this story did not surface until more than two hundred years after her death, but more significant is the fact that Phaon has been found to be a vegetable deity associated with Aphrodite, and a god to whom Sappho wrote hymns. These hymns are thought to have provided the basis for this apocryphal account of her death.

There are, however, some assumptions that can be drawn from Sappho's own words. Her poetry indicates that she was the leader of a group of young women who appear to have studied music, poetry, and dance and who seem to have worshiped Aphrodite and the Muses. As the daughter of an aristocratic family, Sappho would probably not have conducted a formal school, but was more likely the informal leader of a circle of girls and young women. Scholars know from other references in her poetry that there were several such groups on Lesbos, with leaders who were rivals of Sappho.

Many of Sappho's poems also concern her romantic relationships with various women of her group, a fact that has evoked various responses throughout history, ranging from vilification to denial. Her reputation seems to have been first darkened in the fourth century B.C.E., long after her death, when she was the subject of a number of comic and burlesque plays; it is believed that many of the unsavory stories that came to be associated with Sappho were generated during this period. A serious and most unfortunate effect of this created and perhaps inaccurate reputation was that much of Sappho's work was later deliberately destroyed, particularly by Christians whose moral sensibilities were offended by some of the stories that circulated in the second, fourth, and eleventh centuries C.E. Sappho's reputation was also reworked by later scholars who admired her poetry but who were discomfited by her love for women; among their efforts to dissociate Sappho from her sexuality was the widely circulated story that there were in fact two Sapphos, one the licentious and immoral woman to whom all the unsavory tales applied, and the other a faultless and asexual woman who wrote sublime poetry. Most scholars today believe that there was only one Sappho, but they also believe that most of the stories told about her were untrue.

Thus, because of the legendary tales that have come to be associated with Sappho, and because of the lack of reliable historical evidence, there is little knowledgeabout her life that is certain. It seems reasonable to assume that she lived on Lesbos, that she was a poet, and that she valued personal relationships, about which she wrote. Both during her lifetime and after, she was much admired; statues were erected in her honor, coins were minted bearing her likeness, and she is said to have been given a heroine's funeral. Beyond these small pieces of information, scholars must turn to the fragments of her poetry for knowledge and understanding.

ANALYSIS

Since Sappho's poetry is largely personal, it concerns her immediate world: her dedication to Aphrodite, her love of nature and art, and her relationships with lovers, friends, and family. Her poetry reflects her enjoyment of beauty in the natural world and the close connection that existed between that world and the lives of herself and her friends. Their worship of Aphrodite, their festive songs and dances, are all celebrated with flowers from the fields and with branches from the trees. Her poetry also reflects her love of art, whether in the form of poetry, the music of the lyre, or the graceful movement of a maiden in a dance. Since these interests are, however, always presented through the perspective of a personal response, a chief defining characteristic of Sappho's poetry is that it is highly emotional.

"Ode to Aphrodite"

Most of the extant fragments of Sappho's poetry were quoted by later writers to illustrate some point of dialect, rhetoric, grammar, or poetic style, and those writers usually quoted only that portion of Sappho's poem that was pertinent to their point. It is fortunate, then, that Dionysius of Halicarnassus, a Greek writer of treatises who lived in Rome around 30 B.C.E., quoted in its entirety Sappho's "Ode to Aphrodite," to illustrate "the smooth mode of composition." This poem, the longest of several by Sappho honoring Aphrodite, appears to be the most substantial complete work of Sappho that remains.

The ode contains the usual components of a celebration prayer to Aphrodite: the Invocation, the Sanction, and the Entreaty. The Invocation to the goddess consists of a series of epithets, "Dapple-throned Aphrodite,/ eternal daughter of God,/ snare-knitter"; the Sanction asks the goddess's generosity and assistance and reminds her of past favors she has granted; and the Entreaty urgently appeals to the goddess for aid in the present situation. Sappho employs this traditional form in a fresh way, however, not only by her use of vivid metaphors and lyrical language, but also by using the Sanction to reveal something of the goddess's character as well as something of Sappho's own psychology.

As Sappho employs it, the Sanction is a narrative passage within which both she and the goddess move back and forth in time. After describing a past occasion when the goddess came to Earth in a carriage pulled by sparrows, Sappho then recounts the goddess's questioning of her at that time. Using in her narrative the past tense and the indirect question, Sappho recalls the goddess's remarks: "You asked, What ailed me now that/ made me call you again?" Abruptly, then, Sappho places the goddess's gentle chiding within the present context; the poem shifts to direct discourse as the goddess questions Sappho directly: "Whom has/ Persuasion to bring round now/ to your love? Who, Sappho, is/ unfair to you?" This mix of the two temporal perspectives links and blends the present with the past, not only emphasizing Sappho's recurring states of anxiety over new love but also illuminating the special and friendly relationship between the poet and the goddess: Aphrodite has obviously assisted Sappho before in similar matters of the heart. Continuing to reveal Sappho's character, the goddess reminds her that they are beginning a now-familiar pattern: A bemused Aphrodite recalls, "If she [the desired lover] won't accept gifts, she/ will one day give them; and if/ she won't love you—she soon will/love." Sappho, manipulating the tradition of the Sanction for new purposes of self-mockery and character revelation, thus discloses her love for the courting period, as well as the shift in attitudes that will inevitably occur between her and her new lover. After the goddess's assurance that the sought-after lover will very shortly be seeking Sappho, the reader is then returned to the poem's outer frame, the prayer, as Sappho begs the goddess to help at once, to "Come now! Relieve this intolerable pain!"

Within the form of a traditional prayer honoring Aphrodite, the poem thus presents a delightful variety of tone. It discloses not only the intensity of Sappho's passion for the desired lover, but also her wry recognition that this intensity will be limited by time and by her own nature. The poem similarly indicates not only the immensity of the goddess's power but also her gentle amusement at the joys and woes of her followers; although Sappho's present sufferings in love will soon be in the past, a pattern underscored by the poem's movement between present and past time, there is every reason to believe that the goddess will assist Sappho once again in achieving the lover who will end her present suffering. In revealing not only something of the character of Aphrodite but also something of the character of Sappho, the poem thus transcends the limitations of its genre: It is a prayer, to be sure, and a narrative, but it is also a charmingly refreshing analysis of the poet's own psychology.

"ODE TO ANACTORIA"

Although there are a few other fragments of poems honoring Aphrodite, the largest number of Sappho's fragments which remain are concerned with love, a subject that occupied much of Sappho's attention. One love poem that may, like the "Ode to Aphrodite," be nearly complete, is the large fragment sometimes called the "Ode to Anactoria," although the poem may have been written for Atthis or even for some other woman whom Sappho loved. An unknown writer who has been labeled "Longinus," in a Greek work believed to date from the first or second century C.E., quoted this fragment to illustrate Sappho's mastery in depicting physical sensations. Extraordinary in its exquisitely precise delineation of the extremes of passion, the poem is also notable for the contrast between the control of its first section and the revealed intensity of its latter section, with the resulting alternations in tone as the speaker sits in the presence of two people, the woman she loves and the man who is evidently enjoying that woman's attentions.

Concisely and with control, the poem beings:

> He is a god in my eyes—
> the man who is allowed
> to sit beside you—he
> who listens intimately
> to the sweet murmur of
> your voice, the enticing
> laughter that makes my own
> heart beat fast.

This calm and steady beginning establishes an outer mood of control, an atmosphere of containment and casual social interplay; the poem turns, however, on the word "laughter," and the rest of the fragment describes, rapidly and with great intensity, the physical symptoms of the poet's great passion. All her senses are affected: Her "tongue is broken," and she sees nothing; she hears only her "own ears drumming" as she drips with sweat; and, as "trembling shakes" her body, she turns "paler than dry grass." In one of Sappho's most superb lines, she declares that "a thin flame runs under/ my skin." Then, ending this rapid and graphic description of the physical results of intense emotion, the poet remarks, in a powerfully reserved manner, that "At such times/ death isn't far from me."

Scholars have long debated the cause of Sappho's passion, arguing whether it is love or jealousy or both; scholars have also quarreled over the identity of the woman and the relationship between the woman and the man who sits beside her. Such discussions are, however, ultimately irrelevant; the poet's salient point is her own overpowering feeling for the woman to whom she is listening, a feeling that prevents Sappho from exercising over her body any control; it is the physical manifestations of that feeling, the effects on the body of great passion, which Sappho is recording. Within the poem, the effects of that passion are heightened by the contrast that turns on the word "laughter"; just as the poem is divided between the controlled description of the outer situation and the blaze of feelings within the poet, so Sappho and the man are divided in their response to the woman's laughter; he "listens intimately," calmly, while Sappho experiences a whole cascade of violent physical and emotional reactions.

Sappho's description in this poem of the effects of passion has not been surpassed, although a number of later poets, including Catullus, have imitated, translated, or adopted her ideas. None, however, has been able to convey such intensity of feeling with the economy and precision of Sappho. It seems safe to say that there are few who would dispute Longinus's claim that this poem illustrates "the perfection of the Sublime in poetry."

16 L.-P.

In addition to considering the physical effects of love on the individual, Sappho also analyzes love's nature and power. One such poem, 16 L.-P., which refers directly to Anactoria, appears on a papyrus of the second century. The poem begins with a paratactic trope, a common device that presents the theme as the culmination of a series of comparisons:

> Some say a cavalry corps,
> some infantry, some, again,
> will maintain that the swift cars
> of our fleet are the finest
> sight on dark earth; but I say
> that whatever one loves, is.

More than illustrating normal differences of opinion, this means of introducing the theme establishes, as well, a decided difference between male and female values:

Sappho seems clearly to imply that while men would see the ideal of beauty to be things having to do with war, she sees the ideal of beauty to be the thing beloved—in this case, the absent Anactoria.

Sappho then reinforces her contention that the beloved is the world's most beautiful sight by a reference to Helen, who had her pick of the world's men; in contrast to what one would expect, however, Helen was obliged, because of love, to choose "one who laid Troy's honor in ruin," one who "warped" her "to his will," one who caused her even to forget the "love due her own blood, her own/ child." Sappho uses the story of Helen to illustrate love's power to make insignificant all ordinary considerations and constraints. Yet Sappho clearly intends no judgment against Helen; the purpose of her allusion is simply to demonstrate the power of love and, by analogy, Sappho's love for her beloved.

Only then, after establishing by example and comparisons the supremacy and strength of love, does Sappho reveal in an apostrophe the name of her beloved. Addressing Anactoria and expressing her fear that Anactoria will forget her, Sappho confesses that the sound of her footstep, or the sight of her bright face, would be dearer "than glitter/ of Lydian horse or armoured/ tread of mainland infantry." In an intricate linking of end and beginning by means of metaphor and comparisons, the poem thus moves full circle, back to its starting place; the final sentence of the fragment reinforces the idea contained in the opening sentence as it simultaneously contrasts the tread of the infantry with the delightful sound of Anactoria's footstep, and the glitter of armor with the bright shine of Anactoria's face. In such ways, Sappho clearly exposes the conflicting value systems that underlie her poems and those of her male contemporaries.

Several other fragments of varying size also treat the power of love, among them a particularly felicitous line quoted by Maximus of Tyre around 150 C.E.: "As a whirlwind/ swoops on an oak/ Love shakes my heart." An overpowering natural phenomenon, love is presented here as an elemental force that completely overcomes the lover, both physically and emotionally. As the wind physically surrounds the oak, so does love overpower the lover physically as well as emotionally. Love, a force that cannot be denied, is thus depicted as a violent physical and emotional assault, to which one may well respond with mixed feelings.

Sappho explores the ambiguity of the lover's response to love's violent assault in another fragment, quoted by Hephaestion around 150 C.E.: "Irresistible/ and bittersweet/ that loosener/ of limbs, Love/ reptile-like/ strikes me down." Again, love is depicted as an absolute power and as a violent force—in this instance as a reptile that, attacking a passive victim, creates in her a weakened state. That state is not, however, altogether unpleasant, as is indicated by the exquisite sensuality of the adjectival phrase describing love as "that loosener of limbs." Love's duality—its violence and its sweetness—and the lover's ambiguity of response—as the victim of assault and as reveler in love's sensuality—are further underscored by the oxymoronic adjective "bittersweet," an epithet for love that Sappho may have been the first to use.

94 L.-P.

In addition to analyzing the nature and effects of love, Sappho writes of love's termination, of separation, loss, and grief. One such fragment, 94 L.-P., found in a seventh century manuscript in very poor condition, contains many lacunae and uncertain readings. Nevertheless, enough of the poem remains to prove that Sappho was defining the state of bereavement and the effectiveness of memory in alleviating that state. In the course of exploring these themes, however, the poem presents an enchanting account of the life led by Sappho and the members of her group as they worshiped Aphrodite, celebrated the beauty of nature, and gloried in one another.

Like the "Ode to Aphrodite," the poem uses a frame of present time to contain an account of past time; in this poem, however, the past time frames an even earlier period, so that three time periods are represented. Beginning in her present situation, Sappho, alone, reveals her emotional state at the loss of her beloved: "Frankly I wish I were dead." Attempting then to console herself, Sappho recalls the occasion of their parting; at that time, in contrast to the present situation, Sappho controlled her grief to comfort her lover, who was overcome by weeping. On that occasion, Sappho urged her beloved to remember their former happiness and to comfort herself with the memory of their love. At this point in the past, the poem then removes to its third temporal setting, that idyllic period when the two were actually together. In a passage of great lyrical beauty, Sappho recalls the details of their life:

> think
> of our gifts of Aphrodite
> and all the loveliness that we shared
> all the violet tiaras
> braided rosebuds, dill and
> crocus twined around your young neck
> myrrh poured on your head
> and on soft mats girls with
> all that they most wished for beside them
> while no voices changed
> choruses without ours
> no woodlot bloomed in spring without song.

In re-creating, at the moment of their farewell, this earlier time of delight in love, nature, and each other, Sappho consoles her beloved by reminding her that the joys they shared are preserved in memories and that those memories can provide solace. At the same time, from her position in the outer frame of the poem—the present context—Sappho attempts to comfort herself by the same means.

Although the poem, on one hand, asserts the consolation that memory can offer, it testifies as well to memory's limitations. Even though Sappho has shared the joyful events of which she reminds her beloved, the poem indicates all too clearly that memory's ability to ease grief is restricted. As Sappho tersely and flatly demonstrates by her opening statement, in no way can memory truly compensate for the beloved's absence. Still, the enchantment of those memories remains, and even though they cannot totally eliminate the pain of parting, they can provide some surcease by powerfully evoking the time when the lovers' joy in nature and in their love created for them an existence truly idyllic.

In addition to these personal poems, private accounts of her own and her friends' feelings and activities, Sappho also wrote some poems of a more public nature. Notable among these "public" poems are a number of fragments from her epithalamiums, or wedding songs. Some of these are congratulatory pieces honoring bride or groom, some appear to have been part of good-humored songs of mockery or wedding jest, and some seem to have been serious considerations of what marriage meant, especially for a woman. Of the latter, particularly worthy of comment are two fragments thought by some to be part of a single poem concerning the loss of maidenhood. As is true of other poems by Sappho, opinion is divided as to the poem's ultimate meaning, some believing that it alludes to an ungentle lover who does not properly appreciate the maiden whose virginity he destroys, and others believing that the poem refers generally to the destruction of innocence and the loss of girlhood joys that marriage necessitates.

The fragments employ two similes, the first comparing the blushing girl to

> a quince-apple
> ripening on a top
> branch in a tree top
> not once noticed by
> harvesters or if
> not unnoticed, not reached.

The location of the apple high in the tree permits it to ripen without disturbance, perhaps as a girl's careful upbringing or superior social standing might shield her from importunate suitors. The second fragment compares the loss of the virginal state to

> a hyacinth in
> the mountains, trampled by shepherds until
> only a purple stain
> remains on the ground.

Through the powerful image of the delicate hyacinth roughly trod into the earth, the poem clearly delineates the destructive power of love and marriage.

112 L.-P.

That image is countered, however, in another fragment from an epithalamium, 112 L.-P., which rejoices in marriage and celebrates the groom's winning of the girl he desires. The bride is described as "charming to look at,/ with eyes as soft as/ honey, and a face/ that Love has lighted/ with his own beauty." Sappho, clearly indicating her own opinion as to which is the lucky partner in the marriage, reminds the groom, "Aphrodite has surely/ outdone herself in/ doing honor to you!" Such songs were thought to have been written for the weddings of Sappho's friends, and would have been accompanied by music and dance.

Sappho's legacy is meager in size, consisting of one or two poems that may be complete, together with a number of shorter fragments that tantalize by their incompleteness even as they enchant with what they do provide. These few pieces clearly manifest the enormous poetic talent that Sappho possessed: a genius for capturing a mood, for portraying an experience, and for depicting an emotion. Although her poetry is personal in dealing with her own responses to life, it is, paradoxically, also universal; the feelings she describes, even though they are her own, are shared by all human beings who ever love, lose, or grieve, or who experience jealousy, anger, or regret. One of the first poets to explore the range and depth of the human heart, Sappho well deserves Plato's epithet for her, "the tenth Muse."

BIBLIOGRAPHY

Bowra, C. Maurice. *Greek Lyric Poetry: From Alcman to Simonides*. 2d ed. Oxford, England: Clarendon Press, 1961. A classic review of seven Greek lyric poets stressing their historical development and critiquing important works. Offers groundbreaking theories of the poets as a group and as individual writers. Views Sappho as the leader of a society of girls that excluded men and worshiped the Muses and Aphrodite.

Burnett, Anne Pippin. *Three Archaic Poets: Archilochus, Alcaeus, Sappho*. Cambridge, Mass.: Harvard University Press, 1983. Rejects theories of ancient Greek lyrics as either passionate outpourings or occasional verse. Describes Sappho's aristocratic circle and critiques six major poems.

DuBois, Page. *Sappho Is Burning*. Chicago: University of Chicago Press, 1995. The title is taken from part of David A. Campbell's translation of Sappho's fragment 48, in which the poet's heart is "burning with desire." DuBois assumes and examines an aesthetics of fragmentation and veers to a strained "postmodern" appreciation of the poet.

Greene, Ellen, ed. *Reading Sappho* and *Re-reading Sappho*. Berkeley: University of California Press, 1996. A two-volume collection of essays and articles (by writers such as Mary Lefkowitz, Holt N. Parker, and Jack Winkler) important in elucidating Sappho's poetry.

Jenkyns, Richard. *Three Classical Poets: Sappho, Catullus, and Juvenal*. Cambridge, Mass.: Harvard University Press, 1982. Stresses the relativistic view that no one theory can elucidate ancient poetry. Detailed analysis of Sappho's principal poems and fragments, concluding that she is a major poet.

McEvilley, Thomas. *Sappho*. Putnam, Conn.: Spring, 2008. A biography of Sappho that explores her life and works.

Prins, Yopie. *Victorian Sappho*. Princeton, N.J.: Princeton University Press, 1999. Superb study of the presentations of Sappho in nineteenth century English literature. Exposes the imperfections of editions by Dr. Henry Wharton and Michael Field (pseudonym of Katherine Bradley and Edith Cooper). Cogent chapter on Sappho and Swinburne in "Swinburne's Sapphic Sublime."

Rayor, Diane. *Sappho's Lyre: Archaic Lyric and Women Poets of Ancient Greece*. Berkeley: University of California Press, 1991. In most respects, this is the best available translation of Sappho. Includes fragments of nine women poets besides Sappho, along with poems and fragments of seven male lyric poets.

Reynolds, Margaret, ed. *The Sappho Companion*. New York: Palgrave, 2001. Contains narratives of the way societies in different times have accepted or rejected Sappho's works. Includes an introduction as well as translations of the fragments of the poems, a bibliography, and an index.

Snyder, Jane McIntosh. *The Woman and the Lyre: Women Writers in Classical Greece and Rome*. Carbondale: Southern Illinois University Press, 1989. Informative introduction to Sappho and eight female lyric poets of classical antiquity, with representative translations.

Snyder, Jane McIntosh, and Camille-Yvette Welsch. *Sappho*. Philadelphia: Chelsea House, 2005. A woman-centered perspective on Sappho that looks at whether Sappho was a lesbian and how she related to other women.

Yatromanolakis, Dimitrios. *Sappho in the Making: The Early Reception*. Washington, D.C.: Center for Hellenic Studies, Trustees for Harvard University, 2007. An examination of Sappho and the world around her, examining how it shaped her poetry and how poetry was viewed.

Evelyn S. Newlyn

SIEGFRIED SASSOON

Born: Brenchley, Kent, England; September 8, 1886
Died: Heytesbury, England; September 1, 1967
Also known as: Saul Kain; Pinchbeck Lyre; Sigmund Sashun

PRINCIPAL POETRY
The Daffodil Murderer, 1913
The Old Huntsman, and Other Poems, 1917
Counter-Attack, and Other Poems, 1918
War Poems, 1919
Picture Show, 1920
Recreations, 1923
Selected Poems, 1925
Satirical Poems, 1926
The Heart's Journey, 1927
Poems of Pinchbeck Lyre, 1931
The Road to Ruin, 1933
Vigils, 1935
Poems Newly Selected, 1916-1935, 1940
Rhymed Ruminations, 1940
Collected Poems, 1947
Common Chords, 1950
Emblems of Experience, 1951
The Tasking, 1954
Sequences, 1956
Lenten Illuminations and Sight Sufficient, 1958
The Path to Peace, 1960
Collected Poems, 1908-1956, 1961
An Octave, 1966

OTHER LITERARY FORMS

Siegfried Sassoon (suh-SEWN) is nearly as well known for his prose works as for his poetry. From 1926 to 1945, he spent most of his time working on the two trilogies that form the bulk of his work in prose. The first of these was the three-volume fictionalized autobiography published in 1937 as *The Memoirs of George Sherston*. It begins in *Memoirs of a Fox-Hunting Man* (1928), by recounting the life of a well-to-do young country squire in Georgian England up to his first experiences as an officer in World War I. The second volume, *Memoirs of an Infantry Officer* (1930), and the third,

Sherston's Progress (1936), describe the young man's war experiences. In the later trilogy, Sassoon discarded the thinly disguised fiction of the Sherston novels and wrote direct autobiography, with a nostalgic look back at his pleasant pastoral life in prewar England in *The Old Century and Seven More Years* (1938) and *The Weald of Youth* (1942). In *Siegfried's Journey, 1916-1920* (1945), Sassoon looks again at his own experiences during and immediately following the war. These autobiographical works are invaluable to the student of Sassoon's poetry because of the context they provide, particularly for the war poems.

Two other significant prose works should be mentioned. The first is Sassoon's *Lecture on Poetry*, delivered at the University of Bristol on March 16, 1939, in which Sassoon delineated what he considered to be the elements of good poetry. The second work is Sassoon's critical biography of the poet George Meredith, titled simply *Meredith* (1948), which also suggests some of Sassoon's views on poetry.

Achievements

According to Bernard Bergonzi, Siegfried Sassoon was the only soldier-poet to be widely read during the war itself. This gave Sassoon a unique opportunity to influence other war poets, which he did. Though his war poetry has been criticized for being mere description, for appealing to only the senses and not the imagination, and for being uncontrolled emotion without artistic restraint, there can be no doubt than Sassoon's poetry represented a complete break with the war poetry of the past in tone, technique, and subject matter. With uncompromising realism and scathing satire, Sassoon portrayed the sufferings of the front-line soldier and the incompetency of the staff for the express purposes of convincing his readers to protest continuation of the war. His *Counter-Attack, and Other Poems* was nearly suppressed because of poems such as "The General," which broke the prohibition against criticizing those in charge of the war effort.

Unquestionably, Sassoon's realistic subject matter and diction influenced other poets, most notably his friend Wilfred Owen, whose poetry was posthumously published by Sassoon in 1920; but Sassoon failed to influence later poetry because, as John Johnston notes, his war poetry was all negative—he provided no constructive replacement for the myths he had destroyed. Nor did Sassoon influence poetry in the 1930's because, according to Michael Thorpe, he was still a prisoner of war, and through his autobiographies he retreated from the political struggle of W. H. Auden and Stephen Spender and others into his own earlier years.

When in the 1950's Sassoon finally did have something positive to offer, no one was willing to listen. He was no longer well known or critically acknowledged. Certainly his future reputation will rest on the war poems; but in his religious poems of the 1950's, Sassoon did achieve a style of simple expression, compact brevity, and concrete imagery with a universally appealing theme, and this should be noted as a remarkable though largely unrecognized achievement.

BIOGRAPHY

Siegfried Lorraine Sassoon was born in the Kentish weald in 1886, the second of three sons of Alfred Ezra Sassoon and Theresa Georgina Thornycroft. His father was descended from a long line of wealthy Jewish merchants and bankers who, after wandering through Spain, Persia, and India, had come to settle in England. The family was proud of its orthodoxy, and Siegfried's father was the first to marry outside the faith. Siegfried's mother, in contrast, was an artist, the close relative of three well-known sculptors, and a member of the landed gentry. The marriage was a failure, and Alfred Sassoon left when Siegfried was five, leaving the younger Sassoon to be reared by his mother as an Anglican.

Siegfried had no formal schooling as a child, though from the ages of nine to fourteen he learned from private tutors and a German governess. In 1902, he attended Marlborough, and in 1905, he entered Clare College, Cambridge. Sassoon's temperament was not disciplined enough for scholarly pursuits; he began by reading law, switched to history, and ultimately left Cambridge without a degree. He returned to Kent, where, on an inherited income of five hundred pounds a year, he was able to devote his energies to foxhunting, racing, and writing poetry. Sassoon loved the pastoral beauty of the Kentish downs and attempted to portray it in a number of dreamy, sentimental lyrics. Between the ages of nineteen and twenty-six, Sassoon had nine volumes of poetry privately published, before he enjoyed a mild success with *The Daffodil Murderer* in 1913. The poem was chiefly intended as a parody of John Masefield's *The Everlasting Mercy*, but Sassoon's poem had a strong human appeal of its own. By this time, Sassoon had been befriended by Edward Marsh, the editor of *Georgian Poetry*. Marsh encouraged Sassoon's literary endeavors and persuaded him to come to London in May, 1914, where Sassoon began to move in the literary world and to meet such notable authors as Rupert Brooke. Sassoon, however, felt unhappy and lacked a sense of purpose, and when he enlisted in the army on August 3, 1914 (two days before England entered the war), it was to escape a sterile existence.

Sassoon's early life had been extremely sheltered, even pampered, and it was a very immature twenty-eight-year-old who went to war, totally unprepared for what he would find. After convalescence from injuries received in a fall during cavalry training, he accepted a commission and went through training as an infantry officer. Thus, he did not arrive in France until November, 1915, where he became transport officer for the First Battalion of the Royal Welch Fusiliers. Here he met and befriended the poet Robert Graves. In *Goodbye to All That* (1929), Graves describes his first meeting with Sassoon and relates how, when he showed Sassoon his first book of poems, *Over the Brazier* (1916), Sassoon, whose early war poems were idealistic, had frowned and said that war should not be written about in such a realistic way. Graves, who had been in France six months, remarked that Sassoon had not yet been in the trenches.

Graves already knew what Sassoon would soon discover, indeed what all the British troops in France were coming to feel: growing disillusionment at the frustration and the staggering casualties of trench warfare. There were 420,000 British casualties in the Somme offensive beginning on July 1, 1916—an offensive that gained virtually nothing. The Somme was Sassoon's most bitter experience in the trenches; after it, he would never write the old kind of poetry again.

In spite of his pacifist leanings, Sassoon distinguished himself in the war. Called "Mad Jack" by his troops, Sassoon was awarded the Military Cross and recommended for the Distinguished Service Order for his exploits in battle: After a raid at Mametz, he took it upon himself to bring back the wounded; in the Somme in early July, he single-handedly occupied a whole section of an enemy trench, after which he was found in the trench, alone, reading a book of poetry. Ill with gastric fever in late July, he was sent home for three months, where he worked on poems to be included in *The Old Huntsman, and Other Poems*.

While in England, Sassoon met Lady Ottoline Morrell and her liberal husband, Philip, at whose home he spoke with such pacifists as Bertrand Russell, listened to open criticism of the war, and heard of Germany's peace overtures and the impure motives of members of parliament who wanted the war to continue.

Sassoon returned to active service in France in February, 1917, but in April, he was wounded in the Battle of Arras and sent home again. Haunted by nightmares of violence and by what the pacifists were saying, Sassoon resolved to protest the war on a grand scale. In July, Sassoon refused to return to active duty and wrote a formal declaration of protest to his commanding officer, which was reproduced in the press and which Russell arranged to have mentioned in the House of Commons. In his letter, Sassoon charged that the war was being deliberately prolonged by the politicians for ignoble purposes, even though there was a chance for a negotiated settlement with Germany, thus leading the men at the front line to be slaughtered needlessly. Sassoon hoped to be court-martialed, so that his protest would have propaganda value. To his dismay, however, the official reaction was largely to minimize the letter. In a moment of despair, Sassoon flung his Military Cross into the Mersey River and vowed to continue his protest.

At that point, Graves stepped in. Graves agreed with Sassoon's letter, but considered the gesture futile and feared for Sassoon's personal welfare. Graves arranged to have Sassoon appear before a medical board, and chiefly on Graves's testimony, Sassoon was found to be suffering from shell shock. The incident was closed, and Sassoon was sent to Craiglockhart hospital in Edinburgh, where physician W. H. R. Rivers became his counselor and friend, and where in August he met the brilliant young poet Wilfred Owen. Owen knew and idolized Sassoon as the author of *The Old Huntsman, and Other Poems* (which had appeared in May), and Sassoon's encouragement and insistence on realism had greatly influenced him. At Craiglockhart, during the autumn of 1917, Sassoon composed many of the poems of *Counter-Attack, and Other Poems*, which was published the following year.

Owen returned to active duty in November, and Sassoon, feeling that he was betraying his troops at the front by staying away in comfort, returned to duty a few weeks later. He went first to Ireland, then to Egypt, where he became a captain, then back to France in May. On July 15, 1918, Sassoon, returning from an attack on a German machine gun, was wounded in the head by one of his own sentries. He was sent to a London hospital, where he spent the rest of the war.

After the war, Sassoon retreated from the active life, becoming more and more contemplative (he had always been introspective and solitary) until he acquired a reputation as a virtual hermit. Immediately after the war, he joined the Labor Party and became editor of the literary pages of the *Daily Herald*, where he published satirical pieces with a socialist point of view. His satire of the 1920's, however, was uneasy and awkward, stemming from the fact that the issues of the day were not as clear-cut as the right and wrong about the war had been. Besides, he was not really sure of himself, feeling a need to explore his past life and find some meaning in it. Still, as the 1930's grew darker, Sassoon wrote poems warning of the horror of chemical and biological warfare. No one seemed to want to listen, however, and Sassoon, disillusioned, forsook "political" poetry completely. In part, the autobiographies that he worked on in those years were a rejection of the modern world and an idealization of the past. In part, too, they were an effort to look inside himself, and that same urge characterizes most of his later poetry, which is concerned with his personal spiritual struggle and development.

Thus, the incidents of Sassoon's later life were nearly all spiritual. Only a few isolated events are of interest: In 1933, he finally married; he had a son, George, but Sassoon kept his personal relationships private, never mentioning them in his poetry. During World War II, Sassoon's home was requisitioned for evacuees, and later, fifteen hundred American troops were quartered on his large estate. After the war, Sassoon remained very solitary and appears to have cultivated his image as the "hermit of Heytesbury." When his volumes of poetry appeared in the 1950's, they were largely ignored by critics and public alike. The fiery war poet had outlived his reputation, but he had reached a great personal plateau: On August 14, 1957, Sassoon was received into the Catholic Church at Downside Abbey. His last poems, appearing in a privately published collection, *An Octave*, on his eightieth birthday (a year before his death), display a serene and quiet faith.

Analysis

In 1939, Siegfried Sassoon delineated his views on poetry in a lecture given at Bristol College. While what he said was not profound or revolutionary, it did indicate the kind of poetry Sassoon liked and tried to write, at least at that time. First, Sassoon said, poetry should stem from inspiration, but that inspiration needs to be tempered by control and discipline—by art. Second, the best poetry is simple and direct—Sassoon disliked the tendency toward complexity initiated by T. S. Eliot and Ezra Pound. Third,

Sassoon held the Romantic view that poetry should express true feeling and speak the language of the heart. Fourth, poetry should contain strong visual imagery, the best of which is drawn from nature. Finally, the subject matter of the best poetry is not political (again, he was reacting against the avowedly political poetry of Auden and his associates), but rather personal, and this examination of self led Sassoon to write spiritual poetry.

A review of Sassoon's poetry will reveal, however, that even in his best poems he did not always follow all these precepts, and that in his worst poems he seldom followed any. Sassoon's worst poems are most certainly his earliest ones. Sassoon's prewar lyric verses are lush and wordy, in weak imitation of Algernon Charles Swinburne and the Pre-Raphaelites, but full of anachronisms and redundancies. Some, such as "Haunted" and "Goblin Revel," are purely escapist; Lewis Thorpe suggests that Sassoon was looking for escape from his own too-comfortable world. The best thing about these early poems is their interest in nature—an interest that Sassoon never lost and that provided him with concrete images in later pieces. The best poems that Sassoon wrote before the war, *The Daffodil Murderer* and "The Old Huntsman," abandon the poetic diction for a colloquial style, and "The Old Huntsman" reveals a strong kinship with nature.

THE WAR POETRY

Sassoon's early, idealistic war poetry is characterized by an abstract diction and generalized imagery. He was writing in the "happy warrior" style after the manner of Rupert Brooke's famous sonnet sequence and was even able to write of his brother's death early in the war as a "victory" and his ghost's head as "laureled." Perhaps the best example of these early poems is "Absolution," written before Sassoon had actually experienced the war. Sassoon romanticizes war, speaking of the glorious sacrifice of young comrades in arms who go off to battle as "the happy legion," asserting that "fighting for our freedom, we are free." The poem is full of such abstractions, but no concrete images. Its language is often archaic ("Time's but a golden wind"), and it is the sort of thing that Sassoon soon put behind him.

Edward Marsh, after reading some of Sassoon's earlier poetry, had told him to write with his eye directly on the object. As Sassoon began to experience the horrors of trench warfare, he did exactly that. His poems became increasingly concrete, visual, and realistic, his language became increasingly colloquial, and his tone became more and more bitter as the war went on. Early in 1916, he wrote "Golgotha," "The Redeemer," and "A Working Party," in which he tried to present realistically the sufferings of the common soldier. Such realistic depiction of the front lines characterized one of two main types of war poetry that Sassoon was to write in the next few years. The best example of sheer naturalistic description is "Counter-Attack," the title poem of Sassoon's most popular and most scathing volume of poetry. "Counter-Attack" begins with a description of the troops, who, having taken an enemy trench, begin to deepen it with shovels. They uncover a pile of dead bodies and rotting body parts—"naked sodden buttocks, mats of hair,/ Bulged, clotted heads."

"Repression of War Experience"

The horror of this description is without parallel, but where Sassoon really excels is in his realistic portrayal of the psychological effects of the war. Perhaps his best poem in this vein is "Repression of War Experience," from *Counter-Attack, and Other Poems*. The poem, in the form of an interior monologue, explores a mind verging on hysteria, trying to distract itself and maintain control while even the simplest, most serene events—a moth fluttering too close to a candle flame—bring nightmarish thoughts of violence into the persona's mind. In the garden, he hears ghosts, and as he sits in the silence, he can hear only the guns. In the end, his control breaks down; he wants to rush out "and screech at them to stop—I'm going crazy;/ I'm going stark, staring mad because of the guns."

"They"

Sassoon was not merely presenting realistic details; he was being deliberately didactic, trying to use his poetry to incite a public outcry against the war. When home on leave, he had been appalled by the jingoistic ignorance and complacency on the home front. Sassoon's second main type of war poetry made a satirical attack on these civilians, on those who conducted the war, and on the irresponsible press that spread the lying propaganda. Justly the most famous of these poems is "They" (*The Old Huntsman, and Other Poems*), in which Sassoon demolishes the cherished civilian notion that the war was divinely ordained and that the British were fighting on God's side. Sassoon presents a pompous bishop declaring that, since the "boys" will have fought "Anti-Christ," none will return "the same" as he was. The irony of this statement is made clear when the "boys" return quite changed: blind, legless, and syphilitic. The bishop can only remark, "The ways of God are strange." "They" caused a great outcry in England by ruthlessly attacking the Church for forsaking the moral leadership it should have provided.

"They" also illustrates Sassoon's favorite technique in satire: concentration of his ironic force in the last line of the poem. This kind of "knock-out punch" may be seen most vividly in the poem "The One-Legged Man" (*The Old Huntsman, and Other Poems*), which describes a soldier, discharged from the war, watching the natural beauty of the world in autumn and considering the bright, comfortable years ahead. The poem ends with the man's crushingly ironic thought, "Thank God they had to amputate!"

Certainly there are flaws in Sassoon's war poetry. Some of the verses are nothing more than bitter invectives designed merely to attack a part of his audience, such as "Glory of Women," "Blighters," and "Fight to the Finish." Even the best poems often lack the discipline and order that Sassoon himself later advanced as one main criterion of poetry. Further, Sassoon almost never got beyond his feelings about immediate experiences to form theoretical or profound notions about the broader aspects of the war. Sassoon himself realized this lack in 1920, when he brought out his slain friend Wilfred Owen's war poetry, which converted war experiences into something having universal meaning.

"THE DUG OUT"

The war poetry, however, has a number of virtues as well. It uses simple, direct, and clear expression that comes, as Sassoon advocated, from the heart. Further, it uses vivid pictures to express the inexpressible horror of the trenches. "The Dug Out" (*Picture Show*) is an example of Sassoon's war poetry at its best. In its eight lines, Sassoon draws a clear picture of a youth sleeping in an awkward and unnatural position. The simple, colloquial language focuses on the emotional state of the speaker, and much is suggested by what is left unsaid. The speaker's nerves are such that he can no longer bear the sight of the young sleeper because, as he cries in the final lines, "You are too young to fall asleep for ever;/ And when you sleep you remind me of the dead." Arthur Lane compares such poems, in which the ironic effect is achieved through the dramatic situation more than through imagery, to those in the *Satires of Circumstance* (1914) of Sassoon's idol, Thomas Hardy, suggesting an influence at work.

"EVERYONE SANG"

Perhaps the culmination of Sassoon's attempt to transcend his war experience is the much-admired lyric "Everyone Sang" (*Picture Show*). It is a joyous lyric expressing a mood of relief and exultation, through the imagery of song and of singing birds. Sassoon seems to have been expressing his own relief at having survived: "horror/ Drifted away." Lane calls these lines "pure poetry" of "visionary power," comparing them to poems of William Wordsworth and William Blake. He might have also mentioned Henry Vaughan, Sassoon's other idol, whose path toward poetry of a very personal spirituality Sassoon was soon to follow.

"LINES WRITTEN IN ANTICIPATION..."

Unquestionably, it is for his war poetry that Sassoon is chiefly admired. Still, he lived for nearly fifty years after the armistice, and what he wrote in that time cannot be disregarded. He first flirted with socialism after the war; "Everyone Sang" may be intended to laud the coming utopian society. Then he attempted satiric poetry during the 1920's, which must be regarded as a failure. His targets varied from the upper classes to political corruption and newspapers, but the poetry is not from the heart; the satire is too loud and not really convincing. Michael Thorpe points out the wordiness of Sassoon's style in these satires, together with the length of his sentences. One blatant example is "Lines Written in Anticipation of a London Paper Attaining a Guaranteed Circulation of Ten Million Daily." Even the title is verbose, but note the wordy redundancy of the lines:

> Were it not wiser, were it not more candid,
> More courteous, more consistent with good sense,
> If I were to include all, all who are banded
> Together in achievement so immense?

RELIGIOUS SEARCHING AND SPIRITUALITY

Though he soon abandoned the satiric mode, Sassoon did maintain what Joseph Cohen calls the role of prophet that he had assumed in the war years, by continually warning, through *The Road to Ruin* and *Rhymed Ruminations*, of the coming disaster of World War II. His total despair for the modern world is expressed in "Litany of the Lost" (1945), wherein, with the ominous line "Deliver us from ourselves," Sassoon bid farewell to the poetry of social commentary. By now he was more interested in his spiritual quest.

Next to his war poems, Sassoon's poems of religious searching are his most effective. The quest begins with "The Traveller to His Soul" (1933), in which Sassoon asks, as the "problem which concerns me most," the question "Have I got a soul?" He spends over twenty years trying to answer the question. His work, beginning with *The Heart's Journey* and *Vigils*, is concerned with exploration of self and uncertainty about the self's place in the universe, with increasing questioning about what lies behind creation. With *Rhymed Ruminations*, Sassoon ends the 1930's on a note of uneasiness and uncertainty.

SEQUENCES

The questions are answered in the three volumes *Common Chords*, *Emblems of Experience*, and *The Tasking*, which were combined to make the book *Sequences*. In the poem "Redemption" (*Common Chords*), Sassoon yearns for a vision of the eternal, which he recognizes as existing beyond his senses. Sassoon's lines recall Vaughan's mystical visions when he asks for "O but one ray/ from that all-hallowing and eternal day." In *The Tasking*, Sassoon reached what Thorpe calls a spiritual certainty, and his best poems in that volume succeed more clearly than the war poems in satisfying Sassoon's own poetic criteria as expressed in 1939. In "Another Spring," Sassoon speaks in simple, direct, and compact language about feelings of the heart—an old man's emotions on witnessing what may be his last spring. The natural imagery is concrete and visual as well as auditory, concentrating on "some crinkled primrose leaves" and "a noise of nesting rooks." Though the final three lines of the poem add a hint of didacticism, the poem succeeds by leaving much unsaid about the eternal rebirth of nature and its implications for the old man and the force behind the regenerative cycle of nature. It is a fine poem, like many in *The Tasking*, with a simple, packed style that makes these poems better as art, though doomed to be less familiar than the war poems.

Other major works

LONG FICTION: *The Memoirs of George Sherston*, 1937 (includes *Memoirs of a Fox-Hunting Man*, 1928; *Memoirs of an Infantry Officer*, 1930; and *Sherston's Progress*, 1936).

NONFICTION: *The Old Century and Seven More Years*, 1938; *Lecture on Poetry*, 1939; *The Weald of Youth*, 1942; *Siegfried's Journey, 1916-1920*, 1945; *Meredith*, 1948; *Siegfried Sassoon Diaries, 1920-1922*, 1981; *Siegfried Sassoon Diaries, 1915-1918*, 1983; *Siegfried Sassoon Diaries, 1923-1925*, 1985.

EDITED TEXT: *Poems by Wilfred Owen*, 1920.

Bibliography

Bloom, Harold, ed. *Poets of World War I: Rupert Brooke and Siegfried Sassoon*. Philadelphia: Chelsea House, 2003. Contains numerous essays on Sassoon, covering topics such as realism, satire, and spirituality in his poetry.

Caesar, Adrian. *Taking It Like a Man: Suffering, Sexuality, and the War Poets: Brooke, Sassoon, Owen, Graves*. New York: Manchester University Press, 1993. Caesar explores how four British poets reconciled their ideologies inherited from Christianity, imperialism, and Romanticism with their experiences of World War I.

Campbell, Patrick. *Siegfried Sassoon: A Study of the War Poetry*. Jefferson, N.C.: McFarland, 1999. Through primary documents and research, Campbell provides critical analyses of Sassoon's war poetry. Includes bibliographical references and an index.

Egremont, Max. *Siegfried Sassoon: A Life*. New York: Farrar, Straus and Giroux, 2005. This biography of Sassoon examines his life, including his relationship with Stephan Tennant, its breakup, and his subsequent marriage.

Fussell, Paul. *The Great War and Modern Memory*. 1975. Reprint. New York: Oxford University Press, 2000. This classic study of the literature arising from the experience of fighting in World War I pays special attention to Sassoon's fiction, autobiography, and poetry. Provides a useful context for Sassoon's work in comparison to other writers of the period.

Hipp, Daniel. *The Poetry of Shell Shock: Wartime Trauma and Healing in Wilfred Owen, Ivor Gurney, and Siegfried Sassoon*. Jefferson, N.C.: McFarland, 2005. Contains chapters examining the lives and works of three war poets: Sassoon, Wilfred Owen, and Ivory Gurney.

Lane, Arthur E. *An Adequate Response: The War Poetry of Wilfred Owen and Siegfried Sassoon*. Detroit: Wayne State University Press, 1972. Lane highlights the use of satire and parody as he analyzes Sassoon's war verse. Contends that Sassoon and others, when faced with the horrors of trench warfare, were charged with creating a new mode of expression since the traditional modes proved inadequate.

Moeyes, Paul. *Siegfried Sassoon: Scorched Glory—A Critical Study*. New York: St.

Martin's Press, 1997. Moeyes draws on Sassoon's edited diaries and letters to explore Sassoon's assertion that his poetry was his real autobiography. Includes bibliography and an index.

Wilson, Jean Moorcroft. *Siegfried Sassoon: The Journey from the Trenches—A Biography, 1918-1967*. London: Duckworth, 2003. Describes the later years of Sassoon's life, looking at his life after the war.

———. *Siegfried Sassoon: The Making of a War Poet—A Biography*. New York: Routledge, 1999. Details Sassoon's early life, covering the years from his birth through 1918, and in doing so, closely examines his struggle to come to terms with being gay.

Jay Ruud

JAMES SCHUYLER

Born: Chicago, Illinois; November 9, 1923
Died: New York, New York; April 12, 1991

Principal poetry
Salute, 1960
May 24th or So, 1966
Freely Espousing, 1969
The Crystal Lithium, 1972
A Sun Cab, 1972
Hymn to Life, 1974
The Fireproof Floors of Witley Court: English Songs and Dances, 1976
Song, 1976
The Home Book: Prose and Poems, 1951-1970, 1977 (Trevor Winkfield, editor)
The Morning of the Poem, 1980
Early in '71, 1981
A Few Days, 1985
Selected Poems, 1988
Collected Poems, 1993
Last Poems, 1999
Selected Poems, 2007
Other Flowers: Uncollected Poems, 2010

Other literary forms

James Schuyler (SKI-lur) wrote (or cowrote) three novels. Beginning with *Alfred and Guinevere* (1958), the novels deal with the upper middle class and show a good ear for the comic trivialities of ordinary conversation, whether of children and adolescents, sophisticated young adults, or middle-aged couples. They also demonstrate, with their precision in naming, Schuyler's connoisseur's eye for furniture, design, and objects used or displayed in the household. The satiric *A Nest of Ninnies* (1969), cowritten with John Ashbery, lacks the plot and fully developed characters of *What's for Dinner?* (1978), his most substantial novel, giving rich evidence of true command of the form as it traces an alcoholic's recovery in a mental hospital, her husband's simultaneous affair with a widowed friend, and the progress of several other patients on short-term stays in the hospital.

Three of Schuyler's plays have been produced: the one-act pieces *Presenting Jane* (pr. 1952) and *Shopping and Waiting* (pb. 1953), and *Unpacking the Black Trunk*, another collaboration with a fellow poet (Kenward Elmslie), produced off-Broadway in

1965. He wrote the libretto ("mostly collage from newspapers," he says) for *A Picnic Cantata: For Four Women's Voices, Two Pianos, and Percussion* (pr. 1953), for which the writer Paul Bowles composed the music; it was recorded by Columbia Records.

Like fellow New York poets Ashbery and Frank O'Hara, Schuyler also wrote art criticism—particularly for *Art News*, where he served for a time as associate editor.

Achievements

James Schuyler won the Pulitzer Prize in poetry in 1981 for *The Morning of the Poem*. His other awards include the Frank O'Hara Prize from *Poetry* in 1969, the Bernard F. Connors Prize for Poetry from the *Paris Review* in 1985, a Whiting Writers' Award in 1985, and a Lambda Literary Award in 1993. He received grants and fellowships, including a National Endowment for the Arts grant and an Academy of American Poets Fellowship.

Biography

Born in Chicago to a family with extensive roots in the United States, James Marcus Schuyler grew up in Washington, D.C., and Buffalo and East Aurora, New York, the family seat to which he returned. He attended Bethany College in West Virginia, served in the U.S. Navy in World War II, and worked for Voice of America in New York City before traveling to Italy, where he attended the University of Florence and lived in W. H. Auden's house in Ischia, typing some of the elder poet's manuscripts (as he notes in his obituary poem, "Wystan Auden"). After he returned to New York in the early 1950's, he became involved in art and poetry circles and took a curatorial position in the Department of Circulating Exhibitions at the Museum of Modern Art, organizing a number of shows. He also served as associate editor of *Art News*, for which O'Hara and Ashbery also worked. Together, and with a number of other young poets, they changed the poetry scene in New York and became a major force in contemporary American poetry. Close friends as well as colleagues, they often have referred to one another in their books and poems and sometimes collaborated. Painters and musicians are included in this group; various artist friends of Schuyler not only are mentioned in his poems but also have contributed cover illustrations for several of his books. Schuyler suffered personal traumas in the 1970's, and his recovery from a nervous breakdown is recorded in *The Morning of the Poem*; he also sustained severe burns after falling asleep while smoking in bed. Nevertheless, in the late 1970's, he began reading publicly for the first time. Schuyler died in New York City in 1991 after suffering a stroke.

Analysis

James Schuyler was a keen observer of the most intimate details of the world around him and of the sensations they evoked in him. His poetry captures those detailed impressions and sensations, however ephemeral they may be. This very ephemerality is the singular distinction of his world, particularly in his presentation of nature. The individual poem lives not so much as a perfected piece of art, frozen under glass; rather, it shimmers with movement and conveys a sense of being nearly as ephemeral as the impressions it records. Sometimes, of course, the impressions and mood are so fleeting as to leave the reader with virtually nothing but random actions and details—or even only words. This is the danger of Schuyler's method—one which its great advocate, O'Hara, did not always steer clear of himself. Thus, some poems read as little more than notebook jottings.

However, the method is also responsible for the brilliance of his two long poems, "Hymn to Life" and "The Morning of the Poem" (the title poem of the volume for which he was awarded the Pulitzer Prize). These poems ramble, it is true, down the streams of Schuyler's consciousness, across several weeks' time, from place to place, subject to subject, and mood to mood. However, each attains a remarkable unity through the skill and exactness with which Schuyler has captured his own voice, developed over the course of a rather short career (barely two decades of serious publishing), to penetrate and reveal his own mental and emotional states. His highly individual, warmly personal, and frankly intimate voice is characterized by unforced humor, gentle self-deprecation, eagerness, equivocation, wonder, doubt, and fascination. This is the voice, as well, of a series of simple and tender love poems, joyful and physical without being actually erotic, addressing another man with the greatest ease and naturalness imaginable. Schuyler's achievements in evoking the processes of nature, love, and mind are praiseworthy, for producing not only such thought-provoking and appealing major works as the two long poems but also many shorter ones that are sure to enchant readers over the years.

Schuyler was a master of subtle changes—in growing things, in weather, in time of day or year, and in moods and thoughts. These he conveyed appropriately, without big effects, sudden bursts of insight, or harsh contrasts. Rather, his poems have the shimmering magical quality of familiar scenes and objects rendered in watercolor landscapes or still lifes, but they are anything but still: Even his most quiet and peaceful scenes contain movement, even if nearly imperceptible. Such constant, inevitable movement is the manifestation of life for Schuyler, and through his poetry, the reader too gains a more intense appreciation for the many wonders and delights of even the smallest details in this life, once a moment is taken to observe them.

In an interview, Schuyler once said, "Much of my poetry is as concerned with looking at things and trying to transcribe them as painting is. This is not generally true of poetry." Evidence of Schuyler's affinities to painting (which doubtless stem largely from his friendship with many painters as well as his own work in the art world) is abundant throughout his work, in his attention to color, light, texture, and other visual effects.

Besides being "very visual," his work also "seems to be especially musical," he went on to say. Indeed, he counted important composers such as Virgil Thomson and Ned

Rorem among his friends and wrote about music from Johannes Brahms and Sergei Rachmaninoff to Janis Joplin and Carly Simon. His is not the music of the conventional sonneteer, however, although he made an obligatory gesture or two in that direction. Rather, his poetry, almost without exception, ignores regular rhyme and meter in favor of free verse, appropriate for his emphasis on endless change. His styles of free verse change radically too, from lines of only two or three syllables in his self-styled "skinny poems," providing a slow, even, almost hesitant, occasionally fragmented pace appropriate for the meditative stance of some of these poems, to lines as long as each individual sentence unit requires (in "The Cenotaph"), to lines a page wide or more in the long poems. Line breaks are often capricious, but this very unpredictability allows him some splendid effects. For example, the minimally punctuated "Buttered Greens" has lines which make sense in one way, until the next line indicates that the last part of the preceding line is meant not as a completion of the preceding thought but as the beginning of a new statement: "inside all/ is not con-/ tent, yet/ the chance/ of it is/ there, free." A reader automatically assumes that "free" modifies "chance," but the next line suggests that it modifies the botanical noun: "there, free/ leaves fall." Often he abandons punctuation altogether, and a whole series of sensory impressions flows down or across the page as unmediated sensory input ("A Sun Cab"). Sentence fragments, composed of nouns, adjectives, and prepositional phrases, are frequent in many of these shorter poems, reminiscent of William Carlos Williams, whom Schuyler acknowledged as an early influence.

However, musical aspects are present in occasional devices of structure and sound. Words or images are repeated, like leitmotifs; recurring themes and images are particularly important in the long poems, where depiction of rain or of sites in Washington, D.C., acts both as a cohesive device and as a counterpoint to other concerns in the poem. His free-verse lines often emulate the startling and open structures of much modern music. Finally, Schuyler does not neglect the traditional musical devices of sound; pleasing patterns of alliteration, assonance, consonance, and even exact rhyme (though usually internal and never long-sustained) appear casually in occasional poems such as "Song" and "Just Before Fall."

Most of his poems purport to do no more than map the stream of his consciousness, whether it consists chiefly of external impressions which engage his full attention or of thoughts and feelings and whatever sensory recollections they invoke. Sometimes it is a combination of the two—external impressions giving rise to memories, which are in turn interrupted by more sensory input from the present moment. Schuyler's is very much a poetry of the present. Nearly every poem begins directly in the present tense, often indicating the setting of place, time, and weather; recollections of the past may intrude, described in the past tense as appropriate, but their appearance is strongly grounded in the immediacy of the present moment, rather than being a meditation on "remembrance of things past" or "emotion recollected in tranquillity" undertaken as an end in itself.

Time is certainly a central theme for Schuyler, but with an emphasis quite unlike that of most other poets. It passes as quickly (or slowly) for him as for another, but he does not bemoan its passing. He is not without regrets, but these are for friends who have died, lovers who have left: He accepts his move ahead into age, not with resignation but as merely another stage of life, for "Life will change and/ I am part of it and/ will change too."

Such an attitude informs his two longest poems, "Hymn to Life" and "The Morning of the Poem." Each embraces and celebrates change, the prevailing force in his work, the dominant characteristic of all life itself. In the earlier poem, Schuyler takes the reader with him along the paths of his mind and experiences, recording his various thoughts and sensory impressions as time moves on. It begins the day before spring (that is, in March), then moves imperceptibly into April and May. These shifts occur not with an abrupt, secretarial ripping-off of the old month's calendar page but with the gradualism of nature itself: This seventeen-page poem is not broken into sections as the time passes but reveals each new month's presence only in mid-line, appropriately for the subtle recognition of something new in the air, a change that has occurred while one was watching but was perhaps momentarily distracted, watching the many wonderful details all around, so exquisitely conveyed in this poem.

"Song"

Such unremarked changes, so lovingly dwelt on, are Schuyler's stock-in-trade, for the times between (parts of the year or the day) are his favorite poetic subjects. "Song," for example, concentrates on the hour of sunset. It begins: "The light lies layered in the trees" (with melodious alliteration and use of long vowel sounds). Then the sun sets, "not sharply or at once," but in "a stately progress down the sky." Other details around him, however, attract his attention: "Traffic sounds and/ bells resound . . . the grass is violent green." Several color sensations then yield to the sound of a car starting up, as the visual sense surrenders to darkness. Two short lines ("A horsefly vanishes./ A smoking cigarette.") capture the sense of increasing darkness: The normally quite visible insect is lost to sight while the glowing of the cigarette, normally not noticeable in daylight, appears, contrasting with the lack of light around it. Finally, the leaves merge, "discriminated barely/ in light no longer layered," because of the departure of the sun's light.

This poem, like so many others by Schuyler, simply presents a sequence of sensory images, vividly capturing the various components of a particular moment as it is experienced. Schuyler does not pretend to deal with the earth-shattering problems of humanity: That becomes editorial writing, he has said. Consequently, his poetry has often been regarded as trivial. Indeed, many of his poems do fail to register any significant impression. The comic criticism of himself that he quotes in "The Morning of the Poem"— "All he cares about are leaves and/ flowers and weather"—has validity, but not at all as a criticism. These subjects serve as indicators of his own understanding of life—its beauty, its transience, and its variability, qualities that every human being must understand and accept to come fully to terms with existence as well as with such major human concerns as love and death.

These important concerns are not in the least absent from Schuyler's work. He often confronts death as he recalls or writes elegies for friend and fellow poet Frank O'Hara, other friends and lovers (Bill Aalto, his first lover, who died of leukemia after they had broken up), and musicians as diverse as Libby Holman, Janis Joplin, and Bruno Walter. Their deaths may be violent or gentle, but Schuyler accepts them with deepest serenity. He portrays love as "quiet/ ecstasy and sweet content." A lovely series in *Hymn to Life* records with utmost simplicity such joys as lying on the beach beside his lover or eagerly awaiting his return from a trip; later poems reveal with welcome understatement the pain of being without him, once the relationship has ended.

"THE MORNING OF THE POEM"

Love (and sex) and death, in addition to time and change (indeed, in conjunction with them, for the latter are ineluctably implicated with the former) form the major strands of the intricate but not at all impenetrable tapestry of Schuyler's longest poem, "The Morning of the Poem," which reads almost like a run-on, candid, and charmingly intimate conversational journal. Because it proceeds through sixty-one pages with no break other than a dot in the exact middle of the poem (separating an elegy from a grocery list), it would seem to be all of one piece. Schuyler maintains unity of place—that is, the East Aurora room where he sits at his typewriter—although his thoughts may range to New York City, New Brunswick, England, and Paris, and among similarly diverse subjects. Yet the reader discovers, moving through the poem, that these meditations occur not on a single morning or afternoon but over a nearly two-month span.

"The Morning of the Poem" takes Schuyler from the beginning of July to late August, when he leaves his rural family home in western New York to return to Manhattan. As he sits at his typewriter, thinking of his friend painting in New York (and addressing him, as if in a letter, throughout much of the poem), the weather, assorted deliveries, his aged mother's nagging, and many memories from various stages of the past (last night's dream, cruising another middle-aged man in the grocery store, boyhood and adolescent incidents, lovers and friends and a beloved dog now gone) impinge on his consciousness and accordingly enter the poem. Amid the many surrenders to thought and recollection, the recurring descriptions of the rainy weather, several lawn mowings, and a few passing references to the time of month give readers their bearings as to the progression of time—always to their surprise at its speed.

Schuyler has a vested interest in moving time rapidly—he is looking forward to rejoining his painter friend in New York. His recollections of the past enable time to pass more quickly for him, while the present-tense descriptions of the weather and activities around the house slow it down, reminding him only of the stretch of time still facing him. However, this does not deny his ability to find pleasure even in the moments that drag on.

Schuyler keeps imagining his friend painting on his rooftop in New York and praises "the dedication of the artist" which characterizes him. Schuyler's question, "Whoever knows what a painter is thinking?" is echoed near the end of the poem, upon receipt of a postcard from composer Ned Rorem: "I wonder what it's like, being a composer?" He finds these other arts mysterious: painting involves colors whose names he cannot remember; music demands "so much time" to write down "the little notes," whereas his own writing "goes by so fast:/ a couple of hours of concentration, then you're/ spent." Presented in counterpoint to these other artists, one introduced at the very beginning of the poem, the other at the end, Schuyler as poet, seated at his typewriter, is seen by the reader to be every bit as dedicated, even when drinking limeade, or just lost in reverie—dedicated to the pursuit of self-knowledge, of an empathy with the life around him, natural and human. It has certainly demanded great effort to make this poem, composed presumably in countless sittings over two months, flow so smoothly and achieve a unity among the many subjects of its meanderings.

A poetry of sheer stream of consciousness, of simple recording of sensory and mental experiences, would seem to be an easy achievement; many lesser poets have attempted it, but without the aura of mystery, celebration, wonder, and joy that Schuyler brings to such moments. He has no poetic program, no ambition to make his poems "more open," as "a clunkhead" suggests; rather, he wants "merely to say, to see and say, things/ as they are." It thus seems important to name things exactly, and he displays a splendidly precise vocabulary of nouns and verbs when describing his environment (climate, plant life, sea life, forest life, furnishings, and art works). It is understandably frustrating, therefore, when he fails to remember certain names for things, as throughout "The Morning of the Poem." Yet specific names may not be so important when considered against appreciation for the things themselves and the experiences they create, as he tells his "dead best friend" in "The Morning of the Poem":

> this is not
> your poem, your poem I may
> Never write, too much, though it is there and
> needs only to be written down
> And one day will and if it isn't it doesn't matter:
> the truth, the absolute
> Of feeling, of knowing what you know, that is
> the poem . . .

To capture such "truth," such an "absolute of feeling" in words is, of course, far from easy. In "Hudson Ferry," Schuyler writes, with a kind of comic disgust, "You can't talk about the weather"—it is so easily susceptible to clichés. However, Schuyler has paradoxically persisted, as "The Morning of the Poem" makes clear. How? He continues to remark that "You can't get at a sunset naming colors," so he uses other means: For example, noting the effects of the sunset in "Song," he is not afraid to use metaphors and similes—but characteristically with freshness and aptness: "An almost autumn sky, a swimming pool awash/ with cinnamon and gentian." However, he also often mocks the poet's metaphorical and personifying tendencies and can undercut such poeticisms with a deft phrase, like the parenthesis that immediately follows the lines just quoted: "(The sky's the swimming pool, that is)," or the deflation of the grandiose apostrophe "O Day!" with the no less and possibly more appreciative "literal/ and unsymbolic/ day." As he writes in "The Cenotaph": "The hawkweed flowers are an idea about the color of fire./ The hawkweed are one thing and the fire is another." Thus he reminds the reader that the objects compared retain their own identities; it is the human mind that draws such parallels. For that very reason—that the human mind perceives things by making such comparisons—these poetic figures which indicate similarities must not be omitted from the writing of poetry; they are indispensable to the mind's process of perception. What he does seek to avoid poetically are the familiar standard associations: "fall/ equals melancholy, spring,/ get laid." "An Almanac" succeeds in this splendidly, tracing the passage of the seasons in an utterly fresh way—through nothing but discrete details of action, predominantly human, which indicate clearly the particular changes accompanying each new season, from fall to spring: "Shops take down their awnings . . . In cedar chests sheers and seersuckers displace flannels and wools."

Schuyler's poetry revels in the experience of any sort of weather, season, time of day, or environment. He seems equally at home in city and country (though favoring the latter) and can paint a Manhattan street scene as luminously as a Long Island beach or a woodland walk in Vermont. The variety of the scenes he can enjoy and his ability to capture accurately the feel of such a range of experience richly display his appreciation for the fact of change—even in the breakup of love affairs, even in the losses of death. Toward the end of "The Morning of the Poem," he realizes "how this poem seems mostly about what I've lost," yet none of these losses has broken him. He does not elegize them with the typical "life must go on" resolution, for he knows very well that, *sub specie temporis*, there is nothing else life can do: "Life will change and/ I am part of it and/ will change too. So/ will you, and you. . . ." Death is merely another form of this change. The process of life contains "in repetition, change:/ a continuity, the what/ of which you are a part." There is no stability, as each season fades into the next, yet in each season is the promise of the future ones; as Schuyler writes in "Buttered Greens," our life means "leavings and/ the permanence/ of return."

When Schuyler in "The Morning of the Poem" receives a letter from a friend telling of her brother's dying while "the grandchildren and the dogs ran in and out as usual," Schuyler responds quoting the familiar litany, which is no less true: "'In the midst of life we are in death, in the/ Midst of death we are in life.'" This is the essence of Schuyler's attitude toward both life and death, including a healthy recognition of the passage of time and the inevitability of change ("This beauty that I see . . . it goes, it goes."). After he hears about a hurricane on Long Island, Schuyler asks himself in "The Morning of the Poem," "Why so much pleasure in wrack and/ ruin?" It may be the proof it gives of the ephemeral nature of all security and permanence. After all, "the scattered wrack" contains "(always) some cut-up surprise." Change gives no cause for fear or regret, Schuyler suggests through his wonderfully serene poetry; change in nature creates endless sequences of beauty, like the changing days in "Hymn to Life": "each so unique, each so alike." The seasons are predictable, yet full of unexpected variations: a cold, rainy July, a balmy November.

During the course of the marvelous abundance of "The Morning of the Poem," Schuyler, indulging in a favorite pastime, eating ("grapes, oysters/ And champagne"), remarks that "bliss is such a simple thing." So is most of Schuyler's poetry, yet it conveys a rich sense of the world around him and a healthy, joyous approach to existence.

OTHER MAJOR WORKS

LONG FICTION: *Alfred and Guinevere*, 1958; *A Nest of Ninnies*, 1969 (with John Ashbery); *What's for Dinner?*, 1978.

PLAYS: *Presenting Jane*, pr. 1952 (one act); *A Picnic Cantata: For Four Women's Voices, Two Pianos, and Percussion*, pr. 1953 (music by Paul Bowles); *Shopping and Waiting*, pb. 1953; *Unpacking the Black Trunk*, pr. 1965 (one act, with Kenward Elmslie).

NONFICTION: *Two Journals: James Schuyler, Darragh Park*, 1995; *The Diary of James Schuyler*, 1996; *Selected Art Writings*, 1998 (Simon Pettet, editor); *Just the Thing: The Selected Letters of James Schuyler*, 2004 (William Corbett, editor); *The Letters of James Schuyler to Frank O'Hara*, 2006 (Corbett, editor).

EDITED TEXTS: *Broadway: A Poet's and Painter's Anthology*, 1979; *Broadway 2: A Poet's and Painter's Anthology*, 1989.

BIBLIOGRAPHY

Auslander, Philip. *The New York School Poets as Playwrights*. New York: Peter Lang, 1989. Although the focus of this volume is on plays, the chapter on Schuyler also examines his poetry, including his link to the New York School.

Corbett, William, and Geoffrey Young, eds. *That Various Field for James Schuyler*. Great Barrington, Mass.: The Figures, 1991. A good overview.

Schuyler, James. *The Diary of James Schuyler*. Edited by Nathan Kernan. Santa Rosa, Calif.: Black Sparrow Press, 1997. Schuyler's diary is a devastating account of his decline into mental illness and a narrative of his achievements. Includes bibliographical references.

Vinson, James, ed. *Contemporary Poets*. 3d ed. New York: St. Martin's Press, 1980.

The entry on Schuyler, by Michael Andre, identifies his artistic leanings and his prolific writings. Calls *Salute* representative of his poems, which are "sensitive and perceptive." Notes that much of Schuyler's poetry describes what he sees and what he loves—and that is not New York.

Ward, Geoff. *Statutes of Liberty: The New York School of Poets*. 2d ed. New York: Palgrave, 2001. An account of the key figures of the New York School including Schuyler. Ward provides updated material on the group and its influence on postmodern poetics. Includes bibliographical references and index.

Scott Giantvalley

GERTRUDE STEIN

Born: Allegheny (now in Pittsburgh), Pennsylvania; February 3, 1874
Died: Neuilly-sur-Seine, France; July 27, 1946

PRINCIPAL POETRY
Tender Buttons: Objects, Food, Rooms, 1914
Before the Flowers of Friendship Faded Friendship Faded, 1931
Two (Hitherto Unpublished) Poems, 1948
Bee Time Vine, and Other Pieces, 1913-1927, 1953
Stanzas in Meditation, and Other Poems, 1929-1933, 1956

OTHER LITERARY FORMS

Most of Gertrude Stein's works did not appear until much later than the dates of their completion. Much of her writing, including novelettes, shorter poems, plays, prayers, novels, and several portraits, appeared posthumously in the Yale Edition of the Unpublished Writings of Gertrude Stein, in eight volumes edited by Carl Van Vechten. A few of her plays have been set to music, the operas have been performed, and the later children's books have been illustrated by various artists.

ACHIEVEMENTS

Gertrude Stein did not win tangible recognition for her literary achievements, though she did earn the Medal of French Recognition from the French government for services during World War II. Nevertheless, her contribution to art, and specifically to writing, is as great as that of Ezra Pound or James Joyce. It is, however, diametrically opposed to that of these figures in style, content, and underlying philosophy of literature. She advanced mimetic representation to its ultimate, doing away progressively with memory, narration, plot, the strictures of formalized language, and the distinction among styles and genres. Her view of life was founded on a sense of the living present that shunned all theorizing about meaning and purpose, making writing a supreme experience unto itself. For the first fifteen years of her artistic life, she worked at her craft with stubborn persistence while carrying on an active social life among the Parisian avant-garde. She became influential as a person of definite taste and idiosyncratic manners rather than as an artist in her own right. Her parlor became legend, and writers as diverse as Ernest Hemingway and Sherwood Anderson profited from her ideas. In the 1920's, she was the matron of the American expatriates, and her work, by then known to most writers, was either ferociously derided or enthusiastically applauded.

It was the poetry of *Tender Buttons* that first brought Gertrude Stein to the attention of the public. After 1926, however, her novels, critical essays, and prose portraits in-

Gertrude Stein
(Library of Congress)

creasingly circulated. She secured a place in American letters with the publication of *The Autobiography of Alice B. Toklas* (1933), which was also a commercial success. She did not receive any official recognition during her lifetime, except as a curiosity in the world of letters.

Literary criticism has traditionally simply skirted the "problem" of Gertrude Stein, limiting itself to broad generalizations. There exists a group of Stein devotees responsible for preserving the texts; this group includes Robert Bartlett Haas, Carl Van Vechten, Donald Gallup, and Leon Katz. Stein's work has been illuminated by two indispensable scholar-critics, Richard Bridgman and Donald Sutherland; and there are useful interpretive suggestions in studies by Rosalind Miller, Allegra Stewart, Norman Weinstein, and Michael J. Hoffman. Stein's major impact has been on writers of later generations, especially in the late 1950's, through the 1960's, and up to the present time; the poetry of Aram Saroyan, Robert Kelly, Clark Coolidge, Jerome Rothenberg, and Lewis Welch is especially indebted to Stein. New insights into this revolutionary writer in the wake of global revisions of the notion of writing and critical thinking have been offered in short pieces by S. C. Neuman, William H. Gass, and Neil Schmitz. Today, a place of eminence is accorded to Stein's fairy tales and children's stories, the theoretical writings, the major works *The Autobiography of Alice B. Toklas* and *The Making of Ameri-*

cans: Being a History of a Family's Progress (1925, 1934), the shorter works *Three Lives* (1909) and *Ida, a Novel* (1941), and finally *Tender Buttons*, considered by many to be a masterpiece of twentieth century literature.

BIOGRAPHY

Gertrude Stein was born in Allegheny, Pennsylvania, on February 3, 1874. Her grandfather, Michael Stein, came from Austria in 1841, married Hanna Seliger, and settled in Baltimore. One of his sons, Daniel, Gertrude's father, was in the wholesale wool and clothing industry. Daniel was mildly successful and very temperamental. He married Amelia Keyser in 1864 and had five children, Michael (born in 1865), Simon (1867), Bertha (1870), Leo (1872), and Gertrude (1874). In 1875, the family moved to Vienna, and three years later, Daniel returned to the United States, leaving his family for a one-year stay in Paris. In 1879, the family moved back to the United States and spent a year in Baltimore with Amelia Keyser's family. In 1880, Daniel found work in California, and the family relocated again, to Oakland. Memories of these early moves would dot Gertrude's mature works. Leo and Gertrude found that they had much in common, took drawing and music lessons together, frequented the Oakland and San Francisco public libraries, and had time to devote to their intellectual and aesthetic interests. When their mother died of cancer in 1888, Leo and Gertrude found themselves more and more detached from the rest of the family. In 1892, Daniel Stein died, and the eldest son, Michael, took the family back to Baltimore, but the Steins began to scatter. In 1892, Leo entered Harvard, while Gertrude and Bertha stayed with their aunt, Fannie Bachrach. Michael, always patriarchal and the image of stability, married Sarah Samuels and later moved to Paris, where he became a respected member of the intellectual elite, maintaining a Saturday night open house at their apartment in rue Madame. Matisse's portrait of Michael is now in San Francisco.

Gertrude was a coddled and protected child. At sixteen, she weighed 135 pounds, and later in college she hired a boy to box with her every day to help her lose weight. Her niece, Gertrude Stein Raffel, recalls that her heaviness "was not unbecoming. She was round, roly-poly, and angelic looking." During her adolescent years, she became very introspective and critical, and was often depressed and concerned with death. Already emotionally independent, owing to her mother's protracted invalidism and her father's neglect and false representation of authority, Gertrude saw in her brother Leo her only friend. Their bond would not be broken for another twenty years, and she would follow him everywhere, the two delving into matters of mutual interest.

In 1893, Gertrude Stein entered the Harvard Annex, renamed Radcliffe College the following year. She gravitated toward philosophy and psychology, and took courses with such luminaries as George Santayana, Josiah Royce, Herbert Palmer, and William James. In 1894, she worked in the Harvard Psychological Laboratory with Hugo Münsterberg. Her interest in psychology expanded, and in 1896, she published, together with Leon Solomons, a paper on "Normal Motor Automatism," which appeared in the *Psychological Review*. A second article, "Cultivated Motor Automatism," appeared two years later. In 1897, Stein followed her brother to The Johns Hopkins University and began the study of medicine. She specialized in brain research and was encouraged to continue, even though by 1901 her dedication had waned. She attempted four examinations, failed them, and withdrew without a degree.

In 1902, Stein began her travels, first to Italy and then to London, where she met philosopher Bertrand Russell. She spent much time in the British Museum Library studying the Elizabethans, especially William Shakespeare. In the meantime, Leo also abandoned his studies, reverting to an earlier passion for history. A specialist in Renaissance costume, he was drawn to contemporary art, and when, in 1904, he and his sister saw a Paul Cézanne exhibit in Florence, they started buying paintings; Leo would became a major collector of Henri Matisse. The two settled in the now-famous apartment at 27 rue de Fleurus, where Gertrude's literary career began, though her first sustained effort, *Q.E.D.*, written in 1903, remained unpublished until 1950 (as *Things as They Are*). In 1905, while working on a translation of Gustave Flaubert's *Trois contes*, she wrote *Three Lives*. During that period, she met Pablo Picasso, who would be very influential in her thinking about art and with whom she would remain friends for decades. The following year, he painted the famous portrait now at the Metropolitan Museum. These days of intense work and thinking saw Stein fast at work on her first major long novel, *The Making of Americans*, which she completed in 1910.

Gertrude's trips abroad and throughout France from her home base in Paris became an essential part of her existence. In 1907, her brother Michael introduced her to Alice B. Toklas, who soon became her secretary, going to work on the proofs of *Three Lives*. Toklas learned to use a typewriter, and the following year, in Fiesole, Italy, she began to copy parts of the manuscript of *The Making of Americans*. Leo, intellectually independent, was moving toward his own aesthetic, though he was still busy promoting new American and French talents. As a painter, Leo was not successful, and he came eventually to dislike all contemporary painters except the cubists. In 1913, he moved from the rue de Fleurus apartment, and with him went all the Renoirs and most of the Matisses and Cézannes, while Gertrude kept the Picassos. Leo's place had been taken by Toklas, who stayed with Gertrude until her death in 1946.

The writer first began to be noticed as a result of Alfred Stieglitz's publication of her "portraits" of Matisse and Picasso in *Camera Work* in 1912. She spent the summer of that year in Spain, capturing the sense of her idea of the relationship between object and space, with which she had been struggling. Here she began the prose poem *Tender Buttons*, which brought her to the attention of most of her contemporaries, eliciting varying reactions. She continued to write "portraits" while visiting Mabel Dodge in Florence, at the Villa Curonia. At the Armory Show in New York in 1913, Stein was responsible for the presentation of the Pablo Picasso exhibit. When the war broke out, she was in London, where she met the philosopher Alfred North Whitehead. She continued to work intensely, mostly on poetry and plays, and visited Barcelona and Palma de Majorca. In 1916, Stein and Toklas returned to France and the next year did voluntary war relief work in the south. In 1922, Stein was awarded a Medaille de la Reconnaissance Française.

With the appearance of her first collected volume, *Geography and Plays*, in 1922, Stein's fame among the cognoscenti was assured, together with a lively controversy over her truly original style. She was invariably visited by the younger expatriate artists from the United States, and her parlor became a focal point for the exchange of ideas. Sherwood Anderson introduced her to Hemingway in 1922, and the younger writer learned much from her about the craft of writing. Hemingway was influential in securing publication of parts of *The Making of Americans* in Ford Madox Ford's magazine, *Transatlantic Review*. (The nine-hundred-page work was later abridged to half its size by her translator into French, and the shorter version was published in 1925 by Contact Editions, Paris.) Her relationship with Hemingway, however, because of conflicting temperaments, was short-lived; their friendship soon degenerated into bickering.

Stein entered another phase of her life when she was asked to lecture in Oxford and Cambridge in 1926. The text of the conference, "Composition as Explanation," constituted her first critical statement on the art of writing; she subsequently returned to a personal exposition of her ideas in *How to Write* (1931), breaking new ground at the stylistic level. This period of major intellectual and thematic upheaval witnessed several transformations in her art. She began to devote more time to the theater and eventually tackled the difficult task of writing about ideas in the little known *Stanzas in Meditation, and Other Poems, 1929-1933* (not published until 1956). In 1929, she left Paris and moved to Bilignin. Her *Lucy Church Amiably* (1930) had not pleased her, but *Four Saints in Three Acts* (pr., pb. 1934), with music by Virgil Thomson, was successfully produced in New York. After publication of the well-received *The Autobiography of Alice B. Toklas* in 1933, she traveled to the United States for a lecture tour. Her *Lectures in America* (1935) dealt with her philosophy of composition.

Compelled to close her apartment at rue de Fleurus shortly after her return to France, Stein moved with Toklas to rue Christine; with the onset of the war in 1939, however, they returned to Bilignin. During the war, the two women lived for a time in Culoz, where they first witnessed the German occupation and then the arrival of the Americans, which would be recounted in *Wars I Have Seen* (1945). In December, 1944, she returned to Paris, only to leave soon afterward to entertain U.S. troops stationed in occupied Germany. Her views on the U.S. soldier and the society that produced him changed considerably during these two years. In October, 1945, she traveled to Brussels to lecture. Weary and tired, she decided to visit her friend Bernard Fay in the country. Her trip was abruptly interrupted by her illness, and she entered the American Hospital in Neuilly-sur-Seine, where, after an unsuccessful cancer operation, she died on July 27, 1946.

ANALYSIS

It is customary to refer to Gertrude Stein's poetry—and her work in general—with the qualifiers "abstract," "repetitive," and "nonsensical," terms that do little if any justice to a most remarkable literary achievement. The proper evaluation of Stein's work requires a willingness to rethink certain basic notions concerning art, discourse, and life, a task that is perhaps as difficult as the reading of Stein's voluminous production itself. Her work, however, is really not excessively abstract, especially when one considers that her poetic rests on the fundamental axiom of "immediate existing." Nothing could be more concrete than that. Whatever she may be describing, each unit is sure to be a complete, separate assertion, a reality immediately given—in the present, the only time there is.

Repetition is insistence: A rose is a rose is a rose is a rose. Each time it is new, different, unique, because the experience of the word is unique each time it is uttered. Stylistically, this entails the predominance of parataxis and asyndeton, words being "so nextily" in their unfolding. Repetition of the same is often supplanted by repetition of the different, where the juxtaposition is in kind and quality. An example of the latter is the following passage from *A Long Gay Book* (1932):

> All the pudding has the same flow and the sauce is painful, the tunes are played, the crinkling paper is burning, the pot has cover and the standard is excellence.

Whether operating at the syntagmatic or at the paradigmatic level, as above, the repetition serves the purpose of emphasizing and isolating a thing, not simply anything. The break with all previous associations forces one to consider this pudding and this sauce, allowing a concretization of the experience in this particular frame of the present. If the content appears to have no "logical" coherence, it is because it is not meant to, since the experience of the immediate does not warrant ratiocination or understanding of any sort. Art in Stein is perception of the immediate, a capturing of the instantaneity of the word as event, sense, or object. The notion is clearly nonreferential in that art does not need a world to know that it exists. Although it occasionally refers to it, it does not have to—in fact, the less it does, the better. What is of paramount importance is that this self-contained entity comes alive in the continuous present of one's experience of it, and only then. The influence of Stein's painter friends was unequivocal. Not all discourse that links the work of art to history and other realms of life is, properly speaking, a preoccupation of the artist: It does not constitute an aesthetic experience, remaining just that—criticism, sociology, and philosophy. Meaning is something that comes after the experience, thanks to reflection, the mediation of reason, and the standardization of logic and grammar; it is never given in the immediacy of the poetic expression. Stein's writings attempt to produce the feeling of something happening or being lived—in short, to give things (objects, emotions, ideas, words) a sense that is new and unique and momentary, independent and defiant of what an afterthought may claim to be the "true" meaning or sense of an experience or artistic event. From this perspective, can it still be honestly said that Stein's work is "nonsense," with all the negative implications usually associated with the epithet?

THINGS AS THEY ARE

Stein had from very early in her career a keen sense of the distance that naturally exists between objects and feelings as perceived, and their transposition into conventional formalized speech. Her first novel, *Q.E.D.* (for the Latin *quod erat demonstrandum*, meaning "which was to be proved"), written in 1903 and known after 1950 as *Things as They Are*, dealt with the then taboo topic of lesbianism in a ménage à trois of three women. However, the work is already shorn of such typical narrative features as symbolism, character development, climax, and descriptions of setting, though it is cast in an intelligible variation of standard prose. At the limits of the (Henry) Jamesian novel, what happens among the characters and the space of emotional relatedness is more important than the characters as characters. The focal point is the introspection of these human natures, and all elaborations and complications of feelings remain internal, intimate, within the consciousness of the individual being described or, most often, within the dialectic of the relationship. Doing away with all contingent background material meant zooming in on the poetic process itself; but for all practical purposes the author is still struggling within the precincts of the most sophisticated naturalism: She is still representing, in the tradition of Henry James and Gustave Flaubert, two authors whom she admired greatly. The characters are at odds with the author: They are white American college women constantly preoccupied with the propriety of their relationship and therefore demand of the author a polite, cultivated, and literary realization.

THREE LIVES

The problem of the language to employ in writing is dealt with in the next work, *Three Lives*, where the progressive abandonment of inherited expressive forms is much stronger and can be said to constitute a first milestone in Gertrude Stein's stylistic development, especially in "Melanchta," the last of the three stories. Here Stein describes a love story set among lower-class blacks, where she can explore the intensity of "uneducated" speech and where, as Donald Sutherland quite aptly points out, there exists "a direct relationship between feeling and word." Typical of her entire literary career, at the time of publication the printer inquired whether the author really knew English. In *Three Lives*, Stein was "groping for a continuous present and for using everything again and again." This continuous present is immediate and partakes of the human mind as it exists at any given moment when confronted with the object of writing. It is different from the prolonged present of duration, as in Henri Bergson, where aspects of human nature may enter. At the stylistic level, punctuation is rare and the present participle is employed as a substantive for its value in retaining the sense of process, of continuity in a present mode that knows no before and no after. This "subjective time" of writing is paralleled by similar developments in the visual and plastic arts, from which Stein drew copiously. Her admiration and appreciation of what Cézanne had done for painting was matched by the unrelenting support that she bestowed on the upcoming younger generation of artists, such as Picasso, Matisse, Juan Gris, and Francis Picabia. Cézanne had taught her that there are no less important areas on a canvas vis-à-vis the theme or figure that traditionally dominated representational painting, and he returned to "basics," such as color, tone, distribution, and the underlying abstractions, reaching out for those essentials in the welter of external detail to capture a sense without which there would be no painting. Picasso went even further, forsaking three-dimensional composition for the surface purity of plane geometry, ushering in cubism. For Stein, perception takes place against the tabula rasa of immediate consciousness, and cubism offered the flatness of an interior time that could be brought to absolute elementalism, simplicity, and finality.

TENDER BUTTONS

Things as They Are and *Three Lives*, for all their stylistic experimentation, are clearly works of prose. In *Tender Buttons*, however, Stein blurs the distinction between prose and poetry. She works with "meaningless" babble, puns, games, rhymes, and repetitions. Much as in Lewis Carroll and Tristam Tzara, the word itself is seen as magic. In a world of pure existence, dialogue disappears, replaced by word lists and one-word utterances. Interactions of characters are no longer tenable, and people give way to objects. The portrait is supplanted by the still life, and the technique of composition is reminiscent of Picasso's collages, not of automatic writing. The intention seems to be to give the work its autonomy independent of both writer and reader: One sees and reads what one sees and reads, the rest being reconstruction from memory or projections of the viewer's intellect. The effort is ambitious: to see language being born. Disparate critical ideas have been invoked to "interpret" *Tender Buttons*, and it is likely that Norman Weinstein (*Gertrude Stein and the Literature of Modern Consciousness*, 1970) comes closest when he summons the studies of Jean Piaget, the Sapir-Whorf language hypothesis, R. D. Laing, and the dimension of schizophrenia. On the opposite bank, Allegra Stewart (*Gertrude Stein and the Present*, 1967) reads the work as a Jungian mandala and relates the alchemical correspondences to all the literary movements of the epoch, such as Dada, Futurism, and so on.

"A jack in kill her, a jack in, makes a meadowed king, makes a to let." The plastic use of language permits the bypassing of the rule where, for example, a substantive is the object of a preposition. The infinitive "to let" appears as the object of a verb and is modified by the indefinite article "a." If analysis emphasizes the dislocation, the derangement, of standard usage, suggesting that alternative modes of expression are possible and even revealing, no matter how unwieldy, it should also note the foregrounding of "events" in an atemporal framework, where even nouns are objects that do not need the passing of ages to be what they are. Sense, if not altogether certain meanings, can be obtained only in the suspended perception of the reading, especially aloud.

This effort to see and write in the "continuous present" requires, Stein said, a passionate identification with the thing to be described: A steady, trance-like concentration on the object will first of all divest it of all its customary appellations and then permit the issuing forth of words and structures that alone can speak as *that* thing in front of the observer.

"Poetry and Grammar"

In "Poetry and Grammar" (1935), Stein says, "Poetry is concerned with using with abusing, with losing with wanting, with denying with avoiding with adoring with replacing the noun.... Poetry is doing nothing but using losing refusing and pleasing and betraying and caressing nouns." In this spirit of reevaluation of the nature and process of naming things she will then go all out in making sure that the things she looks at will by themselves elicit the way they are to be called, never being for a moment worried that such a process may be at odds with the limited range of possibilities offered by conventional reality; she wanted not only to rename things but also to "find out how to know that they were there by their names or by replacing their names." As Shakespeare had done in Arden, the goal was to create "a forest without mentioning the things that make a forest."

With this new discovery, for the ensuing twenty years Stein kept busy revisiting timeworn forms and models of poetic expression, charging them with fresh blood and impetus. The underlying magic would be constant: "looking at anything until something that was not the name of that thing but was in a way that actual thing would come to be written." This process was possible because Stein had arrived at a particular conception of the essence of language: It is not "imitation either of sounds or colors or emotions," but fundamentally an "intellectual recreation." The problem of mimesis and representation was forever behind her, and the idea of play became fundamental in her work.

1920's and 1930's

The third stage of Stein's poetry came in the late 1920's and early 1930's, when she was both very happy at receiving some recognition and much depressed about some new problems of her craft. Of the three materials that she felt art had to deal with—sight, sound, and sense, corresponding to the spatial, the temporal, and the conceptual dimensions of the mind—she had up to then worked intensely on the first two, relegating the third to the background by ignoring it or by simply rejecting it as a response to conventional grammatical and logical sense. At times, she handled the problem of sense by mediating it through her theoretical writings, especially after 1925.

With the ending of the Roaring Twenties, however, much of the spatiality in literature also disappeared. Painting became intellectual, poets became religious or political, and the newer waves did not seem to hold much promise. Stein had also reached a conclusion concerning works of art: that there are no masterpieces containing ideas; in philosophy, there are no masterpieces. Ideas and philosophy require almost by definition a mediated, sequential array of items over time and in history, ideas being about something or other. For a poetic of the unique, concrete thing—again, against all claims that Stein's is a poetic of the abstract—the task of dealing with ideas, which are by nature abstract, posed no small problem. Still, owing also to her attention to religious thought and the artistic implications of meditation, communion, trance, and revelation, she felt the need to come to terms with this hitherto untrodden ground.

STANZAS IN MEDITATION

Stein set about writing a poem of ideas without all the historical and philosophical underpinnings and referents that accompany works such as Ezra Pound's *The Cantos* (1925-1972) and T. S. Eliot's *The Waste Land* (1922). True to the credo that art is immanent and immediate, she wrote *Stanzas in Meditation*, a long poem made up of five parts and running to 163 stanzas, some a line long, others extending over several pages.

Remarkably little has been written about this forgotten but truly major composition, for the difficulty once again is the unpreparedness of criticism to deal with another of Stein's innovations: Instead of writing about ideas, she writes the ideas themselves: Thinking, in other words, does not occur in the mind after reading the words on the page, but the words themselves are the ideas, making ideas partake of the human mind instead of human nature. The old reliable technique of stopping the momentous thoughts on the page as consciousness becomes aware of them creates once again the typical situation with Stein's art: One experiences ideas as one reads; one cannot lean back and expect to put together a "coherent" whole. There are in fact no philosophical terms in the traditional sense and no organization as such. Norman Weinstein writes that "The poem is not *about* philosophy, but *is* philosophy set into motion by verbal action." The disembodied, fragmentary, and discontinuous vision of the cubists is here interwoven with the process-philosophy of William James and Whitehead.

Stylistically, each line tends to be objective and stable and corresponds to what in prose is the sentence. As the lines build up into a stanza, they swell with tension, and, like the paragraph, constitute a specific unit of attention. The poem will occasionally evidence images and allow symbols, but these are accidental, perhaps because the idea itself can best or only be expressed in that particular fashion. According to Sutherland, the poem can be entered in a tradition that lists Plato, Pindar, the English Metaphysicals, and Gerard Manley Hopkins. The poem can be read by simply beginning at random, which is perhaps the best way for the uninitiated to get a "sense" of it and familiarize themselves with the tone, lyricism, and surprisingly deceiving content. The technique of repetition is still present, revealing new contexts for given words, and Stein coins new expressions for ancient truisms. The text is a gold mine of brilliant aphorisms: "There is no hope or use in all," or "That which they like they knew."

THE AUTOBIOGRAPHY OF ALICE B. TOKLAS

Between the time of the appearance of *The Autobiography of Alice B. Toklas* and the publication, shortly before her death, of *The Gertrude Stein First Reader and Three Plays* (1946), thirteen other books came out, among which were the highly successful and important *The Geographical History of America* (1936) and *Everybody's Autobiography* (1937). During these years, Stein's major efforts were directed to the problem of self-presentation and the formal structure of autobiography. She put the writer on the same ground as the reader, ending the privileged position of both biographer and autobiographer. She continued to elaborate the poetic of impersonal, timeless, and spaceless writing, ensuring that experience, flow, and place remain within the confines of the continuous present of perception. Her poetry during this period was chiefly written for children, rhymed and chanted and playful, with no pretense at being anything more than a momentary flash in the continuum of life, a diversion, a game. Many of these works were published either as limited editions or posthumously in the Yale edition of her uncollected writings, where they can now be read in chronological sequence.

OTHER MAJOR WORKS

LONG FICTION: *Three Lives*, 1909; *The Making of Americans: Being a History of a Family's Progress*, 1925 (abridged, 1934); *Lucy Church Amiably*, 1930; *A Long Gay Book*, 1932; *Ida, a Novel*, 1941; *Brewsie and Willie*, 1946; *Blood on the Dining-Room Floor*, 1948; *Things as They Are*, 1950 (originally known as *Q.E.D.*); *Mrs. Reynolds and Five Earlier Novelettes, 1931-1942*, 1952; *A Novel of Thank You*, 1958.

SHORT FICTION: *As Fine as Melanctha*, 1954; *Painted Lace, and Other Pieces, 1914-1937*, 1955; *Alphabets and Birthdays*, 1957.

PLAYS: *Geography and Plays*, pb. 1922; *Operas and Plays*, pb. 1932; *Four Saints in Three Acts*, pr., pb. 1934; *In Savoy: Or, Yes Is for a Very Young Man (A Play of the Resistance in France)*, pr., pb. 1946; *The Mother of Us All*, pr. 1947; *Last Operas and Plays*, pb. 1949; *In a Garden: An Opera in One Act*, pb. 1951; *Lucretia Borgia*, pb. 1968; *Selected Operas and Plays*, 1970.

NONFICTION: *Composition as Explanation*, 1926; *How to Write*, 1931; *Matisse, Picasso, and Gertrude Stein, with Two Shorter Stories*, 1933; *The Autobiography of Alice B. Toklas*, 1933; *Portraits and Prayers*, 1934; *Lectures in America*, 1935; *Narration: Four Lectures*, 1935; *The Geographical History of America*, 1936; *Everybody's Autobiography*, 1937; *Picasso*, 1938; *Paris, France*, 1940; *What Are Masterpieces?*, 1940; *Wars I Have Seen*, 1945; *Four in America*, 1947; *Reflections on the Atomic Bomb*, 1973;

How Writing Is Written, 1974; *The Letters of Gertrude Stein and Thornton Wilder*, 1996 (Edward Burns and Ulla E. Dydo, editors); *Baby Precious Always Shines: Selected Love Notes Between Gertrude Stein and Alice B. Toklas*, 1999 (Kay Turner, editor).

CHILDREN'S LITERATURE: *The World Is Round*, 1939.

MISCELLANEOUS: *The Gertrude Stein First Reader and Three Plays*, 1946; *The Yale Edition of the Unpublished Writings of Gertrude Stein*, 1951-1958 (8 volumes; Carl Van Vechten, editor); *Selected Writings of Gertrude Stein*, 1962; *The Yale Gertrude Stein*, 1980.

BIBLIOGRAPHY

Curnutt, Kirk, ed. *The Critical Response to Gertrude Stein*. Westport, Conn.: Greenwood Press, 2000. This guide includes quintessential pieces on Stein by Carl Van Vechten, William Carlos Williams, and Katherine Anne Porter, as well as previously obscure estimations from contemporaries such as H. L. Mencken, Mina Loy, and Conrad Aiken.

Dydo, Ulla E., with William Rice. *Gertrude Stein: The Language That Rises, 1923-1934*. Evanston, Ill.: Northwestern University Press, 2003. Dydo, a renowned Stein scholar, provides a comprehensive analysis of the letters, manuscripts, and notebooks Stein generated in a twenty-year period.

Kellner, Bruce, ed. *A Gertrude Stein Companion*. New York: Greenwood Press, 1988. Kellner supplies a helpful introduction on how to read Stein. The volume includes a study of Stein and literary tradition, her manuscripts, and her various styles; and biographical sketches of her friends and "enemies." Includes an annotated bibliography of criticism.

Knapp, Bettina. *Gertrude Stein*. New York: Continuum, 1990. A general introduction to Stein's life and art. Discusses her stylistic breakthrough in the stories in *Three Lives*, focusing on repetition and the use of the continuous present. Devotes a long chapter to *Tender Buttons* as one of Stein's most innovative and esoteric works; discusses the nonreferential nature of language in the fragments.

Malcolm, Janet. *Two Lives: Gertrude and Alice*. New Haven, Conn.: Yale University Press, 2007. Malcolm examines the good and the bad in the life shared by Stein and Alice B. Toklas.

Mitrano, G. F. *Gertrude Stein: Woman Without Qualities*. Burlington, Vt.: Ashgate, 2005. A study of Stein's writing and a look at why it remains relevant to twenty-first century readers.

Murphy, Marguerite S. *A Tradition of Subversion: The Prose Poem in English from Wilde to Ashbery*. Amherst: University of Massachusetts Press, 1992. Devotes a chapter to *Tender Buttons*. Argues that Stein borrowed her genre from painting. Discusses the experimental nature of Stein's prose poems in the collections.

Pierpont, Claudia Roth. *Passionate Minds: Women Rewriting the World*. New York:

Alfred A. Knopf, 2000. Evocative, interpretive essays on the life paths and works of twelve women, including Stein, connecting the circumstances of their lives with the shapes, styles, subjects, and situations of their art.

Simon, Linda. *Gertrude Stein Remembered*. Lincoln: University of Nebraska Press, 1994. Consists of short memoirs of the modernist writer by her colleagues and contemporaries. Selections include pieces by Daniel-Henri Kahnweiler, Sylvia Beach, Sherwood Anderson, Cecil Beaton, and Eric Sevareid, each of whom offer intimate and often informal views of Stein.

Wineapple, Brenda. *Sister Brother: Gertrude and Leo Stein*. Lincoln: University of Nebraska Press, 2008. Wineapple looks at the long and close relationship between Stein and her brother, Leo, and the emergence of her writing voice, which may been in part responsible for the rift between the two siblings.

Peter Carravetta

PAUL VERLAINE

Born: Metz, France; March 30, 1844
Died: Paris, France; January 8, 1896

PRINCIPAL POETRY
Poèmes saturniens, 1866
Fêtes galantes, 1869 (*Gallant Parties*, 1912)
La Bonne Chanson, 1870
Romances sans paroles, 1874 (*Romances Without Words*, 1921)
Sagesse, 1881
Jadis et naguère, 1884
Amour, 1888
Parallèlement, 1889, 1894 (English translation, 1939)
Bonheur, 1891
Chansons pour elle, 1891
Femmes, 1891 (English translation, 1977)
Liturgies intimes, 1892
Élégies, 1893
Odes en son honneur, 1893
Épigrammes, 1894
Dans les limbes, 1894
Chair, dernière poésies, 1896
Invectives, 1896 (English translation, 1939)
Hombres, 1903 (English translation, 1977)
Selected Poems, 1948
Femmes/Hombres, 1977 (includes English translation of *Femmes* and *Hombres*)

OTHER LITERARY FORMS

Most of the other published works of Paul Verlaine (vehr-LEHN) are autobiographical writings and critical articles on contemporary poets. During his lifetime, he published two plays that were performed—*Les Uns et les autres* (pr. 1884; the ones and the others) and *Madame Aubin* (pr. 1886)—and one short story, *Louise Leclercq* (1886). A collection of seven other short stories, *Histories comme ça* (1903; stories like that), was published posthumously.

The most significant of his critical writings were published under the title *Poètes maudits* (1884; *The Cursed Poets*, 2003), which includes articles on Tristan Corbière, Arthur Rimbaud, Stéphane Mallarmé, Villiers de L'Isle-Adam, and others. Verlaine's *Confessions* (*Confessions of a Poet*, 1950) was published in 1895. Many of his previ-

Paul Verlaine
(Library of Congress)

ously unedited writings were published posthumously in a 1903 edition of his works, which includes several autobiographical pieces as well as some original ink drawings. All his prose works were published in the 1972 Pléiade edition.

Achievements

Paul Verlaine is universally recognized as one of the great French poets of the nineteenth century. His name is associated with those of his contemporaries Charles Baudelaire, Rimbaud, and Mallarmé. His most famous and frequently anthologized poems, such as "Chanson d'automne" ("Song of Autumn"), "Mon rêve familier" ("My Familiar Dream"), "Clair de lune" ("Moonlight "), and "Il pleure dans mon coeur" ("It Is Crying in My Heart"), are readily recognized and often recited by persons with any knowledge of French poetry. Many of his poems, including those cited, have been set to music by serious composers.

Verlaine's admirers include both saints and sinners, for Verlaine is at once the author of one of the most beautiful collections of religious poetry ever published and the writer of some explicitly erotic poems. During his lifetime, Verlaine's poetic genius was recognized by only a handful of poets and friends. His penchant for antisocial and occasionally criminal behavior (he was jailed twice for potentially murderous attacks) undoubtedly contributed to his lack of commercial success or popular recognition during his lifetime. By the end of his life, he had gained a small measure of recognition and received some income from his royalties and lecture engagements.

BIOGRAPHY

Paul Marie Verlaine was born in Metz, France, on March 30, 1844, the only child of Captain Nicolas-Auguste Verlaine and Elisa Dehée Verlaine. The family moved often during Verlaine's first seven years, until Captain Verlaine retired from the army to settle in Paris. Verlaine attended the Lycée Bonaparte (now Condorcet) and received his *baccalauréat* in 1862.

Verlaine's adoring mother and equally adoring older cousin Elisa Moncomble, whose death in 1867 affected him profoundly, spoiled the sensitive child, encouraged his demanding capriciousness, and helped him become a selfish, immature, unstable young man.

After his *baccalauréat*, he worked in an insurance office and then found a clerical job in municipal government, which he kept until 1870. In 1863, he published his first poem, "Monsieur Prudhomme." He met Catulle Mendès, an editor of the literary magazine *Le Parnasse contemporain*, in which Verlaine published eight poems. In 1866, he published his first volume of poetry, *Poèmes saturniens*, and in 1869, a second volume, *Gallant Parties*.

Alcoholism began to take its toll on his personal life. Twice in drunken rages, he threatened to kill his mother . His family tried to marry him to a strong-willed cousin, a fate that he avoided by proposing to Mathilde Mauté, whom he married in 1870 and who inspired his third volume of poetry, *La Bonne Chanson*.

Having served as press officer to the Commune of Paris during the 1870 insurrection, Verlaine subsequently fled Paris and lost his government job. He helped to found a new journal, *La Renaissance*, in which he published many of the poems included in his 1874 volume, *Romances Without Words*.

Verlaine's drinking and his friendship with Rimbaud led to violent domestic scenes. Following several fights and reconciliations with Mathilde, Verlaine ran off to Brussels with Rimbaud in July, 1872. During the following year, the two poets lived together in Brussels and London and then returned to Brussels. On July 10, 1873, Verlaine, in a drunken rage, fired a revolver at Rimbaud, who had threatened to leave him. Verlaine was convicted of armed assault and sentenced to two years in prison.

In prison, Verlaine converted to a mystical form of Roman Catholicism and began to write the poems for the volume *Sagesse*, published in 1881. After his release in 1875 and until 1879, he held teaching positions in England and France. He formed a sincere and probably chaste relationship with one of his students, Lucien Létinois. They attempted a joint farming venture, which failed, and then returned to Paris, where

Verlaine tried to get back his old government job but was turned down because of his past record. This disappointment, coupled with the sudden death of Létinois in 1883, caused Verlaine to become profoundly discouraged.

After another ill-fated farming venture, Verlaine abandoned himself for a long period to drinking and sordid affairs. A drunken attack on his mother cost him a month in prison in 1885. During his last ten years, his economic distress was somewhat eased by his growing literary reputation. He continued writing and published several more significant volumes of verse.

From 1890 to his death in 1896, Verlaine moved in and out of several hospitals, suffering from a swollen, stiffened leg, the terminal effects of syphilis, diabetes, rheumatism, and heart disease. He lived alternately with two women who cared for him and exploited him. During his last years, he was invited to lecture in Holland, Belgium, and England.

Analysis

In two articles on Baudelaire published in *L'Art* in 1865, Paul Verlaine affirms that the overriding concern of a poet should be the quest for beauty. Without denying the role of inspiration and emotion in the process of poetic creation, Verlaine stresses the need to master them by poetic craftsmanship. Sincerity is not a poetic virtue. Personal emotion must be expressed through the combinations of rhyme, sound, and image that best create a poetic universe in which nothing is the result of chance.

The most obvious result of Verlaine's craftsmanship is the musicality of his verse. Sounds flow together to create a sonorous harmony that repetitions organize and structure as in a musical composition. In his 1882 poem "L'Art poétique," Verlaine gives a poetic recipe that begins with the famous line, "Music above everything else." He goes on to counsel using odd-syllabled lines, imprecise vocabulary and imagery (as if veiled), and nuance rather than color. The poet should avoid wit, eloquence, and forced rhyme. Poetic verse should be light and fugitive, airborne and slightly aromatic. The poem ends with the somber warning, "Anything else is literature."

The subject matter of Verlaine's carefully crafted poetry is frequently his personal experience, certainly dramatic and emotionally charged material. The prologue to *Poèmes saturniens* reveals his consciousness of his miserable destiny. Throughout the rest of his poetry, he narrates the various permutations of his self-fulfilling expectation of unhappiness. "Moonlight," which serves as a prologue to his second volume of verse, presents gallant eighteenth century lovers "who don't appear to believe in their happiness." This skepticism clouds the fugitive moments of happiness throughout Verlaine's poetic pilgrimage. *La Bonne Chanson* is Verlaine's homage to marital bliss. Poem 17, filled with images of love and faithfulness, begins and ends with the question, "Isn't it so?" Poem 13 ends with a similar worry: "A vain hope . . . oh no, isn't it so, isn't it so?" In *Sagesse*, which proposes Roman Catholic mysticism as the ultimate form of happiness, the fear of a return to his old ways haunts the poet's peaceful communion with God.

Because sex, love, God, and wine all fail to provide a safe haven from his saturnine destiny, Verlaine must seek another refuge. What he finds, perhaps not entirely consciously, is sleep. With surprising frequency the final images of Verlaine's poems are images of sleep; many of his musical pieces are thus lullabies whose delicate, soothing images—from which color, laughter, pompousness, loudness, and sharpness have been banished—lead the poet's battered psyche to the unthreatening harbor of sleep. Often, a maternal figure cradles the poet in his sleep or stands by watchfully. In many poems in which the sleep motif is not explicit, the imagery subsides at the end of the poem, leaving an emptiness or absence analogous to the oblivion of sleep.

Poèmes saturniens

Verlaine's first volume of poetry, *Poèmes saturniens*, was published by Lemerre in November, 1866, at the author's expense. It drew very little critical or popular attention. The title refers to the astrological contention, explained in the prologue, that those like Verlaine who are born under the sign of Saturn are doomed to unhappiness, are bilious, have sick, uneasy imaginations, and are destined to suffer.

The volume is the work of a very young poet, some of the poems having been written as early as 1861. They are consequently of uneven quality, but among them is the poem "My Familiar Dream," which is perhaps the most frequently anthologized of all Verlaine's poems and which, according to Verlaine's friend and admirer H. Suquet, the poet preferred to all his others. It is a haunting evocation of an imaginary woman who loves the poet, who understands him, and who is capable of soothing his anguish.

The central section of the volume, titled "Paysages tristes" ("Sad Landscapes"), contains the poems most typical of Verlaine: vague, melancholy landscapes, inspired by his memories of the Artois region, whose fading colors, forms, and sounds reflect the poet's soul and whose ultimate disappearance translates as an innate desire for oblivion.

The first of these poems, "Soleils couchants" ("Setting Suns"), a musical poem of sixteen five-syllable lines, describes a rising sun so weakened that it casts a sunset-like melancholy over the fields, inspiring strange raddish ghosts in the poet's imagination. The short, odd-syllabled lines create a musical effect reinforced by alliteration and repetition—the phrase "setting suns," for example, is repeated four times in a poem about dawn.

"Promenade sentimentale" ("Sentimental Walk") presents a twilight scene through which the wounded poet passes. The vaguely lit water lilies that glow faintly through the fog in the evening light are swallowed up by the shroudlike darkness in the poem's final image.

"Nuit du Walpurgis classique" (" Classical Walpurgis Night") is full of allusions. Phantoms dance wildly throughout the night in a landscape designed by Johann Wolfgang von Goethe, Richard Wagner, Antoine Watteau, and André Le Nôtre. At dawn's approach, the

Wagnerian music fades and the phantoms dissolve, leaving "absolutely" nothing except "a correct, ridiculous, charming Le Nôtre garden." Another noteworthy tone poem, "Song of Autumn," a melodic eighteen-line lyric composed of four- and three-syllable lines, combines *o*'s and nasal sounds to reproduce a melancholy autumn wind that carries off the mournful poet like a dead leaf.

Verlaine's first collection of verse reveals the influence of Baudelaire, Victor Hugo, Charles-Marie Leconte de Lisle, Théodore de Banville, and Théophile Gautier—and of Verlaine's young friends Louis de Ricard and Joseph Glatigny. It is a carefully crafted and original volume, demonstrating that at the age of twenty-four, Verlaine had already mastered the art of poetry and discovered most of the themes of his later works.

GALLANT PARTIES

The mid-nineteenth century's rediscovery of the paintings of Watteau is confirmed by several works dedicated to that artist and to his times, including one by the Edmond de Goncourt and Jules de Goncourt, *L'Art du dix-huitième siècle* (1859-1875; *French Eighteenth Century Painters*, 1948), which undoubtedly had a strong influence on Verlaine's choice of this subject and his interpretation of it. During the composition of the poems of *Gallant Parties*, Verlaine undoubtedly consulted some of the published reproductions of Watteau's works as well as his one painting in the Louvre collection, *Embarkation for Cythère*, a vast work devoted to eighteenth century gallantry, its rites, costumes, myths, poetry, and fashionable devotees. These aristocratic gallants and the characters from *The Italian Comedy*, also painted by Watteau, come alive in Verlaine's second published volume of poetry.

The often-anthologized "Moonlight" opens the volume and sets the mood. This musical evocation of the songs and dances of the masked characters and the relationship between their costumes and their souls insist on the underlying sadness of both. The gallant aristocrats are somewhat sad beneath their fantastic disguises because they do not really believe in the love and life of which they sing. Their dispersed song is absorbed by the moonlight.

These same characters sing, dance, walk, skate, and love through the rest of the volume, sometimes assuming stock character names from commedia del l'arte—Pierrot, Clitandre, Cassandre, Arlequin, Colombine, Scaramouche, and Pulcinella—and sometimes classical names—Tircis, Aminte, Chloris, Eglé, Atys, and Damis.

The landscapes of *Gallant Parties* are very different physically and psychologically from those of the *Poèmes saturniens*. They are sculpted, landscaped, arranged, and peopled. Paths are lined by rows of pruned trees and mossy benches. Fountains and statues are harmoniously placed around well-kept lawns. The relationship between the characters and the landscape is no longer a natural sympathetic mirroring. Nature has been artificially subdued to reflect the characters' forced gaiety and becomes a mocking image of the vanity of their pursuits. One of the obvious formal characteristics of the volume is the presence of dialogue and monologue, couched in the artificial, erotic language of gallantry. There are many allusions to "former ecstasies," "infinite distress," and "mortal languors."

The volume's overriding pessimism is orchestrated by the arrangement of the poems. The latent sadness of the apparently carefree gallants in "Moonlight" becomes the dominant feeling in the second half of the work. While humorous love play and inconsequential erotic exchanges dominate the first half, several disturbing images—such as the statue of a snickering faun who anticipates eventual unhappiness and the sad spectacle of a statue of Cupid overturned by the wind—foreshadow the volume's disastrous conclusion, the poem "Colloque sentimentale" ("Sentimental Colloquium"), in which a ghostly "form" tries to recall a past sentimental adventure. The cold, solitary park, witness to the scarcely heard dialogue, swallows up the desperate efforts to recall a past love as well as the negations of those efforts. One of the lovers tries unsuccessfully to awaken memories of their past love, which the other negates repeatedly: "Do you remember our former ecstasy?" "Why do you want me to remember it?" "Does your heart still beat at the sound of my name?" "No."

ROMANCES WITHOUT WORDS

The Franco-Prussian War of 1870 and the Commune separated Verlaine from his Parnassian friends and led him toward new friendships and a new form of poetry, toward a modernistic vision that replaced the artificiality of Parnassian inspiration with an attempt to capture the essence of contemporary life. During 1872 and 1873, Verlaine wrote the poems of *Romances Without Words*, which was published in 1874. All the poems precede the episode with Rimbaud that resulted in Verlaine's imprisonment. The period was emotionally difficult for Verlaine. Torn between love for Mathilde and dependence on Rimbaud, Verlaine was tormented by his vacillations. *Romances Without Words* fuses his new poetic ideal with his personal struggle.

The sad, lilting songs that make up the first part of the volume, titled "Ariettes oubliées" ("Forgotten Melodies"), include one of the most frequently quoted of Verlaine's poems, "It Is Crying in My Heart," in which the gentle sound of the rain falling on the town echoes the fall of tears within his heart. A more interesting poem, however, is the musical twelve-line poem "Le Piano que baise une main frêle" ("The Piano Kissed by a Fragile Hand"), in which the light, discreet melody rising from the piano corresponds to the faintness in the fading evening light of the visual impression of slight hands on a barely discernible piano. A series of vague, fleeting adjectives seep out of the perfumed boudoir to disappear through a slightly opened window into a small garden. The hushed sonorities of the poem coincide with the diminished intensity of the images. One remarkable phrase in the tenth line embodies both the musical effects and the characteristic tone of Verlaine's verse: "fin refrain incertain" ("delicate, uncertain refrain").

While the influence of music on Verlaine's poetry is certain, the importance of painting is no less significant. *Gallant Parties* is to a great extent a tribute to the painting of Watteau. The "Paysages belges" ("Belgian Landscapes") that Verlaine paints into *Romances Without Words*, are a tribute to the Impressionist school of painting, whose birth corresponds with the date of composition of the collection. Verlaine knew Édouard Manet and Ignace Henri Fantin-Latour and was certainly interested in their technique. The Impressionistic Belgian landscapes that Verlaine has painted are carefree and happy, carrying no reflection of the shadow of Mathilde that haunts the rest of the volume. The first poem in the section, "Walcourt" (a small, industrial town in Belgium), reflects the gaiety of the two vagabond poets (Verlaine and Rimbaud) in a series of brightly colored images that flash by, without help of a verb, in lively four-syllabled lines: tiles and bricks, ivy-covered homes, and beer drinkers in outdoor bars.

The gaiety of the Belgian countryside is interrupted by a bitter poem, "Birds in the Night" (original title in English), which Verlaine had first titled "La Mauvaise Chanson" ("The Bad Song") as an ironic counterpart to his previous book of poems, *La Bonne Chanson*, devoted to marital bliss. "Birds in the Night" accuses Mathilde of a lack of patience and kindness as well as of treachery. The suffering poet offers his forgiveness. The poem suggests a singular lack of understanding of the real causes of their marital discord.

The last section of *Romances Without Words* contains visions of Verlaine's London experience, but the image of Mathilde pierces through the local color with haunting persistence. All six of the poems have English titles. The most interesting is "Green," in which the poet presents to his mistress fruits, flowers, leaves, branches, and then his heart, which he commends to her care. The poem ends with the desire for a restful oblivion on the woman's bosom.

SAGESSE

Only seven of the poems in *Sagesse* were actually composed while Verlaine was in prison. The rest were written between the time of his release in 1875 and the spring of 1880. The title refers to Verlaine's intention to live virtuously according to the principles of his new faith and should perhaps be translated not as "wisdom" but as "good behavior." The volume is divided into three parts, the first of which dwells on the difficulty of converting to a virtuous life, the almost daily battles with overwhelming temptation. The second part narrates the poet's mystic confrontation with God, primarily through a cycle of ten sonnets. The last part describes the poet's return to the world and contains many of the themes and images of his earlier nature poetry. These poems are not overtly religious; the prologue to this part, "Désormais le sage, puni" ("Henceforth, the Virtuous, Punished"), explains the virtuous poet's return to a contemplative love of nature.

Poems 6 and 7 of the first part, both sonnets, are the most poetic of Verlaine's evocations of the contrast between his former and his present preoccupations. Poem 6 presents his former joys as a line of clumsy geese limping off into the distance on a dusty road. Their departure leaves the poet with a welcome emptiness, a peaceful sense of abandonment as his formerly proud heart now burns with divine love. Poem 7 warns of the prevailing appeal of the "false happy days" that have tempted his soul all day. They have glowed in his memory as "long hailstones of flame" that have symbolically ravaged his blue sky. The last line of the poem exhorts the poet's soul to pray against the storm to forestall "the old folly" that threatens to return.

Three of the most moving poems of the third part were written in prison, one on the very day of Verlaine's sentencing: "Un Grand Sommeil noir" ("A Great Black Sleep"). This poem, as well as "Le Ciel est, par-dessus le toit" ("The Sky Is, Beyond the Roof") and "Gaspard Hauser chante" ("The Song of Kaspar Hauser"), sings of the poet's despair, plaintively expressing his self-pity, his regrets, and his total sense of shock in the early days of his imprisonment. The third part of *Sagesse* also contains two of Verlaine's most finely crafted sonnets. "L'Espoir luit comme un brin de paille dans l'étable" ("Hope Glistens Like a Blade of Straw in a Stable") is perhaps his most Rimbaudian and most obscure poem. An unidentified protector speaks to the poet reassuringly as he rests in a country inn. The voice is maternal and encourages the poet to sleep, promising to cradle him. The voice shoos away a woman whose presence threatens the poet's rest. The poem opens and closes with a fragile image of glistening hope, which, in the final line, opens up into a hoped-for reflowering of the roses of September.

The sonnet "Le Son du cor" ("The Sound of the Hunting Horn") is perhaps the best example of Verlaine's poetic art. It was written before his imprisonment, probably in the spring of 1873. This very musical poem blends the sound of the hunting horn, the howling of the wind, and the cry of a wolf into a crescendo that subsides to a mere autumn sigh as the falling snow blots out the last colors of the setting sun. The painful notes of the opening stanza are completely obliterated as day gives way to a cradling, monotonous evening.

OTHER MAJOR WORKS
SHORT FICTION: *Louise Leclercq*, 1886; *Histoires comme ça*, 1903.
PLAYS: *Les Uns et les autres*, pr. 1884; *Madame Aubin*, pr. 1886.
NONFICTION: *Poètes maudits*, 1884 (*The Cursed Poets*, 2003); *Mes hôpitaux*, 1891; *Quinze jours en Hollande*, 1892; *Mes prisons*, 1893; *Confessions*, 1895 (*Confessions of a Poet*, 1950); *Les Mémoires d'un veuf*, 1896; *Charles Baudelaire*, 1903; *Critiques et conférences*, 1903; *Souvenirs et promenades*, 1903; *Voyage en france par un français*, 1903.

BIBLIOGRAPHY
Blackmore, A. M., and E. H. Blackmore, eds. *Six French Poets of the Nineteenth Century: Lamartine, Hugo, Baudelaire, Verlaine, Rimbaud, Mallarmé*. New York: Oxford University Press, 2000. This anthology of poetry is preceded by an introduc-

tion, notes on text and translations, a select bibliography, and a chronology. Contains poems by and background information on Verlaine.

Ivry, Benjamin. *Arthur Rimbaud*. Bath, Somerset, England: Absolute Press, 1998. A biography of Rimbaud that details his two-year affair with Verlaine. Ivry delves deeply into the relationship, especially its sexual aspects, including possible dalliances with other men, misogynist outbursts, and graphically sexual poems.

Lehmann, John. *Three Literary Friendships: Byron and Shelley, Rimbaud and Verlaine, Robert Frost and Edward Thomas*. New York: Henry Holt, 1984. An examination of the way these friendships influenced each poet's work. Verlaine and Arthur Rimbaud each produced more poetry after their relationship.

Lepelletier, Edmond Adolphe de Bouhelier. *Paul Verlaine: His Life, His Work*. Translated by E. M. Lang. New York: AMS Press, 1970. The only English translation of the hefty 1909 biography.

Nicolson, Harold George. *Paul Verlaine*. 1921. Reprint. New York: AMS Press, 1997. This venerable biography remains useful.

Robb, Graham. *Rimbaud: A Biography*. New York: W. W. Norton, 2001. This biography of Arthur Rimbaud contains discussion of his affair with Verlaine, including the altercation at its end.

Sorrell, Martin. Introduction to *Selected Poems*, by Paul Verlaine. 1999. Reprint. New York: Oxford University Press, 2009. Sorrell's introduction is useful for beginning students in this bilingual edition of 170 newly translated poems by Verlaine.

Whidden, Seth Adam. *Leaving Parnassus: The Lyric Subject in Verlaine and Rimbaud*. Amsterdam: Rodopi, 2007. Notes the influence of Parnassian poetry on Verlaine and Arthur Rimbaud, even as they departed from it. One multichapter section is devoted to various aspects of Verlaine's poetry.

Paul J. Schwartz

ALICE WALKER

Born: Eatonton, Georgia; February 9, 1944

PRINCIPAL POETRY
Once, 1968
Five Poems, 1972
Revolutionary Petunias, and Other Poems, 1973
Good Night, Willie Lee, I'll See You in the Morning, 1979
Horses Make a Landscape Look More Beautiful, 1984
Her Blue Body Everything We Know: Earthling Poems, 1965-1990 Complete, 1991
Absolute Trust in the Goodness of the Earth: New Poems, 2003
A Poem Traveled Down My Arm: Poems and Drawings, 2003

OTHER LITERARY FORMS

Although Alice Walker's poetry is cherished by her admirers, she is primarily known as a fiction writer. The novel *The Color Purple* (1982), generally regarded as her masterpiece, achieved both popular and critical success, winning the Pulitzer Prize and the National Book Award. The Steven Spielberg film of the same name, for which Walker acted as consultant, reached an immense international audience.

Other Walker fiction has received less attention. Her first novel, *The Third Life of Grange Copeland* (1970), depicts violence and family dysfunction among people psychologically maimed by racism. *Meridian* (1976) mirrors the Civil Rights movement, of which the youthful Walker was actively a part. Later novels, *The Temple of My Familiar* (1989), *Possessing the Secret of Joy* (1992), and *By the Light of My Father's Smile* (1998) have employed narrative as little more than a vehicle for ideas on racial and sexual exploitation, abuse of animals and the earth, and New Age spirituality. *In Love and Trouble: Stories of Black Women* (1973) and *You Can't Keep a Good Woman Down* (1981) revealed Walker to be one of the finest of late twentieth century American short-story writers. She also has written an occasional children's book (*To Hell with Dying*, 1988, is particularly notable) and several collections of essays (*In Search of Our Mothers' Gardens: Womanist Prose*, 1983, is the most lyrical) that present impassioned pleas for the causes Walker espouses.

ACHIEVEMENTS

At numerous colleges, as a teacher and writer-in-residence, Alice Walker established herself as a mentor, particularly to young African American women. Her crusades became international. To alert the world to the problem of female circumcision in Africa, she collaborated with an Anglo-Indian filmmaker on a book and film. She has been a voice for artistic freedom, defending her own controversial writings and those of others, such as Salman Rushdie. In her writings and later open lifestyle, she affirmed lesbian and bisexual experience. However, the accomplishment in which she took the most pride was her resurrection of the reputation of Zora Neale Hurston, a germinal African American anthropologist and novelist, whose books had gone out of print.

Walker won the Rosenthal Award of the National Institute of Arts and Letters for *In Love and Trouble* and received a Charles Merrill writing fellowship, a National Endowment for the Arts award, and a Guggenheim Fellowship. Her second book of poetry, *Revolutionary Petunias, and Other Poems*, received the Lillian Smith Award and was nominated for a National Book Award. Her highest acclaim came with the novel *The Color Purple*, for which she won the National Book Award and the 1983 Pulitzer Prize. She received the Fred Cody Award for lifetime achievement in 1990. Walker was inducted into the California Hall of Fame in 2006.

Biography

Alice Malsenior Walker was the youngest of eight children born to a Georgia sharecropper and his wife. Her father earned about three hundred dollars per year, while her mother, the stronger figure, supplemented the family income by working as a maid. Walker herself was a bright, confident child until an accident at age eight blinded her in one eye and temporarily marred her beauty. At this time, she established what was to become a lifelong pattern of savoring solitude and making the most of adversity. She started reading and writing poetry.

Because of her partial blindness and her outstanding high school record, Walker qualified for a special scholarship offered to disabled students by Spelman College, the prestigious black women's college in Atlanta. When she matriculated there in 1961, her neighbors raised the bus fare of seventy-five dollars to get her to Atlanta.

As a Spelman student, Walker was "moved to wakefulness" by the emerging Civil Rights movement. She took part in demonstrations downtown, which brought her into conflict with the conservative administration of the school. Finding the rules generally too restrictive and refreshed with her new consciousness, she secured a scholarship at Sarah Lawrence College in Bronxville, New York. She then felt closer to the real action that was changing the country. At Sarah Lawrence College, she came under the influence of the poet Muriel Rukeyser, who recognized her talent and arranged for her first publications. She also took a summer off for a trip to her "spiritual home," Africa. She returned depressed and pregnant, contemplated suicide for a time, but instead underwent an abortion and poured her emotions into poetry.

After graduation, Walker worked for a time in the New York City Welfare Department before returning to the South to write, teach, and promote voter registration. She married Melvyn Leventhal, a white Jew, and worked with him on desegregation legal cases and Head Start programs. Their child, Rebecca, was born during this highly productive period. By the time the marriage ended in 1976, Walker was already becoming recognized as a writer, though she did not become internationally famous until after the publication of *The Color Purple*.

Walker continued to write during the 1980's and 1990's, though never again achieving the acclaim or the notoriety that *The Color Purple* brought her. Critics complained of her stridency, the factual inaccuracies in her writings, and her tendency to turn her works of fiction into polemics. Many African Americans felt that her writings cast black society in a grim light. Walker moved to California and lived for several years with Robert Allen, the editor of *Black Scholar*. Times had changed; the motto was no longer "black and white together": marriages between Jews and African Americans were out, and black-black relationships were in.

Walker also became more alert to the problems women of color faced throughout the world. Taking a female partner, she decided to devote her time and talents to celebrating women and rectifying wrongs committed against them. In March of 2003, Walker was arrested for protesting the Iraq War. In 2009, Walker visited Gaza to promote peace and friendlier relations between Egypt and Israel. Walker has always encouraged awareness of important issues in her writing, but she has attracted attention to issues such as problems in the black culture, violence against women, and the ravages of war by personally participating in or protesting events about which she feels passionately.

Analysis

Alice Walker writes free verse, employing concrete images. She resorts to few of the conceits, the extended metaphors, the Latinate language, and other common conventions of poetry. Readers frequently say that her verses hardly seem like poetry at all; they resemble the conversation of a highly articulate, observant woman. Although her poetry often seems like prose, her fiction is highly poetic. The thoughts of Miss Celie, the first-person narrator of *The Color Purple*, would not have been out of place in a book of poetry. Boundaries between prose and poetry are minimal in the work of Walker. Her verse, like her prose, is always rhythmic; if she rhymes or alliterates, it seems to be by accident. The poetry appears so effortless that its precision, its choice of exact image or word to convey the nuance the poet wishes, is not immediately evident. Only close scrutiny reveals the skill with which this highly lettered poet has assimilated her influences, chiefly E. E. Cummings, Emily Dickinson, Robert Graves, Japanese haiku, Li Bo, Ovid, Zen epigrams, and William Carlos Williams.

Walker's poetry is personal and generally didactic, generated by events in her life, causes she has advocated, and injustices over which she has agonized. The reader feels that it is the message that counts, before realizing that the medium is part of the message. Several of her poems echo traumatic events in her own life, such as her abortion. She remembers the words her mother uttered over the casket of her father, and she makes a poem of them. Other poems recall ambivalent emotions of childhood: Sunday school lessons which, even then, were filled with discrepancies. Some poems deal with the creative process itself: She calls herself a medium through whom the Old Ones, formerly mute, find their voice at last.

Some readers are surprised to discover that Walker's poems are both mystical and socially revolutionary, one moment exuberant and the next reeking with despair. Her mysticism is tied to reverence for the earth, a sense of unity with all living creatures, a bond of sisterhood with women throughout the world, and a joyous celebration of the female principle in the divine. On the other hand, she may lament that injustice reigns in society: Poor black people toil so that white men may savor the jewels that adorn heads of state.

ONCE

Walker's first collection of poetry, *Once*, communicates her youthful impressions of Africa and her state of mind during her early travels there and the melancholy and thoughts of death and suicide she felt on her return to United States, where racism persisted. Perhaps the epigram from French philosopher Albert Camus, which prefaces the book, expresses its mood best: "Misery kept me from believing that all was well under the sun, and the sun taught me that history wasn't everything."

The title poem of the collection contains several loosely connected scenes of injustice in the American South, small black children run down by vans because "they were in the way," Jewish Civil Rights workers who cannot be cremated because their remains cannot be found, and finally a black child waving an American flag, but from "the very/ tips/ of her/ fingers," an image perhaps of irony or perhaps of hope. There are meditations on white lovers—blond, Teutonic, golden—who dare kiss this poet who is "brown-er/ Than a jew." There are memories of black churches, where her mother shouts, her father snores, and she feels uncomfortable.

The most striking poem is certainly "African Images," an assortment of vignettes from the ancestral homeland: shy gazelles, the bluish peaks of Mount Kenya, the sound of elephants trumpeting, and rain forests with red orchids. However, even when viewed in the idealism of youth, Africa is not total paradise. The leg of a slain elephant is fashioned into an umbrella holder in a shop; a rhinoceros is killed so that its horn may be made into an aphrodisiac.

REVOLUTIONARY PETUNIAS, AND OTHER POEMS

Revolutionary Petunias, and Other Poems is divided into two parts. The first is titled "In These Dissenting Times . . . Surrounding Ground and Autobiography." She proposes to write "of the old men I knew/ And the young men/ I loved/ And of the gold toothed women/ Mighty of arm/ Who dragged us all/ To church." She writes also "To acknowledge our ancestors" with the awareness that "we did not make/ ourselves, that the line stretches/ all the way back, perhaps, to God; or/ to Gods." She recalls her baptism "dunked . . . in the creek," with "gooey . . . rotting leaves,/ a greenish mold floating." She was a slight figure, "All in white./ With God's mud ruining my snowy/ socks and his bullfrog spoors/ gluing up my face."

The last half of the collection, "Revolutionary Petunias . . . the Living Through," begins with yet another epigram from Camus, reminding the reader that there will come a time when revolutions, though not made by beauty, will discover the need for beauty. The poems, especially those referred to as "Crucifixions," become more anguished, more angered. Walker becomes skeptical of the doctrine of nonviolence, hinting that the time for more direct action may have come. The tone of the last poems in the collection may be expressed best by the opening lines to the verse Walker called "Rage." "In me, " she wrote, "there is a rage to defy/ the order of the stars/ despite their pretty patterns."

GOOD NIGHT, WILLIE LEE, I'LL SEE YOU IN THE MORNING

Good Night, Willie Lee, I'll See You in the Morning expands on earlier themes and further exploits personal and family experiences for lessons in living. The title poem is perhaps the most moving and characteristic of the collection. Walker shared it again on May 22, 1995, in a commencement day speech delivered at Spelman College. As a lesson in forgiveness, she recalled the words her mother, who had much to endure and much to forgive, uttered above her father's casket. Her last words to the man with whom she had lived for so many years, beside whom she had labored in the fields, and with whom she had raised so many children were, "Good night, Willie Lee, I'll see you in the morning." This gentle instinctive act of her mother taught Walker the enduring lesson that "the healing of all our wounds is forgiveness/ that permits a promise/ of our return/ at the end."

HORSES MAKE A LANDSCAPE LOOK MORE BEAUTIFUL

Horses Make a Landscape Look More Beautiful took its title from words of Lame Deer, an Indian seer who contemplated the gifts of the white man—chiefly whiskey and horses—and found the beauty of horses almost made her forget the whiskey. This thought establishes the tone of the collection. These are movement poems, but as always, they remain intensely personal and frequently elegiac. The poet seems herself to speak:

> I am the woman
> with the blessed
> dark skin
> I am the woman
> with teeth repaired
> I am the woman
> with the healing eye
> the ear that hears.

There is also lamentation for lost love:

> When I no longer have your heart
> I will not request your body
> your presence
> or even your polite conversation.
> I will go away to a far country
> separated from you by the sea
> —on which I cannot walk—
> and refrain even from sending
> letters
> describing my pain.

HER BLUE BODY EVERYTHING WE KNOW

Her Blue Body Everything We Know contains a selection of poems written between 1965 and 1990, along with a few new verses and revealing commentary. This collection includes poems from *Once*; *Revolutionary Petunias, and Other Poems*; *Good Night, Willie Lee, I'll See You in the Morning*; and *Horses Make a Landscape Look More Beautiful*. Walker provides readers with insights on the art of poetry (in poems such as "How Poems Are Made: A Discredited View" and "I Said to Poetry"). In her introduction to the final section of the collection, Walker relates how she once felt jealous of how musicians connect with their work and seem to be one with it, but that during career as a writer, she has learned that poets share a similar relationship with their poetry. Walker, a woman of passion, shows how her personal beliefs about Africa (in the first section of this collection, "African Images: Glimpses from a Tiger's Back"), multiracial relationships (in the poem "Johann"), and the pangs of love (in poems such as "Did This Happen to Your Mother? Did Your Sister Throw Up a Lot?") are intricately intertwined and evident in her poetic creations.

Walker calls the final section "We Have a Beautiful Mother: Previously Uncollected Poems." The poems in this section, including "Some Things I Like About My Triple Bloods," "If There Was Any Justice," "We Have a Map of the World," and "Telling," are deeply personal and challenge readers to think about boundaries between cultures, countries, and hearts.

ABSOLUTE TRUST IN THE GOODNESS OF THE EARTH

In the preface to *Absolute Trust in the Goodness of the Earth*, Walker confides that she thought that she had reached the end of her career as a poet and was at peace with this, but after the terrorist attacks of September, 11, 2001, on the United States, Walker found herself writing poems regularly. After the attacks, Walker feared imminent war, and her poems in this book reflect that anxiety, including pieces such as "Thousands of Feet Below You," "Not Children," and "Why War Is Never a Good Idea." The narrator of "Thousands of Feet Below You" mentions a boy, running away from the bombs of war, who eventually is shredded to pieces in a violent explosion. Walker shares similar feelings about the concept of war in "Not Children," in which she refers to war as a cowardly act and an event that the world can do without. The title of "Why War Is Never a Good Idea" is self-explanatory, the subtitle of which ("A Picture Poem for Children Blinded by War") emphasizes Walker's stance on the issue.

Walker also continuously challenges readers to think about race relations in the United States, and how they might be improved. For example, "Patriot" encourages readers to respect all Americans, no matter what their country of origin is (she mentions Middle Eastern men, American Indian men, and African women, in particular), because these people all combine to make and define the United States. "Projection" encourages readers to look beyond the stereotypes associated with certain ethnicities (such as Indians, Germans, and Arabs) and remember that, inside each person, exists an innocent child.

In the preface to *Absolute Trust in the Goodness of the Earth*, Walker also shares her interest in and admiration for the environment and plants in particular. These feelings about the natural world are represented clearly in the title of this collection, which praises the earth for its beauty and righteousness. Walker, like many writers, associates nature with an inherent sense of peace. Natural imagery abounds in this collection, appearing in poems such as "Even When I Walked Away," "Red Petals Sticking Out," "Inside My Rooms," and "The Tree." Walker's plant and flower images remind readers of her belief that humankind is deeply rooted in and connected to the earth.

A POEM TRAVELED DOWN MY ARM

In the introduction to *A Poem Traveled Down My Arm*, Walker explains that her publisher sent her blank pages to autograph; these pages would later be bound into copies of *Absolute Trust in the Goodness of the Earth* to save Walker time at forthcoming book signings. Tired of signing her own name so many times, Walker says that she suddenly started drawing little sketches on the pieces of paper. Soon, she was scrambling to keep up with writing down poems that sprang to mind, inspired by the images she had drawn. Walker feels this collection is strange when compared with her others, especially because she thought she was done writing poetry a few years earlier. Instead, she published two collections of poetry in a single year.

The poems in *A Poem Traveled Down My Arm* typically hover around ten words each. These succinct poetic creations address topics prevalent in the rest of Walker's canon, including love, peace, nature, and war. The untitled poems function almost like a series of proverbs, offering her readers advice about living a healthy spiritual life while respecting Earth and all of humanity.

OTHER MAJOR WORKS

LONG FICTION: *The Third Life of Grange Copeland*, 1970; *Meridian*, 1976; *The Color Purple*, 1982; *The Temple of My Familiar*, 1989; *Possessing the Secret of Joy*, 1992; *By the Light of My Father's Smile*, 1998; *Now Is the Time to Open Your Heart*, 2004.

SHORT FICTION: *In Love and Trouble: Stories of Black Women*, 1973; *You Can't Keep a Good Woman Down*, 1981; *The Complete Stories*, 1994; *Alice Walker Banned*, 1996 (stories and commentary).

NONFICTION: *In Search of Our Mothers' Gardens: Womanist Prose*, 1983; *Living by the Word: Selected Writings, 1973-1987*, 1988; *Warrior Marks: Female Genital Mutilation and the Sexual Blinding of Women*, 1993 (with Pratibha Parmar); *The Same River Twice: Honoring the Difficult*, 1996; *Anything We Love Can Be Saved: A Writer's Activism*, 1997; *The Way Forward Is with a Broken Heart*, 2000; *Sent by Earth: A Message from the Grandmother Spirit After the Attacks on the World Trade Center and Pentagon*, 2001; *We Are the Ones We Have Been Waiting For: Light in a Time of Darkness*, 2006; *The World Has Changed: Conversations with Alice Walker*, 2010 (Rudolph P. Byrd, editor).

CHILDREN'S LITERATURE: *Langston Hughes: American Poet*, 1974; *To Hell with Dying*, 1988; *Finding the Green Stone*, 1991; *There Is a Flower at the Tip of My Nose Smelling Me*, 2006; *Why War Is Never a Good Idea*, 2007.

EDITED TEXT: *I Love Myself When I Am Laughing . . . and Then Again When I Am Looking Mean and Impressive: A Zora Neale Hurston Reader*, 1979.

BIBLIOGRAPHY

Bates, Gerri. *Alice Walker: A Critical Companion*. Westport, Conn.: Greenwood Press, 2005. A well-crafted biography that discusses Walker's major works, tracing the themes of her novels to her life.

Bloom, Harold, ed. *Alice Walker*. New York: Chelsea House, 1989. An important collection of critical essays examining the fiction, poetry, and essays of Walker from a variety of perspectives. The fourteen essays, including Bloom's brief introduction, are arranged chronologically. Contains useful discussions of her first three novels, brief analyses of individual short stories, poems, and essays, and assessments of Walker's social and political views in connection with her works and other African American female authors. Chronology and bibliography.

Bloxham, Laura J. "Alice (Malsenior) Walker." In *Contemporary Fiction Writers of the South*, edited by Joseph M. Flora and Robert Bain. Westport, Conn.: Greenwood Press, 1993. A general introduction to Walker's "womanist" themes of oppression of black women and change through affirmation of self. Provides a brief summary and critique of previous criticism of Walker's work.

Gates, Henry Louis, Jr., and K. A. Appiah, eds. *Alice Walker: Critical Perspectives Past and Present.* New York: Amistad, 1993. Contains reviews of Walker's first five novels and critical analyses of several of her works of short and long fiction. Also includes two interviews with Walker, a chronology of her works, and an extensive bibliography of essays and texts.

Gentry, Tony. *Alice Walker.* New York: Chelsea House, 1993. Examines the life and work of Walker. Includes bibliographical references and index.

Lauret, Maria. *Alice Walker.* New York: St. Martin's Press, 2000. Provocative discussions of Walker's ideas on politics, race, feminism, and literary theory. Of special interest is the exploration of Walker's literary debt to Zora Neale Hurston, Virginia Woolf, and even Bessie Smith.

Simcikova, Karla. *To Live Fully, Here and Now: The Healing Vision in the Works of Alice Walker.* Lanham, Md.: Lexington Books, 2007. Simcikova focuses on Walker's spirituality, her relationship with nature, and how these beliefs and connections present themselves in her oeuvre of work.

Smith, Lindsey Claire. "Alice Walker's Eco-'Warriors.'" In *Indians, Environment, and Identity on the Borders of American Literature: From Faulkner and Morrison to Walker and Silko.* New York: Palgrave Macmillan, 2008. Smith analyzes boundaries delineating cultural, geographical, and racial differences in Walker's canon.

Walker, Rebecca. *Black, White, and Jewish: Autobiography of a Shifting Self.* New York: Riverhead, 2001. A self-indulgent but nevertheless insightful memoir by Alice Walker's daughter, Rebecca Walker. She describes herself as "a movement child," growing up torn between two families, two races, and two traditions, always in the shadow of an increasingly famous and absorbed mother.

White, Evelyn C. *Alice Walker: A Life.* New York: Norton, 2004. The life and accomplishments of Walker are chronicled in this biography through interviews with Walker, her family, and friends.

Allene Phy-Olsen
Updated by Karley K. Adney

WALT WHITMAN

Born: West Hills, New York; May 31, 1819
Died: Camden, New Jersey; March 26, 1892

PRINCIPAL POETRY
"Song of Myself," 1855
Leaves of Grass, 1855, 1856, 1860, 1867, 1871, 1876, 1881-1882, 1889, 1891-1892
Drum-Taps, 1865
Sequel to Drum-Taps, 1865-1866
After All, Not to Create Only, 1871
Passage to India, 1871
As a Strong Bird on Pinions Free, 1872
Two Rivulets, 1876
November Boughs, 1888
Good-bye My Fancy, 1891
Complete Poetry and Selected Prose, 1959 (James E. Miller, editor)

OTHER LITERARY FORMS

Walt Whitman published several important essays and studies during his lifetime. *Democratic Vistas* (1871), *Memoranda During the War* (1875-1876), *Specimen Days and Collect* (1882-1883, autobiographical sketches), and the *Complete Prose Works* (1892) are the most significant. He also tried his hand at short fiction, collected in *The Half-Breed, and Other Stories* (1927), and a novel, *Franklin Evans* (1842). Many of his letters and journals have appeared either in early editions or as parts of the New York University Press edition of *The Collected Writings of Walt Whitman* (1961-1984; 22 volumes).

ACHIEVEMENTS

Walt Whitman's stature rests largely on two major contributions to the literature of the United States. First, although detractors are numerous and the poet's organizing principle is sometimes blurred, *Leaves of Grass* stands as the most fully realized American epic poem. Written in the midst of natural grandeur and burgeoning materialism, Whitman's book traces the geographical, social, and spiritual contours of an expanding nation. It embraces the science and commercialism of industrial America while trying to direct these practical energies toward the "higher mind" of literature, culture, and the soul. In his preface to the first edition of *Leaves of Grass*, Whitman referred to the United States itself as "essentially the greatest poem." He saw the self-esteem, sympa-

Walt Whitman
(Library of Congress)

thy, candor, and deathless attachment to freedom of the common people as "unrhymed poetry," which awaited the "gigantic and generous treatment worthy of it." *Leaves of Grass* was to be that treatment.

The poet's second achievement was in language and poetic technique. Readers take for granted the modern American poet's emphasis on free verse and ordinary diction, forgetting Whitman's revolutionary impact. His free-verse form departed from stanzaic patterns and regular lines, taking its power instead from individual, rolling, oratorical lines of cadenced speech. He subordinated traditional poetic techniques, such as alliteration, repetition, inversion, and conventional meter, to this expansive form. He also violated popular rules of poetic diction by extracting a rich vocabulary from foreign languages, science, opera, various trades, and the ordinary language of town and country. Finally, Whitman broke taboos with his extensive use of sexual imagery, incorporated not to titillate or shock, but to portray life in its wholeness. He determined to be the poet of procreation, to celebrate the elemental and primal life force that permeates humans and nature. Thus, "forbidden voices" are unveiled, clarified, and transfigured by the poet's vision of their place in an organic universe.

Whitman himself said he wrote but "one or two indicative words for the future." He expected the "main things" from poets, orators, singers, and musicians to come. They would prove and define a national culture, thus justifying his faith in American democracy. These apologetic words, along with the early tendency to read Whitman as "untranslatable," or barbaric and undisciplined, long delayed his acceptance as one of America's greatest poets. In fact, if judged by the poet's own test of greatness, he is a failure, for he said the "proof of a poet is that his country absorbs him as affectionately as he has absorbed it." Whitman has not been absorbed by the common people to whom he paid tribute in his poetry. However, with recognition from both the academic community and such poets as Hart Crane, William Carlos Williams, Karl Shapiro, and Randall Jarrell, his *Leaves of Grass* has taken its place among the great masterworks of American literature.

Biography

Walter Whitman, Jr., was born in West Hills, Long Island on May 31, 1819. His mother, Louisa Van Velsor, was descended from a long line of New York Dutch farmers, and his father, Walter Whitman, was a Long Island farmer and carpenter. In 1823, the father moved his family to Brooklyn in search of work. One of nine children in an undistinguished family, Whitman received only a meager formal education between 1825 and 1830, when he turned to the printing trade for the next five years. At the age of seventeen, he began teaching at various Long Island schools and continued to teach until he went to New York City to be a printer for the *New World* and a reporter for the *Democratic Review* in 1841. From then on, Whitman generally made a living at journalism. Besides reporting and freelance writing, he edited several Brooklyn newspapers, including the *Daily Eagle* (1846-1848), the *Freeman* (1848-1849), and the *Times* (1857-1859). Some of Whitman's experiences during this period influenced the poetry that seemed to burst into print in 1855. While in New York, Whitman frequented the opera and the public library, both of which furnished him with a sense of heritage and of connection with the bards and singers of the past. In 1848, Whitman met and was hired by a representative of the New Orleans *Crescent*. Although the job lasted only a few months, the journey by train, stagecoach, and steamboat through what Whitman always referred to as "inland America" certainly helped to stimulate his vision of the country's democratic future. Perhaps most obviously influential was Whitman's trade itself. His flair for action and vignette, as well as descriptive detail, surely was sharpened by his journalistic writing. The reporter's keen eye for the daily scene is everywhere evident in *Leaves of Grass*.

When the first edition of his poems appeared, Whitman received little money but some attention from reviewers. Included among the responses was a famous letter from

Ralph Waldo Emerson, who praised Whitman for his brave thought and greeted him at the beginning of a great career. Whitman continued to write and edit, but was unemployed during the winter of 1859-1860, when he began to frequent Pfaff's bohemian restaurant. There he may have established the "manly love" relationships that inspired the "Calamus" poems of the 1860 edition of *Leaves of Grass*. Again, this third edition created a stir with readers, but the outbreak of the Civil War soon turned everyone's attention to more pressing matters. Whitman himself was too old for military service, but he did experience the war by caring for wounded soldiers in Washington, D.C., hospitals. While in Washington as a government clerk, Whitman witnessed Abraham Lincoln's second inauguration, mourned over the president's assassination in April, printed *Drum-Taps* in May, and later added to these Civil War lyrics a sequel, which contained "When Lilacs Last in the Dooryard Bloom'd."

The postwar years saw Whitman's reputation steadily increasing in England, thanks to William Rossetti's *Selections* in 1868, Algernon Swinburne's praise, and a long, admiring review of his work by Anne Gilchrist in 1870. In fact, Gilchrist fell in love with the poet after reading *Leaves of Grass* and even moved to Philadelphia in 1876 to be near him, but her hopes of marrying Whitman died with her in 1885. Because of books by William D. O'Connor and John Burroughs, Whitman also became better known in the United States, but any satisfaction he may have derived from this recognition was tempered by two severe blows in 1873. He suffered a paralytic stroke in January, and his mother, to whom he was very devoted, died in May. Unable to work, Whitman returned to stay with his brother George at Camden, New Jersey, spending summers on a farm at Timber Creek.

Although Whitman recuperated sufficiently to take trips to New York or Boston, and even to Colorado and Canada in 1879-1880, he was never again to be the robust man he had so proudly described in early editions of *Leaves of Grass*. His declining years, however, gave him time to revise and establish the structure of his book. When the seventh edition of *Leaves of Grass* was published in Philadelphia in 1881-1882, Whitman had achieved a total vision of his work. With the money from a centennial edition (1876) and an occasional lecture on Lincoln, Whitman was able by 1884 to purchase a small house on Mickle Street in Camden. Although he was determined not to be "house-bound," a sunstroke in 1885 and a second paralytic stroke in 1888 made him increasingly dependent on friends. He found especially gratifying the friendship of his secretary and companion, Horace Traubel, who recorded the poet's life and opinions during these last years. Despite the care of Traubel and several doctors and nurses, Whitman died of complications from a stroke on March 26, 1892.

Analysis

An approach to Walt Whitman's poetry profitably begins with the "Inscriptions" to *Leaves of Grass*, for these short, individual pieces introduce the main ideas and methods of Whitman's book. In general, they stake out the ground of what Miller has called the prototypical New World personality, a merging of the individual with the national and cosmic, or universal, selves. That democratic principles are at the root of Whitman's views becomes immediately clear in "One's-Self I Sing," the first poem in *Leaves of Grass*. Here, Whitman refers to the self as a "simple separate person," yet utters the "word Democratic, the word En-Masse." Citizens of America alternately assert their individuality—obey little, resist often—and yet see themselves as a brotherhood of the future, inextricably bound by the vision of a great new society of and for the masses. This encompassing vision requires a sense of "the Form complete," rejecting neither body nor soul, singing equally of the Female and Male, embracing both realistic, scientific, modern humanity and the infinite, eternal life of the spirit.

LEAVES OF GRASS

Whitman takes on various roles to lead his readers to a fuller understanding of this democratic universal. In "Me Imperturbe," he is at ease as an element of nature, able to confront the accidents and rebuffs of life with the implacability of trees and animals. As he suggests in *Democratic Vistas*, the true idea of nature in all its power and glory must become fully restored and must furnish the "pervading atmosphere" to poems of American democracy. Whitman must also empathize with rational things—with humanity at large and in particular—so he constructs what sometimes seem to be endless catalogs of Americans at work and play. This technique appears in "I Hear America Singing," which essentially lists the varied carols of carpenter, boatman, shoemaker, woodcutter, mother, and so on, all "singing what belongs to him or her and to none else" as they ply their trades. In longer poems, such as "Starting from Paumanok," Whitman extends his catalog to all the states of the Union. He intends to acknowledge contemporary lands, salute employments and cities large and small, and report heroism on land and sea from an American point of view. He marks down all of what constitutes unified life, including the body, sexual love, and comradeship, or "manly love." Finally, the poet must join the greatness of love and democracy to the greatness of religion. These programs expand to take up large parts of even longer poems, such as "Song of Myself" or to claim space of their own in sections of *Leaves of Grass*.

Whitman uses another technique to underscore the democratic principle of his art: He makes the reader a fellow poet, a "camerado" who joins hands with him to traverse the poetic landscape. In "To You," he sees the poet and reader as passing strangers who desire to speak to one another and urges that they do so. In "Song of the Open Road," Whitman travels the highways with his "delicious burdens" of men and women, calling them all to come forth and move forever forward, well armed to take their places in "the procession of souls along the grand roads of the universe." His view of the reader as fellow traveler and seer is especially clear in the closing lines of the poem:

> Camerado, I give you my hand!
> I give you my love more precious than money,
> I give you myself before preaching or law;
> Will you give me yourself? will you come travel with me?
> Shall we stick by each other as long as we live?

Finally, this comradeship means willingness to set out on one's own, for Whitman says in "Song of Myself" that the reader most honors his style "who learns under it to destroy the teacher." The questions one asks are one's own to puzzle out. The poet's role is to lead his reader up on a knoll, wash the gum from his eyes, and then let him become habituated to the "dazzle of light" that is the natural world. In other words, Whitman intends to help his reader become a "poet" of insight and perception and then release him to travel the public roads of a democratic nation.

This democratic unification of multiplicity, empathic identification, and comradeship exists in most of Whitman's poems. They do not depend on his growth as poet or thinker. However, in preparing to analyze representative poems from *Leaves of Grass*, it is helpful to establish a general plan for the various sections of the book. Whitman revised and reordered his poems until the 1881 edition, which established a form that was to remain essentially unchanged through succeeding editions. He merely annexed materials to the 1881 order until just before his death in 1892, then authorized the 1891-1892 version for all future printings. Works originally published apart from *Leaves of Grass*, such as *Drum-Taps* or *Passage to India*, were eventually incorporated in the parent volume. Thus, an analysis of the best poems in five important sections of this final *Leaves of Grass* will help delineate Whitman's movement toward integration of self and nation, within his prescribed portals of birth and death.

"SONG OF MYSELF"

"Song of Myself," Whitman's great lyric poem, exemplifies his democratic "programs" without diminishing the intense feeling that so startled his first readers. It successfully combines paeans to the individual, the nation, and life at large, including nature, sexuality, and death. Above all, "Song of Myself" is a poem of incessant motion, as though Whitman's energy is spontaneously bursting into lines. Even in the contemplative sections of the poem, when Whitman leans and loafs at his ease observing a spear of summer grass, his senses of hearing, taste, and sight are working at fever pitch. In the opening section, he calls himself "nature without check with original energy." Having once begun to speak, he hopes "to cease not till death." Whitman says that although others may talk of the beginning and the end, he finds his subject in the now—in the "urge and urge and urge" of the procreant world.

One method by which Whitman's energy escapes boundaries is the poet's ability to "become" other people and things. He will not be measured by time and space, nor by physical form. Rather, he effuses his flesh in eddies and drifts it in lacy jags, taking on new identities with every line. His opening lines show that he is speaking not of himself alone but of all selves. What he assumes, the reader shall assume; every atom of him, and therefore of the world, belongs to the reader as well. In section 24, he represents himself as a "Kosmos," which contains multitudes and reconciles apparent opposites. He speaks the password and sign of democracy and accepts nothing that all cannot share. To stress this egalitarian vision, Whitman employs the catalog with skill and variety. Many parts of "Song of Myself" list or name characters, places, occupations, or experiences, but section 33 most clearly shows the two major techniques that give these lists vitality. First, Whitman composes long single-sentence movements of action and description, which attempt to unify nature and civilization. The poet is alternately weeding his onion patch, hoeing, prospecting, hauling his boat down a shallow river, scaling mountains, walking paths, and speeding through space. He then follows each set of actions with a series of place lines, beginning with "where," "over," "at," or "upon," which unite farmhouses, hearth furnaces, hot-air balloons, or steamships with plants and animals of land and sea. Second, Whitman interrupts these long listings with more detailed vignettes, which show the "large hearts of heroes"—a sea captain, a hounded slave, a fireman trapped and broken under debris, an artillerist. Sections 34-36 then extend the narrative to tales of the Alamo and an old-time sea fight, vividly brought forth with sounds and dialogue. In each case, the poet becomes the hero and is actually in the scene to suffer or succeed.

This unchecked energy and empathy carry over into Whitman's ebullient imagery to help capture the physical power of human bodies in procreant motion. At one point Whitman calls himself "hankering, gross, mystical, nude." He finds no sweeter flesh than that which sticks to his own bones, or to the bones of others. Sexual imagery, including vividly suggestive descriptions of the male and female body, is central to the poem. Although the soul must take its equal place with the body, neither abasing itself before the other, Whitman's mystical union of soul and body is a sexual experience as well. He loves the hum of the soul's "valved voice" and remembers how, on a transparent summer morning, the soul settled its head athwart his hips and turned over on him. It parted the shirt from the poet's "bosom-bone," plunged its tongue to his "bare-strip heart," and reached until it felt his beard and held his feet. From this experience came peace and the knowledge that love is fundamental to a unified, continuous creation. Poetic metaphor, which identifies and binds hidden likenesses in nature, is therefore emblematic of the organic world. For example, in answering a child's question, "What is the grass?" the poet offers a series of metaphors that join human, natural, and spiritual impulses:

> I guess it must be the flag of my disposition, out of
>   hopeful green stuff woven.
> Or I guess it is the handkerchief of the Lord,
> A scented gift and remembrancer designedly dropt,
> Bearing the owner's name someway in the corners,
>   that we may see and remark, and say *Whose?*

The grass becomes hair from the breasts of young men, from the heads and beards of old people, or from offspring, and it "speaks" from under the faint red roofs of mouths. The smallest sprout shows that there is no death, for "nothing collapses," and to die is "luckier" than anyone had supposed. This excerpt from the sixth section of "Song of Myself" illustrates how image making signifies for Whitman a kind of triumph over death itself.

Because of its position near the beginning of *Leaves of Grass* and its encompassing of Whitman's major themes, "Song of Myself" is a foundation for the volume. The "self" in this poem is a replica of the nation as self, and its delineation in the cosmos is akin to the growth of the United States in the world. Without putting undue stress on this nationalistic interpretation, however, the reader can find many reasons to admire "Song of Myself." Its dynamic form, beauty of language, and psychological insights are sufficient to make Whitman a first-rate poet, even if he had written nothing else.

CELEBRATION OF SELF AND SEXUALITY

The passionate celebration of the self and of sexuality is Whitman's great revolutionary theme. In "Children of Adam," he is the procreative father of multitudes, a champion of heterosexual love and the "body electric." In "From Pent-Up Aching Rivers," he sings of the need for superb children, brought forth by the "muscular urge" of "stalwart loins." In "I Sing the Body Electric," he celebrates the perfection of well-made male and female bodies. Sections 5 and 9 are explicit descriptions of sexual intercourse and physical "apparatus," respectively. Whitman does not shy away from the fierce attraction of the female form or the ebb and flow of "limitless limpid jets of love hot and enormous" that undulate into the willing and yielding "gates of the body." Because he sees the body as sacred, as imbued with divine power, he considers these enumerations to be poems of the soul as much as of the body.

Indeed, "A Woman Waits for Me" specifically states that sex contains all—bodies and souls. Thus, the poet seeks warm-blooded and sufficient women to receive the pent-up rivers of himself, to start new sons and daughters fit for the great nation that will be these United States. The procreative urge operates on more than one level in "Children of Adam"—it is physical sex and birthing, the union of body and soul, and the metaphorical insemination of the poet's words and spirit into national life. In several ways, then, words are to become flesh. Try as some early Whitman apologists might to explain them away, raw sexual impulses are the driving force of these poems.

"CALAMUS" POEMS

Whitman's contemporaries were shocked by the explicit sexual content of "Children of Adam," but modern readers and critics have been much more intrigued by the apparent homoeroticism of the poems in the "Calamus" section of the 1860 edition of *Leaves of Grass*. Although it is ultimately impossible to say whether these poems reflect Whitman's gay associations in New York, it is obvious that comradeship extends here to both spiritual and physical contact between men. "In Paths Untrodden" states the poet's intention to sing of "manly attachment" or types of "athletic love," to celebrate the need of comrades. "Whoever You Are Holding Me Now in Hand" deepens the physical nature of this love, including the stealthy meeting of male friends in a wood, behind some rock in the open air, or on the beach of some quiet island. There the poet would permit the comrade's long-dwelling kiss on the lips and a touch that would carry him eternally forth over land and sea. "These I Singing in Spring" refers to "him that tenderly loves me" and pledges the hardiest spears of grass, the calamus-root, to those who love as the poet himself is capable of loving.

Finally, two of Whitman's best lyrics concern this robust but clandestine relationship. "I Saw in Louisiana a Live-Oak Growing" is a poignant contrast between the live oak's ability to "utter joyous leaves" while it stands in solitude, without companions, and the poet's inability to live without a friend or lover near. There is no mistaking the equally personal tone of "When I Heard at the Close of the Day," probably Whitman's finest "Calamus" poem. The plaudits of others are meaningless and unsatisfying, says Whitman, until he thinks of how his dear friend and lover is on his way to see him. When his friend arrives one evening, the hissing rustle of rolling waves becomes congratulatory and joyful. Once the person he loves most lies sleeping by him under the same cover, face inclined toward him in the autumn moonbeams and arm lightly lying around his breast, he is happy.

Other short poems in "Calamus," such as "For You O Democracy," "The Prairie Grass Dividing," or "A Promise to California," are less obviously personal. Rather, they extend passionate friendship between men to the larger ideal of democratic brotherhood. Just as procreative love has its metaphorical implications for the nation, so too does Whitman promise to make the continent indissoluble and cities inseparable, arms about each other's necks, with companionship and the "manly love of comrades." Still other poems move this comradeship into wider spans of space and time. "The Moment Yearning and Thoughtful" joins the poet with men of Europe and Asia in happy brotherhood, thus transcending national and continental boundaries. "The Base of All Metaphysics" extends this principle through historical time, for the Greek, Germanic, and Christian systems all suggest that the attraction of friend to friend is the basis of civilization. The last poem in the "Calamus" section, "Full of Life Now," completes Whitman's panoramic view by carrying friendship into the future. His words communicate the compact, visible to readers of a century or any number of centuries hence. Each seeking the other past time's invisible boundaries, poet and reader are united physically through Whitman's poetry.

"CROSSING BROOKLYN FERRY"

"Crossing Brooklyn Ferry" is the natural product of Whitman's idea that love and companionship will bind the world's peoples to one another. In a sense it gives the poet immortality through creation of a living artifact: the poem itself. Whitman stands motionless on a moving ferry, immersed in the stream of life and yet suspended in time through the existence of his words on the page. Consequently, he can say that neither time nor place nor distance matters, because he is with each reader and each fellow traveler in the future. He points out that hundreds of years hence others will enter the gates of the ferry and cross from shore to shore, will see the sun half an hour high and watch the seagulls floating in circles with motionless wings. Others will also watch the endless scallop-edged waves cresting and falling, as though they are experiencing the same moment as the poet, with the same mixture of joy and sorrow. Thus, Whitman confidently calls upon the "dumb ministers" of nature to keep up their ceaseless motion—to flow, fly, and frolic on—because they furnish their parts toward eternity and toward the soul.

Techniques match perfectly with these themes in "Crossing Brooklyn Ferry." Whitman's frequent repetition of the main images—sunrise and sunset, ebb and flow of the sea and river, seagulls oscillating in the sky—reinforces the belief in timeless, recurring human experience. Descriptions of schooners and steamers at work along the shore are among his most powerful evocations of color and sound. Finally, Whitman's employment of pronouns to mark a shift in the sharing of experiences also shows the poem's careful design. Whitman begins the poem with an "I" who looks at the scenes or crowds of people and calls to "you" who are among the crowds and readers of present and future. In section 8, however, he reaches across generations to fuse himself and pour his meaning into the "you." At the end of this section, he and others have become "we," who understand and receive experience with free senses and love, united in the organic continuity of nature.

"SEA-DRIFT" POEMS

The short section of *Leaves of Grass* entitled "Sea-Drift" contains the first real signs of a more somber Whitman, who must come to terms with hardship, sorrow, and death. In one way, this resignation and accommodation follow the natural progression of the self from active, perhaps callow, youth to contemplative old age. They are also an outgrowth of Whitman's belief that life and death are a continuum, that life is a symphony of both sonatas and dirges, which the true poet of nature must capture fully on the page. Whereas in other poems the ocean often signifies birth and creation, with fish-shaped Paumanok (Manhattan) rising from the sea, in "Tears," it is the repository of sorrow. Its white shore lies in solitude, dark and desolate, holding a ghost or "shapeless lump" that cries streaming, sobbing tears. In "As I Ebb'd with the Ocean of Life," Whitman is distressed with himself for daring to "blab" so much without having the least idea who or what he really is. Nature darts on the poet and stings him, because he has not understood anything and because no man ever can. He calls himself but a "trail of drift and debris," who has left his poems like "little wrecks" on Paumanok's shores. However, he must continue to throw himself on the ocean of life, clinging to the breast of the land that is his father, and gathering from the moaning sea the "sobbing dirge of Nature." He believes the flow will return, but meanwhile he must wait and lie in drifts at his readers' feet.

"Out of the Cradle Endlessly Rocking"

"Out of the Cradle Endlessly Rocking" is a fuller, finally more optimistic, treatment of the poet's confrontation with loss. Commonly acknowledged as one of Whitman's finest works, this poem uses lyrical language and operatic structure to trace the origin of his poetic powers in the experience of death. Two "songs" unite with the whispering cry of the sea to communicate this experience to him. Central to the poem is Whitman's seaside reminiscence of a bird and his mate, who build and tend a nest of eggs. When the female fails to return one evening, never to appear again, the male becomes a solitary singer of his sorrows, whose notes are "translated" by the listening boy-poet. The bird's song is an aria of lonesome love, an outpouring carol of yearning, hope, and finally, death. As the boy absorbs the bird's song, his soul awakens in sympathy. From this moment forward, his destiny will be to perpetuate the bird's "cries of unsatisfied love." More important, though, Whitman must learn the truth that this phrase masks, must conquer "the word" that has caused the bird's cries:

> Whereto answering, the sea,
> Delaying not, hurrying not,
> Whisper'd me through the night, and very plainly
>   before daybreak,
> Lisp'd to me the low and delicious word death,
> And again death, death, death, death.

Whitman then fuses the bird's song and his own with death, which the sea, "like some old crone rocking the cradle," has whispered to him. This final image of the sea as an old crone soothing an infant underscores the central point of "Out of the Cradle Endlessly Rocking": Old age and death are part of a natural flux. Against the threat of darkness, one must live and sing.

Drum-Taps

Like the tone of the "Sea-Drift" section, darker hues permeate Whitman's Civil War lyrics. His experiences as a hospital worker in Washington, D.C., are clearly behind the sometimes wrenching imagery of *Drum-Taps.* As a wound dresser, he saw the destruction of healthy young bodies and minds at first hand. These spectacles were in part a test of Whitman's own courage and comradeship, but they were also a test of the nation's ability to survive and grow. As Whitman says in "Long, Too Long America," the country had long traveled roads "all even and peaceful," learning only from joys and prosperity, but now it must face "crises of anguish" without recoiling and show the world what its "children enmasse really are." Many of the *Drum-Taps* lyrics show Whitman facing this reality, but "The Wound Dresser" is representative. The poet's persona is an old man who is called on years after the Civil War to "paint the mightiest armies of earth," to tell what experience of the war stays with him latest and deepest. Although he mentions the long marches, rushing charges, and toils of battle, he does not dwell on soldiers' perils or soldiers' joys. Rather, he vividly describes the wounded and dying at battlegrounds, hospital tents, or roofed hospitals, as he goes with "hinged knees and steady hand to dress wounds." He does not recoil or give out at the sight of crushed heads, shattered throats, amputated stumps of hands and arms, the gnawing and putrid gangrenous foot or shoulder. Nevertheless, within him rests a burning flame, the memory of youths suffering or dead.

Confronted with these horrors, Whitman had to find a way to surmount them, and that way was love. If there could be a positive quality in war, Whitman found it in the comradeship of common soldiers, who risked all for their fellows. In "As Toilsome I Wander'd Virginia's Woods," for example, Whitman discovers the grave of a soldier buried beneath a tree. Hastily dug on a retreat from battle, the grave is nevertheless marked by a sign: "Bold, cautious, true, and my loving comrade." That inscription remains with the poet through many changeful seasons and scenes to follow, as evidence of this brotherly love. Similarly, "Vigil Strange I Kept on the Field One Night" tells of a soldier who sees his comrade struck down in battle and returns to find him cold with death. He watches by him through "immortal and mystic hours" until, just as dawn is breaking, he folds the young man in a blanket and buries him in a rude-dug grave where he fell. This tale of tearless mourning perfectly evokes the loss caused by war.

Eventually, Whitman finds some ritual significance in these deaths, as though they are atonement for those yet living. In "A Sight in Camp in the Daybreak Gray and Dim," he marks three covered forms on stretchers near a hospital tent. One by one he uncovers their faces. The first is an elderly man, gaunt and grim, but a comrade nevertheless. The second is a sweet boy "with cheeks yet blooming." When he exposes the third face, however, he finds it calm, of yellow-white ivory, and of indeterminable age. He sees in it the face of Christ himself, "dead and divine and brother of all." "Over the Carnage Rose Prophetic a Voice" suggests that these Christian sacrifices will finally lead to a united Columbia. Even though a thousand may have to "sternly immolate themselves for one," those who love one another shall become invincible, and "affection shall solve the problems of freedom." As in other sections of *Leaves of Grass,* Whitman believes the United States will be held together not by lawyers, paper agreements, or force of arms, but by the cohesive power of love and fellowship.

"When Lilacs Last in the Dooryard Bloom'd"

"When Lilacs Last in the Dooryard Bloom'd," another of Whitman's acknowledged masterpieces, repeats the process underlying *Drum-Taps*. The poet must come to terms with the loss of one he loves—in this case, the slain President Lincoln. Death and mourning must eventually give way to consolation and hope for the future. Cast in the form of a traditional elegy, the poem traces the processional of Lincoln's coffin across country, past the poet himself, to the president's final resting place.

To objectify his emotional struggle between grief, on one hand, and spiritual reconciliation with death on the other, Whitman employs several vivid symbols. The lilac blooming perennially, with its heart-shaped leaves, represents the poet's perpetual mourning and love. The "powerful fallen star," which now lies in a "harsh surrounding could" of black night, is Lincoln, fallen and shrouded in his coffin. The solitary hermit thrush that warbles "death's outlet song of life" from a secluded swamp is the soul or spiritual world. Initially, Whitman is held powerless by the death of his departing comrade. Although he can hear the bashful notes of the thrush and will come to understand them, he thinks only of showering the coffin with sprigs of lilac to commemorate his love for Lincoln. He must also warble his own song before he can absorb the bird's message of consolation. Eventually, as he sits amidst the teeming daily activities described in section 14, he is struck by the "sacred knowledge of death," and the bird's carol thus becomes intelligible to him. Death is lovely, soothing, and delicate. It is a "strong deliveress" who comes to nestle the grateful body in her flood of bliss. Rapt with the charm of the bird's song, Whitman sees myriad battle corpses in a vision—the debris of all the slain soldiers of the war—yet realizes that they are fully at rest and no longer suffering. The power of this realization gives him strength to let go of the hand of his comrade. An ever-blooming lilac now signifies renewal, just as death takes its rightful place as the harbinger of new life, the life of the eternal soul.

Matters of spirit

Whitman's deepening concern with matters of the spirit permeates the last sections of *Leaves of Grass*. Having passed the test of the Civil War and having done his part to reunite the United States, Whitman turned his attention to America's place in the world and his own place in God's design. As he points out in "A Clear Midnight," he gives his last poems to the soul and its "free flight into the wordless," to ponder the themes he loves best: "Night, sleep, death and the stars." Such poems as "Chanting the Square Deific" and "A Noiseless Patient Spider" invoke either the general soul, the "Santa Spirita" that pervades all created life, or the toils of individual souls, flinging out gossamer threads to connect themselves with this holy spirit.

"Passage to India"

Whitman was still able to produce fine lyrics in his old age. One of these successful poems, "Passage to India," announces Whitman's intention to join modern science to fables and dreams of old, to weld past and future, and to show that the United States is but a "bridge" in the "vast rondure" of the world. Just as the Suez Canal connected Europe and Asia, Whitman says, America's transcontinental railroad ties the eastern to the western sea, thus verifying Christopher Columbus's dream. Beyond these material thoughts of exploration, however, lies the poet's realm of love and spirit. The poet is a "true son of God," who will soothe the hearts of restlessly exploring, never-happy humanity. He will link all human affections, justify the "cold, impassive, voiceless earth," and absolutely fuse nature and humanity. This fusion takes place not in the material world but in the swelling of the soul toward God, who is a mighty "centre of the true, the good, the loving." Passage to these superior universes transcends time and space and death. It is a "passage to more than India," through the deep waters that no mariner has traveled, and for which the poet must "risk the ship, ourselves and all."

"Prayer of Columbus"

Whitman also uses a seagoing metaphor for spiritual passage in "Prayer of Columbus," which is almost a continuation of "Passage to India." In the latter, Whitman aggressively flings himself into the active voyage toward God, but in "Prayer of Columbus" he is a "batter'd, wreck'd old man," willing to yield his ships to God and wait for the unknown end of all. He recounts his heroic deeds of exploration and attributes their inspiration to a message from the heavens that sped him on. Like Columbus, Whitman is "old, poor, and paralyzed," yet capable of one more effort to speak of the steady interior light that God has granted him. Finally, the works of the past fall away from him, and some divine hand reveals a scene of countless ships sailing on distant seas, from which "anthems in new tongues" salute and comfort him. This implied divine sanction for his life's work was consolation to an old poet, who, at his death in 1892, remained largely unaccepted and unrecognized by contemporary critics and historians.

Legacy

The grand design of *Leaves of Grass* appears to trace self and nation neatly through sensuous youth, crises of maturity, and soul-searching old age. Although this philosophical or psychological reading of Whitman's work is certainly encouraged by the poet's tinkering with its structure, many fine lyrics do not fit into neat patterns, or even under topical headings. Whitman's reputation rests more on the startling freshness of his language, images, and democratic treatment of the common American citizen than on his success as epic bard. Common to all his poetry, however, are certain major themes: reconciliation of body and soul, purity and unity of physical nature, death as the "mother of beauty," and above all, comradeship or love, which binds and transcends all else. In fact, Whitman encouraged a complex comradeship with his readers to bind his work to future generations. He expected reading to be a gymnastic struggle and the reader to be a re-creator of the poem through imaginative interaction with the poet. Perhaps that is why he said in "So Long" that *Leaves of Grass* was no book, for whoever touches his poetry "touches a man."

OTHER MAJOR WORKS
LONG FICTION: *Franklin Evans*, 1842.
SHORT FICTION: *The Half-Breed, and Other Stories*, 1927.
NONFICTION: *Democratic Vistas*, 1871; *Memoranda During the War*, 1875-1876; *Specimen Days and Collect*, 1882-1883; *Complete Prose Works*, 1892; *Calamus*, 1897 (letters; Richard M. Bucke, editor); *The Wound Dresser*, 1898 (Bucke, editor); *Letters Written by Walt Whitman to His Mother, 1866-1872*, 1902 (Thomas B. Harned, editor); *An American Primer*, 1904; *Walt Whitman's Diary in Canada*, 1904 (William S. Kennedy, editor); *The Letters of Anne Gilchrist and Walt Whitman*, 1918 (Harned, editor).
MISCELLANEOUS: *The Collected Writings of Walt Whitman*, 1961-1984 (22 volumes).

BIBLIOGRAPHY
Canning, Richard. *Whitman*. London: Hesperus, 2010. Part of the Poetic Lives series, this is a basic biography that examines Whitman's life and poetry.
Folsom, Ed. *Re-scripting Walt Whitman: An Introduction to His Life and Work*. Malden, Mass.: Blackwell, 2005. A good starting point for readers of Whitman, delving into his life and literary works.
Genoways, Ted. *Walt Whitman and the Civil War: America's Poet During the Lost Years of 1860/1862*. Berkeley: University of California Press, 2009. Uses unpublished letters and manuscripts to explore Whitman's involvement in the war, debunking his supposed indifference.
Herrero-Brassas, Juan A., ed. *Walt Whitman's Mystical Ethics of Comradeship: Homosexuality and the Marginality of Friendship at the Crossroads of Modernity*. Albany: State University of New York Press, 2010. This collection of essays examines Whitman's mystical religious beliefs, his concept of comradeship, and his homosexuality.
Killlingsworth, M. Jimmie, ed. *The Cambridge Introduction to Walt Whitman*. New York: Cambridge University Press, 2007. A comprehensive work that covers Whitman's life and presents extensive analysis of his poetry, including his prewar poetry, *Leaves of Grass*, "Calamus," "Children of Adam," earth and body poems, and elegies. Also looks at critical reception of his works and the image that was created around him.
Kummings, Donald D., ed. *A Companion to Walt Whitman*. Malden, Mass.: Blackwell,

2006. These thirty-five essays by prominent scholars delve into the life and writing of Whitman. The essays are classified under four sections, concentrating on the author's life, the cultural and literary contexts of his writing, and the texts themselves. Topics such as nature, the city, gender, civil war, and pop culture are discussed at length in relation to Whitman and his writing. Readers will also find this book valuable for the publication history it provides, as well as the thorough bibliography of criticism of Whitman's prose.

Reynolds, David S. *Walt Whitman*. New York: Knopf, 2005. Part of the Lives and Legacies series, this work examines the life and work of Whitman. Reynolds calls Whitman the founder of free verse and the first poet to treat sex candidly.

Robertson, Michael. *Worshipping Walt: The Whitman Disciples*. Princeton, N.J.: Princeton University Press, 2008. In his later years, Whitman developed "disciples," people who admired and supported him. This work examines his disciples, including Anne Gilchrist, John Burroughs, John Addington Symonds, and Horace Traubel.

Stacey, Jason. *Walt Whitman's Multitudes: Labor Reform and Persona in Whitman's Journalism and the First "Leaves of Grass," 1840-1855*. New York: Peter Lang, 2008. Focuses on the political views of Whitman as expressed in his journalism and in the first edition of *Leaves of Grass*. Whitman wrote on artisans who had lost their economic status, blaming them in part for becoming involved in consumerism and affectation.

Williams, C. K. *On Whitman*. Princeton, N.J.: Princeton University Press, 2010. Part of the Writers on Writers series, this work looks at Whitman from the standpoint of another poet and delves into Whitman's influence.

Perry D. Luckett

OSCAR WILDE

Born: Dublin, Ireland; October 16, 1854
Died: Paris, France; November 30, 1900

PRINCIPAL POETRY
Ravenna, 1878
Poems, 1881
Poems in Prose, 1894
The Sphinx, 1894
The Ballad of Reading Gaol, 1898

OTHER LITERARY FORMS

Oscar Wilde wrote a number of plays produced successfully in his lifetime: *Lady Windermere's Fan* (pr. 1892), *A Woman of No Importance* (pr. 1893), *An Ideal Husband* (pr. 1895), and *The Importance of Being Earnest: A Trivial Comedy for Serious People* (pr. 1895). Banned in London, his play *Salomé* was produced in 1893 in Paris with Sarah Bernhardt. Two plays, *Vera: Or, The Nihilists* (pb. 1880) and *The Duchess of Padua* (pb. 1883), were produced in New York after publication in England. Finally, two plays, *A Florentine Tragedy* (pr. 1906) and *La Sainte Courtisane*, were published together in the collected edition of Wilde's works in 1908. Wilde published one novel, *The Picture of Dorian Gray* (1891), serially in *Lippincott's Magazine*. Commercially and artistically successful with a number of his plays and his one novel, Wilde reached his peak in the early 1890's when he wrote little poetry. Wilde also wrote short stories and a number of fairy tales. His last prose work is a long letter, *De Profundis*, an apologia for his life. Parts of it were published as early as 1905, but the full work was suppressed until 1950.

ACHIEVEMENTS

G. F. Maine states that the tragedy of Oscar Wilde is that he is remembered more as a criminal and a gay man than as an artist. Readers still feel overwhelmed by Wilde's life just as his personality overwhelmed his contemporaries. His greatest achievement is in drama, and his only novel–*The Picture of Dorian Gray*—is still widely read. In comparison, his poetry is essentially derivative.

Wilde modeled himself on the poets of a tradition that was soon to end in English literature, and most of his poetry appears in the earlier part of his career. Within this Romantic tradition, Wilde had a wider range than might be expected; he could move from the limited impressions of the shorter poems to the philosophic ruminations of the longer poems. Yet behind each poem, the presence of an earlier giant lurks: John Keats,

Oscar Wilde
(Library of Congress)

William Wordsworth, Algernon Charles Swinburne. Wilde's most original poem, *The Ballad of Reading Gaol*, is not derivative, and its starkness shows a side of Wilde not generally found in his other poems. Wilde's poetry is a coda, then, to the end of a tradition.

BIOGRAPHY

Oscar Fingal O'Flahertie Wills Wilde was born in Dublin, Ireland, on October 16, 1854. Flamboyance, so characteristic of the adult Wilde, was an obvious quality of both of his parents. His father was noted for physical dirtiness and love affairs, one of which led to a lawsuit and public scandal. Something of a social revolutionary, his mother published poetry and maintained a salon for intellectual discussion in her later years. Wilde grew up in this environment, showing both insolence and genius. He was an excellent student at all his schools. He attended Portora Royal School, Trinity College in Dublin, and then won a scholarship to Magdalen College, Oxford. At this time, John Ruskin was lecturing, and Wilde was influenced by Ruskin's ideas and style. More important, he heard and met Walter Pater, who had recently published his *Studies in the History of the Renaissance* (1873). It is Pater's influence that is most obvious in Wilde's development as a poet. While at Oxford, Wilde visited Italy and Greece, and this trip strengthened the love of classical culture so obvious in his poetry.

In the 1880's, as he developed as a writer, he also became a public personality. He toured the United States for about a year, and in both the United States and England, he preached an aesthetic doctrine that had its origins in the Pre-Raphaelites and Pater. He married in 1883 and had two sons. Wilde serially published his only novel, *The Picture of Dorian Gray*, which immediately created a sensation with the public. Thereafter, he wrote a number of plays, most notably *Lady Windermere's Fan* and *The Importance of Being Earnest*.

Wilde's last decade involved the scandal over his sexuality. His chief male lover was Lord Alfred Douglas, whose father, the marquess of Queensberry, tried to end Wilde's liaison with his son and ruin Wilde socially. Consequently, Wilde sued the marquess of Queensberry for libel but lost the case and also had his sexuality revealed. Tried twice for homosexuality, a crime in England at the time, he was found guilty and sentenced to two years at hard labor. From his prison experiences, Wilde wrote his most famous poem, *The Ballad of Reading Gaol*. Released from prison, he wandered over the Continent for three years, broken physically and ruined financially. He died in Paris at the age of forty-six.

Analysis

Oscar Wilde's poetry derives from the rich tradition of nineteenth century poetry, for, as Richard Aldington shows, Wilde imitated what he loved so intensely in the great poets of his century. Drawing from John Keats, Dante Gabriel Rossetti, William Morris, and Algernon Charles Swinburne, Wilde demonstrated an aestheticism like theirs in his lush imagery and in his pursuit of the fleeting impression of the moment. His poetry tries to capture the beautiful, as the Victorian critic John Ruskin had urged a generation earlier, but generally lacks the moral tone that Ruskin advocated. Wilde's poetry best fulfills the aesthetic of Walter Pater, who, in his *Studies in the History of the Renaissance*, advocated impressionism and art for art's sake. Indeed, Wilde paraphrased Pater's famous line of burning with a "hard, gemlike flame" in several of his poems.

Wilde published many poems individually before 1881, but his *Poems* of 1881 included almost all these poems and many new ones. With this collection, he published more than half of the poetry that he was to produce. The collection of 1881 is a good representation of his aestheticism and his tendency to derivativeness. Wilde avoided the overtly autobiographical and confessional mode in these poems, yet they mirror his attitudes and travels as impressions of his life. The forms he tried most often in the collection were the Italian sonnet and, for longer poems, a six-line stanza in pentameter with an *ababcc* rhyme scheme. The smaller poetic output that followed the 1881 collection consists of a number of shorter poems, two longer poems, and *Poems in Prose*. The short poems break no new ground, *The Sphinx* heralds a decadence and a celebration of pain unequaled in the nineteenth century except by Swinburne a generation earlier. *The Ballad of Reading Gaol*, however, builds on Wilde's earlier efforts. Again, he avoids the confessional mode that one would expect, considering the horrors of incarceration out of which the poem grew. The persona of the poem is no longer an urbane mind observing nature and society, but a common prisoner at hard labor generalizing about the cruelties of humans and their treatment of those they love. In this poem, despite its shrillness and melodrama, Wilde struck a balance between his own suffering and art, a balance that the impressionism of his poetic talents made easier. He dealt, as an observer, with the modern and the sordid as he had dealt earlier with art and nature. *Poems in Prose* is Wilde's effort at the short parable, offering neither the impressionism nor the formal qualities of his other poems, but ironic parables that refute the pieties of his era. Here Wilde is at his wittiest.

Ravenna

Ravenna was Wilde's first long poem to be published, and it won the Newdigate prize for poetry while he was still at Oxford. Written in couplets, the poem deals with many of the themes that he developed for the 1881 collection; thus, *Ravenna* is the starting point in a study of Wilde's poetry. Like the later long poems, *Ravenna* develops through contrasts: northern and southern European cultures, innocence and experience, past and present, classical and Christian. As a city, Ravenna evokes all these contrasts to the youthful Wilde.

The opening imagery is of spring, with a tendency to lushness typical of Keats. The boyish awe that Wilde felt in Ravenna is tempered, however, by recollection, for in the poem he is recalling his visit a year later. It is through recollection that he understands the greatness of the city, for in his northern world he has no such symbol of the rich complexity of time. What he learns from the English landscape is the passage of seasons that will mark his aging. He is sure, though, that with his love for Ravenna he will have a youthful inspiration despite his aging and loss of poetic powers.

Most of the poem is a poetic recounting of Ravenna's history. Wilde discusses the classical past of the city with reference to Caesar, and when he refers to Lord Byron's stay in the city, by association with Byron's last days in Greece, he imagines the region peopled with mythological figures; but the evening convent bell returns him to a somber Christian world. Recounting the Renaissance history of the city, Wilde is most moved by Dante's shrine. He closes the poem with references to Dante and Byron.

Wilde published twenty-eight sonnets in the 1881 collection, *Poems*, all of them Italian in form. Like his mentor Keats, Wilde used the sonnet to develop themes that he expanded in his longer poems.

SONNETS

"Hélas," an early sonnet not published in the 1881 collection, is his artistic manifesto that sets the tone for all the poems that followed. "Hélas" finds Wilde rhetorically questioning whether he has bartered wisdom for the passion or impression of the moment. In the sonnets that follow, he clearly seems to have chosen such moments of vivid impression.

In several sonnets, Wilde alludes to the poets who molded his style and themes, including two sonnets about visiting the graves of Keats and Percy Bysshe Shelley in the Protestant cemetery in Rome. He identifies himself with Keats as he never identifies with Shelley, and rightly so, for Keats's style and themes echo throughout the 1881 collection. Wilde also refers directly to Keats in another sonnet, "Amor Intellectualis," and to other poets important to him: Robert Browning, Christopher Marlowe, and particularly Dante and John Milton. The sonnet "A Vision" is a tribute to Aeschylus, Sophocles, and Euripides. On a larger scale than the sonnets, the longer poem "The Garden of Eros" presents Wilde's pantheon of poets with his feelings about them.

Some of the sonnets have political themes; in a number of these, Wilde advocates freedom, occasionally sounding like a Victorian Shelley. He is concerned with the political chaos of nineteenth century Italy, a land important to him for its classical past; "Italia" is a sonnet about the political venality in Italy, but it stresses that God might punish the corrupt. In his own country, Wilde idealizes the era of the Puritans and Oliver Cromwell; the sonnet "To Milton" laments the loss of democracy in England and advocates a return to the ideals of the Puritan revolution. In "Quantum Mutata," he admires Cromwell for his threat to Rome, but the title shows how events have changed, for Victorian England stands only for imperialism. This attack on British imperialism informs the long poem "Ave Imperatrix," which is far more emotional in tone than the political sonnets.

A number of Wilde's sonnets express his preference for the classical or primitive world and his antipathy for the modern Christian world. These poems have a persona visiting Italy, as Wilde did in 1877, and commenting on the Christian elements of the culture; "Sonnet on Approaching Italy" shows the speaker longing to visit Italy, yet, in contemplating far-off Rome, he laments the tyranny of a second Peter. Three other sonnets set in Italy, "Ave Maria, Gratia Plena," "Sonnet Written in Holy Week in Genoa," and "Urbs Sacra Aeterna," have Wilde contrasting the grandeur and color of the classical world with the emptiness and greyness of the Christian world. It is in these poems that Wilde is most like Swinburne. In other sonnets, he deals with religious values, often comparing the Christian ideal with the corruption of the modern Church he sees in Italy, or Christ's message with the conduct of his sinful followers. In "Easter Day," Wilde depicts the glory of the Pope as he is borne above the shoulders of the bearers, comparing that scene with the picture of Christ's loneliness centuries before. In "E Tenebris," the speaker appeals for help to a Christ who is to appear in weary human form. In "Sonnet, On Hearing the Dies Irae Sung in the Sistine Chapel," Wilde criticizes the harsh picture of a fiery day of judgment and replaces it with a picture of a warm autumn harvest, in which humankind awaits reaping by and fulfillment in God.

Wilde's best religious sonnet, "Madonna Mia," avoids the polemicism of some of his other religious sonnets, showing instead an affinity with the Pre-Raphaelite painting and poetry of a generation earlier. This sonnet is Pateresque in its hard impression, and it fulfills the credo suggested by the sonnet "Hélas." The picture Wilde paints in words is detailed: braided hair, blue eyes, pale cheeks, red lips, and white throat with purple veins; Wilde's persona is a worshiper of Mary, as Dante was of Beatrice.

"THE BURDEN OF ITYS"

"The Burden of Itys" is one of several long philosophic poems about nature and God to be found in the 1881 collection. Each of these poems has the same stanza form, a six-line stanza with an *ababcc* rhyme scheme; the first five lines are iambic pentameter, and the sixth is iambic heptameter. The stanza form gives a lightness which does not perfectly fit the depth of the ideas the poems present; it seems a form better suited to witticism than to philosophy.

Set in England close to Oxford, "The Burden of Itys" is similar in imagery and setting to Matthew Arnold's poems "The Scholar Gypsy" and "Thrysis." Wilde piles image on image of the flora of the region to establish the beauty of the setting, suggesting that the beauty of the countryside (and thus of nature in general) is holier than the grandeur of Rome. Fish replace bishops and the wind becomes the organ for the persona's religious reverie. By stanza 13, Wilde shifts from his comparison between Rome and nature to a contrast between the English landscape and the Greek. Because England is more beautiful than Greece, he suggests that the Greek pantheon could fittingly be reborn in Victorian England. A bird singing to Wilde, much like the nightingale singing to Keats, is the link between the persona imagining a revival of classical gods and actually experiencing one in which he will wear the leopard skin of a follower of Bacchus. This spell breaks, though, with another contrast, for a pale Christ and the speaker's religion destroy the classical reverie.

Brought back then to the Victorian world, as Keats was brought back to his world at the end of "Ode to a Nightingale," Wilde philosophizes and fixes the meaning of his experience in a way Keats never would have done. He stresses that nature does not represent the lovely agony of Christ but warm fellowship both in and between the worlds of humankind and animal. Even Oxford and nature are linked to each other, Wilde implies, as the curfew bell from his college church calls him back.

PHILOSOPHICAL POEMS

"Panthea" also works through dissimilarity, this time between southern and northern Europe, passion and reason, and classical and Christian thought. Wilde's rejection of the Church in "The Burden of Itys" is gentle, but in "Panthea" it is blatant. The gods have simply grown sick of priests and prayer. Instead, people should live for the passion and pleasure of an hour, those moments being the only gift the gods have to give. The poem emphasizes that the Greek gods themselves dwell in nature, participating fully in all the pleasures there. Their natural landscape, though, is not the bleak landscape of northern Europe, but the warm rich landscape of southern Europe.

Wilde proceeds to the philosophical theme of the poem, that one great power or being composes nature, and Nature, thus, subsumes all lives and elements and recycles them into various forms. For people to be reborn as flower or thrush is to live again without the pain of mortal existence; yet, paradoxically, without human pain, nature could not create beauty. Pain is the basis of beauty, for nature exists as a setting for human passion. Nature, in Wilde's words, has one "Kosmic Soul" linking all lives and elements. Wilde echoes lines of Keats and Pater, and, uncharacteristically, William Wordsworth; Wilde's affirmation proceeds with lines and images from Wordsworth's "Ode: Intimations of Immortality from Recollections of Early Childhood."

"Humanitad" is the longest of the philosophical poems in the 1881 collection, and it has much less in common with the other two philosophical poems than they have with each other. While spring is imminent, the speaker responds only to the winter elements still persisting. He emphasizes (paraphrasing Pater) that he has no fire to burn with a clear flame. The difference here is with the renewal of spring and spiritual exhaustion, and the speaker must look outside himself for some source of renewal. At one point, the poem turns topical by referring to ideals of simplicity and freedom: Switzerland, Wordsworth, and Giuseppe Mazzini. Wilde invokes the name of Milton as epitomizing the fight for freedom in the past; and, at the same time, he laments that there are no modern Miltons. Having no modern exemplar, Wilde also dismisses death and love as possible solutions for his moribund life. Turning to science, Wilde also rejects it. Wilde then has no recourse, and he faces a meaningless universe until he touches on mere causality after having rejected science.

Causality leads to God and creed, for causality is a chain connecting all elements. Nature, as in "Panthea," cannot help the speaker, for he has grown weary of mere sensation. Accordingly, he turns to the force behind nature (in this instance, God as Christ), although he rejects orthodoxy. He sees modern humanity's creed as being in process, for humanity is in the stage of crucifixion as it tries to discover the human in Christ and not the divine. The persona then sees his emptiness as the suffering leading to renewal. It is the full discovery of Christ's humanity that will make modern human beings masters of nature rather than tormented, alienated outcasts.

THE SPHINX

Just as Wilde drew from classical mythology for many of his poems and then contrasted the gray Christian world with the bright pagan world, he used Egyptian mythology in *The Sphinx* to picture a decadent sadistic sensuality as distinguished from a tortured Christian suffering. The situation in the poem is that a cat has crept into the speaker's room; to the speaker, the cat represents the Sphinx. Now, giving his imagination play, the speaker reveals his own sadistic eroticism, a subject that Wilde had not developed in other poems. The style also represents a departure for him; the stanzas consist of two lines of iambic octameter with no rhyme, resulting in a languorous slow rhythm in keeping with the speaker's ruminations about sensuality and sadism.

The cat as Sphinx represents the lush, decadent, yet appealing sensuality found in Egyptian mythology. In half of the poem, Wilde rhetorically questions the Sphinx about mythological figures of ancient Egypt, asking who her lovers were and at the same time cataloging the most famous myths of Egypt. Wilde settles on Ammon as the Sphinx's lover, but then he discusses how Ammon's statue has fallen to pieces, thus suggesting that the lover might be dead. Yet the Sphinx has the power to revive her lover; Ammon is not really dead. Having earlier referred to the holy family's exile in Egypt, Wilde now mentions that Christ is the only god who died, having let his side be pierced by a sword. Christ then is weaker than Ammon, and, in this way, Wilde suggests that pagan mythology is more vital than Christian mythology. The speaker's reflections on love become orthodox at the end; he feels he should contemplate the crucifix and not the Sphinx. He returns to a world of penitence where Christ watches and cries for every soul, but the speaker sees the tears as futile. The poem then raises the question of whether human beings can be redeemed from their fallen condition.

THE BALLAD OF READING GAOL

Wilde's most famous poem, *The Ballad of Reading Gaol*, is a departure from any of the poems he had published previously. Sometimes overdone emotionally, the poem uses the prison as a metaphor for life and its cruelties. Wilde is the observer rather than the subject; in this way, he distances himself from his own experiences. The poem raises the thematic question of why humans are cruel to other human beings, so cruel that they always destroy what they love. It is through cruelty that people kill or destroy the ones they love, just as the prisoner whom Wilde observes, and who is soon to hang, murdered his lover. The mystery of human cruelty was the mystery of the Sphinx in Wilde's previous poem, but here the issue is the agony of the mystery rather than the decadent glory of cruelty, as in *The Sphinx*.

Wilde exploits the Gothic elements of the situation, dwelling on the macabre details of the grave of quicklime that dissolves the murderer's body. He uses the dread and gloom of the prisoners' lives to heighten the tone, but he often becomes shrill and melodramatic by emphasizing details such as the bag that covers the head of the condemned, tears falling like molten lead from the other prisoners as they observe the condemned, terror personified as a ghost, and the greasy rope used for the hanging. Ironically, the surviving prisoners are bedeviled by terror and horror, while the condemned dies calmly and serenely. Wilde uses a simple six-line stanza for a forcefully direct effect.

The short lines alternate three and four feet of iambic pentameter with masculine rhyming of the second, fourth, and sixth lines. The stanza form is not one that suggests a reflective tone but rather a direct, emotional one.

The concluding motif of the poem is religious. The prison is a place of shame, where brother mistreats brother. Christ could feel only shame at what he sees his children do to each other there; but he rescues sinful humankind when he is broken by suffering and death. Even though the body of the hanged had no prayers said over it before interment in the quicklime, Christ rescued his soul. The surviving prisoners, their hearts broken and contrite, also gain salvation from the effects of their suffering.

POEMS IN PROSE

Wilde's *Poems in Prose* was the last collection published of all his poems except *The Ballad of Reading Gaol*, and the reader hears a different voice from that of the other poems, satirical and paradoxical like William Blake's in *The Marriage of Heaven and Hell* (1790). In Wilde's hands, the prose poem is a debonair and provocative parable on religious subjects. More often than not in his six prose poems, Wilde is trying to shock the bourgeoisie out of complacency and religious orthodoxy.

"The Artist" sets the tone of the prose poems; in this piece, the artist forsakes the oppressive sorrow of Christianity for the pursuit of hedonism. It is this kind of ironic reversal that the other prose poems also develop. In "The Doer of Good," Christ returns to find sinners and lepers he has saved or cured delighting in the sin, no longer wrong, from which he saved them. The one person whom Christ saved from death wishes that Christ had left him dead. "The House of Judgment" ironically shows the sinner complaining that his earthly life was hellish, and confronted now with Heaven, he has no conception of it after his life of suffering. The most moving of the six is "The Teacher of Wisdom," in which Wilde shows that the finest act of humankind is to teach the wisdom of God. A hermit, having attained the knowledge of God, refuses to part with it by giving it to the young sinner who is imploring him. Frustrated, the sinner returns to sin, but, in so doing, extracts the knowledge from the hermit, who hopes to turn the sinner away from more sin. Fearing that he has parted with his knowledge, the hermit is consoled by God, who now, for his sacrifice, grants him a true love of God. In this parable, Wilde has transcended the satiric wit of the other parables to teach through irony.

OTHER MAJOR WORKS

LONG FICTION: *The Picture of Dorian Gray*, 1890 (serial), 1891 (expanded).

SHORT FICTION: "The Canterville Ghost," 1887; *The Happy Prince, and Other Tales*, 1888; *A House of Pomegranates*, 1891; *Lord Arthur Savile's Crime, and Other Stories*, 1891.

PLAYS: *Vera: Or, The Nihilists*, pb. 1880; *The Duchess of Padua*, pb. 1883; *Lady Windermere's Fan*, pr. 1892; *Salomé*, pb. 1893 (in French), pb. 1894 (in English); *A*

Woman of No Importance, pr. 1893; *An Ideal Husband*, pr. 1895; *The Importance of Being Earnest: A Trivial Comedy for Serious People*, pr. 1895; *A Florentine Tragedy*, pr. 1906 (one act; completed by T. Sturge More); *La Sainte Courtisane*, pb. 1908.

NONFICTION: *Intentions*, 1891; *De Profundis*, 1905; *The Letters of Oscar Wilde*, 1962 (Rupert Hart-Davis, editor); *The Complete Letters of Oscar Wilde*, 2000 (Merlin Holland and Hart-Davis, editors).

MISCELLANEOUS: *Works*, 1908; *Complete Works of Oscar Wilde*, 1948 (Vyvyan Holland, editor); *Plays, Prose Writings, and Poems*, 1960.

BIBLIOGRAPHY

Belford, Barbara. *Oscar Wilde: A Certain Genius*. New York: Random House, 2000. An examination of Wilde's life with a somewhat revisionist view of Wilde's postprison years.

Bloom, Harold, ed. *Oscar Wilde*. New York: Bloom's Literary Criticism, 2008. A collection of literary criticism on Wilde's body of work.

Canning, Richard. *Brief Lives: Oscar Wilde*. London: Hesperus, 2008. A biography of Wilde that covers his short life and his works.

Guy, Josephine, and Ian Small. *Studying Oscar Wilde: History, Criticism, and Myth*. Greensboro, N.C.: ELT Press, 2006. This volume attempts to provide a guide to studying the poet that distinguishes between the myth and history as well as provides literary criticism.

Harris, Frank. *Oscar Wilde: Including My Memories of Oscar Wilde by George Bernard Shaw*. 2d ed. New York: Carroll & Graf, 1997. Harris was one of the few friends who remained loyal to Wilde after his downfall. His biography, although highly readable and full of interesting anecdotes, is not always reliable. Shaw's afterward is a shrewd assessment of Wilde.

McKenna, Neil. *The Secret Life of Oscar Wilde*. New York: Basic Books, 2005. This controversial and groundbreaking biography focuses on how Wilde's homosexuality influenced the writer's life and work. Illustrated.

Nunokawa, Jeff, and Amy Sickels. *Oscar Wilde*. Philadelphia: Chelsea House, 2005. A portrait of Wilde that examines his rise to fame, his sexuality, and the difficulties he experienced, especially after his fall.

Pearce, Joseph. *The Unmasking of Oscar Wilde*. San Francisco: Ignatius Press, 2004. Pearce avoids lingering on the actions that brought Wilde notoriety and instead explores Wilde's emotional and spiritual search. Along with a discussion of *The Ballad of Reading Gaol* and the posthumously published *De Profundis*, Pearce also traces Wilde's fascination with Catholicism.

Stokes, Anthony. *Pit of Shame: The Real Ballad of Reading Gaol*. Winchester, England: Waterside Press, 2007. Looks at Wilde's poem and also the actual jail that held the poet.

Wilde, Oscar. Interviews. *Oscar Wilde in America: The Interviews*. Edited by Matthew Hofer and Gary Scharnhorst. Urbana: University of Illinois Press, 2009. A collection of interviews from the time Wilde spent in the United States.

Dennis Goldsberry

CHECKLIST FOR EXPLICATING A POEM

I. The Initial Readings

A. Before reading the poem, the reader should:
 1. Notice its form and length.
 2. Consider the title, determining, if possible, whether it might function as an allusion, symbol, or poetic image.
 3. Notice the date of composition or publication, and identify the general era of the poet.

B. The poem should be read intuitively and emotionally and be allowed to "happen" as much as possible.

C. In order to establish the rhythmic flow, the poem should be reread. A note should be made as to where the irregular spots (if any) are located.

II. Explicating the Poem

A. *Dramatic situation.* Studying the poem line by line helps the reader discover the dramatic situation. All elements of the dramatic situation are interrelated and should be viewed as reflecting and affecting one another. The dramatic situation serves a particular function in the poem, adding realism, surrealism, or absurdity; drawing attention to certain parts of the poem; and changing to reinforce other aspects of the poem. All points should be considered. The following questions are particularly helpful to ask in determining dramatic situation:
 1. What, if any, is the narrative action in the poem?
 2. How many personae appear in the poem? What part do they take in the action?
 3. What is the relationship between characters?
 4. What is the setting (time and location) of the poem?

B. *Point of view.* An understanding of the poem's point of view is a major step toward comprehending the poet's intended meaning. The reader should ask:
 1. Who is the speaker? Is he or she addressing someone else or the reader?
 2. Is the narrator able to understand or see everything happening to him or her, or does the reader know things that the narrator does not?
 3. Is the narrator reliable?
 4. Do point of view and dramatic situation seem consistent? If not, the inconsistencies may provide clues to the poem's meaning.

C. *Images and metaphors.* Images and metaphors are often the most intricately crafted vehicles of the poem for relaying the poet's message. Realizing that the images and metaphors work in harmony with the dramatic situation and point of view will help the reader to see the poem as a whole, rather than as disassociated elements.
 1. The reader should identify the concrete images (that is, those that are formed from objects that can be touched, smelled, seen, felt, or tasted). Is the image projected by the poet consistent with the physical object?
 2. If the image is abstract, or so different from natural imagery that it cannot be associated with a real object, then what are the properties of the image?
 3. To what extent is the reader asked to form his or her own images?
 4. Is any image repeated in the poem? If so, how has it been changed? Is there a controlling image?
 5. Are any images compared to each other? Do they reinforce one another?
 6. Is there any difference between the way the reader perceives the image and the way the narrator sees it?
 7. What seems to be the narrator's or persona's attitude toward the image?

D. *Words.* Every substantial word in a poem may have more than one intended meaning, as used by the author. Because of this, the reader should look up many of these words in the dictionary and:
 1. Note all definitions that have the slightest connection with the poem.
 2. Note any changes in syntactical patterns in the poem.
 3. In particular, note those words that could possibly function as symbols or allusions, and refer to any appropriate sources for further information.

E. *Meter, rhyme, structure, and tone.* In scanning the poem, all elements of prosody should be noted by the reader. These elements are often used by a poet to manipulate the reader's emotions, and therefore they should be examined closely to arrive at the poet's specific intention.
 1. Does the basic meter follow a traditional pattern such as those found in nursery rhymes or folk songs?
 2. Are there any variations in the base meter? Such changes or substitutions are important thematically and should be identified.
 3. Are the rhyme schemes traditional or innovative, and what might their form mean to the poem?
 4. What devices has the poet used to create sound patterns (such as assonance and alliteration)?
 5. Is the stanza form a traditional or innovative one?
 6. If the poem is composed of verse paragraphs rather than stanzas, how do they affect the progression of the poem?

7. After examining the above elements, is the resultant tone of the poem casual or formal, pleasant, harsh, emotional, authoritative?

F. *Historical context.* The reader should attempt to place the poem into historical context, checking on events at the time of composition. Archaic language, expressions, images, or symbols should also be looked up.

G. *Themes and motifs.* By seeing the poem as a composite of emotion, intellect, craftsmanship, and tradition, the reader should be able to determine the themes and motifs (smaller recurring ideas) presented in the work. He or she should ask the following questions to help pinpoint these main ideas:
   1. Is the poet trying to advocate social, moral, or religious change?
   2. Does the poet seem sure of his or her position?
   3. Does the poem appeal primarily to the emotions, to the intellect, or to both?
   4. Is the poem relying on any particular devices for effect (such as imagery, allusion, paradox, hyperbole, or irony)?

BIBLIOGRAPHY

BIOGRAPHICAL SOURCES

Colby, Vineta, ed. *World Authors, 1975-1980*. Wilson Authors Series. New York: H. W. Wilson, 1985.

_____. *World Authors, 1980-1985*. Wilson Authors Series. New York: H. W. Wilson, 1991.

_____. *World Authors, 1985-1990*. Wilson Authors Series. New York: H. W. Wilson, 1995.

Cyclopedia of World Authors. 4th rev. ed. 5 vols. Pasadena, Calif.: Salem Press, 2003.

Harper, Anthony, and Margaret C. Ives. *Sappho in the Shadows: Essays on the Work of German Women Poets of the Age of Goethe, 1749-1832*. New York: Peter Lang, 2000.

International Who's Who in Poetry and Poets' Encyclopaedia. Cambridge, England: International Biographical Centre, 1993.

Seymour-Smith, Martin, and Andrew C. Kimmens, eds. *World Authors, 1900-1950*. Wilson Authors Series. 4 vols. New York: H. W. Wilson, 1996.

Shucard, Alan. *American Poetry: The Puritans Through Walt Whitman*. Twayne's Critical History of Poetry Series. Boston: Twayne, 1988.

Thompson, Clifford, ed. *World Authors, 1990-1995*. Wilson Authors Series. New York: H. W. Wilson, 1999.

Wakeman, John, ed. *World Authors, 1950-1970*. New York: H. W. Wilson, 1975.

_____. *World Authors, 1970-1975*. Wilson Authors Series. New York: H. W. Wilson, 1991.

Willhardt, Mark, and Alan Michael Parker, eds. *Who's Who in Twentieth Century World Poetry*. New York: Routledge, 2000.

CRITICISM

Brooks, Cleanth, and Robert Penn Warren. *Understanding Poetry*. 4th ed. Reprint. Fort Worth, Tex.: Heinle & Heinle, 2003.

Classical and Medieval Literature Criticism. Detroit: Gale Research, 1988- .

Contemporary Literary Criticism. Detroit: Gale Research, 1973- .

Day, Gary. *Literary Criticism: A New History*. Edinburgh, Scotland: Edinburgh University Press, 2008.

Draper, James P., ed. *World Literature Criticism 1500 to the Present: A Selection of Major Authors from Gale's Literary Criticism Series*. 6 vols. Detroit: Gale Research, 1992.

Habib, M. A. R. *A History of Literary Criticism: From Plato to the Present*. Malden, Mass.: Wiley-Blackwell, 2005.

Jason, Philip K., ed. *Masterplots II: Poetry Series, Revised Edition.* 8 vols. Pasadena, Calif.: Salem Press, 2002.

Literature Criticism from 1400 to 1800. Detroit: Gale Research, 1984- .

Lodge, David, and Nigel Wood. *Modern Criticism and Theory.* 3d ed. New York: Longman, 2008.

Magill, Frank N., ed. *Magill's Bibliography of Literary Criticism.* 4 vols. Englewood Cliffs, N.J.: Salem Press, 1979.

MLA International Bibliography. New York: Modern Language Association of America, 1922- .

Nineteenth-Century Literature Criticism. Detroit: Gale Research, 1981- .

Twentieth-Century Literary Criticism. Detroit: Gale Research, 1978- .

Vedder, Polly, ed. *World Literature Criticism Supplement: A Selection of Major Authors from Gale's Literary Criticism Series.* 2 vols. Detroit: Gale Research, 1997.

Young, Robyn V., ed. *Poetry Criticism: Excerpts from Criticism of the Works of the Most Significant and Widely Studied Poets of World Literature.* 29 vols. Detroit: Gale Research, 1991.

POETRY DICTIONARIES AND HANDBOOKS

Carey, Gary, and Mary Ellen Snodgrass. *A Multicultural Dictionary of Literary Terms.* Jefferson, N.C.: McFarland, 1999.

Deutsch, Babette. *Poetry Handbook: A Dictionary of Terms.* 4th ed. New York: Funk & Wagnalls, 1974.

Drury, John. *The Poetry Dictionary.* Cincinnati, Ohio: Story Press, 1995.

Kinzie, Mary. *A Poet's Guide to Poetry.* Chicago: University of Chicago Press, 1999.

Lennard, John. *The Poetry Handbook: A Guide to Reading Poetry for Pleasure and Practical Criticism.* New York: Oxford University Press, 1996.

Matterson, Stephen, and Darryl Jones. *Studying Poetry.* New York: Oxford University Press, 2000.

Packard, William. *The Poet's Dictionary: A Handbook of Prosody and Poetic Devices.* New York: Harper & Row, 1989.

Preminger, Alex, et al., eds. *The New Princeton Encyclopedia of Poetry and Poetics.* 3d rev. ed. Princeton, N.J.: Princeton University Press, 1993.

Shipley, Joseph Twadell, ed. *Dictionary of World Literary Terms, Forms, Technique, Criticism.* Rev. ed. Boston: George Allen and Unwin, 1979.

INDEXES OF PRIMARY WORKS

Frankovich, Nicholas, ed. *The Columbia Granger's Index to Poetry in Anthologies.* 11th ed. New York: Columbia University Press, 1997.

_____. *The Columbia Granger's Index to Poetry in Collected and Selected Works.* New York: Columbia University Press, 1997.

Guy, Patricia. *A Women's Poetry Index*. Phoenix, Ariz.: Oryx Press, 1985.

Hazen, Edith P., ed. *Columbia Granger's Index to Poetry*. 10th ed. New York: Columbia University Press, 1994.

Hoffman, Herbert H., and Rita Ludwig Hoffman, comps. *International Index to Recorded Poetry*. New York: H. W. Wilson, 1983.

Kline, Victoria. *Last Lines: An Index to the Last Lines of Poetry*. 2 vols. Vol. 1, *Last Line Index, Title Index*; Vol. 2, *Author Index, Keyword Index*. New York: Facts On File, 1991.

Marcan, Peter. *Poetry Themes: A Bibliographical Index to Subject Anthologies and Related Criticisms in the English Language, 1875-1975*. Hamden, Conn.: Linnet Books, 1977.

Poem Finder. Great Neck, N.Y.: Roth, 2000.

POETICS, POETIC FORMS, AND GENRES

Attridge, Derek. *Poetic Rhythm: An Introduction*. New York: Cambridge University Press, 1995.

Brogan, T. V. F. *Verseform: A Comparative Bibliography*. Baltimore: Johns Hopkins University Press, 1989.

Fussell, Paul. *Poetic Meter and Poetic Form*. Rev. ed. New York: McGraw-Hill, 1979.

Hollander, John. *Rhyme's Reason*. 3d ed. New Haven, Conn.: Yale University Press, 2001.

Jackson, Guida M. *Traditional Epics: A Literary Companion*. New York: Oxford University Press, 1995.

Padgett, Ron, ed. *The Teachers and Writers Handbook of Poetic Forms*. 2d ed. New York: Teachers & Writers Collaborative, 2000.

Pinsky, Robert. *The Sounds of Poetry: A Brief Guide*. New York: Farrar, Straus and Giroux, 1998.

Preminger, Alex, and T. V. F. Brogan, eds. *New Princeton Encyclopedia of Poetry and Poetics*. 3d ed. Princeton, N.J.: Princeton University Press, 1993.

Spiller, Michael R. G. *The Sonnet Sequence: A Study of Its Strategies*. Studies in Literary Themes and Genres 13. New York: Twayne, 1997.

Turco, Lewis. *The New Book of Forms: A Handbook of Poetics*. Hanover, N.H.: University Press of New England, 1986.

Williams, Miller. *Patterns of Poetry: An Encyclopedia of Forms*. Baton Rouge: Louisiana State University Press, 1986.

GUIDE TO ONLINE RESOURCES

WEB SITES

The following sites were visited by the editors of Salem Press in 2010. Because URLs frequently change, the accuracy of these addresses cannot be guaranteed; however, long-standing sites, such as those of colleges and universities, national organizations, and government agencies, generally maintain links when their sites are moved.

Academy of American Poets
http://www.poets.org

The mission of the Academy of American Poets is to "support American poets at all stages of their careers and to foster the appreciation of contemporary poetry." The academy's comprehensive Web site features information on poetic schools and movements; a Poetic Forms Database; an Online Poetry Classroom, with educator and teaching resources; an index of poets and poems; essays and interviews; general Web resources; links for further study; and more.

Contemporary British Writers
http://www.contemporarywriters.com/authors

Created by the British Council, this site offers profiles of living writers of the United Kingdom, the Republic of Ireland, and the Commonwealth. Information includes biographies, bibliographies, critical reviews, and news about literary prizes. Photographs are also featured. Users can search the site by author, genre, nationality, gender, publisher, book title, date of publication, and prize name and date.

LiteraryHistory.com
http://www.literaryhistory.com

This site is an excellent source of academic, scholarly, and critical literature about eighteenth, nineteenth, and twentieth century American and English writers. It provides individual pages for twentieth century literature and alphabetical lists of authors that link to articles, reviews, overviews, excerpts of works, teaching guides, podcasts, and other materials.

Literary Resources on the Net
http://andromeda.rutgers.edu/~jlynch/Lit

Jack Lynch of Rutgers University maintains this extensive collection of links to Web sites that are useful to researchers, including numerous sites about American and English literature. This collection is a good place to begin online research about poetry, as it links to other sites with broad ranges of literary topics. The site is organized chronologically, with separate pages about twentieth century British and Irish literature. It also has separate pages providing links to Web sites about American literature and to women's literature and feminism.

LitWeb
http://litweb.net
  LitWeb provides biographies of hundreds of world authors throughout history that can be accessed through an alphabetical listing. The pages about each writer contain a list of his or her works, suggestions for further reading, and illustrations. The site also offers information about past and present winners of major literary prizes.

The Modern Word: Authors of the Libyrinth
http://www.themodernword.com/authors.html
  The Modern Word site, although somewhat haphazard in its organization, provides a great deal of critical information about writers. The "Authors of the Libyrinth" page is very useful, linking author names to essays about them and other resources. The section of the page headed "The Scriptorium" presents "an index of pages featuring writers who have pushed the edges of their medium, combining literary talent with a sense of experimentation to produce some remarkable works of modern literature."

Outline of American Literature
http://www.america.gov/publications/books/outline-of-american-literature.html
  This page of the America.gov site provides access to an electronic version of the ten-chapter volume *Outline of American Literature*, a historical overview of poetry and prose from colonial times to the present published by the Bureau of International Information Programs of the U.S. Department of State.

Poetry Foundation
http://www.poetryfoundation.org
  The Poetry Foundation, publisher of *Poetry* magazine, is an independent literary organization. Its Web site offers links to essays; news; events; online poetry resources, such as blogs, organizations, publications, and references and research; a glossary of literary terms; and a Learning Lab that includes poem guides and essays on poetics.

Poet's Corner
http://theotherpages.org/poems
  The Poet's Corner, one of the oldest text resources on the Web, provides access to about seven thousand works of poetry by several hundred different poets from around

the world. Indexes are arranged and searchable by title, name of poet, or subject. The site also offers its own resources, including "Faces of the Poets"—a gallery of portraits—and "Lives of the Poets"—a growing collection of biographies.

Representative Poetry Online
http://rpo.library.utoronto.ca
This award-winning resource site, maintained by Ian Lancashire of the Department of English at the University of Toronto in Canada, has several thousand English-language poems by hundreds of poets. The collection is searchable by poet's name, title of work, first line of a poem, and keyword. The site also includes a time line, a glossary, essays, an extensive bibliography, and countless links organized by country and by subject.

Voice of the Shuttle
http://vos.ucsb.edu
One of the most complete and authoritative places for online information about literature, Voice of the Shuttle is maintained by professors and students in the English Department at the University of California, Santa Barbara. The site provides countless links to electronic books, academic journals, literary association Web sites, sites created by university professors, and many other resources.

Voices from the Gaps
http://voices.cla.umn.edu/
Voices from the Gaps is a site of the English Department at the University of Minnesota, dedicated to providing resources on the study of women artists of color, including writers. The site features a comprehensive index searchable by name, and it provides biographical information on each writer or artist and other resources for further study.

ELECTRONIC DATABASES

Electronic databases usually do not have their own URLs. Instead, public, college, and university libraries subscribe to these databases, provide links to them on their Web sites, and make them available to library card holders or other specified patrons. Readers can visit library Web sites or ask reference librarians to check on availability.

Canadian Literary Centre
Produced by EBSCO, the Canadian Literary Centre database contains full-text content from ECW Press, a Toronto-based publisher, including the titles in the publisher's Canadian fiction studies, Canadian biography, and Canadian writers and their works se-

ries; *ECW's Biographical Guide to Canadian Novelists*; and *George Woodcock's Introduction to Canadian Fiction*. Author biographies, essays and literary criticism, and book reviews are among the database's offerings.

Literary Reference Center

EBSCO's Literary Reference Center (LRC) is a comprehensive full-text database designed primarily to help high school and undergraduate students in English and the humanities with homework and research assignments about literature. The database contains massive amounts of information from reference works, books, literary journals, and other materials, including more than 31,000 plot summaries, synopses, and overviews of literary works; almost 100,000 essays and articles of literary criticism; about 140,000 author biographies; more than 605,000 book reviews; and more than 5,200 author interviews. It contains the entire contents of Salem Press's MagillOnLiterature Plus. Users can retrieve information by browsing a list of authors' names or titles of literary works; they can also use an advanced search engine to access information by numerous categories, including author name, gender, cultural identity, national identity, and the years in which he or she lived, or by literary title, character, locale, genre, and publication date. The Literary Reference Center also features a literary-historical time line, an encyclopedia of literature, and a glossary of literary terms.

MagillOnLiterature Plus

MagillOnLiterature Plus is a comprehensive, integrated literature database produced by Salem Press and available on the EBSCOhost platform. The database contains the full text of essays in Salem's many literature-related reference works, including *Masterplots, Cyclopedia of World Authors, Cyclopedia of Literary Characters, Cyclopedia of Literary Places, Critical Survey of Poetry, Critical Survey of Long Fiction, Critical Survey of Short Fiction, World Philosophers and Their Works, Magill's Literary Annual,* and *Magill's Book Reviews*. Among its contents are articles on more than 35,000 literary works and more than 8,500 poets, writers, dramatists, essayists, and philosophers; more than 1,000 images; and a glossary of more than 1,300 literary terms. The biographical essays include lists of authors' works and secondary bibliographies, and hundreds of overview essays examine and discuss literary genres, time periods, and national literatures.

Rebecca Kuzins; updated by Desiree Dreeuws

GEOGRAPHICAL INDEX

ASIA MINOR
    Sappho, 147

ENGLAND
    Gunn, Thom, 81
    Housman, A. E., 94
    Mew, Charlotte, 107
    Sassoon, Siegfried, 159
    Wilde, Oscar, 228

FRANCE
    Rimbaud, Arthur, 135
    Stein, Gertrude, 180
    Verlaine, Paul, 193

GREAT BRITAIN
    Gunn, Thom, 81
    Housman, A. E., 94
    Mew, Charlotte, 107
    Sassoon, Siegfried, 159
    Wilde, Oscar, 228

GREECE
    Sappho, 147

IRELAND
    Wilde, Oscar, 228

UNITED STATES
    Allen, Paula Gunn, 9
    Ashbery, John, 15
    Bishop, Elizabeth, 30
    Crane, Hart, 41
    Cullen, Countée, 54
    Ginsberg, Allen, 64
    Gunn, Thom, 81
    O'Hara, Frank, 112
    Rich, Adrienne, 121
    Schuyler, James, 170
    Stein, Gertrude, 180
    Walker, Alice, 203
    Whitman, Walt, 212

CATEGORY INDEX

AESTHETIC POETS
    Wilde, Oscar, 228
AFRICAN AMERICAN CULTURE
    Cullen, Countée, 54
    Walker, Alice, 203
AMERICAN EARLY NATIONAL POETS
    Whitman, Walt, 212
AVANT-GARDE POETS
    Ashbery, John, 15
    O'Hara, Frank, 112
    Schuyler, James, 170
    Stein, Gertrude, 180

BEAT POETS
    Ginsberg, Allen, 64
    Gunn, Thom, 81
BLACK ARTS MOVEMENT
    Walker, Alice, 203

CHILDREN'S/YOUNG ADULT POETRY
    Stein, Gertrude, 180
CONFESSIONAL POETS
    Ginsberg, Allen, 64
CUBISM
    Stein, Gertrude, 180

DECADENT POETS
    Rimbaud, Arthur, 135
    Verlaine, Paul, 193
    Wilde, Oscar, 228
DIALECT POETRY
    Cullen, Countée, 54
DRAMATIC MONOLOGUES
    Gunn, Thom, 81
    Mew, Charlotte, 107

ECOPOETRY
    Whitman, Walt, 212
EKPHRASTIC POETRY
    Ashbery, John, 15
    Bishop, Elizabeth, 30
    Gunn, Thom, 81
EPICS
    Crane, Hart, 41
    Whitman, Walt, 212
EXPERIMENTAL POETS
    Rimbaud, Arthur, 135
    Stein, Gertrude, 180

FEMINIST POETS
    Allen, Paula Gunn, 9
    Mew, Charlotte, 107
    Rich, Adrienne, 121
    Stein, Gertrude, 180
    Walker, Alice, 203

GEORGIAN POETS
    Housman, A. E., 94
    Sassoon, Siegfried, 159
GHAZALS
    Rich, Adrienne, 121

HAIKU
    Ginsberg, Allen, 64
HELLENISTIC POETS
    Sappho, 147
HYMNS
    Sappho, 147

IMPRESSIONISM
    Verlaine, Paul, 193

JEWISH CULTURE
    Ginsberg, Allen, 64
    Rich, Adrienne, 121
    Sassoon, Siegfried, 159
    Stein, Gertrude, 180

LOST GENERATION
    Crane, Hart, 41
    Stein, Gertrude, 180

LOVE POETRY
    Crane, Hart, 41
    Cullen, Countée, 54
    Sappho, 147
    Verlaine, Paul, 193

LYRIC POETRY
    Crane, Hart, 41
    Housman, A. E., 94
    Sappho, 147
    Wilde, Oscar, 228

MODERNISM
    Crane, Hart, 41
    Cullen, Countée, 54
    Mew, Charlotte, 107
    Sassoon, Siegfried, 159

MOVEMENT POETS
    Gunn, Thom, 81

NARRATIVE POETRY
    Crane, Hart, 41
    Cullen, Countée, 54
    Wilde, Oscar, 228

NATIVE AMERICAN CULTURE
    Allen, Paula Gunn, 9

NATURE POETRY
    Verlaine, Paul, 193
    Walker, Alice, 203
    Whitman, Walt, 212

NEO-ROMANTICISM
    Housman, A. E., 94

NEW YORK SCHOOL
    Ashbery, John, 15
    O'Hara, Frank, 112
    Schuyler, James, 170

OCCASIONAL VERSE
    Schuyler, James, 170

ODES
    O'Hara, Frank, 112
    Sappho, 147

ORAL TRADITION
    Sappho, 147

PARNASSIANISM
    Verlaine, Paul, 193

POLITICAL POETS
    Queer Theory, 1
    Rich, Adrienne, 121
    Walker, Alice, 203

POSTCONFESSIONAL POETS
    Bishop, Elizabeth, 30
    Rich, Adrienne, 121

POSTMODERNISM
    Ginsberg, Allen, 64
    Gunn, Thom, 81

RELIGIOUS POETRY
    Sassoon, Siegfried, 159
    Verlaine, Paul, 193

RENAISSANCE, AMERICAN
    Whitman, Walt, 212

ROMANTICISM, AMERICAN
    Whitman, Walt, 212

SATIRIC POETRY
    Rimbaud, Arthur, 135

SONGS
    Sappho, 147

SONNETS
    Verlaine, Paul, 193
    Wilde, Oscar, 228

SURREALIST POETS
    Ashbery, John, 15
SYMBOLIST POETS
    Rimbaud, Arthur, 135
    Verlaine, Paul, 193

TOPOGRAPHICAL POETRY
    Whitman, Walt, 212

VICTORIAN ERA
    Housman, A. E., 94
    Mew, Charlotte, 107
    Wilde, Oscar, 228

VISIONARY POETRY
    Crane, Hart, 41
    Ginsberg, Allen, 64
    Rimbaud, Arthur, 135

WAR POETS
    Sassoon, Siegfried, 159
WOMEN POETS
    Allen, Paula Gunn, 9
    Bishop, Elizabeth, 30
    Mew, Charlotte, 107
    Rich, Adrienne, 121
    Sappho, 147
    Stein, Gertrude, 180
    Walker, Alice, 203

SUBJECT INDEX

16 L.-P. (Sappho), 153
94 L.-P. (Sappho), 155
112 L.-P. (Sappho), 156

Absolute Trust in the Goodness of the Earth (Walker), 208
Allen, Paula Gunn, 9-14
    A Cannon Between My Knees, 11
    Shadow Country, 12
And the Stars Were Shining (Ashbery), 26
April Galleons (Ashbery), 25
Art for art's sake, 230
"Art poétique, L'" (Verlaine), 196
Ashbery, John, 15-29
    And the Stars Were Shining, 26
    April Galleons, 25
    Houseboat Days, 24
    Self-Portrait in a Convex Mirror, 22
    Some Trees, 18
    The Tennis Court Oath, 20
    Three Poems, 20
    A Wave, 25
    Where Shall I Wander, 26
    A Worldly Country, 27
    Your Name Here, 26
"Atlantis" (Crane), 52
Autobiography of Alice B. Toklas, The (Stein), 190
"Ave Maria" (Crane), 46

"Bad Blood" (Rimbaud), 141
Ballad of Reading Gaol, The (Wilde), 235
Beauvoir, Simone de, 1
"Birdbrain" (Ginsberg), 75
Bishop, Elizabeth, 30-40
    "The Fish," 33
    "In the Waiting Room," 38

"The Man-Moth," 34
"The Map," 37
"The Monument," 36
"Objects and Apparitions," 33
"Over 2000 Illustrations and a Complete Concordance," 34
Questions of Travel, 34
"The Riverman," 35
"Sandpiper," 32
Black Christ, The (Cullen), 59
Boss Cupid (Gunn), 92
Bridge, The (Crane), 45
"Burden of Itys, The" (Wilde), 233
Butler, Judith, 1

Cannon Between My Knees, A (Allen), 11
"Cape Hatteras" (Crane), 48
Change of World, A (Rich), 124
Collected Poems, 1947-1997 (Ginsberg), 77
Cosmopolitan Greetings (Ginsberg), 75
Crane, Hart, 41-53
    "Atlantis," 52
    "Ave Maria," 46
    The Bridge, 45
    "Cape Hatteras," 48
    "Cutty Sark," 48
    "The Dance," 47
    "For the Marriage of Faustus and Helen," 44
    "Indiana," 48
    "Powhatan's Daughter," 46
    "Quaker Hill," 50
    "The River," 47
    "Three Songs," 49
    "To Brooklyn Bridge," 45
    "The Tunnel," 51
    "Van Winkle," 46

"Crossing Brooklyn Ferry" (Whitman), 221
Cullen, Countée, 54-63
   The Black Christ, 59
   "From the Dark Tower," 61
   "Harlem Wine," 60
   "Heritage," 59
   "Yet Do I Marvel," 57
"Cutty Sark" (Crane), 48

"Dance, The" (Crane), 47
"Day Lady Died, The" (O'Hara), 118
"Deliria I" (Rimbaud), 142
"Deliria II" (Rimbaud), 142
Derrida, Jacques, 2
Diamond Cutters, The (Rich), 124
Diving into the Wreck (Rich), 128
Dream of a Common Language, The (Rich), 129
Drum-Taps (Whitman), 222
"Drunken Boat, The" (Rimbaud), 139
"Dug Out, The" (Sassoon), 166

"Everyone Sang" (Sassoon), 166

Fall of America, The (Ginsberg), 74
"Farewell" (Rimbaud), 142
Farmer's Bride, The (Mew), 109
Fêtes galantes. See *Gallant Parties*
Fighting Terms (Gunn), 84
"Fish, The" (Bishop), 33
"For the Marriage of Faustus and Helen" (Crane), 44
Foucault, Michel, 5
Fox (Rich), 132
"From an Old House in America" (Rich), 128
"From the Dark Tower" (Cullen), 6

Gallant Parties (Verlaine), 198
Gender, 1, 5

Ginsberg, Allen, 64-80
   "Birdbrain," 75
   Collected Poems, 1947-1997, 77
   Cosmopolitan Greetings, 75
   The Fall of America, 74
   "Howl," 69
   "Kaddish," 70
   "Kral Majales," 72
   Mind Breaths, 74
   Plutonian Ode, 74
   White Shroud, 75
   "Witchita Vortex Sutra," 72
Good Night, Willie Lee, I'll See You in the Morning (Walker), 207
Gunn, Thom, 81-93
   Boss Cupid, 92
   Fighting Terms, 84
   Jack Straw's Castle, and Other Poems, 89
   The Man with Night Sweats, 91
   Moly, 88
   My Sad Captains, and Other Poems, 85
   The Passages of Joy, 89
   Positives, 87
   The Sense of Movement, 85
   Touch, 87
   Undesirables, 90

"Harlem Wine" (Cullen), 60
Her Blue Body Everything We Know (Walker), 208
"Heritage" (Cullen), 59
Horses Make a Landscape Look More Beautiful (Walker), 207
Houseboat Days (Ashbery), 24
Housman, A. E., 94-106
   Last Poems, 100
   More Poems, 100
   A Shropshire Lad, 100
   "With rue my heart is laden," 101
"Howl" (Ginsberg), 69

Illuminations (Rimbaud), 143
"Impossible, The" (Rimbaud), 142
"In the Waiting Room" (Bishop), 38
"Indiana" (Crane), 48
Irigaray, Luce, 1
"It Is Crying in My Heart" (Verlaine), 199

Jack Straw's Castle, and Other Poems (Gunn), 89

"Kaddish" (Ginsberg), 70
"Kral Majales" (Ginsberg), 72

Last Poems (Housman), 100
Leaflets (Rich), 126
Leaves of Grass (Whitman), 216
"Lightning" (Rimbaud), 142
"Lines Written in Anticipation . . ." (Sassoon), 166

"Man-Moth, The" (Bishop), 34
Man with Night Sweats, The (Gunn), 91
"Map, The" (Bishop), 37
Mew, Charlotte, 107-111
   The Farmer's Bride, 109
   The Rambling Sailor, 110
Midnight Salvage (Rich), 132
Mind Breaths (Ginsberg), 74
Moly (Gunn), 88
"Monument, The" (Bishop), 36
More Poems (Housman), 100
"Morning" (Rimbaud), 142
"Morning of the Poem, The" (Schuyler), 175
"My Familiar Dream" (Verlaine), 197
"My Heat" (O'Hara), 115
My Sad Captains, and Other Poems (Gunn), 85

Necessities of Life (Rich), 126
"Night in Hell" (Rimbaud), 141

O'Hara, Frank, 112-120
   "The Day Lady Died," 118
   "My Heat," 115
   "Poem (Lana Turner has collapsed!)," 118
   "Savoy," 117
"Objects and Apparitions" (Bishop), 33
"Ode to Anactoria" (Sappho), 152
"Ode to Aphrodite" (Sappho), 151
Once (Walker), 206
"Out of the Cradle Endlessly Rocking" (Whitman), 222
"Over 2000 Illustrations and a Complete Concordance" (Bishop), 34

"Passage to India" (Whitman), 225
Passages of Joy, The (Gunn), 89
Pater, Walter, 230
"Piano Kissed by a Fragile Hand, The" (Verlaine), 199
Plutonian Ode (Ginsberg), 74
"Poem (Lana Turner has collapsed!)" (O'Hara), 118
Poem Traveled Down My Arm, A (Walker), 209
Poems (Rich), 128
Poems in Prose (Wilde), 236
"Poetry and Grammar" (Stein), 188
Positives (Gunn), 87
"Powhatan's Daughter" (Crane), 46
Poèmes saturniens (Verlaine), 197
"Prayer of Columbus" (Whitman), 225
Psappho. *See* Sappho

"Quaker Hill" (Crane), 50
Queer theory, 1-8
Questions of Travel (Bishop), 34

Rambling Sailor, The (Mew), 110
Ravenna (Wilde), 231

"Repression of War Experience" (Sassoon), 165
Revolutionary Petunias, and Other Poems (Walker), 206
Rich, Adrienne, 121-134
  A Change of World, 124
  The Diamond Cutters, 124
  Diving into the Wreck, 128
  The Dream of a Common Language, 129
  Fox, 132
  "From an Old House in America," 128
  Leaflets, 126
  Midnight Salvage, 132
  Necessities of Life, 126
  Poems, 128
  Snapshots of a Daughter-in-Law, 125
  Time's Power, 131
  "Transcendental Etude," 130
  A Wild Patience Has Taken Me This Far, 130
  The Will to Change, 127
  Your Native Land, Your Life, 131
Rimbaud, Arthur, 135-146
  "Bad Blood," 141
  "Deliria I," 142
  "Deliria II," 142
  "The Drunken Boat," 139
  "Farewell," 142
  Illuminations, 143
  "The Impossible," 142
  "Lightning," 142
  "Morning," 142
  "Night in Hell," 141
  A Season in Hell, 140
  "Seer Letter," 138
  "Vowels," 140
"River, The" (Crane), 47
"Riverman, The" (Bishop), 35
Romances Without Words (Verlaine), 199

Sagesse (Verlaine), 200
Saison en enfer, Une. See *Season in Hell, A*
"Sandpiper" (Bishop), 32
Sappho, 147-158
  16 L.-P., 153
  94 L.-P., 155
  112 L.-P., 156
  "Ode to Anactoria," 152
  "Ode to Aphrodite," 151
Sassoon, Siegfried, 159-169
  "The Dug Out," 166
  "Everyone Sang," 166
  "Lines Written in Anticipation . . . ," 166
  "Repression of War Experience," 165
  Sequences, 167
  "They," 165
Saturday Market. See *Farmer's Bride, The*
Saussure, Ferdinand de, 2
"Savoy" (O'Hara), 117
Schuyler, James, 170-179
  "The Morning of the Poem," 175
  "Song," 174
Season in Hell, A (Rimbaud), 140
Sedgwick, Eve Kosofsky, 1
"Seer Letter" (Rimbaud), 138
Self-Portrait in a Convex Mirror (Ashbery), 22
Sense of Movement, The (Gunn), 85
Sequences (Sassoon), 167
Shadow Country (Allen), 12
Shropshire Lad, A (Housman), 100
Signifiers and signifieds, 2
Snapshots of a Daughter-in-Law (Rich), 125
Some Trees (Ashbery), 18
"Song" (Schuyler), 174
"Song of Myself" (Whitman), 217
"Sound of the Hunting Horn, The" (Verlaine), 201
Sphinx, The (Wilde), 234
Stanzas in Meditation (Stein), 189